Oaks of Righteousness

by
Gloria Blowers

Precious Debbie
5 Mar 2010

I pray this book will be a source of "Hope,
comfort & assurance" for you.

I love you dearly♡!!

In Jesus,
Gloria Blowers
(Is. 61:1-3)

First printing: July 2008
Second printing: November 2008

ISBN-13: 978-0-9796289-1-7
ISBN-10: 0-9796289-1-1

All Scripture taken from NASB (New American Standard Version) except where designated otherwise.

Unless otherwise indicated, names in the personal examples and anecdotal material have been changed to protect the privacy of those involved.

This book is a discipleship Bible Study and is not meant to be a professional medical manual. One's own personal health and the decisions regarding how it is managed is each person's responsibility. The author and publisher accept no responsibility for any decisions made that may affect one's health.

Note: Poetic expressions of the NASB are written in narrow columns in original text. This format has been modified to utilize the full length of the line in this study book. The words, "Heaven" and "Hell" are capitalized to underscore the fact that these are real places. (Just as we would capitalize New Orleans, Kansas, Romania.) I have also capitalized "Word" when it refers directly to Jesus or the written or spoken Word of God.

Cover Design - Janell Robertson, Farewell Communications
Interior Layout - Judy Lewis

<u>Rivers of Joy Bible Study Series</u>:

Oaks of Righteousness is book two of a three-part series. Book one, *Free Indeed*, was released in August 2007. Tentative release date for book three, *That Your Joy May Be Full*, is December 2009.

MGB Publishing
58 Misty Creek Cove
Sautee Nacoochee, GA 30571

This book is lovingly dedicated to these cherished women in my life:

To my mother, Rosanna Upham: Thank you for bearing me in your womb and for giving me LIFE! Without that, there would have been no story to tell, no book to write and no opportunity to experience all the wonderful plans God had for me. Thanks also for always "being there" for Dad and for us kids. That meant more than anything—especially when life hurt and things didn't make any sense. You listened, encouraged, gave the wise counsel I needed, and somehow after that, I knew that things would be OK again. And they always were! Thank you for teaching me so much about courage, perseverance…and singing through the storms. Thanks, Mom, for <u>all</u> you did for me and for our family!

To my sister, Kathy Albers: Your faith and courage in adversity has been an endless source of inspiration to me. Thanks for being the best sister I could have possibly had as you walked with me through many difficult and confusing times through the years. Your wisdom, understanding heart, and kind words of encouragement kept me going so often!

To my dear Aunt Lois Strauss and my long time friend, Charlene Caspar, whose lives radiate the meaning of Jesus' words: *I was hungry, and you gave Me something to eat; I was thirsty and you gave Me drink (Matt. 25:35).* Oh, what *treasures* you have *stored up in heaven (Matt. 6:20)* for the incalculable times you have extended the loving hand of Jesus to others in the form of a hot cooked meal, homemade pie, or cookies; or in providing practical help—cleaning the home of an infirmed sister, picking up groceries for a sick neighbor, or taking the elderly to an appointment. Your liberal, untiring, joyful sharing of Jesus' love is something I greatly admire and deeply desire to emulate.

To Ms. Blanche Thurmond, my precious 93 year old spiritual mom, confidant and prayer partner. Thanks for the endless times you provided a patient, listening ear, shoulder to cry on, or word of wisdom from God when I so desperately needed it. Your love, godly counsel, and faithful prayers have meant more than I could ever possibly express!

I love you all dearly and pray God's most merciful, gracious and bountiful blessings on you always!

Acknowledgments and Special Thanks

The list of individuals that follows is but a very abbreviated sampling of the countless numbers who played a significant role in my life—encouraging me, praying for me, giving godly wisdom and counsel—throughout the writing of this book…and the lifetime that preceded it! To all of you that I will not be able to mention individually, please accept my personal word of thanks and appreciation. You know who you are…and God knows. My prayer is that He will bless you and your families in every rich and bountiful way!

To my dear husband, Mel. Thank you once again for standing by me every step of the way with words of encouragement and endless expressions of love and support. You continue to be for me God's most precious gift and endless example of Christlike love, patience, and joyful service to others. I am, of all women, most blessed!

To Annelie, Sam, Rhonda, Ruth, Surendra, Joey, Delphine, Igor, Dana, Sam-Nair, Seth, Anji, Anu, and Marius. Thank you for completing my life by giving me the precious privilege of experiencing the incomparable joys of motherhood…and being a grandma!

To Janell Robertson of Farewell Communications for your creative work on the cover; to Judy Lewis for your professional and prompt, yet always personal, work on the interior layout; to Phyllis Bassett for your ever so faithful, skillful editorial assistance…and to you all for your above and beyond patience and loving and encouraging friendship!

To our Romanian "extended family", Pastor Liviu and Lavinia, Natanael, Andrei, and Emanuel Costea for your unceasing love, support and prayers through the years. You truly are "family". We cherish the times of ministry and fellowship we have enjoyed together!

To Mama and Papa Patru, our adopted Romanian parents for your special love and faithful prayers that have *availed much (James 5:16),* giving the strength needed so often to *press on.* Special thanks also to the Voineas, Didina and Fira, Lili, Mihaela and Mari, Marcel and Lili, Carmen…and our many other Romanian friends who encourage and pray for us faithfully.

To my brothers and sister (and their spouses), Billy and Terri Upham, Kathy and Kenny Albers, Kenny and Kathy Upham for your continued love, support and prayers.

To my Uncle Bill Strauss, who at the age of 81, is a modern day Caleb, still serving the Lord with strength and joy and doing more for God's people—and others—than most half his age!...and to Kenny Albers who endlessly teaches us all, through his beautiful example, the true meaning of hard work, kindness and humility.

To Mrs. Lois Albers, 93, who still bakes homemade cookies for the farm hands—and whoever else might stop by for a visit. Thanks for refreshing my soul so often through the years with your delicious cookies and a cup of tea!

Table of Contents

Foreword 9

Abbreviations of Bible Translations and Books of the Bible 10

Bible Study Instructions 11

Chapter 1 13
    Day 1: Personal Testimony 14
    Day 2: Introduction to Book Two – Oaks of Righteousness 27
        A Word from Mel 29
    Day 3: In the Beginning…GOD 32
    Day 4: The Authority, Inerrancy, Immutability and Sufficiency of the
        Word of God—Part One (The Essential Importance of God's Word) 37
    Day 5: The Authority, Inerrancy, Immutability and Sufficiency of the
        Word of God—Part Two (Three Irrefutable Facts) 42
    Day 6: God's Eternal Plan 49

Chapter 2 55
    Day 1: Tradition vs. True Saving Faith—Part One 56
        The Danger and Power of Demonic Deception Through Tradition
    Day 2: Tradition vs. True Saving Faith—Part Two 62
        To My Catholic Friends Whom I Love Dearly
    Day 3: Proofs of Salvation - The Most Important Test You Will Ever Take 67
        Examine Yourself—Have You Truly been Born of the Spirit?
    Day 4: Progressive Sanctification 71
Day 5: Man's Wisdom Versus God's Wisdom 76

Chapter 3 83
    Day 1: The Psychologization of Sin 84
    Day 2: The Problem of Self-Esteem 89
    Day 3: God's Solution to the Self-Esteem Problem 95
    Day 4: Spirtual Warfare – An Introduction 102
        Be A Good Soldier: Alert, Prepared, Armed
    Day 5: The War Within—The Conflict of the Two Natures 108

Chapter 4 117

    Day 1: It Takes Faith! Learning to walk by Faith, not Sight … or *Feelings* 118

    Day 2: Faith that Perseveres 124

    Day 3: The Obedience of Faith 130

    Day 4: The Patience of Faith 136

    Day 5: The Inexhaustible Supply of Faith—Grace 140

Chapter 5 147

    Day 1: The Heart/Mind Connection 148

    Day 2: The Problem of Pride/The Joy of Discipline 153

    Day 3: Holy, Holy, Holy 158

    Day 4: The Surprising Side of Holy Love 165

    Day 5: God's Blessed Remnant 172

Chapter 6 177

    Day 1: Possessing Our Possessions – The Believer's Rest 178

    Day 2: As Sparks Fly Upward 184

    Day 3: You Have Need of Endurance 190

        Fighting the Good Fight … Finishing Well

    Day 4: Sweet Hour of Prayer – Part One 198

    Day 5: Sweet Hour of Prayer – Part Two 204

Chapter 7 211

    Day 1: Biblical Health and Healing – An Overview – Part One 212

    Day 2: Biblical Health and Healing – An Overview – Part Two 217

    Day 3: The Sons of Issachar and the Signs of the Times 222

    Day 4: Heaven – Better By Far! – Part One 227

    Day 5: Heaven – Better By Far! – Part Two 233

    Epilogue 239

End Notes 240

Appendix 241

    Gospel Presentation 242

    Catholic Doctrines vs. The Word of God 244

    Biblical Proofs of Salvation 246

    Psychology: A Biblical Analysis 248

    Update on Personal Testimony 251

    Resources 253

Foreword

Knowing God and becoming conformed to the image of His Son is the ultimate goal of our faith in Jesus as our Savior, accomplished through His Grace. Growing into the image of Jesus is a freedom and joy increasing process as intimacy in a trusting, obedient relationship with God is developed. God uses each person's life circumstances to fulfill His purposes and to develop the character of Christ.

In this book series, God uses Gloria, and her life circumstances, to "come alongside" you as a friend and encourager in this process. As you read the graphic descriptions of her pilgrimage, you will experience a deep assurance of God's goodness and overcoming Grace. Gloria shares valuable lessons that will help you draw closer to God and experience His abiding presence in your life. You will also gain a greater awareness of the depth and power of God's Word in giving strength, assurance and the counsel needed to be victorious in every day living.

This is not just another book about a woman who wants to tell about her difficult, pain-filled life. Rather, it is a book about God's triumphant love, mercy and grace in the life of one who has placed her total trust in Him and in the unfailing promises of His Word. Whether you are experiencing the normal challenges of life in a fallen world or a more difficult, intense physical, spiritual, or mental warfare, you will relate to what Gloria shares as you see yourself in similar situations that she experienced. You will hear words of comfort and hope. You will be encouraged. You will receive solid, practical biblical solutions to life's most challenging problems and God will show you the path to true freedom and joy in Him.

Darrel L. Anderson, TH.D
Positions Held: Pastor, First Baptist Church, Minneapolis MN
VP/Field Director, National Association of Evangelicals
Executive Director, Romanian Missionary Society
Currently Pastoring in DesMoines, Iowa.

Abbreviations of Bible Translations and Books of the Bible

Please note the following abbreviations of Bible Translations and the books of the Bible used in this study:

cf. – Indicates comparative references; references making similar point.

sel. – designates "selected" portions of text listed.

Bible Translations

NASB – New American Standard Bible
KJV – King James Version
NKJV – New King James Version Bible

NIV – New International Version
TLB – The Living Bible (A Paraphrase)

Books of the Bible

Old Testament

Genesis – Gen.
Exodus – Ex.
Leviticus – Lev.
Numbers – Num.
Deuteronomy – Deut.
Joshua – Josh.
Judges – Judges
Ruth – Ruth
1 and 2 Samuel
    1 and 2 Sam.
1 and 2 Kings
    1 and 2 Kings

1st and 2nd Chronicles
    1st and 2nd Chron.
Ezra – Ezra
Nehemiah – Neh.
Esther – Esther
Job – Job
Psalms – Ps.
Proverbs – Prov.
Ecclesiastes – Eccles.
Song of Solomon – Song of Sol.
Isaiah – Is.
Jeremiah – Jer.
Ezekiel – Ezek.

Daniel – Dan.
Hosea – Hosea
Joel – Joel
Amos – Amos
Obadiah – Ob.
Jonah – Jonah
Micah – Micah
Nahum – Nah.
Habakkuk – Hab.
Zephaniah – Zeph.
Haggai – Hag.
Zechariah – Zech.
Malachi – Mal.

New Testament

Matthew – Matt.
Mark – Mark.
Luke – Luke
John – John
Acts – Acts
Romans – Rom.
1 and 2 Corinthians
    1 and 2 Cor.
Galatians – Gal.

Ephesians – Eph.
Philipians – Phil.
Colossians – Col.
1 and 2 Thessalonians
    1 and 2 Thess.
1 and 2 Timothy
    1 and 2 Tim.
Titus – Titus
Philemon – Philemon

Hebrews – Heb.
James – James
1 and 2 Peter
    1 and 2 Pet.
1, 2 and 3 John
    1, 2 and 3 John
Jude – Jude
Revelation – Rev.

BIBLE STUDY INSTRUCTIONS

Welcome to book two, *Oaks of Righteousness,* of the three-part Bible Study series, *Rivers of Joy.* I'm excited about all that God is going to teach us as we continue to *grow in His wisdom, knowledge and grace (2 Pet. 3:18).*

> *Everyone who hears these words of Mine, and acts upon them, may be compared to a wise man, who built his house upon the rock. And the rain descended, and the floods came, and the winds blew, and burst against that house; and yet it did not fall, for it had been founded upon the rock (Matt. 7:24-25).*

In book one of this series, *Free Indeed,* we began to build a strong house of faith that would stand firm and protective regardless of the difficulties or trials (storms of life) encountered. As God's Word exhorts us, we carefully laid a firm foundation of the central doctrines (biblical teachings) of our Christian faith. Each of these truths was anchored in *Jesus,* the *chief cornerstone (Ps. 118:22; Eph. 2:20)*—His life, (example and teachings), death, and resurrection. Some of the topics we covered in book one were: The Awesome Creation of the Universe; In the Image of God—the wonderful truth about all that this means; You Must be Born Again—the absolute necessity of the second birth; The Person and Ministry of the Holy Spirit; The Unpardonable Sin; The Problem of Fear…and What to do About It; *Come, Let Us Go Up to the Mountain of the Lord*—discovering an ever-increasing security, peace and joy through a growing, trusting, obedient walk with God (Micah 4:2; Prov. 4:18).

If you do not already have this first book of the series, it would be helpful to obtain a copy to strengthen and fortify your own faith through a review of these foundational doctrines of our Christian faith. It is also an excellent evangelistic/discipleship tool that you can use with unsaved friends or new believers.

And you shall remember all the way which the Lord your God has led you (Deut. 8:2).

Because a thorough understanding of the pivotal truths of God's Word is essential for building a *strong house of faith,* we will spend the first few weeks reviewing key topics studied in book one. Upon this solid foundation, we will build *walls and rooms* and begin to *fill them with all pleasant and precious riches (Prov. 24:3).*

How to Use this Study

As with book one, this is an interactive study of the Word of God. Devotional material discussing the topic of the day is followed by a Bible Study Supplement with applicable Scripture that will help you apply the principles taught in the study material. This is, by far, the most important part and it is crucial to complete the questions to gain the lasting benefits intended.

Whenever a Bible verse is given with a small "a" or "b"—for example, Isaiah 31:3a or Isaiah 31:3b—it is referring to the first part of the verse (a) or the last part of the verse (b).

Abbreviations for the translations and books of the Bible are given preceding these introductory instructions. Please note these.

The study is designed for five days per week—except for week one which contains an extra day to accommodate introductory material. This will leave one day to review what you have learned or to "catch up." The other day is for preparing your heart to worship God in your local assembly.

On the cover sheet of each new week, (the cover sheet appears at the beginning of each chapter and contains a summary of the topics to be studied for that week), there will be two verses given for memorization *(hiding in your heart - Ps. 119:11).* Please ask God to help you to be faithful in memorizing at least one of these verses, and if possible, try to memorize both of them. As you do, you will be amazed at how often God uses these Scriptures to encourage, strengthen, and guide you. Also, there will be a Bible verse(s) listed at the top of each day's meditation. Please read these carefully. They are the *focus verse(s)* for the day and will set your mind on the biblical truth that will be studied.

Before you begin each day's study, it is important to start with a word of prayer. Sit for a moment in quietness before the Lord. Ask the Holy Spirit to remove any distracting thoughts so that you may give your attention fully to the study of God's Word. Also ask God, through His Holy Spirit, to give you true biblical clarity in your understanding, and to guard your heart from deception or inaccurate interpretation. There are several prayers in Scripture that are excellent for this: *Open my eyes that I may behold wonderful things from Thy (Word) (Ps. 119:18). Speak, Lord, for Thy servant is listening (1 Sam. 3:9). Search me, O God and know my heart; try me and know my anxious thoughts, and see if there be any hurtful way in me and lead me in the everlasting way (Ps. 139:23-24).*

Assignment for Day 1

To encourage each student regarding the amazing love, mercy and grace of God, I shared my personal testimony in book one, *Free Indeed*. If you did not go through that study and read the testimony then, or if you would like to review it—the testimony has been revised to include new material—you will do that today. Please go to the next page, look over the outline and memory instructions for chapter one, then proceed to My Personal Testimony. There is no Bible Study Supplement for today. We will begin that tomorrow.

Chapter 1

> Memory Bible Verse: *The Spirit of the Lord God is upon me, because the Lord has anointed me to bring good news to the afflicted; He has sent me to bind up the brokenhearted, to proclaim liberty to captives, and freedom to prisoners…To comfort all who mourn, giving them a garland instead of ashes, the oil of gladness instead of mourning, the mantle of praise instead of a spirit of fainting. So they will be called* **oaks of righteousness**, *the planting of the Lord, that He may be glorified* (Is. 61:1-3).
>
> Bonus Memory Verse: *… therefore, a strong people will glorify (the Lord)* (Is. 25:3a).

Note: Isaiah 61:1-3 is the theme for this study. You do not have to memorize all of it the first week. If you memorize it according to the schedule below, it will not be difficult and by the end of the study you will have this beautiful promise in your heart to strengthen and encourage. (See below for memory schedule).

Day 1
<u>Bible Study Instructions</u> – If you have not already done so, please read. (Important info)
Personal Testimony

Day 2
Introduction to Book Two: Oaks of Righteousness

Day 3
In the Beginning…GOD

Days 4 and 5
The Authority, Inerrancy, Immutability and Sufficiency of the Word of God

Day 6
God's Eternal Plan

Week One: The Spirit of the Lord God is upon me, because the Lord has anointed me to bring good news to the afflicted;

Week Two: (Add) He has sent me to bind up the brokenhearted,

Week Three: (Add) to proclaim liberty to captives, and freedom to prisoners…

Week Four: (Add) To comfort all who mourn, giving them a garland instead of ashes,

Week Five: (Add) the oil of gladness instead of mourning, the mantle of praise instead of a spirit of fainting.

Week Six: (Add) So they will be called **oaks of righteousness**, the planting of the Lord, that He may be glorified.

Week Seven: Review all.

Chapter 1 — Day 1
Personal Testimony

> *Then Jesus said to those who believed, "If you continue in My Word, then are you My disciples indeed. And you shall know the Truth, and the Truth shall make you free... If the Son, therefore, shall make you free, you shall be **free indeed*** (John 8:31,32,36).

The following is my personal testimony. I pray that as you read it you will be reminded of the greatness of our heavenly Father's love, mercy, and faithfulness in your life just as He demonstrated these again and again in mine, long before I *knew* Him.—Gloria Blowers

Broken Pieces

I stared at the image in the mirror. I did not recognize the stranger before me. The face was drawn, contorted into a frightening countenance reflecting the intensity of the destructive battle going on inside. A loud voice within screamed: *"Hopeless, hopeless, hopeless!"* Suddenly, fisted hands began beating mercilessly upon my stomach: *"Destroy! Destroy!!"* I doubled over, collapsing into a heap of agonizing pain and...helpless hopelessness.

It was a scary experience. Just one of many in the fourteen-year battle with the various eating disorders—first bulimia, then anorexia, and finally, compulsive eating—that threatened to destroy my marriage, my life, and my eternal destiny. I couldn't understand what was happening. I had always prided myself on being intelligent, assertive, strong-willed, able to handle whatever came my way—not just successfully, but commendably. But on this day, reality struck me in the face as clearly as the image that stood before me. I could finally see that all the outward success was in itself a huge

mockery serving as a cloak of deceit over what was happening inside. I was not the happy, together, stable person I projected to others. I was, in reality, a powerless prisoner, held captive by a host of life-dominating obsessions and addictions. And I was too proud to admit it to anyone. So began the tormenting, endless charade of the dual life. I became, as it were, two people: on the outside—intelligent, high achiever, successful. But inwardly, I was a miserable, tormented failure, incessantly plagued by uncontrollable compulsions, mental and emotional turmoil—and *fear.*

I've struggled for a long time with just how much of my story I should share. There's so much that I would prefer not to talk about, for to do so means embarrassing humiliation. And it is certainly *not* politically correct to talk about such things. We are all supposed to be happy, together, paradigms of success who can handle anything life throws at us confidently and with a smile on our face. To admit anything less is social suicide. But the Bible says we are to *speak the truth in love (Eph. 4:15)* even if it hurts or is momentarily embarrassing, because only the truth—God's truth—sets people *free,* ourselves and others (John 8:31-32, 36). So I am going to take that risk of ridicule and rejection. I am going to be painfully honest, and as I do, it is my fervent prayer that all who read this testimony will be encouraged by the greatness of God's love, mercy, and grace. I pray also that many who are discouraged—who have endured too much pain for too long—will find hope and a renewed strength to press on to the true freedom and joy that Jesus came to bring us all (*John 8:31-32, 36; 15:11*).

I grew up on a small farm near Junction City in eastern Kansas. I was the second of four children—two brothers and a sister. Life was hard on the farm and beset with difficulties and losses. On two separate occasions, within three years, in a matter of a few terrifying moments, tornados ravaged our farm, destroying not only our barns, animals, and my mom's pretty flowers and white picket fence, but also years of hard work, hopes, dreams…and my parents' financial stability. Still in the process of rebuilding from these, just two years later a third tornado struck, adding to the heartaches and financial pressures. Looking back on all this today, I am totally amazed at my mom and dad's courage and perseverance. I can never remember them grumbling or complaining or losing heart in any way. They just kept working hard, rebuilding, and doing the best they could. This memory would later serve as a stabilizing influence in my most difficult trials.

My earliest recollections of life were characterized by loneliness, fear of rejection, mental and emotional turmoil, and physical pain. Even at an early age, I sensed I was different from other kids. I felt things deeper. When others hurt, I hurt. I cried a lot. Sometimes I would lock myself in my room and just cry and cry until I had such a pulsating headache I couldn't see straight. At other times, the relentless turmoil manifested itself in the form of grand mal seizures.

Because the inner pain was so great, I longed for comfort and affirmation. Neither of my parents were, by nature, outwardly affectionate, so I soon *perceived* great deprivation in this area. I know now that my parents were expressing their love in the best way they could through their hard work and doing all they could to keep our family together and as stable as possible, given all the humanly

overwhelming difficulties and losses. But I was too absorbed in my own battle—the never-ending mental and emotional turmoil accompanied almost continually by physical pain and problems—to see beyond this.

I mistakenly interpreted my mother and father's lack of affection as rejection. This introduced at a very early age, an obsessive preoccupation with earning approval and acceptance through achievement. This "drivenness" for achievement invaded every area of life. In my schoolwork, my *best* was never good enough. It had to be straight A's or I considered myself a total failure. Sports soon joined academics in my quest for affirmation. As early as junior high, I was a captain and leading scorer on school and community soccer and softball teams. I was also a record setting track competitor. One year, at a regional tournament, I swept the girls' track competition, taking first place in all the major running events and setting a new record. But in my sports endeavors, as in my academics, I could not participate for the sheer joy of competing. I had to win! The destructive seeds of self-imposed perfectionism had already taken root.

In high school, my pursuit of approval and significance through academic achievement continued. I was determined to acquire as much of the world's knowledge as I possibly could. Every night, I brought home a stack of books. I quickly changed clothes, did my chores, then barricaded myself in my room and studied until my brain hurt.

My successes in academics and sports contributed to the popularity I also longingly craved. I was an officer in several extracurricular clubs as well as secretary of my senior class. But each and every brief moment of acknowledgment faded ever so quickly into a preoccupation with the next needed quest for recognition. Like a dark cloud over a Fourth of July parade, the fear of future failure in achieving the needed praise and approval dampened every joy of the moment.

With a number of scholarships to support my academic ambitions, I began my college career at

St. John's College, Winfield, Kansas. After earning my A.A. degree—graduating magna cum laude—I continued my education at the prestigious, academically acclaimed River Forest University, Chicago, Illinois. My college experience followed a similar pattern as high school. As a cheerleader, accomplished athlete, consistent high honor student, and officer in several popular collegiate clubs, my social and academic life flourished, giving all the external markings of success. Yet, the peace and contentment for which my turmoiled heart yearned continued to elude me. Big was never big enough. Perfect wasn't perfect enough. Enough was never enough! The accusations of futile insignificance beat mercilessly upon me night and day. "More…more…more!" the cruel taskmaster within screamed with relentless painful lashings.

During my teen years, and early adult life, I was hospitalized a number of times for mental and emotional-related problems.

"Religion" played a significant part in my early years. Mom and Dad were very active in a formal, liturgical church. They faithfully took us to Sunday school and church every week and read to us from the denominational devotional literature every night at bedtime. I was taught that I was "saved" (going to heaven) at the time of my baptism as a baby through a statement of faith made by my sponsors. This was "confirmed" by correctly answering questions from the Catechism and reciting designated Bible verses at the time of my confirmation in the eighth grade. But there was never any discussion about the *new birth* or what it meant to have a *personal relationship* with God through faith in Jesus so I did not understand what this really meant and I certainly did not have one. With no personal commitment to God or to His Word, after leaving home for college, I began to drift away from my religious moorings. In time, I abandoned them all together.

My attention to academics led to another magna cum laude graduation from River Forest in May, 1969, at which time I received the exciting job opportunity to be the Director of Counseling at a prominent private academy in Denver, Colorado. I pursued graduate studies at Kansas State University in the summer, then moved to Colorado to begin my new career in the fall. I enjoyed the students, counseling, and teaching Senior Psychology. But something was still missing. Finally, after a year of yet more restless mental turmoil, I decided that academics had been my life too long! I needed to expand my horizons. So I left my teaching career to seek something *bigger*—more exciting and challenging.

The field of aeronautics and space exploration was at that time a relatively new, exciting career field with virtually limitless possibilities. I decided that was the place to be. I joined the ranks of Martin Marietta Aerospace Corporation, pursued specialized training in aeronautical engineering, then helped pioneer the role of women in this previously male-dominated field. Within one year I had climbed the corporate ladder to hold the position of release department head for all Martin Marietta's contractual drawings. Soon, I was winning awards and enjoying social contacts with the astronauts and upper management. Life was good! At age twenty-four, I had acquired all the trappings that the world claimed would satisfy those deepest human longings for love, acceptance, and fulfilment. Yet, the inner turmoil persisted. There was still something missing. As I battled to subdue the growing agitation, another siren call beckoned me away. It was the call to world travel. I wrestled long and hard with giving up my successful, highly regarded career. Yet the call persisted, tempting and cajoling day and night until I could resist it no more. I gave my notice, put my belongings in storage, and set out on my new adventure to travel the world. Surely I would find it—the peace, the contentment—somewhere… out there!

My plane touched down in Stockholm, Sweden. My cousin was waiting and drove me to Orebro where I stayed with my mother's incredibly kind, hospitable relatives, Maj-Britt and Yngve Larsson. They lovingly took me into their family and treated me like one of their own for over three months! I shall never forget their unselfish, daily deeds of kindness, and will be forever grateful to them and their family! But, again, the yearning to move on compelled me to pack my bags. I hitchhiked and traveled by train, crisscrossing the European continent for a year picking up exciting jobs along the way: working in a beautiful après ski lodge in Aufham, (Bad Reichenall) Germany, in the heart of the majestic Alps, and tutoring a wealthy European entrepreneur's children in France where I lived in a luxurious French provincial mansion with a lavishly landscaped courtyard, fountains, and lavender gardens. This gracious couple even offered the use of their spacious condo in Cavalier on the beautiful French Riviera near Cannes. I spent two months in this glorious paradise during the exciting Mimosa Festival and world-famous Monte Carlo Road Race.

Even all this—the lavish accommodations and Eden-like surroundings—could not quiet the discontent that yet stirred within. I longed for more independence, my own place, and a stable, well-paying income that would enable me to continue in the flagrant lifestyle to which I had become accustomed. By this time, I spoke four languages, which landed me another exciting job: a top security position with the Drug Enforcement Administration, International Division, Frankfurt, Germany. I traveled extensively throughout Europe and Asia on business and pleasure-related trips. My social life flourished. I was wined and dined in some of the most elegant restaurants on the European continent. Yet, even then, the inner turmoil and mental harassment refused to be quieted. There was never any real, lasting peace or contentment. It was just one outward charade after another. How long could I keep this up?

Then, finally, the most wonderful thing in all the world happened. It was, I was sure, the missing piece to the proverbial happiness/contentment puzzle. Into my life walked the man of my fondest, most romantic dreams—tall, *very* handsome, promising career. His 6'5" stature, dark hair, piercing brown eyes, and warm, congenial smile would melt any woman's heart. He was a captain (pilot) in the US Air Force,

with the prestigious 7th Special Ops Squadron—the Fulton Recovery/James Bond-type rescue guys who worked with the Green Berets and Navy Seals. Captain Blowers was also very intelligent, kind, and courteous. He brought me beautiful flowers and took me to fine restaurants, on picnics in the countryside, and on weekend excursions exploring castles and walled cities. Then one night in the quaint, romantic Tzigone Cave Restaurant in Brussels, Belgium, his eyes glistening in the soft candlelight, he pulled from beneath the table a small black velvet box. As I opened it, a large beautifully cut, perfectly hued diamond, surrounded by nearly a dozen smaller diamonds, sparkled like stars on a clear summer night. The long-awaited question followed: "Will you . . . ?" "Yes!"

Surely, this was what I had been searching for all my life: someone special with whom I could live and learn and laugh and share my dreams and aspirations. Like a schoolgirl anticipating her first prom, I excitedly began to make preparations for the upcoming wedding which included a trip to London and the John Lewis Bridal Salon for purchase of my wedding dress. There were showers and going-away parties as we prepared to return to the United States for the wedding and Mel's transfer to Hurlburt Air Force Base, Fort Walton Beach, Florida. Back home in Kansas and Pennsylvania (where Mel's family lived), there were more showers and open houses to wish us well. I was easily caught up in the momentary excitement, keeping the inner turmoil at bay.

The wedding was an idyllic sunset ceremony at Vesper Point, Rock Springs Ranch, overlooking the tranquil, Eastern Kansas rolling-hills countryside. The breathtaking purple and crimson sky provided the perfect backdrop to the wedding service. Afterward, at the reception, an elaborate multi-tiered cake surrounding a sparkling fountain, made by my dear and very talented Aunt Lois, served as an elegant centerpiece to the festivities. Everything was—outwardly—*perfect*.

Then it was off to Hawaii and our luxurious honeymoon condo on Waikiki Beach. But a pulsating migraine and the return of the agonizing agitation inside greatly dampened my joy of the celebration.

We returned to Fort Walton Beach where we began our married life together. I loved our first cozy apartment not far from the base. I wanted so much to be a good wife and make my husband happy and proud. Three months into our marriage something wonderful—and frightening—happened. I got sick! I went to the doctor, where I received the news. I was pregnant! There came with the news a dichotomy of intense emotion: ecstatic joy mingled with a paralyzing fear. As a little girl I loved to play with dolls and dreamed of the day when I would be a mother and have a real baby to hold and care for. Now that dream was about to come true. Yet, *doubt* and *fear* flooded my mind. I was not ready to be a mom.

As I struggled to prepare for my new role, just two short months into the pregnancy, tragedy struck for which I was not prepared. I had a spontaneous miscarriage. Rather than feeling a sense of relief as I thought I would (when I wished so often that I were not pregnant), I was devastated! I realized then that I really did want this baby more than any of the other dreams and ambitions of the past. It was as if a part of me died with our baby that day. A dark, overpowering depression set in, along with that all-too-familiar agitation in my heart. Try as I might to convince myself that I still had Mel and together we possessed all for which I had ever dreamed—and so much more—I could not quiet the inner turmoil or overcome the awful depression.

One day, in an attempt to break through the ever-thickening clouds, Mel called from work and asked me to join him for dinner at the Officer's Club. As we enjoyed our favorite meal—chateaubriand for two—in the lovely, candlelit dining room overlooking beautiful Okaloosa Bay, he told me about a graduate program in counseling that was about to begin on base. I'd been longing to return to school and complete my master's, so this news was very exciting. The next day I enrolled in the program.

I threw myself into my studies and completed my master's in Clinical/Agency Counseling with a perfect 4.0. Soon after graduation, I was hired as director of Okaloosa county CETA (Comprehensive Employment and Training Act), a vocational-training program. In a short time, I developed a model program for the state of Florida. I traveled extensively serving as a consultant to other executive directors. More awards, recognitions and featured front-page newspapers articles followed, fueling the insatiable flames of discontent once more. I could not understand what was happening. The more I achieved, the less content—and more depressed—I became. Would this oppressive cycle ever end?

When Mel's service obligation was over, I terminated my job with CETA, and we moved to Kansas City where he flew for the Air Force Reserves, and I tried desperately to cope with the deepening depression. I enjoyed cooking and had attended culinary arts classes in Cordon, France while living there, so in an attempt to keep my mind occupied and alleviate the pain of the internal agony, I started a culinary arts school. Then I got pregnant again. A paralyzing fear gripped me once more. How could I bring a baby into this state of chronic depression and relentless mental turmoil? I was unfit as a wife. I could never make it as a mom. Moms are strong and happy and love their kids and find unending joy in caring for and nurturing them. I couldn't even care for myself and Mel. I was miserable and I would make my child miserable. What kind of a life would that be?

The paralyzing fear and all the questions and uncertainties were soon complicated by a very serious flu-like illness. I ran a high fever and was continually nauseous with extreme vertigo for several weeks. After a number of visits to the doctor, he, in a very concerned voice let me know that what was happening had nothing to do with any normal morning sickness but that something very serious was going on. He suspected a life-threatening uterine infection. After several more weeks of trying unsuccessfully to treat the infection, he told me that the baby was probably dead or severely damaged because of the long-term high fever and other complications.

He advised a therapeutic abortion. Depressed or not, I was *not* ready for that! I must have time to think about it and discuss it with my husband. For two long, painful, nearly sleepless weeks, I wrestled with the decision to follow the doctor's advice or to carry the baby to full-term. When I became so exhausted from the emotional battle that I began to have blackouts, the doctor insisted that I have the abortion.

Mel, fearing he would lose me if something were not done soon, agreed. In desperation for relief, I gave in and signed the papers. In a few hours, I was being prepped for the surgery. To this day I can not find words to adequately describe the horrors of this experience—the pain, the guilt, the depression that settled in, darker than anything I had experienced previously. (Just a side note here. Anyone who says that an abortion does not affect the life of the mother is believing a very tragic and destructive lie. It affects her very much, for the rest of her life: the nightmarish pain/recovery of the procedure itself haunts for years; far greater, however, is the inevitable consequences of never being able to hold her precious baby, or of experiencing the love, joy and blessing he (or she) would have brought, bringing painful tears often! For weeks after the procedure, I could not sleep, adding further to the mental and emotional torment.

A few months later, by the grace of God alone—there were over a thousand applications for every commerical airline pilot position at that time—Mel was hired by Delta. A flicker of hope was rekindled. Maybe now, at last, with this fresh new start, things would get better. We moved to Atlanta—the flourishing, emerging city of culture, entertainment and exciting job opportunities. I very quickly landed yet another promising position with IBM (International Business Machines). As a system support specialist, I enjoyed an exceptionally successful career, winning the prestigious Southeastern Division System Support Rep of the Year after just one year of joining the company. This was followed by numerous other local, regional and national awards. What more could I possibly want! I had a wonderful husband, a beautiful home, a successful career, and even unlimited flying privileges, which we took advantage of frequently—romantic get-aways to San Juan (Puerto Rico), Cancun and Mazatlan (Mexico); the World's Fair in Seattle; Broadway shows in New York; ski trips to Colorado and the Alps of Austria, Switzerland and Northern Italy; bed and breakfast tours of Ireland and Scotland…and dozens more. Once we flew to San Francisco (from Atlanta) for dinner! Wine became a regular part of our meals, and any time in between when we felt like kicking back and relaxing. It seemed to numb the emptiness. There were spas, exotic weekend excursions, luxury cruises, and every other pleasurable indulgence my heart desired in an attempt to ameliorate the relentless turmoil inside. But it didn't work. The agonizing inner battle continued no matter the momentary outward pleasure.

In fact, the more we made and the more we acquired, the greater became the emotional upheavals. There were times the mental torment became so intense, I would beat myself mercilessly with fisted hands or bite my arm until the blood came, in a convoluted attempt to bring relief to the hellish pain inside. At this point, there were several serious suicide attempts. It was obvious that I could no longer handle what was going on alone. I needed help. So I turned to psychotherapy—along with its accompanying liberal use of psychotropic drugs—as my last hope to end the relentless inner war. Now, I added to alcohol and all the other pleasures and distractions, uppers to get me up, downers to calm me down, and tranquilizers to help me sleep.

I spent two years undergoing intensive psychotherapy. I was labeled at one time or another along the rocky road of treatment: epileptic, mentally and emotionally unstable, clinically depressed, bipolar (manic-depressive), obsessive/compulsive, co-dependent, neurotic, psychotic, schizophrenic. I had every major symptom listed in the DSM (Diagnostic and Statistical Manual of Mental Disorders) for all these disorders.

Even though the more socially acceptable labels—such as clinical depression or bipolar—

offered a comforting excuse when needed in my public life for a short while, pride would not allow me to live with such labels for long, for I considered them terribly demeaning and reserved for the real "crazies". So I began a campaign of deception that rivaled the best of Broadway productions. On the outside, I was all smiles and exuded a life-is-great attitude. I had become a master at deceit, pretending to be what I was not: happy, content.

Though incredibly effective on the outside, the deception could not fool nor ameliorate the conflict and torment within. So I turned to a former "god" for relief—food. Only this time the devastating control it had over me was far more intense than ever before. And thus began the most hellish mental and emotional battle ever! I had so often thought in the previous years that the only good thing about my life was that I had certainly reached the bottom of the pit, so the next move would have to be up. Little did I know that all the pain and problems endured thus far would soon pale in comparison to the horror I was about to enter: a horror that lasted nearly fourteen long, truly indescribably miserable, life-threatening years! First it was bulimia, then anorexia, and finally, compulsive eating with its typical endless binge/starve cycles. Unless you have been in the grips of a life-dominating obsession such as this, you cannot even begin to imagine the totality of such misery! Life ceases to be, and you exist in a pseudo world of pretend and make-believe, because if anyone knew how bound and helplessly enslaved to the compulsion you were, they would either walk as far away as they could or else they would do all in their power to get you committed, because happy, healthy, together people don't act like that! And they are right. They don't!

I certainly wasn't happy, healthy, or together. My latest "god," food, like all the others—education, sports, success, pleasure—could not deliver on its promise to satisfy, though I worshipped faithfully at its altar day after endless day. In fact, food became my life. I did not *eat to live* as healthy, happy, together people do. I *lived to eat*. Food was the first thought on my mind when I awoke in the morning and the last thought before I went to sleep—*if* I fell asleep at all, as chronic insomnia robbed me of more and more of that. My life—more accurately, my intensely miserable *existence*—consisted of but two dismal choices from which I was forced to choose daily and throughout the oft long, sleepless nights of nocturnal cravings. I could choose to eat what I wanted, which always resulted in an uncontrollable binge and the physical misery—the bloated stomach and agonizing emotional guilt that accompanied it—or I could starve myself and remain even more miserable in my self-imposed deprivation and hunger. There was absolutely no choice in between. I was incapable of sitting down to a normal, nutritious meal, enjoying it, and then leaving the table satisfied. I was never satisfied—whether I ate enough for twelve people or only enough to keep a starving sparrow alive. The self-inflicted beatings and bitings intensified, as did the suicide attempts.

Yet, convolutedly, I was at the same time, as a "qualified", degreed professional, heavily involved in therapeutic counseling in the evenings and weekends, counseling other people how to solve their problems throughout those fourteen years!

I knew (human knowledge) all the physiological and psychological reasons why I was doing what I was doing, and what I needed to do to change it. Yet, I was absolutely and utterly powerless to do it, and I was passing on to others this same head knowledge of powerless, empty solutions.

After more soul-searching, I concluded that there was only one thing that I had not yet done that I had always wanted to do, and that was to own my own business. After all, I was a hard worker and I'd done so much for all those *other* people; now I wanted to do something for *me* and be personally rewarded accordingly.

Just four years into my successful, rapidly climbing career with IBM, I gave my resignation notice. We moved to the quaint Alpine village resort town of Helen in the beautiful North Georgia mountains, where I designed, built and operated a riverside restaurant, Cafe International. The restaurant flourished and, during Octoberfest and the Fall Leaf Season, it was one of the most popular gathering places in town. People waited in line almost continually to get a seat on the picturesque covered deck overlooking the Chattahoochee River. The Atlanta Journal/Constitution even featured the restaurant as the cover story in its weekend leisure magazine. Surely, I could rest now in this latest success.

At this point, Mel was flying as Second Officer on the L-1011 with Delta. We built a lovely new home. It is hard to imagine that there would be any room for discontent or inner turmoil with all that we had going for us! But there was. I can vividly remember stopping at the bank's night deposit box night after endless night and hearing the hollow, clanging sound of the bulging money bag making its way to the bottom of the chute. And as it did, I could hear the question of a popular song echoing through the deepest chambers of my own hollow, empty heart: "Is that all there is, my friend?"

It was never a matter of not wanting to change. I wanted to change more than life itself, for I knew that if I did not change—soon—there would be no future, for there would be no life. My destructive eating habits had begun to take a heavy toll on my health. I began to develop serious problems: relentless strep throat, swelling and intense pain in muscles and joints, nausea, vertigo, fever, stomach and intestinal problems. Endless visits to doctors and specialist added to the list of labels ascribed to my condition: CFIDS (Chronic Fatigue Immune Dysfunction Syndrome), Fibromyalgia, Lupus, Rheumatoid Arthritis, and a few other strange names of rare diseases I cannot even remember now. The endless series of antibiotics and other drug therapies destroyed what little was left of my already weakened, overstressed immune system. Recurring infections added to the out-of-control downward spiral toward total destruction. Death seemed imminent, and at this point, welcomed, because of the chronic insomnia that accompanied all the other problems. There was never any break from the pain day after day, night after sleepless night. A dark impenetrable sense of *helpless hopelessness* permeated every futile attempt to find relief. Truly, there are no words to adequately describe the relentless, torturous hellishness of it! As so often before, suicide seemed to be the only way out. And I am sure, but for the grace of God, at that point, I would have been successful. But a pervasive and powerful *fear* (that I now know was the mercy of God!) kept me from completing a number of well-laid plans. I did not know God. Yet I knew there was a God and there was life after death—*He has planted eternity in their hearts (Eccles. 3:11)*. There was a heaven and there was a hell, which was exactly where I was headed! And I'd experienced enough *hell on earth* to know I did not want to go there forever!

My marriage was as rocky as my physical, mental, and spiritual condition. Totally obsessed for so many years with *my* needs, *my* wants, *my* quests for fulfillment, *my* compulsions, and now, *my* pain, I totally neglected my responsibilities as a wife and helpmate for my husband. Consequently, one cold, blustery February morning, the inevitable happened. Mel, who had received little more than the crumbs of my time and attention, while at the same time enduring my emotionally bizarre, unstable, self-centered mania for all those years, had taken all he could take! He had his own masculine needs that were not being met. Slamming his fist upon the breakfast bar, he said without a hint of mercy in his eyes: "Your restaurant, or me! No compromises!" He turned and walked away. He was going on a three-day trip. I had three days to decide my future marital status and my forever-after destiny.

I went to work in a daze. The threat of the inevitable destruction of my world hung over me like a guillotine about to drop. How could I give up my restaurant, which had become my identity in my deluded quest for significance? On the other hand, I knew my husband was the best thing that had ever happened to me. He had brought a sense of stability to my life, a buffer to the unmitigating pain and confusion. I knew he was inextricably linked to any hope for future security, stability—peace. I was at the proverbial crossroads in life where I was forced to choose one direction or the other. Yet, I wanted and I *needed* both.

When I got to work, the pressure of the no-win situation became overwhelming. I was nauseas and faint. Suddenly, the distressing vertigo sent me to the floor. My manager ran quickly for a cold cloth, which she pressed against my pallid brow as she issued her own instructions: "Go home and get some rest!"

Having no recollection of how I actually got there, I pulled up in front of our house, staggered to the front door, and with shaky hand fumbled for the keyhole. I stumbled through the bedroom door, tripping on an object in my path to the bed. To this day, neither my husband nor I have any idea of how that yellow suitcase got there, but there is not a doubt regarding the fact that it was mysteriously, strategically located directly in my path, for it was the instrument God used to start the life-altering series of events about to transpire. Tripping on the suitcase, I fell flat on my face. As my tense, pain-wracked body slammed against the hard floor, the pent-up anger, the hurt, the confusion, the long years of endless strivings, the growing awareness of the vanity in the self-deception flooded through me from deep within like torrents over a broken dam. Angrily, I jumped to my feet, grabbed the yellow suitcase and whirled around the room: round and round and round—then recklessly let it go. Leaning against the wall in the path of the projectile was a beautiful, two-hundred-year-old antique stained glass window, imported from a judge's chamber in Ireland, which we had purchased for the bedroom in our new home. The suitcase crashed through the center of the glass, shattering it into a myriad of jagged pieces. I fell on the floor, shaking and weeping uncontrollably. Finally, I lifted my head peering at the broken glass. "Oh, God," I cried, "That's my life! Broken pieces. Nothing but *broken pieces*. That's all it's ever been: broken pieces! If you think it's worth putting back together, you are going to have to do it this time,

because I can't. I can't do it any longer. I quit! Help me, God. Please, God. Save me, Jesus!"

I shall never forget that moment as long as I live. God heard my prayer, and He answered so compassionately, so quietly, I cannot yet fully describe it. Every cruel, demanding voice inside was stilled. There was a calm and there was a peace, a deep, tranquil peace I'd never before experienced, a *peace that passed all human understanding (Phil. 4:7)*. After sitting totally absorbed in the sweet, restful, serenity of the moment, I suddenly had a compelling desire to read the Word of God. "I must find God's Word, and I must read it! I must learn about God and what life is really all about. I must find out who God created me to be, *His* plans for my life and how to have real, lasting love, joy, peace, and purpose."

As I began to obey the prompting to go to God's Word, the sweet quietness was broken. The familiar accusing voice that had controlled my life all those years reared its ugly head in determined defiance: "Stupid idea! Stupid! Stupid! Stupid! The Bible is no more than an ancient archaic book that weak, ignorant Christians read and hang on to for a crutch because they aren't smart enough—like you!—to figure life out on their own." For so many years, I had believed that lie and was thoroughly convinced in my own mind that this *ancient archaic book* could not possibly teach me anything I did not already know. Yet, somehow, the quiet prompting would not go away. At one point, I seriously considered the temptation to forget it. Fear and trembling came upon me at that thought, however, as something inside seemed to warn me that this very well could be the last time I would be able to hear the quiet voice, the gentle prompting.

I ran upstairs, pulled down boxes from the attic, searching until I found the green-covered, paperback Bible I had picked up—somewhere—in my desperate search for peace. As I began to read, my eyes stared in unbelief. The words were so plain, so understandable, so personal!

"Woe to My rebellious children", says the Lord; "you ask advice from everyone but me,

and decide to do what you want to do without consulting Me… adding sin to sin. For without consulting me you have gone down to Egypt to find aid and have put your trust in Pharaoh for his protection. But in trusting Pharaoh, you will be disappointed, humiliated and disgraced, for he cannot deliver on his promises to save you!" (Is. 30:1–3 TLB)

In these few sentences, I saw my life clearly. Egypt was the world and all the places to which I ran to find the peace, joy, and happiness for which my troubled heart longed. Pharaoh was my knowledge, my achievements, my accumulated material goods—and later, food—that had become my *gods* to which I ran for comfort, for satisfaction, for deliverance. And there were so many carefully executed plans along the way. How often I asked for advice from unbelievers—others just as lost and far from God as I. Not once had I ever stopped to read God's Word, talk to Him, or ask Him what *His* plans for my life might be. With every new self-directed plan, I only widened the gap between my heavenly Father and me—*adding sin to sin*. I continued…

Therefore, the safety of Pharaoh will be your shame, and the shelter… of Egypt, your humiliation. Through a land of distress and anguish you travail… (You) carry your riches… and your treasure...to a people who cannot profit;… And you felt secure in your wickedness and said, 'No one sees me'… Your wisdom and your knowledge… deluded you. For you have said in your heart, 'I am, and there is no one besides me.' But evil will come on you; and disaster will fall on you for which you cannot atone. You are wearied with your many counsels;… (you) cannot deliver (yourself) from the power of the flame;… There is no one to save you (Is. 30:3–5, 47:10–15, sel.).

The broken pieces were coming together.

They weary themselves committing iniquity. "Your dwelling is in the midst of deceit; through deceit you refuse to know Me," declares the Lord. "Your ways and your deeds have brought these things to you. How bitter! How it has touched your heart!" (Jer. 9:5b, 6, 4:18).

Hear, O earth: behold, I am bringing disaster on this people, the fruit of their plans, because they have not listened to My Words. As for my law, they have rejected it also. (Jer. 6:19)

Every man is stupid, devoid of knowledge… In their discipline of delusion, (they) worship worthless idols… idols (that) are deceitful; there is no breath in them; they are worthless, a work of mockery. Who would not fear Thee, O King of the nations?...For among all the wise men… and in all their kingdoms, there is none like Thee (Jer. 10:14-15, 7-8, sel.).

I am the Lord your God, who teaches you to profit, who leads you in the way you should go. If only you had paid attention to My commandments. Then your well-being would have been like a river, and your righteousness like the waves of the sea (Is. 48:17).

How I would set you among My sons, and give you a pleasant land, the most beautiful inheritance of the nations. And I said, You shall call Me… Father, and not turn away from following Me... For thus the Lord God, the Holy One of Israel, has said, In repentance and rest you shall be saved, in quietness and trust is your strength… But you were not willing (Jer. 3:19; Is. 30:15).

The words continued, offering hope.

For Thou, O Lord, art our Father, our Redeemer from of old… He said surely, they are My people, sons...so he became their Savior… Come now, let us reason together, though your sins be as scarlet, they shall be white as snow. If you consent and obey, you will eat the best of the land; but if you refuse and rebel, you will be devoured by the sword. Truly the mouth of the Lord has spoken (Is. 63:16, 64:8-9, 1:18–20).

Having totally neglected the Word of God for so long, my weak, hungry soul was famished. I could not get enough of its life-giving nourishment! I read and read through the night...

For God so loved the world that He sent His only begotten Son, that whosoever believeth in Him might not perish but have everlasting life... Repent... and believe in the Lord Jesus Christ (John 3:16 KJV; Acts 2:38, 16:31).

So right there, at my kitchen table, as the first early morning rays broke through the darkness of the night, I *believed*. I confessed and repented of my sins of pride and rebellion, of rejecting God and stubbornly going my own way all those years. I thanked Jesus for dying on the cross for my sins and for making a way back to God. I asked Him to forgive me, to come into my heart to be my Lord and Savior— to help me live for Him and fulfill God's purposes for my life. And He did come into my heart that very moment to be my own personal Lord and Savior. It was so simple and so *real*. I know it was real because in that moment that I made this simple, genuine, confession of faith, God gave me the *seal of His Holy Spirit, (Eph. 1:14)*—that *blessed assurance* that says: "I know that I <u>know</u> that I <u>know</u> that I have been born again by the Spirit of the living God. I am His redeemed, blood-bought child and have *eternal life* with Him...forever." (John 11:25-26). This assurance of the Holy Spirit's presence became an immediate and unending source of stability, strength, and security.

Finally, I realized that salvation was not joining a church, memorizing Bible verses, or even baptism and partaking in the sacraments. It was a *personal relationship with God* through faith in Jesus and what He accomplished for us on the cross—salvation (forgiveness of sins) and eternal life. It was a precious living, loving, interactive *relationship.*

I had fallen into the trap so very common: mistakenly assuming that "religion" and "salvation" were one and the same. But now I could see the nearly fatal delusion in this assumption. *Religion* is man's attempt to get to God, or, as is even more common, to *be his own God (Gen. 3:5; Is. 14:13). Salvation*

is God's grace reaching down to lost man, offering forgiveness, unconditional love, and acceptance through the sacrificial, redemptive work of Jesus on the cross. I had been very *religious* at times, looking to an institution (a church) with its religious traditions—infant baptism, confirmation, church membership, the sacraments—to somehow save me. But it didn't, and it couldn't. That's why my life remained so empty and full of turmoil. When I got my eyes off myself, off religious traditions and off other people—most of whom were just as lost and living under the same delusions as I—and onto God and His Word, the pieces of my fractured, broken life began to fit together. At last the real missing piece to the puzzle of contentment and inner peace had been found—a loving, forgiven, *relationship* with God. Into my life flowed for the first time, unconditional love and acceptance and the assurance of a glorious sure and secure future. Finally, I knew who I really was, why I was here, and where I was going! I could, for the first time truly *enjoy the present moment* and *smile at the future (1 Tim. 6:17; Prov. 31:25).*

Then Jesus said to those who believed: If you continue in My Word then are you my disciples indeed and you shall know the truth, and the truth shall make you free. If the Son, therefore, shall make you free, you shall be free indeed" (John 8:31-32, 36). I believed that promise; and I *continued* in God's Word every day from that beautiful beginning until now...and I *continue* still. God, through the wisdom and truth found in His Word, has already set me free from so much. He liberated me from the awful torment of bulimia, anorexia, and compulsive eating, along with all sorts of other destructive habits that kept me bound in a world of oppressive sin and guilt. How can I ever thank Him enough for bringing me from a weak, unstable, drug-dependent mental and emotional basket case who spent the majority of her days sick—in bed, or in a state of total non-productive debilitation—to one who is *completely drug free, active in ministry, and has not spent one single day in bed for sickness in more than seventeen years!* To me, this is nothing short of a very real miracle. To God be the glory!

The Bible says: *If any man be in Christ, he is a new creature, old things pass away, behold all things become new" (2 Cor. 5:17).* My life is a dramatic, living testimony of this profound truth. God has overcome the destructive power of the former labels: neurotic, psychotic, manic-depressive, bipolar, etc., and has given me new names: *Redeemed, Born Again, Saved by Grace, Child of God, Joint Heir of Heaven, The King's Daughter - Glorious Within, Bride of Christ (Gal. 4:4-5; John 3:3; Eph. 2:8-9; John 1:12; Gal. 4:7; Eph. 1:18; Ps. 45:13; Rev. 18:23, 19:7, 21:2).*

There is much more I wish I had time to tell you about the way God put back together our nearly destroyed marriage, giving us a beautiful relationship and a wonderful home permeated with His love, joy, and peace; or the many other ways He has worked in my life to bring yet more freedom and joy-producing purpose. But that would take many more pages and much too much of your precious time. You've already been so very patient. Thank you so much for that!

However, before I close, I must take just a moment to share something far more important than anything I've said to this point. For thirty-five years of my life, I cannot remember one person coming to me personally to share the gospel and tell me (biblically) how I could receive forgiveness of my sins and eternal life with God in Heaven when I die, or how I could understand God's plan for my life and why this was so important. As mentioned earlier, my parents faithfully took us to church every Sunday and I even attended a parochial school, so I heard a lot of Bible stories and sermons on good moral living. But there was never any instruction concerning a *personal relationship with Jesus* that comes only with the new birth (genuine repentance and personal faith in Jesus' redemptive work on the cross), and the <u>necessity</u> of this for *eternal life (John 3:3–16; Rom. 10:9-10,* etc.). I am truly *deeply* grateful for all that my parents did in their loving and sincere desire to raise us children right. They were diligently following what they had been taught, as did their parents before them. And I am sure that seeds were planted that played a significant role in my salvation (Is. 55:11). But I also know now that the faith of a parent, diligent, strict adherence to religious tradition and practice—including infant baptism with the confessions of a "sponsor" or "godparent" on one's behalf, and partaking of the sacraments, or even *being good* (doing "good works"), will not get one person into Heaven. The Word of God could not be clearer: *Truly, truly, I say to you, unless one is born again, he cannot see the kingdom of God...My people perish for lack of knowledge (John 3:3; Hosea 4:6).* This *lack of knowledge* nearly cost me, not only my present life, but also eternal separation from God. I was perishing because I did not understand what the Bible says about salvation, the new birth, God's plan for my life…and many other things.

> *"Lies and not Truth prevail in the land" declares the Lord… From the prophet even to the priest, everyone practices deceit. And they heal the brokenness of My people superficially, saying, 'Peace, peace,' But there is no peace" (Jer. 9:3; 8:10–11).*

I lived in that dreadful, terrible condition all those long painful years of mental and emotional instability, superficial healing, self-manufactured (false) peace. It was God's Word that broke through the darkness of the deception and illumined the way back to God in whom I found real, lasting healing and the filling up of all those empty places in my heart for love, acceptance, purpose.

Jesus said: *I am the Way, the Truth, and the Life; no one comes to the Father (to Heaven) except through Me (John 14:6).* People have tried for centuries to ignore or argue against this basic foundational truth to their own hurt and eventual eternal damnation. But argue as they will, ignore as they choose, it will never alter the reality of this truth nor the consequence of its rejection. I cannot help but think often of how very close I came to this point, because the Bible also clearly teaches that there comes a time when God will close the door of salvation to those who continue to reject His Son…*trampling underfoot His precious blood and the suffering He endured for our redemption… and there will never again be an opportunity to turn back, to repent (Heb. 6:4–6, 10:26–29, sel.).* This is a very sobering fact that yet sends me to my knees in overwhelming gratitude to God for His *patience and longsuffering (Ex. 34:6)* towards me. It is also the reason I cannot help but share the wonderful good news with others before it might be *too late* for them.

And that is what this Bible study is all about. It is not only about true salvation—forgiveness of sins and eternal life with God in Heaven one day—it is also about *freedom* and *joy* and *showers of blessings* along the way.

And I will make a covenant of peace with them and eliminate harmful beasts from the land, so that they may live securely… And I will cause showers to come down… they will be showers of blessing (Ezek. 34:25–26).

These things I have written that My joy may be in you and your joy may be full (John 15:11).

*If you continue in My Word, then are you My disciples indeed. And you shall know the Truth, and the Truth shall make you free… If the Son, therefore, shall set you free, you shall be **free indeed** (John 8:31-32, 36).*

Chapter 1 — Day 2
Introduction to Oaks of Righteousness

> *Then I will make to cease from the cities of Judah and from the streets of Jerusalem the voice of joy and the voice of gladness, the voice of the bridegroom and the voice of the bride; for the land will become a ruin (Jer. 7:34).*
>
> *My people are destroyed for lack of knowledge (Hosea 4:6).*

"Lies and not truth prevail in the land; for they proceed from evil to evil, and they do not know Me," declares the Lord… And everyone deceives his neighbor, and does not speak the truth;… they weary themselves committing iniquity. Your dwelling is in the midst of deceit; through deceit they refuse to know Me," declares the Lord… Then I will make to cease from the cities of Judah and from the streets of Jerusalem the voice of joy and the voice of gladness, the voice of the bridegroom and the voice of the bride;… the land will become a ruin (Jer. 9:3-6, Jer. 7:34, 9:12).

We live in a land devastated by the results of abandoning God and His Word. Gone from many homes is *the voice of joy and the voice of gladness (Jer. 7:34).* Demonic deception, uncertainty, and a joy-robbing oppression have invaded even Christian homes and churches (perhaps not outwardly, but inwardly behind the façade of superficial smiles). There is far more fear than faith; more gloom than joy; more anxiety than peace.

Is this the way God intended it to be for His redeemed children? According to the Word of God, the answer is a resounding, "No!"

The people who walk in darkness will see a great light; those who live in a dark land, the light will shine on them… Thou shalt increase their gladness… (they will) proclaim the excellencies of Him who has called (them) out of darkness into His marvelous light (Is. 9:2-3; 1 Pet. 2:9).

The world may be growing dark, lies may prevail in our land, but we have the light of the unfailing truths and promises of the Word of God *as an anchor of the soul, a hope both sure and steadfast (Heb. 6:19).* Far from the *gloom and doom* lies of Satan that he has deceived many into believing—all is hopeless, all is futile, there is nothing we can do—things are far from hopeless! And there is something we can do. These are not *gloom and doom* days for the people of God. They are days of hope and anticipation (Titus 2:13; Luke 21:28), and they are opportune days to shine the light of God's love and truth more brightly than ever before. Light always shines brightest in the darkness!

Jesus Christ is the same yesterday, today and forever (Heb. 13:6). And so are His promises. The Bible says: *where sin increased, grace abounded all the more (Rom. 5:20).*

Because of the grace that is ours in Jesus, all His promises to us are still *yes and amen in Him (1 Cor.*

1:20), including the promises found in Is. 63:1-3. And these particular promises are perhaps, more needed and more relevant now than at any other time in history. Listen to Jesus—I mean really *listen*—as He calls out to us today:

> *The Spirit of the Lord God is upon me, because He has anointed me to bring good news to the afflicted... to bind up the brokenhearted, to proclaim liberty to captives, and freedom to prisoners;... to comfort all who mourn... giving them the oil of gladness instead of mourning, the mantle of praise instead of a spirit of fainting. So they will be called oaks of righteousness, the planting of the Lord, that He may be glorified (Is. 61:1-3).*

And that is what this Bible Study is all about. It's about *binding up broken hearts* and *proclaiming liberty to captives;* it's about *comfort and gladness and mantles of praise.* It's about *walking in the light as He is in the light,* and *increasing our joy* (John 8:12; Is. 9:2-3). It's about *restoring what the locusts have eaten,* and *being delivered from our enemies* that *we might serve God without fear... all the days of our lives* (Joel 2:25; Luke 1:75). It's about finding, *in Christ,* an inexhaustible *river of living water,* and *joys inexpressible and full of glory* (John 7:38; 1 Pet. 1:8, cf. John 15:11; Neh. 8:10; Ps. 46:4-5).

Won't you join me today in committing to diligently study God's Word that we might know His life-giving truths and promises, and in the power and strength of the Holy Spirit, live them! In so doing, the broken places of our lives will be restored, chains of bondage will be broken, and we will become strong, secure *oaks of righteousness, the planting of the Lord that He may be glorified (Is. 61:3).* To all who share this heartfelt longing, God says:

> *But you, Israel, My servant...whom I have chosen, and not rejected... Do not fear, for I am with you; do not anxiously look about you, for I am your God. I will strengthen you; surely I will help you; surely I will uphold you with My righteous right hand (Is. 41:8-10, sel.).*

> *The people who survived the sword found grace in the wilderness... I will build you, and you shall be rebuilt. Again you shall take up your tambourines, and go forth to the dances of the merrymakers... I will lead them; I will make them walk by streams of waters, on a straight path in which they shall not stumble; for I am a father to Israel (Jer. 31:2, 4, 9).*

> *I (Jesus) came that (you) might have life, and have it more abundantly... and you shall go out with Joy be led forth in peace... these things I have spoken to you, that My Joy may be in you, and your Joy may be full... the Joy of the Lord is my strength... Serve the Lord with gladness! (John 10:10; Is. 55:12; John 15:11; Neh. 8:10; Ps. 100:2).*

May these promises and the assurance of their fulfillment (2 Cor. 1:20) fill your heart with hope and joyful anticipation as we begin this study.

[Please read "A Word from Mel" (next page) before proceeding to the Bible Study Supplement.]

A Word from Mel

It is with joy that I affirm this Bible Study. Gloria has taught this study for a number of years and the women in each class have encouraged her to put it into a book so they could share it with others. When Gloria came to me to discuss this possibility, she expressed deep concerns over her place as a woman to publish a book such as this, realizing that it was an interactive Bible Study that could be used by both men and women to help them understand and apply God's Word. Gloria is totally committed to the biblical teaching of male headship in the church, as well as her role as my wife and helpmate—that God has placed her under my authority. She has sought my counsel and approval on every chapter. I know the contents of this book, and I've seen how it has already helped many others who have gone through it.

As I think of Gloria, two Scriptures come to mind. The first is from Proverbs 31. *She rises also while it is still night (Prov. 31:15)* in order to spend uninterrupted time in God's Word and prayer. This she has done consistently since becoming a Christian more than 25 years ago. Her knowledge of scripture, love for God and others, and courage and perseverance in the midst of trials and difficulties reflect this.

The other scripture that comes to mind is Phil. 2:16-17: *Holding fast to the Word of life… I rejoice and share my joy with you all.* Gloria treasures God's Word… *hiding it in her heart* and *holding fast* to it. She has experienced the power it has to transform lives—hers and others—bringing God's love, joy and peace into the hearts and homes of all who live by it. Therefore, one of her greatest joys is sharing the truths and promises of God's Word with others.

God, according to His perfect providence, has taken Gloria through many difficult trials. I have watched her weather these often humanly overwhelming situations with her strong faith and deep desire to honor and glorify God through a life of trust and perseverance—no matter the degree of difficulty or depth of pain. Through these experiences, God has purified and strengthened her faith and equipped her to communicate to others His life-giving truths. For Gloria **not** to share this godly wisdom would be tantamount to hoarding these treasures (Matt. 25:14-30).

I join Gloria in praying that God will use this study to strengthen, encourage, and bless all who go through it. To God be the glory in and through all that is accomplished.

Mel Blowers

Mel Blowers, Gloria's husband, is a Deacon and Sunday School Teacher at Mt. Yonah Baptist Church. He is active in ministry and missions—at home and abroad. Mel is a 777 Captain with Delta Airlines, flying internationally.

Bible Study Supplement
Chapter 1 — Day 2 — Introduction to *Oaks of Righteousness*

1 Read Is. 61:1-3. (Please use NASB text below):

1. The Spirit of the Lord God is upon me, because the Lord has anointed me to bring good news to the afflicted; He has sent me to bind up the brokenhearted, to proclaim liberty to captives, and freedom to prisoners; …

2. to comfort all who mourn…

3. giving them a garland instead of ashes, the oil of gladness instead of mourning, the mantle of praise instead of a spirit of fainting. So they will be called oaks of righteousness, the planting of the Lord, that He may be glorified (Is. 61:1-3).

   a. What was Jesus sent by the Father to do for all who would put their faith and trust in Him? (eight things - Be very specific, listing every phrase separately as each one deals with a different aspect of freedom, comfort and joy - vs. 1-3).

   b. Why does Jesus do all these things? (Again, be very specific – three reasons – vs. 3b)

2. Read Jer. 17:5-8.
   a. Who is cursed? (three characteristics – vs. 5)

   b. Describe what he will be like. (three characteristics – vs. 6)

   c. Who is blessed? (vs. 7)

   d. What will his life be like? (six characteristics – vs. 8)

3. Read Psalm 1.
   a. Who is blessed? (The man who does <u>not</u>…three things) (vs. 1)

Note: We learn here the importance of choosing our friends wisely. We should be careful not to seek important counsel from those who are not walking closely to God. We put ourselves in grave danger when we fail to heed this good biblical instruction.

　　b. In what does the psalmist find his greatest delight and upon what does he meditate day and night? (vs. 2)

In verse 3, we are told that the man who loves and meditates upon God's Word will be like a strong tree that is firmly planted by a stream (God's Word) from which it continually draws nourishment and strength to remain vibrant and strong.

　　c. What are the wicked like? (vs. 4)

　　d. What will happen to the wicked? (vs. 6b)

Note: Whenever the word *wicked* is used in the Bible, it is rarely referring to murderers, thieves, or other vile criminals. It most often refers to anyone who is not in a right, obedient relationship with God, but is, instead, walking *according to his own stubborn heart without listening to God (Jer. 16:12)*. In other words, it is anyone who is in outward or inward rebellion against Him. We can be in rebellion inwardly by exercising an unsubmissive, unyielded (demanding/controlling) spirit or by nursing an ungrateful, unforgiving, bitter attitude. This kind of rebellion against God is a sin and grieves the Holy Spirit who instructs us in God's Word to be *thankful in all things (1 Thess. 5:18)*, to *rejoice always (Phil. 4:4)*, and to *offer sacrifices of praise from the rising of the sun to its setting (Heb. 13:15; Ps. 113:3)*. God gives us these good instructions because He knows that if we don't meditate on God's Word, filling our hearts continually with the hope and joy of its promises, we will focus upon ourselves and our insatiable fleshly lusts and desires. We will, as a result, be discontent, devoid of real peace and joy. Please take note of this so you will have a correct biblical understanding of "wicked" when you encounter it in your studies.

　4. Read Is. 25:1, 3a
　　a. What kind of people honor and glorify God? (vs. 3a) A _____ people.

Would you consider yourself a strong person, who, like a stately, secure, deep-rooted oak tree, flourishes in the righteousness, freedom and victory that Jesus procured for you? Does your life manifest a radiant, trusting joy that brings honor and glory to Him? If not, take heart. This Bible Study will help you *fortify weak places* and *strengthen the hands that hang limp (Heb. 12:12)*.

Write out a Bible verse that had special meaning to you today.

Based upon what you have learned today, write a prayer to God expressing the desires of your heart in applying these truths to your life.

Chapter 1 — Day 3
In the Beginning...GOD

The heavens declare the glory of God, and their expanse is declaring the work of His hands (Ps. 19:1).

Hear, O Israel! The Lord is God, the Lord is one! I am the LORD, and there is no other; Apart from me there is no God (Deut. 6:4, Is. 45:5).

The fool has said in his heart, "There is no God." (Ps. 14.1)

... But realize this, that in the last days, difficult times will come, for men will be lovers of self, lovers of money... lovers of pleasure rather than lovers of God (2 Tim. 3:2-3).

We live in a world obsessed with the love of self and pleasure rather than loving God. Because man is consumed with seeking his own pleasure, he has little time to consider God...*who to know is life eternal (John 17:3)*. Because of the world's preoccupation with self and rejection of God:

"Lies and not truth prevail in the land; for they proceed from evil to evil, and they do not know Me," declares the Lord;...they weary themselves committing iniquity. "Your dwelling is in the midst of deceit; through deceit they refuse to know Me," declares the Lord (Jer. 9:3-6).

Of all the lies being foisted upon our land, the greatest, naturally, are the lies about God—His nature, His character, His purposes and plans for the world, and every individual in it. Satanically spawned, the evolution/humanism movement—the philosophy that believes man, not God is the center of the Universe and the controller of his destiny—is now the ruling religion of the world. Presumptuously assuming the role of "God", this new religion rejects the idea of a sovereign Creator and proudly

and mockingly discounts even His existence. Thus, convolutedly, it has become "God", not man who is *on trial* and must prove Himself. But it is very foolish to place man at the center of the universe and deny the existence and authority of God.

The fool hath said in his heart: There is no God (Ps. 14.1).

To every fool who, through demonic deception, or just plain pride and willful rebellion, has chosen to reject Him, God, in His infinite love reaches out. He welcomes even the haughty, rebellious ones to come into His presence and to sit before Him as He asks a few penetrating questions:

Where were you when I laid the foundation of the earth? Tell Me...Who set its measurements, since you know? Or who stretched the line (of the equator) on it? Who enclosed the sea... and said, "Thus far you shall come, but no farther and here shall your proud waves stop?" (separating the dry land from the oceans)...Have you ever in your life commanded the morning, and caused the dawn to know its place... Have you entered into the springs of the sea? Or have you walked in the recesses of the deep?...Tell Me, if you know all this...Where is the way to the dwelling of light? And darkness, where is its place, that you may take it to its territory... and that you may discern the paths to its home? (Surely) you know, for (you claim) *you were born then,* (unsubstantiated evolutionary theories presented as "fact", as if one were "born then") *and the number of your days is great! (10 billion years?!)...Have you entered the storehouses of the snow... or hail? Who has cleft a channel for the flood, or a way for the thunderbolt...to bring rain on a... desert...to satisfy the waste and desolate land, and to make the seeds of grass to sprout?*

... Or who has begotten the drops of dew? From whose womb has come the ice... and the frost of heaven?...Can you... loose the cords of Orion? Can you lead forth a constellation in its season, and guide the Bear with her satellites? (the two northern hemisphere constellations, the Great Bear and the Little Bear). *Do you know the ordinances of the heavens, or fix their rule over the earth? Can you lift up your voice to the clouds, so that an abundance of water may cover you?... or tip the water jars of the heavens, when the dust hardens into a mass and the clods stick together?...Who prepares for the raven its nourishment, when its young cry to God? (Job 38:1-41, sel.).*

Only a fool would respond affirmatively to all these questions. No human was "there" when God laid the foundations of the earth. And no human has the kind of authority over the universe described here. Only God has that kind of power. And only God, day after faithful day, continues to rule and sustain this vast universe. Therefore, we need to settle once and for all...

In the beginning...God

God, the Creator and sovereign ruler of the universe, does not have to *prove Himself*.

He's already done that!

The heavens declare the glory of God and their expanse is declaring the work of His hands; day to day pours forth His speech, and night to night reveals knowledge (Ps. 19:1-2).

The vastness of the universe with its incalculable galaxies of stars and planets—along with thousands of *other infallible proofs within it (Acts 1:3)—declare the glory of God* by day and by night, pouring forth proof of His power and sustaining presence. Consider for just a moment:

The expanse of creation is staggering. Have you ever reflected on the size of the universe?

A ray of light travels 186,000 miles a second, so a beam of light from here will reach the moon in a second and a half. Imagine traveling that fast! You could reach Mercury in four and a half minutes, Jupiter in thirty-five minutes. If you decided to go farther, you could reach Saturn in about an hour, but it would take four years and four months to make it to the nearest star. Traveling just to the edge of our galaxy, the Milky Way, would take you about 100,000 years! If you could count the stars as you travel, they would number about 100 billion in the Milky Way alone. If you wanted to explore other galaxies, you would have billions to choose from. The size of our universe is understandably incomprehensible. If you refuse to recognize a Creator, it's difficult to explain how this marvelous, intricate, immeasurable universe came into being.[1]

In his video, "The Young Age of the Earth", Dr. Kent Hovind reveals similar mind boggling facts:

Our solar system, the Milky Way, contains more than 100,000,000,000 (one hundred billion!) stars, and the Milky Way is but one very small "page" of God's huge catalogue of the heavens. There are literally more than a billion other galaxies, most of which are many times larger than our galaxy! If the stars (most of which are hundreds of times larger than our sun, which is hundreds of times larger than our earth) were evenly divided among every inhabitant of the earth today, every man, woman and child would have more than two trillion (2,000,000,000,000) stars!

And God knows them all by name! (Is. 40:26).

Lift up your eyes on high and see who has created these stars; The One who leads forth their host by number, He calls them all by name; because of the greatness of His might and the strength of His power, not one of them is missing...When I consider your heavens, the work of your fingers, the moon and the stars, which you have set in place, what is man that you are mindful of him... that you care for him... O Lord, our Lord, how majestic is your Name in all the earth... I will praise you, O Lord... I will tell of all your wonders... The heavens (and earth and all they contain!) *declare the glory of God, and their expanse confirms the work of His hands, day to day pours forth speech! (Is. 40:26; Ps. 8:3, 19:1-2).*

God has further proven Himself in the complex, perfect design of every species in His vast beast, birds and beautifying flora kingdoms. Scientist Paul Bartz of Creation Moments has written several volumes of books on the unique design of animals that irrefutably defy evolutionary explanation. He clearly demonstrates how it is scientifically impossible to explain these unique creatures—of which there are thousands—apart from intelligent design by a Creator. In doing research for this book, I obtained several of Bartz's books. As I began to read, I could not put the books down because the information was so fascinating and the evidence so unarguably supportive of God's divine creative ingenuity—far beyond human ability, and certainly beyond any scientifically debunked "random selection" theory of evolution.

I wish we had time to look in detail at a number of these—they are so interesting, and even humorous at times giving us a glimpse of God's witty, whimsical nature—but there just won't be time for that today. I could not leave this subject, however, without mentioning just a few examples of God's amazing creative genius that clearly demonstrate the abject absurdity of the nonsensical theory of evolution. One of my favorites is the amazing process of metamorphosis. An ugly gray larva (caterpillar) builds a cocoon (chrysalis) around itself. Its body then completely disintegrates into a thick, pulp-like liquid. Days or weeks later an adult insect emerges—one that is dramatically different from it's original form and, as in the case of a butterfly, exquisitely beautiful.

Eighty percent of all insects pass through this metamorphosis process. Food, habitat, and behavior of the larva differ drastically from the adult, once again defying every possible explanation based upon the scientifically unsubstantiated theory of evolution.[2]

And there are literally thousands of other complex, uniquely designed animals, birds, and flora that possess similar evolution defying characteristics, such as the Rove Beetle that "walks on water" gliding gracefully across its surface, stopping, turning and starting up again without moving any part of his body; the Venus flytrap, the incredible plant that snatches its lunch by closing around it instantly through astonishingly rapid cell growth; a sophisticated Bombardier beetle whose protective defense system would rival even the most sophisticated military strategy; the incredible aerodynamic abilities of the tiny hummingbird, and so many more! I hope you will consider getting a couple of the inexpensive paperback books from Creation Moments. You will be blessed as you are reminded again and again of the incredible genius of our great and awesome Creator God. For information on how to obtain Paul Bartz's intriguing *Let God Create Your Day* books, contact Creation Moments.[3]

It is interesting to note that in recent years, some of the world's most renowned scientists in the fields of genetics and origins are standing up and publicly rejecting the theory of evolution, stating emphatically that it is *scientifically absurd* to explain all the uniqueness in plant, animal, and human life without "intelligent design." And the majority of these are non Christians!

These *infallible proofs* in themselves would be more than enough to prove God's existence, His intelligent design of the Universe and His sovereign rulership over it.

There is, however, one more *infallible proof (Acts 1:3)* of God's divine creation that we must mention. It is the greatest *proof* of all that rises far above the arguments of even the most hardened skeptic. It is His masterpiece, His crowning glory, the human body and mind, created... *in His image.*

For Thou didst form my inward parts. Thou didst weave me in my mother's womb. I will give thanks to Thee, for I am fearfully and wonderfully made (Ps. 139:13-14).

There are more than 30 trillion cells that make up every human body. Inside each cell is a nucleus. There is an incredible plethora of activity going on in this nucleus at every second of the day and night. Within each nucleus of a cell are 23 pairs of chromosomes. These form the genetic code that makes every individual unique—color of hair, height, complexion etc. They also, through input from the brain, tell every cell how to act in various situations from birth to death. There is so much information stored in each cell that if you could write it down, it would equal 4,000 volumes of written material—per cell. So how much is 4,000 volumes? It is 20 billion bits of information which is 3 billion letters. At 6 letters per word that is 500,000,000 words. Taking an average of 300 words per page that would equal 2,000,000 pages. Considering 500 pages per book, that would equal 4,000 volumes. You could fill the Grand Canyon several times with the information contained in the cells of one human body. And all of that is working together at any one moment. We are, indeed, *fearfully and wonderfully made!*

A few summers ago, 50 mathematicians, biologists, and physicists came together at the Wister Institute in Philadelphia and for the entire summer scientifically studied the theory of evolution. Spokesman, Dr. Eden from MIT, (Massachusetts Institute of Technology), wrote the following conclusion: "Based on our understanding of the laws of chemistry, physics and what we know about randomness, we see no way that the complexity of life could come about (through) evolutionary processes.[4]

Think for just a moment about what God has allowed us to accomplish with the use of the computer, and satellite communications! Sports fans can watch the Super Bowl while waiting in the airport in Singapore. In the time it takes to blink your eye, a computer can access any subject in the entire Encyclopedia Britannica or scan a nationwide telephone directory. In a few seconds, an e-mail sent from a computer in Georgia arrives at a remote village in Africa. It can also store the information found in dozens of Encyclopedia Britannicas on a memory chip smaller than a baby's thumbnail!

Who has put wisdom in the innermost being, or has given understanding to the mind? (Job. 38:36).

It is, undeniably, GOD who formed man's mind ... *in His image (Gen. 1:26)*—not just so he could create computers and satellites and other such amazing phenomena, but He gave him an intelligent, communicative mind primarily for the glorious purpose of having an intimate, loving, interactive *relationship with Him!* And in the intimacy of that relationship, to share His love and reflect His glory to others.

May God help us all to recognize the eternal privilege and joy of entering into such a relationship ... and the grave danger of rejecting it.

For even though they knew God, they did not honor Him as God, or give thanks, but they became futile in their speculations, and their foolish heart was darkened. Professing to be wise, they became fools, and exchanged the glory of the incorruptible God for an image in the form of corruptible man (whatever he wanted God to be—education, intellect, money, popularity, pleasure). Therefore God gave them over to the impurity of the lusts of their hearts. For they exchanged the truth of God for a lie and worshiped and served the creature rather than the Creator (Rom. 1:21–26).

You, too ... have done evil ... for behold, you are each one walking according to the stubbornness of his own evil heart, without listening to Me ... So I will hurl you out of this land into the land which you have not known ... and there you will serve other gods day and night, for I shall grant you no favor (Jer. 16:12-13).

Return, O faithless sons; I will heal your faithlessness ... .surely in the Lord our God is salvation (Jer. 3:22-23).

Bible Study Supplement
Chapter 1 — Day 3 — In the Beginning…God!

1. Read Ps. 19:1-2.

    a. What is telling of the glory of God? (vs. 1)

    b. What do various aspects of God's creation do day and night? (vs. 2)

God is talking to us *day and night* through His creation: the delicate beauty of a forest trillium, an unfolding rose…or a thousand other masterfully and exquisitely designed flora; the cheerful chirping of a chickadee or melodic refrain of a meadowlark; a gentle breeze; the peaceful sound of a cascading brook; a glorious sunset; a star-studded night. If only we would open our eyes to see and our ears to listen. God is "speaking" to us through it all, reminding us continually of His presence, beauty, and love.

2. Read Ps. 14:1a.

    a. Who has said in his heart, "There is no God"?

3. Read Is. 40:18, 25-26.

    a. What does God invite us to do? (vs. 26a)

    b. What is God able to do concerning the vast galaxies of stars? (vs. 26 – middle of verse)

4. Read Ps. 104:24-28, 33-34.

    a. How has God created all that He has made? (vs. 24)

    b. What should be our response to all that God has done and continues to do? (vs. 33, 34b)

Write out a Bible verse that had special meaning to you today.

Based upon what you have learned today, write a prayer to God expressing the desires of your heart in applying these truths to your life.

Chapter 1 — Day 4
The Authority, Inerrancy, Immutability and Sufficiency of the Word of God—Part One

> *Take to your heart all the words with which I am warning you today, which you shall command your sons to observe carefully; For it is not an idle word for you; indeed it is your life! (Deut. 32:46-47).*

(Note: Immutable means steadfastly secure, not subject to change, unalterable).

A popular saying among Christians a few years ago was "God said it, I believe it, and that settles it for me." But that is a biblically inaccurate statement. It should be: "God said it—that settles it!" Whether I choose to *believe it* or not, I can be sure that every *thus saith the Lord*—and every word in between, from Genesis to Revelation—is true, and it will happen just as God says. *For as many as are the promises of God, in Christ they are yes and Amen! (2 Cor. 1:20).* God is who He says He is and He will do what He says He will do. I find that wonderfully reassuring in an age of ever increasing instability and uncertainty.

As many have rightly said, the Bible is "God's Love Book" to His children. In it, God reveals Himself to us—His nature, His character, His love for us. He tells us how we can enter into and enjoy a secure, loving, protective relationship with Him. He also tells us the wonderful good news of all that He has in store for those who believe and obey His Word as well as the bad news of what will happen if we ignore or rebel against it.

One of the most frequently asked questions through the ages has always been: "Why am I here? What is my purpose in life?" People ask this question because they know they were created for a purpose. God lovingly planted that seed in their hearts as a way of drawing them to Himself—into a personal relationship with Him in which He loves and cares for them and guides them in all the good plans He has for them.

> *He has set eternity in their hearts... For I know the plans I have for you," declares the Lord, "plans for welfare and not for calamity to give you a future and a hope. Then you will call upon Me and come and pray to Me, and I will listen to you. And you will seek Me and find Me, when you search for Me with all your heart" (Eccles. 3:11; Jer. 29:11-13).*

The wise ones, therefore, seek after God. He gladly listens to their searching heart and bids them to enter into a personal relationship with Him. They accept His invitation, then, with deep gratitude, set their hearts on knowing, loving and obeying Him for they realize that the greatest joys in all of life will be found only in an ongoing, growing relationship with God as His good purposes are fulfilled.

These things I have spoken to you, that My joy may be in you and your joy may be full (John 15:11).

They also realize that if they fail to do this, they'll be most miserable, and they will make a lot of others around them miserable as well!

The way of the transgressor is hard… It is hard to kick against the goad (God's will/purpose for one's life) (Prov. 13:15b; Acts 9:5).

Whether we recognize it or not, there are only two concepts that drive us in all that we do: our concept of God and our concept of the purpose for our existence: Why am I here? The answer to these two questions—who is God and what is my purpose—will be at the heart of every man and woman's thoughts, motivations, actions, and eternal destiny.

There is only one place we can go to discover the answer to these fundamental questions of life—the authoritative, inerrant, immutable Word of God.

We can choose to embrace this truth and cherish the Word of God—reading it, studying it, obeying it—or we can reject it. But be sure if we choose the latter, our lives will be superficial and barren of real, lasting peace and contentment—even though we may, with the help of Satan, do a masterful job of deceiving ourselves into believing that "all is well" and we are satisfied and content. It is a lie—a huge, sad, pitiful lie.

Because you say, I am rich and have become wealthy, and have need of nothing. But you do not realize that you are wretched and miserable and poor and blind (Rev. 3:17 Nasb, Niv).

When we who have had free access to the Word of God stand before God one day, there will be no excuse for not knowing Him or fulfilling His will because God has made Himself and His will for our lives perfectly clear in His Word. No wonder Jesus told us: *Seek ye first the Kingdom of God and His righteousness, and all these things (for which your heart yearns—fulfillment, meaning, purpose, peace, joy, etc.) will be added to you (Math. 6:33).*

Sadly, few read and study God's Word diligently so that they can truly know God and enjoy the daily blessings and joys of walking with Him in an intimate, trusting relationship in which He fulfills their deepest needs and longings as they trust and obey Him. Just as the French philosopher Blaise Pascal said centuries ago: "There is a God-shaped vacuum in all of us that only God can fill." It is that part of us that has been created in the image of God to have fellowship with Him, to fulfill His good plans, and to share these with others as we enjoy and reflect His love and glory. Refusing to acknowledge this or trying to fulfill our lives by seeking after our own selfish ambitions apart from God, will only leave us *wretched and miserable (Rev. 3:17),* just as we have all experienced in our own lives and have seen in the lives of countless others.

You, too, have done evil, even more than your forefathers; for behold, you are each one walking according to the stubbornness of his own evil heart, <u>without listening to Me</u> (Jer. 16:12).

These words yet ring often in my heart, reminding me of my previous condition, and of the tendency even now in my fallen state to desire to walk *according to the stubbornness of my own evil heart, without listening to God.* It is also a sad but accurate picture of many in God's family today who think that going to church once a week is all they need in order to *listen to God* and develop a loving, growing relationship with Him. Can you imagine trying to have an intimate, fulfilling marriage if you only spent one hour a week with your spouse? How can you possibly come to know and understand the heart of your spouse if you never spend time with him/her? It won't work. And neither can we develop an intimate and fulfilling relationship with God by spending only one hour with Him a week (or less, if we are sporadic in our worship). It is impossible to *know God* and to *love God* apart from spending time daily in fellowship with Him—in His Word and prayer.

We also need to be in God's Word on a regular, consistent basis in order to keep our minds alert and discerning—able to cut through Satan's crafty lies and deceptions that appear so innocent and enticing but lead only to agonizing disappointment and destruction (Prov. 14:12; John 10:10a). It breaks my heart when I see people stubbornly resist setting aside time to be in God's Word every day, because without the Word of God we are powerless to stand against the enemy, being without *sword or shield (Eph. 6:10–17)*. Whoever walks out into the day without a fresh renewing of their minds through the reading and study of God's Word will be unprotected and vulnerable to the enemy's deceptions and temptations and the wounds inflicted will often be painful and deep. And the even sadder part is that the consequences of our own willful rebellion (sin) affects those around us, causing yet more hurt and suffering. Guilt-driven outbursts of anger and impatience nearly always follow sinful acts—it is the nature of guilt to produce this kind of fruit. Therefore, it is my fervent prayer that if nothing else is accomplished throughout this study, every person who participates will realize how desperately we all need the truths of God's Word refreshing and renewing our hearts and minds daily, and will begin to set aside a consistent time for study and prayer fellowship with God. After all, at the heart of God's plan for our lives is a living, loving, growing, relationship with Him. It is impossible to develop such a relationship without spending time getting to know God through *the one thing needful*—His precious Word (Luke 10:42).

As with God, the Bible does not have to *prove itself*. It was established and *settled* long before any of us arrived on the planet!

Forever, O Lord, Thy Word is settled in Heaven. Thy faithfulness continues throughout all generations. Thou didst establish the earth, and it stands (Ps. 119:89-90).

We would be wise also to remind ourselves daily that there is a consequence for all who discount, ignore, and defame the one and only true God, by refusing to come to Him, seeking to know and to fulfill His good purposes for their lives.

Be not deceived; God is not mocked. For whatever a man sows, this he will also reap. For the one who sows to his own flesh shall from the flesh reap corruption…We have sown the wind. We are reaping the whirlwind. The standing grain has no heads; it yields no grain (Gal. 6:7; Hosea 8:7).

The condition of our world today confirms the truth of God's loving warning here. We have *sown the wind* and we are *reaping the whirlwind*. There is a lot of *standing grain* with no *fruit bearing heads*.

But it doesn't have to be like that for us and for our families. Let's take a few moments today to *look intently into the Word of God (James 1:25)* to confirm in our hearts once again its authority, inerrancy, immutability, sufficiency…and necessity.

Take to your heart all the words I have solemnly declared to you today… For it is not an idle word for you; indeed it is your life (Deut. 32:46-47a, NIV, NASB).

Bible Study Supplement
Chapter 1 — Day 4 — The Authority of the Word of God—Part One

1. Read 2 Tim. 3:16-17.

   Note: The word translated as "inspired" or "by inspiration" in some translations comes from the Greek, *theos* (God) and *pneo* (to breath) and actually means "God-breathed". In other words, the words of the Bible had their origin in the heart of God who then "breathed" them, through the Holy Spirit, into the minds of the writers. They are, therefore, <u>God's words</u>.

   a. How much of the Bible (Scripture) is inspired/God-breathed? (vs. 16)

   b. For what is the Word of God profitable? (four things – vs. 16)

   c. What does it do for the student who diligently studies it in order to obey it? (vs. 17)

Do you see the vital role the Word of God plays in equipping us to do the job to which God calls us? In fact, it is impossible to be adequately equipped without it. That is why we need the Word of God each day in our lives to keep us on God's path and to give us wisdom and discernment in dealing wisely and confidently with every situation that comes to us.

2. Read Psalm 119:1–5, 9–11.

   a. Who is blessed? (four characteristics – vs. 1-2…note especially 2b)

   b. For what does the psalmist long? (vs. 5)

   c. How can a young man keep his way pure? (vs. 9b)

   d. What has the psalmist hidden in his heart?…Why? (vs. 11)

3. Read Ps. 119:89–93.

   a. How does the psalmist describe God's Word and His faithfulness? (vs. 89-90a)

   b. What did God do that confirms this? (vs. 90b)

   c. What would have happened to the psalmist if God's Word hadn't been his delight? (vs. 92b)

   d. What have God's precepts done for him? (vs. 93b)

4. Read Ps. 119:97-105.

   a. What does the psalmist love? (vs 97a) What is this to him (what does he do with it) all day, every day? (vs. 97b)

    b. What do God's commandments make the psalmist? (Three things - vs. 98a, 99a, 100a)

    c. From what has the psalmist restrained his feet? (vs. 101a)

    d. Who has taught him? (vs. 102b)

    e. Describe God's words to him. (vs. 103)

    f. What do God's words provide as he walks through life? (two things - vs. 105)

5. Read Ps. 119:111-112.

    a. What are the testimonies of God to the psalmist? (vs. 111b)

    b. What has he inclined his heart to do? For how long? (vs. 112)

6. Read Ps. 119:129-130.

    a. How does he view (think of) God's testimonies? (vs. 129a)

    b. What does the unfolding (entrance into his heart) of God's words do? (two things – vs. 130)

7. Read Ps. 119:160 - Please use NASB translation below to answer the question that follows.

The sum of Thy word is truth, and every one of Thy righteous ordinances is everlasting (Ps. 119:160).

    a. What is truth? (vs. 160a)

8. Read Ps. 119:165.

    a. What happens to those who love God's law? (two things)

9. Read Deut. 32:45-47.

    a. What are we to take to our hearts?...and what are we to do with it? (vs. 46)

    c. Why is this so important? (vs. 47a).

Write out a Bible verse that had special meaning to you today.

Based upon what you have learned today, write a prayer to God expressing the desires of your heart in applying these truths to your life.

Chapter 1 — Day 5
The Authority, Inerrancy, Immutability and Sufficiency of the Word of God—Part Two

But know this first of all, that no prophecy of Scripture is a matter of one's own interpretation, for no prophecy was ever made by an act of human will, but men moved by the Holy Spirit spoke from God (2 Pet. 1:20,21).

Remember the former things long past, for I am God, and there is no other; I am God, and there is no one like Me, declaring the end from the beginning, and from ancient times things which have not been done, saying, My purpose will be established (Is. 46:9-10).

Three Irrefutable Facts That Affirm that the Bible is Exactly What It Claims to be: The Infallible, Authoritative Word of God

Having been a diligent and faithful student of the Word of God for over 25 years, I can say with total honesty that there is not one shred of doubt in my mind concerning its authority, inerrancy, immutability and sufficiency. In fact, I believe this so strongly that I would give my life before I would deny God, the author of the Bible, or His precious Word that He has given us. Why? Why would I, like thousands before me, literally stake my life on the authority and inerrancy of the Word of God? There are many reasons for that. We won't have time to examine all of them today, but let's consider just three, that in themselves, prove the authority and trustworthiness of the Word of God.

1. **The Continuity and Antiquity of the Bible –** The Bible is unique from all other books that have ever been written in that it contains 66 unique, separate books written by 40 authors over a period of 1500 years on three different continents

and in three distinct languages. People who, in most cases, never met together, never talked, and were separated from each other by time, space, occupation, and language, all write with complete unity. Without question, it would have been impossible for fallible, mortal man to have accomplished such a feat. Only God, Himself, who was present throughout those 1500 years could have orchestrated this kind of transcendent symmetry as He omnisciently *breathed* His Words through His chosen vessels (2 Tim. 3:16; 2 Pet. 1:21).

The original manuscripts of the Bible are by far the oldest, most consistent, historically verified writings in existence. No other book of its size and detail comes even close to the age of the earliest manuscripts of the Bible, as authenticated by scientific dating methods and corroborating historic documentation. The discovery of the Dead Sea Scrolls in the Qumran Caves on the northwestern edge of the Dead Sea in 1947 further validates the antiquity and authenticity of the Word of God. Only divine intervention in the protection and locating of these manuscripts, some of which date one thousand years earlier than any previous manuscripts, could account for this unique preservation and discovery.

The fact that the Bible has survived thousands of years of history, including countless wars, collapses of entire civilizations, rebellions, godless men who tried to destroy it, persecutions, martyrdom, the Dark Ages, and dozens of other destructive obstacles, further proves its God-breathed origin and divine preservation. There is no other book that even remotely compares to the antiquity, consistency (in the hundreds of manuscripts found), and historical authenticity of the Bible. And just the fact that it remains, by far, the most read book in the world, proves that there is a loving Heavenly Father who desires to communicate with His children and has preserved His Word through which He does this faithfully from generation to generation.

As I was preparing this meditation, I could not help but think of one of my cherished historical treasures. It is an old Swedish Bible that is nearly two hundred years old. But the cover is worn, the pages are frayed, and parts of it are already illegible. To think that this precious keepsake (and hundreds like it) is only two hundred years old while some of the original Hebrew manuscripts of the Bible are more than two thousand years old and still perfectly legible and historically accurate, presents even further evidence of divine intervention and protection.

2. **Prophecy** – God says in His Word: *Remember this, and be assured; … Recall it to mind, you transgressors. Remember the former things long past, For I am God, and there is no other; I am God, and there is no one like Me; Declaring the end from the beginning, and from ancient times things which have not been done, saying, 'My purpose will be established, and I will accomplish all… I have planned, surely I will do it.' Listen to Me, you stubborn-minded, who are far from righteousness. I bring near My righteousness… and my salvation (Is. 46:8-10, 12-13).*

No other "god" through the ages could ever make and keep such a claim—to be able to *declare the end from the beginning.* Only God could do this. From the very beginning of time, He has told us all the major events that would transpire down through the ages until the very end of time. And so history has unfolded precisely as God has said it would with 100% accuracy! Those who have attempted to replicate this kind of prophetic declaration, even during very brief windows in time, have consistently been proven false in the fulfillment of their prognostications. God's prophecies have never failed. Not once! And we can be sure they never will. The first time I read the entire Bible through I found myself in total awe again and again at the hundreds of prophecies that were fulfilled to the minutest detail: prophecies that would have been impossible to feign, having been written hundreds, and in some cases, thousands of years before their fulfillment. And every major prophecy has been substantiated—both the circumstances and times of the prophecy and its fulfillment—by closely examined and dated historical records.

The Bible contains more than *two thousand prophecies,* each and every one of which has been fulfilled *exactly* as God said it would happen—except for the very few remaining that await fulfillment in the final days just before and at the time of Jesus' return (2nd coming). When God says, *thus saith the Lord,* you can be sure that *and it was so* will inevitably follow. I never once doubted one word of God's Word after that first read-through-the-Bible experience. And every subsequent year that I have read it through from Genesis to Revelation that assurance has been reinforced all the more. I have not found one promise or one significant statement of fact (truth) refutable. God is Who He says He is; He has always done what He said He would do and He will continue to be true to every promise He has made both for the present and for the future. We can count on that!

3. **Changed lives!** – Though the above two reasons alone should be more than enough to thoroughly convince any thinking, intelligent mind to *take heed* and put faith and trust in the authority of God's Word, the power that it holds to change lives is irrefutable. You just can't argue against a radically changed life. It is living, on-going proof of the power of the Spirit of God working through the Word of God as it is read, believed, and obeyed. I know what God's Word has done (and continues to do) in my life. The changes have been nothing short of miraculous—*humanly* impossible. And history is replete with examples of that same power working in the lives of others, just as it continues to work in countless more lives today. Its power to totally change a life—from one of chaos and destruction, to one of order, confidence, purpose, and peace—is irrefutable evidence of its divine origin and power. (For nearly 3,000 documented testimonies of such irrefutable evidences of changed lives, see appendix, Resources, "Unshackled").

No wonder the Word of God warns that only *fools despise wisdom* (the wisdom of God's Word) (Prov. 1:7). One would have to have a totally depraved mind to examine all the evidence and then conclude that the Bible is anything less than the inspired, inerrant, infallible, *God-breathed* Word of the Creator of the Universe—the only true sovereign, living God *(2 Tim. 3:16-17; 2 Pet. 1:21)*.

> *For the Word of God is living and active and sharper than any two-edged sword...able to judge the thoughts and intentions of the heart ... moreover by (God's Word) Thy servant is warned; in keeping (it) there is great reward (Heb. 4:12; Ps. 19:11).*

The Word of God remains as *living and active* today as the days in which it was written. It still has the power to change, encourage and strengthen lives. How often this precious truth was proven in my own life. When I was going through the darkest times of pain and confusion associated with the mysterious affliction that sapped every ounce of energy and kept my body wracked in pain, threatening to destroy my hope that I would even survive—it was God's Word alone that kept my heart encouraged and gave me the strength to *press on.* I can remember so vividly endless days when I was so weak and so sick that I could not get out of bed or hold my head up in my own strength. But as I prayed and trusted God to help me, He gave the strength to get up and move—ever so slowly and with great effort—to my quiet time corner. There I would prop my head in my own cupped hands resting on the table for strength, and I would read God's Word through blurry eyes. And every day—*every day*—God would speak life-giving promises to me through His Word—promises that gave encouragement and strength—*living, empowering strength*:

> *There is a river whose streams make glad the (children) of God... God is in the midst of her, she will not be moved; God will help her when morning dawns... How precious is Thy lovingkindness, O God!...the children of men take refuge in the shadow of Thy wings. They drink their fill of the abundance of Thy house; and Thou dost give them to drink of the river of Thy delights. For with Thee is the fountain of life (Ps. 46:4-5, 36:7-9).*

> *Now on the last day... of the feast, Jesus stood and cried out, "He who believes in Me, as the Scripture (says), From his innermost being shall flow rivers of living water" (John 7:37-38).*

Through the Holy Spirit resident in me, the *living waters* of God's love, mercy and grace, began to flow into every depleted cell reviving my languishing body and soul. My spirit would be renewed and refreshed—to not just make it through another day, but to be productive and accomplish God's good purposes in it (Ps. 119:153-159; Heb. 4:12). Then, when the evening shadows fell, and I had completed the work God has given me for that day, I would go to bed with a sweet sense of God's presence and cherished affirmation: *Well done, good and faithful servant (Math. 25:23).* And I can say without hesitation that had I not remained faithful to reading, studying, desiring and seeking to obey God's Word daily, this book would never have been written, nor would I even "be here" to tell of it. I would, instead be: 1) dead (suicide), 2) totally disabled or 3) a non-productive, mental and emotional prescription-drug-crazed zombie by this point. There is not a shred of doubt in my mind about this! Not one! God's Word is not only *living and active*, it is *powerful*, imparting *life-giving wisdom and strength!*

Before closing today's meditation, I just want to say a few words concerning the *sufficiency* of Scripture. Sadly, just as the Bible warned would happen *in the last days, many deceivers* (false teachers) have *crept in unnoticed* as *savage wolves, leading My people astray (2 Peter 2:1–12; Acts 20:29–32; 1 John 4:1–6; 2 John 1:7–9, sel.).* God warns us and bids our vigilance concerning these *wolves in sheep's clothing (Matt. 7:15),* so that we are not seduced by their enticing temptations to abandon or doubt the Word of God. Under the influence and deception of Satan, these false teachers (some of whom are actually well-meaning, born-again believers who have been blinded by the incredible power of Satan through the false teaching of respected, powerful leaders in the Christian community) have stirred the hearts of many so that there is a great battle waging against the *sufficiency* of Scripture. Many modern day "biblical scholars" say that they affirm the accuracy and the authority of Scripture but quickly cast doubt upon its *sufficiency* for guiding us in our complex 21ˢᵗ Century lives. They claim that we need the additional "revelation" of humanistic

(man-centered rather than God-centered) psychology, psychotherapy, and any of a number of other rebellious modern man's intellectual enlightenments. They thus raise doubt in the minds of many who do not know Scripture nor its thorough, divinely powerful *sufficiency:*

> *…His divine power has granted to us everything pertaining to life and godliness, through the true knowledge of Him who called us by His own glory and excellence (2 Pet. 1:3).*

God says here that He has given us *everything* we need *pertaining to life and godliness.* Therefore, we can confidently put our trust in the sufficiency of Scripture for *all* matters of life. God has always known about every problem, concern and need we would ever encounter and He has given us instructions concerning all these in His Word. That means there is nothing that I will ever experience in this life concerning which the Word of God does not speak, giving wisdom and direction. Nothing! I find that truth incalculably reassuring.

May God help us all to love and cherish His Word for what it is: God's eternal, *living and active* (life-giving) wisdom, power and unfailing promises to us. It is through God's Word that He fellowships with us and guides us in all His good plans daily, blessing our lives and filling them with *precious and pleasant riches (Prov. 24:3-4).*

> *Thy testimonies are wonderful; therefore my soul observes them. The unfolding of Thy words gives light; it gives understanding to the simple. (Ps. 119:129-130)*

Bible Study Supplement
Chapter 1 — Day 5 — The Authority of the Word of God—Part Two
**Three Irrefutable Facts That Affirm that the Bible is Exactly What It Claims to be:
The Infallible, Authoritative Word of God**

Just a short reminder before we begin today's Bible Study. As mentioned in the instructions at the beginning of the book, because of the extra introductory material, we have an added day for this week—Day 6. (All other weeks will have only five lessons). Please keep this in mind and come back again tomorrow as Day 6 is one of the most important lessons in this entire study. You definitely will not want to miss it.

1. Read 2 Pet. 1:19–21.

   a. What do we do well to "pay attention to"? (vs. 19)

Note: In the early days of God's revelation of Himself to man, He called prophets through whom He spoke to the people. Later, God spoke to us directly through Jesus (Heb. 1:1-2). And today, He continues to speaks to us through His Word and through His Holy Spirit who is present in the Word instructing and guiding, comforting and strengthening us (John 14:16-17; John 16:7-15).

   b. What does God say that we are to know, understand? (vs. 20)

   c. Whose words were actually "spoken" through the prophets? (vs. 21)

2. Read Is. 46:8–10.

   a. What has God done that distinguishes Him from all other "gods"? (vs. 10a)

3. Read Ps. 19:7-11. (Please use NIV text below to answer the questions):

   7. The law of the Lord is perfect, reviving the soul; The statutes of the Lord are sure, making wise the simple.

   8. The precepts of the Lord are right, giving joy to the heart; the commands of the Lord are radiant, giving light to the eyes.

   9. The fear of the Lord is pure, enduring forever.

   10. They are more precious than gold, than much pure gold; they are sweeter than honey, than honey from the comb.

   11. By them is your servant warned; in keeping them there is great reward (Ps. 19:7-11, NIV).

Fill in the blanks and answer the questions:

   a. (vs. 7a) *The law of the Lord* is _____. What does it do for the soul?

   b. (vs. 7b) *The statues of the Lord* are _____. What do they do?

    c. (vs. 8a) *The precepts* (teachings) *of the Lord* are _____. What do they do?

    d. (vs. 8b) The *commands of the Lord* are _____. What do they do?

    e. Together, how valuable are all these things? (vs. 10a)

    f. How sweet are they? (vs. 10b)

    g. What do they do for the servant who reads and studies them? (vs. 11a)

    h. What do they do for the servant who *keeps* (obeys) them? (vs. 11b)

4. Read Heb. 4:12.

    a. List three major characteristics of the Word of God. (vs. 12a)

    b. What is it able to judge/discern? (vs. 12b)

5. Read Is. 40:8.

    a. How long will the Word of God stand?

6. Read 2 Pet. 1:2-3.

    a. What has God given/granted us? (vs. 3).

Please note this text—2 Pet. 1:3—carefully. It is a pivotal verse confirming the sufficiency of God's Word. God is saying to us here that He has given us everything we need to make wise, life-giving decisions and to live righteous, godly lives through His divine power (the Holy Spirit) working in and through the truths of His Word (the true knowledge of Him). I find this promise wonderfully encouraging and reassuring.

We have talked about three "irrefutable facts" that establish the inerrancy and authority of God's Word: (1) The antiquity and continuity of the original manuscripts, (2) Prophecy, and (3) The power of the Word of God to change lives. I want to close today's study by focusing for just a few moments upon the second proof—Prophecy. I believe this is important because it is such a powerful testimony to the supreme, eternal, omniscient rule of God.

As mentioned in the meditation, there are more than two thousand specific, detailed prophecies in the Bible. In preparation for this study I did an in-depth study of prophetic Scriptures. I was continually awed at the minute detail in which God gave and fulfilled every prophecy. I wish we could take a look at several of these, but there just won't be time for that today. However, I want to share just a brief overview of one of my favorite prophetic events so you can catch a glimpse of God's amazing faithfulness in doing exactly what He said He would do. It involves the "handwriting on the wall."

Because of their wickedness, blatant idolatry and <u>repeated</u> rejection of God and His patient, loving warnings and calls to return to Him, God had allowed the southern Kingdom of Judah to be invaded by the Babylonians under wicked King Nebuchadnezzar. Judah was soundly defeated and carried away into exile where they were treated with oppressive cruelty. In agony, they cried out to God.

And God, in His compassionate mercy and faithfulness, just as He had done so many times before, heard and answered their cry. He raised up *His servant, Cyrus, the Mede (Is. 44:28, 45:1-6),* (who, by the way, was a pagan idolater), to deliver His rebellious, wayward children from captivity.

One night, as was his frequent custom Belshazzar, the current ruling king of Babylon, was giving a bacchanalia (wild, drunken orgy). He had brought out *the gold and silver vessels* that *Nebuchadnezzar, his father had taken from the temple in Jerusalem* and he and his concubines were defiling them by drinking out of them and getting drunk. It was during this profane revelry that the mysterious hand appeared and began writing on the wall: *Mene, Mene, Tekel Upharsin.* When none of the kings "wise men" could interpret the meaning of the strange script, the Hebrew captive, Daniel, who now served in the king's court, was summoned. After *praying to his God for wisdom,* Daniel gave the meaning of the dream to King Belshazzar: *God has numbered your kingdom and put an end to it... your kingdom has been divided and given over to the Medes and Persians* (because of the King's continual rejection of God, blatant blasphemies, idolatry, and leading God's precious people astray to worship foreign gods). Under the direction of God, Himself, (Is. 44:28, 45:1-6), Cyrus was at that very moment marching up to the impregnable city of Babylon with its 187-feet thick walls and towers that extended to a height of three hundred feet, enclosing an area of 196 square miles. In one short night, Cyrus, fulfilling to the minutest detail a number of prophecies made by God through His prophet Isaiah years earlier, invaded this invincible city, overcame the king, and destroyed the iron-fisted rule of the Babylonians. Amazing story! But it doesn't end there. Cyrus (Persian name for Darius) became the King of the new Persian Empire. Through a series of events only God could have orchestrated, He brought into King Darius' life the prophet Daniel who shared his faith and the true knowledge of God with Darius. Darius respected Daniel and he listened. His heart began to soften. Then after Daniel's miraculous deliverance from the jaws of the lions, King Darius recognized that Daniel's God was indeed the one and only true God. He then joined Daniel in worshipping God, making this bold declaration: *I, (King Darius) make a decree that in all the dominion of my kingdom men are to fear... the God of Daniel; For He is the living God and enduring forever; His kingdom is one which will not be destroyed, and His dominion will be forever. He delivers and rescues and performs signs and wonders in heaven and on earth (Dan. 6:26-27).*

Every time I read this story I am reminded of the magnitude of the length, breadth and depth of God's love in reaching out to rebellious, lost sinners (King Darius) to draw them to Himself.

And there are hundreds of other similar prophetic accounts that are equally as fascinating as this one giving yet further evidence of God's matchless sovereign rule, and of His never failing love, protection and faithfulness to His children from generation to generation.

Write out a Bible verse that had special meaning to you today.

Based upon what you have learned today, write a prayer to God expressing the desires of your heart in applying these Truths to your life.

Chapter 1 — Day 6
God's Eternal Plan
The Gospel...God's Plan of Salvation and Eternal Life

> *Jesus answered and said to him, "Truly, truly, I say to you, unless one is born again, he cannot see the kingdom of God" (John 3:3).*

God has a plan. He's always had a plan. It's a good plan, a beautiful plan. And He wants you and me to have the glorious privilege of participating with Him in carrying out that plan. So what is God's plan and how can we join Him in it's fulfillment?

Carefully and prayerfully read the following Scriptures.

In the beginning...God (Gen 1:1)

Holy, holy, holy, is the Lord God, the Almighty, who was and who is and who is to come (Rev. 4:8).

God created the heavens and the earth...Then God said, "Let Us make man in Our image, according to Our likeness; and let them rule over all the earth...And God blessed them; and God said to them, "Be fruitful and multiply, and fill the earth"...and God saw all that He had made and behold, it was very good (Gen. 1:3, 26-28; Gen. 13:1, sel.).

And the Lord God commanded the man, saying, "From any tree of the garden you may eat freely; but from the tree of the knowledge of good and evil you shall not eat, for in the day that you eat from it you shall surely die" (Gen. 2:16-17).

Now the serpent was more crafty than any beast of the field which the Lord God had made. And he said to the woman, "You surely shall not die"...When the woman saw that the tree was good for food, and that it was a delight to the eyes, and that the tree was desirable to make one wise, she took from its fruit and ate; and she gave also to her husband with her, and he ate (Gen. 3:1-6, sel.).

...then the man and his wife (were afraid) and hid themselves from the presence of the Lord God...your sins have made a separation between you and your God...the wages of sin is death (Gen. 3:8, 10; Is. 59:2; Rom 6:23).

Therefore...through one man sin entered into the world, and death through sin, and so death spread to all men...all of us like sheep have gone astray. Each of us has turned to his own way...all have sinned and fall short of the glory of God (Rom.5:12, 3:23).

But God demonstrates His own love toward us, in that while we were yet sinners, Christ died for us...For God so loved the world, that He gave His only begotten Son, that whosoever believeth in Him should not perish, but have everlasting life (Rom. 5:8; John 3:16, KJV).

He made Him who knew no sin to be sin on our behalf, that we might become the righteousness of God in Him (2 Cor. 5:21).

Truly, truly, I say to you, unless one is born again, he cannot see the kingdom of God (John 3:3).

What must I do to be saved (born again)? (Acts 16:30).

Repent...and ... Believe on the Lord Jesus Christ and you shall be saved ... I am the way, the truth and the life. No one comes to the Father, except through Me (Acts 2:38, 16:30-31; John 14:6).

... if you confess with your mouth Jesus as Lord, and believe in your heart that God raised Him from the dead, you shall be saved; for with the heart man believes, resulting in righteousness, and with the mouth he confesses, resulting in salvation ... as many as received Him, to them He gave the right to become children of God (Rom. 10:9-10; John 1:12).

Therefore, if any man is in Christ, he is a new creature; the old things passed away; behold, new things have come ... for we are His workmanship, created in Christ Jesus for good works which God prepared beforehand that we should walk in them ... "I know the plans that I have for you," declares the Lord, "plans for welfare and not for calamity, to give you a future and a hope" (2 Cor. 5:17; Eph. 2:10; Jer. 31:29:11).

Now all these things are from God, who reconciled us to Himself through Christ, and gave us the ministry of reconciliation...Therefore, we are ambassadors for Christ, as though God were entreating through us; we beg you on behalf of Christ, be reconciled to God (2 Cor. 5:18-20).

For whom He foreknew, He also predestined to become conformed to the image of His Son ... through sanctification by the Spirit and faith in the truth ... As obedient children, do not be conformed to the former lusts which were yours in your ignorance, but like the Holy One who called you, be holy yourselves also in all your behavior; because it is written, "You shall be holy, for I am holy" (Rom. 8:29; 2 Thess. 2:13; 1 Peter 1:14-16).

"Therefore, come out from them and be separate, and do not touch what is unclean; and I will welcome you ... And I will dwell in them and walk among them ... I will be their God, and they shall be My people. And I will be a father to you and you shall be sons and daughters to Me," says the Lord Almighty (2 Cor. 6:16-18).

But we all, with unveiled face beholding as in a mirror the glory of the Lord, are being transformed into the same image from glory to glory (2 Cor. 3:18).

These things I have spoken to you, that My joy may be in you, and that your joy may be made full ... He who believes in Me, as the Scripture said, "From his innermost being shall flow rivers of living water" (John 15:11, 7:38).

Let not your heart be troubled; believe in God, believe also in Me. In My Father's house are many dwelling places ... I go to prepare a place for you ... And I will come again, and receive you to Myself; that where I am, there you may be also (John 14:1-3).

And nothing unclean ... shall ever come into it, but only those whose names are written in the Lamb's book of life ... And if anyone's name was not found written in the book of life, he was thrown into the lake of fire ... and brimstone ... and they will be tormented day and night forever and ever. This is the second death, the lake of fire (Rev. 21:27, 20:10, 14-15).

Rejoice that your name is recorded in heaven (Luke 10:20).

Bible Study Supplement
Chapter 1 — Day 6 — God's Plan of Salvation and Eternal Life

What you have just read is the glorious gospel—God's eternal plan of redemption for mankind. I hope (and pray) that you have received this good news and are now a redeemed child of God. If you do not have this assurance, I beg you, do not put off this critical decision one more day for none of us is guaranteed "tomorrow". We only have "today":

...just as the Holy Spirit says, "Today if you hear His voice, do not harden your hearts"... for He says, "At the acceptable time I listened to you, and on the day of salvation I helped you"; behold, now is the acceptable time, now is the day of salvation" (Heb. 3:7-9; 2 Cor. 6:2).

Therefore having overlooked the times of ignorance, God is now declaring to men that all people everywhere should repent... For God would that all be saved and come to a knowledge of the truth (Acts 17:30; 1 Tim. 2:4).

Please hear God's compassionate cry:

"Come now, and let us reason together," says the Lord, "Though your sins are as scarlet, they will be as white as snow; though they are red like crimson, they will be like wool...Repent... and believe on the Lord Jesus Christ... for as many as received Him, to them He gave the right to become children of God (Is. 1:18; Acts 2:38, 16:31; John 1:12).

God is offering you the gift of forgiveness of sins and life eternal. He loves you and He wants to have a personal relationship with you. He wants to give you eternal life—not just *some day* when you die and go to heaven—but now, today and everyday that you live. Jesus said: *The thief comes to rob, to kill and to destroy, but I have come that they might have life and that more abundantly (John 10:10).* Please don't let the devil (the thief) rob you of one more day of true—abundant and eternal—life and joy. Ask God to help you understand the eternity-altering importance of the *good news* of the gospel that you read in today's

meditation—then open your heart to receive Jesus as your personal Lord and Savior so that you, too, will become a child of God and can be assured that you will spend eternity with Him and with all who have been born again into His eternal family.

If you already have made this decision, God has called you to be His ambassador to share this good news with others:

Now all these things are from God, who reconciled us to Himself through Christ, and gave us the ministry of reconciliation...Therefore, we are ambassadors for Christ (2 Cor. 5:18-20).

When is the last time you shared the good news of God's salvation with someone outside the family of God? Has it been awhile? And don't you just long to do this? Don't you earnestly desire to tell someone else about God's wonderful plan of salvation and have them—through the Holy Spirit working in them as you share the good news—receive Jesus as their personal Lord and Savior and come into His kingdom? I have now lived nearly six decades and I can tell you without a moment's hesitation that there is nothing in all the world that even remotely compares to the JOY that comes from leading another soul into the kingdom of God!

The reason many people don't share the gospel is because they have never taken the time to really solidify in their own minds exactly what the "good news" is. They have a general idea but to be able to verbalize it to another, they are at a loss. Maybe this has been a hindrance to you, also. So today we will spend our "Bible Study Supplement" time doing something about that so that we can begin to confidently *give a reason for the hope that is in us (1 Pet. 3:15).*

Please take a moment now to first of all thank God for your salvation and for the precious privilege of sharing the word of reconciliation (the gospel) with others. Ask the Holy Spirit to help you as you seek to become a better witness for the Lord. Ask Him to fill you with wisdom, boldness and confidence so that you are ever ready and eager to share the gospel with others as God gives opportunity.

It is important that you have a clear understanding of the gospel so that you are prepared to share it with different people in different situations and according to specific individual needs. There will be times when you will need to present a comprehensive, detailed explanation to those who may be hardened by false teachings or "bad experiences" in the past, as well as for those who may not understand that they even have a *need* for salvation. There will also be times when you only have a few minutes to share the good news or to plant a seed in a lost heart. Regardless of the exact situation, we should, like Paul, the apostle, keep in mind at all times the main message of the gospel:

> *For I delivered to you as of first importance… that Christ died for our sins according to the Scriptures… was buried, and was raised on the third day according to the Scriptures (1 Cor. 15:3-6, sel).*

This simple, but profound truth is the "heart" of the gospel and we must make sure that people understand this fact that is of *first importance*. It is "the gospel in a nutshell".

There are a number of special Gospel presentation programs and tracts that have been developed through the years to help people share the gospel: Campus Crusade's "Four Spiritual Laws", "Evangelism Explosion", the "Step of FAITH" Acronym, and a number of others. Most of these are fine and can be helpful, but the best preparation for presenting the gospel is your own personal, thorough understanding directly from the Bible. That is why I encourage you to review the verses in today's meditation in the days and weeks to come, so that you know them and can clearly share them with others.

As soon as you are able, write out your own gospel presentation. Writing it down solidifies it in your mind. Then practice it as often as God gives opportunity. As you work on your gospel presentation, keep in mind that when the Bible speaks of "death"

it is speaking of "separation". There are two kinds of death—physical and spiritual. Physical death is separation of the soul from the body. Spiritual death is separation of the soul from God. Physical death is merely a transition from the temporal to the eternal. For the child of God (born again believer), this separation marks the happiest day of his life, when at last he will be forever set free: free of his fallen sin nature with all its destructive lusts, free of the world with its trials and tribulations, and free of the devil with his relentless demonic deceptions and harassments. The now totally and forever free believer will be in the very presence of God, Himself, who will *wipe away every tear from (his) eyes; and there shall no longer be any mourning or crying, or pain, or death.* It is this *blessed hope (Titus 2:13)* that keeps his heart encouraged and ever pressing forward to that glorious day! For those who do not have a personal relationship with God, this will be the most horrible, terrible, tragic day of their temporal and eternal existence for they will experience not only physical death, but a second, permanent spiritual death as well—the separation of their soul from God in a place called Hell—*the lake of fire… that burns with fire and brimstone* where *all* (who have rejected God's offer of salvation) *will be tormented day and night forever and ever (Rev. 20:10, 21:8, 14:11).*

You should not wait until you have "perfected" your ability to confidently share the gospel. You know enough today to begin and I would encourage you to never pass up the opportunity to share the gospel whenever you sense the Holy Spirit's prompting you to do so. The more you share it, the clearer it will become and the more *ready* you will always be *to give a reason for the hope that is in you (1 Pet. 3:15).* Don't be afraid of *making a mistake.* This is God's message and He will be with you to help you. And, even if you "blow it" (or feel that you have), God is a redemptive God and He will use even times like these to touch the soul of another with the gospel when your heart is filled with a sincere desire to obey Him and a genuine love for the person to whom you are witnessing.

An inseparable part of sharing the gospel nearly always includes some aspect of your own personal testimony—how the gospel has changed your life. You read earlier my personal testimony. Feel free to share this with others who might benefit from it. However, I strongly urge you to write out your own personal testimony and keep this handy for sharing with those to whom you witness. <u>Be sure it includes a clear presentation of the plan of salvation.</u> (You can use the plan of salvation that you write out for this part. You may have to reword it slightly to fit your particular personal testimony).

What God has done in your life and the changes He has made are a part of the miracle of the "New Birth". It is personal and it is real. Therefore, it is something that cannot be argued against. You will undoubtedly find yourself in situations in the future where someone could really benefit from hearing your personal testimony, but there just isn't time to share it. If you have it written out, you can hand it to the person who can read it later. Who knows but that God might use your written testimony to draw someone (or many someone's) to Himself. I carry several copies of my personal testimony with me whenever I travel and also keep a copy in my briefcase and in my car, so that I have it handy at all times. I have shared it with a number of people this way and God has really used it to draw people "to" or "closer to" Himself.

The Bible says that God's Word *will not return void, without accomplishing what I desire (Is. 55:11).* It is God's desire *that all be saved and come to a knowledge of the truth (1 Tim. 2:4).* Whenever we share the plan of salvation from God's Word, the Holy Spirit uses it to accomplish God's good purposes—the salvation of the lost. In some cases, He uses what we share to plant a seed; at other times He may use us to nurture or water a seed already planted; and on yet other occasions, God gives us the glorious privilege of bringing home (into His kingdom) the precious fruit (1 Cor. 3:6). In the appendix, I have included an outline of my own gospel presentation that I have used in sharing the gospel with many people through the years. After reading the concluding paragraph below, please turn to this sample gospel presentation, "He has Planted Eternity in their Hearts", and review it. It may give you an idea for putting together your own gospel presentation.

There really is nothing that brings more JOY in all the world than being used of God to lead a lost soul to Jesus, our wonderful Lord and Savior. God bless you as you share His "good news" with others! May your JOYS be many!

(Please turn to the appendix to review the sample gospel presentation).

Chapter 2

Bible Memory Verse: *Not everyone who says to Me, 'Lord, Lord,' will enter the kingdom of heaven (Matt. 7:21).*

Bonus Bible Verse: *For the wisdom of this world is foolishness before God (1 Cor. 3:19).*

Day 1

Tradition Versus True Saving Faith – Part One

The Danger and Power of Demonic Deception Through Tradition

Day 2

Tradition Versus True Saving Faith – Part Two

To My Catholic Friends Whom I Love Dearly

Day 3

Proofs of Salvation

Examine Yourself – Have You Truly Been Born of the Spirit?

The Most Important Test You Will Ever Take

Day 4

Progressive Sanctification

Day 5

Man's Wisdom Versus God's Wisdom

Chapter 2 — Day 1
Tradition vs. True Saving Faith — Part One
The Danger and Power of Demonic Deception Through Tradition

They went out from us, (because) they were not really of us; for if they had been of us, they would have remained; but they went out, in order that it might be shown that they all are not of us (1 John 2:19).

Who is the liar, but the one who denies that Jesus is the Christ (1 John 3:22).

And the Pharisees and some of the scribes gathered together around Him when they had come from Jerusalem, and had seen that some of His disciples were eating their bread with impure hands, (not washed according to the ceremonial tradition as taught and practiced by the Pharisees). And the Pharisees and the scribes asked Him, "Why do Your disciples not walk according to the tradition of the elders, but eat their bread with impure hands?" And He said to them, "Rightly did Isaiah prophesy of you hypocrites, as it is written, 'This people honors Me with their lips, but their heart is far away from Me… in vain do they worship Me, <u>teaching as doctrines the precepts of men</u>' … Neglecting the commandment of God, you hold to the tradition of men…" <u>You… set aside the commandment of God in order to keep your tradition</u>" (Mark 7:1-9, sel.).

Jesus had much to say about *the traditions of man* as opposed to *the commandment of God* throughout His ministry… and it was never good. Jesus continually warned of the seriousness of this problem. He did this because Jesus knew how powerful *tradition* is in the hearts of all people. It is a common tendency of every fallen nature to *hold to tradition*… to the familiar, that with which

we are "comfortable". We don't like change and we especially don't like change that involves long standing *traditions* upon which we have been raised that have become a stabilizing factor in our lives. It is as if the *tradition* becomes a part of our very being—who we are and what identifies us. Thus changing a long practiced *tradition* is often tantamount to taking away a part of one's identity. And that can be very frightening. Every fallen nature finds security and comfort in tradition. The devil knows this and he uses it to keep us bound to tradition. Once he gets an unbiblical *tradition* deeply ingrained within us, it becomes a *stronghold*. This deceptive ploy—playing to people's hearts and comfort levels—is incredibly effective since there is so much in this world that is *not* comfortable or secure; we fight to hold on to those few things that are. Religious traditions are undoubtedly at the top of this list.

This deception is most dangerous when it comes to the matter of salvation, for false teaching based on the *traditions of man* rather than the *commandment of God* has the very tragic potential of leading a person away from true saving faith and eventually…to Hell. Though this is a topic that few dare to broach today in the name of tolerance and the quest to be "loved and accepted" by all, it is a serious matter and we must, in obedience to God, warn our brothers when we see them going astray:

When a righteous man turns away from his righteousness (obedience to the truths of God's Word) *and commits iniquity...*(and continues down this path until he dies) *he shall die in his sin, and his righteous deeds which he has done shall not be remembered; but his blood I will require at your hand* (because you failed to warn him). *However, if you have warned the righteous man that the righteous should* (turn from his sin), *and he does… he shall surely live because he took warning; and you have delivered yourself* (Ezek. 3:20-21, sel.).

In obedience to this clear command from Scripture, we must take a few moments today and tomorrow to examine carefully this matter of the *traditions of man* versus the *commandments of God.*

In book one of this series, *Free Indeed,* we introduced the very powerful danger of *demonic deception.* We noted that demonic deception is a spiritual blindness that totally obliterates the *understanding* (ability to comprehend reality accurately) of the person under its influence. As long as this veil remains over his eyes, it is impossible for him to recognize that he is being "deceived". In other words, he is so deceived that he cannot perceive that he is deceived.

The heart is more deceitful than all else and is desperately sick; Who can understand it? (Jer. 17:9)

Demonic deception strikes directly at the "deceived, sick" heart. It is there that a spiritual blindness is cast upon the desperately sick *understanding.* Thus human intellect—regardless of its training and daily exercise to expand it's capacity—is incapable of comprehending the deception. Nor is the human will—no matter how resolute and determined it may be—powerful enough to stand against demonic deception. Only the Spirit of God working through the Word of God can expose such powerful deception and give us the wisdom and courage to stand against it.

Because of the potentially grave consequences of three demonically perpetuated deceptions regarding salvation, we must take a close biblical look at these today with a prayer that God will help us all to examine our own hearts regarding them, take the necessary action to rectify what might be wrong, and then have the courage to share the truth about these dangerous *traditions of man* with all our friends and loved ones who may have been deceived by Satan into believing them. These extremely powerful—and dangerous—traditions are:

1. Salvation by works
2. Salvation by participation in "saving" traditions: One is "saved" and assured a place in Heaven by a*) making a public profession of faith, b) being baptized, c) having his name on a church roll, d) attending church regularly, e) participating in the sacraments.*
3. Infant baptismal regeneration

Salvation by Works

This cunning and very enticing argument regarding salvation is accepted by followers of nearly all the major world religions and even in many Christian denominations. The deceptive argument goes like this: God is love. A loving God would never send a "good person" to Hell. Therefore, all good people who are kind to others and make the world a better place to live will go to Heaven.

This tradition teaches that it is not so much what one *believes* that will get him to Heaven, it is what one *does.* Biblically, this teaching is referred to as salvation by works. Being fully deceived by the traditions of the church they faithfully attend, many *say* they "believe in Jesus", but they are *trusting* in their works to actually *save* them and get them to heaven. In many cases, because of the deception associated with it, this tradition-based belief is not so much formally *taught* as silently *caught* by the examples of others and the deafening "silence" in the church concerning it. Because it is so logical and sounds so *right,* and because there is little direct teaching concerning it, salvation by works is perhaps the most widespread—and believed—demonic lie concerning salvation. Since this is a matter of *eternal life and death*, we must take a serious look at some of the crafty, enticing deceptions associated with this *tradition*, then examine God's Word to see what God says about it.

Remember, <u>one of Satan's most effective tools is to mix a little truth into a dangerous lie</u>, making it unarguably rational from an intellectual standpoint. For the Christian, Satan carries the demonic deception one step further with misplaced (out of context) Scripture to make the argument *appear* not only *believable*, but *biblical*. And so he has done here. Let's look at the deceptive mixing of lies with truth in this nearly universally accepted myth concerning salvation. There are two parts to the lie:

Part 1: God would never <u>send</u> a good person to Hell.

Part 2: God would never send a <u>good person</u> to Hell.

Biblical answer to Part 1: It is true! God doesn't <u>send</u> anyone to Hell.

> *For God so loved the world that He gave His only begotten Son that whosoever believeth on Him should not perish but have everlasting life… God would that all be saved and come to a knowledge of the truth… All who call upon the name of the Lord will be saved… As many as received Him, to them He gave the right to become children of God (John 3:16 KJV; 1 Tim.2:4; Rom. 10:13; John 1:12).*

Not one person will be in Hell because God *sent* him there. Every man and every woman who wakes up in Hell one day will be there because they *chose* to reject God's loving offer of grace: forgiveness of sins and salvation through faith in the sacrificial death and resurrection of Jesus.

For those who have never heard the true gospel of Christ, the Bible makes it clear that God has revealed Himself to them—to everyone!—through His creation and through each individual's own *conscience* (*Rom. 1:18–20*). Every person, therefore, is responsible for what they did with the revelation they were given.

In this country there will be no excuse for not knowing and responding to the gospel. We live in a nation replete with opportunities to hear the gospel: a plethora of Bibles and other gospel teaching books, tapes, videos, radio and television programs, Bible-teaching churches and the personal witness of others. Every person in this country has access to the Bible and knows at least one person—usually a number of people—who are genuine born again believers who would be happy to answer any questions they may have about salvation and how they, too, can come into God's kingdom.

Biblical answer to Part 2: God would never send a *good* person to Hell. So the question is: How good is good enough? Exactly how good does man have to be to merit Heaven?

> *Every one of them has turned aside; they have all become corrupt; There is no one who does good, not even one. All of us like sheep have gone astray, each of us has turned to his own way; For all of us have become… unclean, and all our righteous deeds are like filthy rags; <u>all have sinned and fall short of the glory (holiness) of God</u> (Ps. 53:3, 6, 64:6; Rom. 3:23 KJV/ NASB).*

Man judges everything by his own fallen, sinful standards. God's standard is absolute, perfect, unflawed *holiness*. Nothing less will enter Heaven. There is not one person who has ever walked the face of this earth (apart from Jesus) who meets this standard: *All have sinned and come short of the glory (holiness) of God (Rom. 6:23).* How then, can any man be saved?

> *He made Him who knew no sin to be sin on our behalf, that we might become the righteousness of God in Him (2 Cor. 5:21).*

By faith in Christ's completed work for us on the cross, Christ's righteousness is imputed (given to, "put on") every believer. Therefore, when God looks at the true believer, He no longer sees his sinful imperfections, but Christ's holiness, and that is the only way anyone will enter the portals of Heaven, because

Heaven is a holy place and only holy people will live there.

Salvation by Participation in "Saving" Traditions of the Church

Deceptive belief: One is assured a place in Heaven by any one, or a combination, of the following: 1) making a public *profession of faith*; 2) being baptized; 3) having his name on a church roll; 4) attending church regularly; 5) participating in the sacraments.

Though people who are saved *will* make a public profession of faith, get baptized, join a church, participate in the sacraments and attend church regularly, none of these things will, in themselves, save anyone if there has been no genuine true repentance and personal faith in Jesus which always results in a change of heart and desires. Combined with the false teaching of salvation by good works, these common lies have deceived myriads. It truly breaks my heart to realize that there are people who sit in pews in churches faithfully every Sunday who, because of demonic deception in believing these lies concerning salvation, are perishing. Tears still come to my eyes as I think how close I came to believing these myself—all the way to Hell! And my heart aches for all the precious, sincere, well-meaning people who remain under its cloud, for the Bible clearly and lovingly warns:

> *Not everyone who says to Me, 'Lord, Lord,' will enter the kingdom of Heaven…many will say to Me on that day, 'Lord, Lord, did we not (sit in church every Sunday, get baptized, have our name on a church roll, take Holy Communion, live a noble, good life, helping people)…And I will declare to them, 'I never knew you; depart from Me' (Matt. 7:21–23).*

Infant Baptismal Regeneration

This is another very tender heart issue for me. I was raised in a church that practiced this unbiblical tradition. I was told that I was *saved* when I was baptized (sprinkled with water) as a baby and *sponsors* who *spoke for me* made a profession of faith in Jesus on my behalf. This is an especially appealing teaching because it is very comforting for parents to think that their children are "saved" and assured a place in Heaven by having them "sprinkled" while "faith" is expressed through a sponsor when they are babies. But this is "man's tradition" not "God's commandment". The Word of God is clear. Salvation is by *personal repentance* and *confession of faith* on the part of every individual:

> *For God so loved the world, that He gave His only begotten Son, that whoever <u>believes</u> in Him should not perish, but have everlasting life (John 3:16 KJV).*

> *"Sirs, what must I do to be saved?" And they said, "<u>Believe in the Lord Jesus,</u> and you shall be saved" (Acts 16:30-31)*

> *…that if you <u>confess with your mouth Jesus as Lord,</u> and <u>believe in your heart that God raised Him from the dead,</u> you shall be saved; for with the heart man believes, resulting in righteousness, and with the mouth he confesses, resulting in salvation (Romans 10:9-10).*

> *(Paul) kept declaring…throughout all the region of Judea, and even to the Gentiles, that they should <u>repent</u> and <u>turn to God</u> (Acts 26:20).*

It is impossible for a baby whose intellect and discerning capabilities are not yet developed to even understand the concept of sin and separation from God, let alone, true repentance and faith.

I spent several years discussing this crucial topic of *saving faith* with a pastor of a liturgically formal church whose denomination was steeped in various long-held traditions including the unbiblical practice of infant baptism for regeneration. This man was a very intelligent, kind, congenial man who seemed to really care about people and wanting to help them. I grew to love him and his family very much. I prayed for them faithfully. I was actually very surprised when I began to notice a definite "hardness of heart" that clinging to this tradition of the church had caused through the years. He never could seem to open his heart completely to the truth of Scripture even though he was not able to present solid biblical evidence for the false teaching of infant baptismal regeneration. He gave me books that were written by leading "theologians" in the denomination to help persuade me to his way of thinking, but these only convinced me further that the foundations of the *salvation doctrine* this denomination taught were built upon errant, unbiblical *traditions of man* rather than upon the *commandments of God.* The "authority" that was nearly always quoted was the revered "father" of that denomination and his writings, rather than the *Word of God (Acts 20:27).* It was very sad to me because this was, I truly believe, a very "sincere" man who had fallen under the veil of demonic deception through the traditions of the church which had been rooted in him from the time he was born (and in his parents and grandparents before him), then nurtured by formal training in the denomination's theological institutions. Even sadder, however was the fact that he, along with countless other pastors in this denomination continue to lead myriads of vulnerable sheep astray and to develop within them a false sense of security based upon the unbiblical practice of infant baptismal regeneration. Along with the false security comes almost invariably a "hardness of heart" that refuses to examine Scripture to *see if these things* (they are being taught) *are so (Acts 11:17).* Let's continue to pray for our brothers and sisters who may be caught in this kind of powerful deception for it is very, very serious. Indeed, the eternal destiny of many is at stake.

We, like Paul must lovingly, prayerfully, and as often as God gives us opportunity continue to *declare the truth:*

> *(Paul) kept declaring…throughout all the region of Judea, and even to the Gentiles, that they should <u>repent</u> and <u>turn to God</u>… <u>Believe in the Lord Jesus,</u> and you shall be saved…for there is salvation in no one else; there is no other name* (or tradition) *under heaven that has been given among men, by which we must be saved (Acts 26:20, 16:31, 4:12).*

Bible Study Supplement
Chapter 2 — Day 1 — Tradition vs. True Saving Faith - Part One
The Danger and Power of Demonic Deception Through *Tradition*

We've covered a lot of material today. Thank you for your courage and perseverance in examining this crucial topic from a biblical (God's) perspective. I pray that God will bless you for your diligence and that He will use the material to better equip you to minister to others who may yet be caught in the very dangerous deceptions of unbiblical man-made *traditions*. Because you have already read a lot, we will be looking at only one Scripture in today's supplement which confirms the importance of guarding our own hearts from following deceptive *traditions of man*.

1. Read Mark 7:1-9

    a. What did Jesus call the Pharisees when they accused Him of doing wrong by allowing His disciples to eat with ceremonially unclean hands? (vs. 6 – Fill in blank) H_____

    b. How did Jesus describe all who cling to tradition over the Word of God? (vs. 6-7 – Please use the NASB below and fill in the blanks that follow).

       6. And He said to them, "Rightly did Isaiah prophesy of you hypocrites, as it is written: 'This people honors Me with their lips, but their heart is far away from Me.'
       7. But in vain do they worship Me, teaching as doctrines the precepts of men (Mark 7:6-7).

       This people honors Me with their _____, but their _____ is far from me. But in _____ do they worship Me, teaching as _____ the precepts of _____.

This is a very serious indictment from Jesus. He is saying here that those who insist on following the precepts of man over the Word of God are hypocrites, and God will not honor their worship. They *worship in vain*. God will not hear it and they will not be saved by it.

    c. In verses 8 and 9 Jesus says that people who hold to the traditions of man over the Word of God do two things. What are these? (vs. 9)

May God help us all to see the seriousness of *neglecting the commandment of God* in order to *hold to the tradition of men (Mark 7:8),* so that we are careful to examine our worship and our lives by what God's Word teaches rather than blindly following man-made traditions that will not "save" anyone.

Write out a Bible verse that had special meaning to you today.

Based upon what you have learned today, write a prayer to God expressing the desires of your heart in applying these Truths to your life.

Chapter 2 — Day 2
Tradition vs. True Saving Faith — Part Two
To My Catholic Friends Whom I Love Dearly

> *And when you are praying, do not use meaningless repetition, as the Gentiles do, for they suppose that they will be heard for their many words (Matt. 6:7).*
>
> *There is one God, and one mediator between God and man, Christ Jesus (1 Tim. 2:5).*

Ruby was one of the sweetest, kindest, most loving and hard working women I knew. She was always volunteering for some charitable project at her parish or in our community.

I first met Ruby when she moved into our neighborhood. I visited her to introduce myself and to welcome her and her husband. God gave me a special love for her at that first meeting, which only grew with each subsequent visit. I soon learned that Ruby was a devout Roman Catholic. I could relate to that because of my own involvement in the Catholic church.

I prayed for Ruby and her husband in my daily prayers and I shared my faith with her as God gave opportunity. One day, as I was praying for her, the Lord put upon my heart to visit her and share the true gospel with her. At first I did not want to do this because I knew how devout she was and I loved her dearly and did not want to take the risk of any possible negative affect on our relationship. But as I continued to pray, I recognized that my fear was based on a selfish concern about my own desire to be "loved and accepted by all", not on a genuine love for Ruby. I asked God to forgive me and I called Ruby to set up a time when we could meet.

What a wonderful visit the Lord gave us that day. I don't think I will ever forget it. I could sense the Holy Spirit with us, blessing and guiding the conversation and increasing our love for one another as we shared together. I learned a lot about Ruby: where she was born, how she was raised, how she met her husband. The conversation flowed very naturally into a discussion about faith and church and how she had become a Catholic. I shared my own personal testimony with her. Then I asked her if she knew where she would go when she died. She said that she did not know…that no one could know. She hoped that she would go to heaven, but she certainly could not say for sure that she would. I shared with her that the Bible is very clear that we can know…and God wants us to know that we will go to heaven when we die, if we have repented of our sins and placed our faith and trust in Jesus and His redemptive work on the cross. I shared with her God's promise to us in 1 John 5:13:

> *These things I have written to you who believe in the name of the Son of God, in order that you may **know** that you have eternal life (1 John 5:13).*

It was the first time she had heard that. But the tradition of "working out" or "completing" one's salvation" through the various "means of grace"—participation in the sacraments, prayers, indulgences, good works—was so deep and so strong, she could not fully embrace this simple truth. I don't think I will ever forget the troubled look on Ruby's face as I continued to share the liberating good news of complete and full salvation offered to us by God's grace (available to all), through faith in Jesus and His work on the cross. She *wanted* to believe and be liberated from the endless strivings of the many unbiblical "requirements" placed upon all who followed the traditions of the Catholic faith, yet she just could not break free of the nearly invincible shackles. But I knew that God's Spirit working through His Word could. I encouraged her to read and study the Bible for herself—as it was originally given, not the "Catholic version" with so much added to it, or the "catechism", which was man's interpretation of the Bible tainted with many unbiblical doctrines. And I shared with her God's promise in Jer. 29:13, that if we *seek Him with a whole heart, He will be found by us* and He will give us the wisdom and faith to *know* and *believe.* Ruby found comfort in this promise. She asked me to pray for her, and I did. I prayed that God would honor her tender, seeking heart; that He would help her to understand the true gospel and to receive His free gift of salvation, placing her faith and trust completely in what Jesus did for her on the cross, not in the traditions of her church. When I left she thanked me for the visit and asked that I please continue to remember her in prayer. I did.

Shortly after this, Ruby moved away from our neighborhood and I was sad for that because I would miss her sweet spirit and precious fellowship so much. But there was also joy, knowing that Ruby left with an open, seeking heart and I know that God keeps His promises. I truly believed that as Ruby continued to *seek Him with a whole heart*—through the Word and sincere prayers for wisdom and understanding—God would give her victory in her battle against the stronghold of tradition and she would open her heart to receive Jesus as her personal Lord and Savior finding the freedom and peace her longing heart desired. And that is exactly what happened! To God be the glory!

I share this story because we all know people like Ruby, who are kind and loving people who have been indoctrinated in the traditions of the Catholic faith. I hasten to add that people in Catholic churches are not the only ones who have been affected by the deceptive, demonic power of church tradition. Many in protestant main line denominations and even "Bible Churches" have fallen into similar traps in which church tradition is elevated over the Word of God. Faithful church attendance and adherence to the traditions of the church have replaced <u>genuine repentance</u> and <u>personal faith in Jesus, without which no man will enter the Kingdom of heaven</u> *(John 3:16, 14:6; Acts 4:12, Rom. 3:20a, 24, 28).* It is crucial to remember here what we said earlier about demonic deception. It always results in *spiritual blindness.* In this case, people who have been steeped in strong *church tradition* cannot "see" that they are actually putting their faith in the *traditions of the church* to "save" them rather than in Jesus and His finished work of redemption on the cross, the **only** means of salvation. Only the Holy Spirit working through the Word of God can open the blind eyes, expose the lie, and give the power to overcome it.

I have a very tender heart for people caught in the very powerful demonic deception of tradition because I lived there myself for the first 35 years of my life. Because the Catholic church was so much like the church in which I was raised, I attended a Catholic church and held to its teachings and practices in my early adult life. And I can clearly see that if it were not for the prayers of others, and God's merciful grace in opening my heart as the Spirit of God spoke to me through His Word, I would still be there, with my faith, not in Jesus and in His finished work on the cross, but in my own "good works" and faithful participation in the various church traditions.

Before we close this discussion on the *traditions of man* versus the *commandments of God*, we need to clarify one important matter. In some of Paul's epistles he refers to the "traditions <u>of the faith</u>". He encourages Timothy, and others, to be careful to <u>uphold</u> these. What he is referring to in such cases, however, is the "tradition" of the faithful preaching, teaching, and practice of (obeying) the <u>Word of God</u>. This is a "good" tradition in keeping with the *commandment of God.* By context, it is very clear whether what is being referred to is a "tradition of man" (which Jesus condemned), or a "tradition of the faith" in agreement with the Word of God— the "good tradition" which Jesus Himself practiced, faithfully teaching the commandments of God, not the traditions of men.

I now belong to a Bible believing, preaching, practicing church that holds to the authority of Scripture and is committed to teaching and practicing the *whole counsel of the Word of God (Acts 20:27).* I further nurture my faith through daily Bible Study and prayer. I could never again join any church that clings to and practices the *traditions of man* over the *commandments of God.* And I, personally, cannot understand how any truly *born again* believer can, since he has the Holy Spirit living in him and the primary purpose of the Holy Spirit is to *glorify Christ, (John 16:14),* not the church or church tradition. Another purpose of the Holy Spirit is to make known to us the Word of God as the final authority for *life and godliness (2 Pet. 1:3),* not human traditions—especially those which oppose what the Word of God teaches. However, I also know that breaking free of the heavy chains of *church tradition* is not an easy undertaking. Through demonic deception and our own fallen human craving for acceptance and 'belongingness' (which characterizes churches built upon the traditions of man), breaking those bonds can be a very difficult and oft painful ordeal. Being ostracized by family and friends who remain in the tradition and look upon us with disdain as if we were "traitors" of the family because of our commitment to God's Word, hurts very much because we love these people deeply and we desire to have fellowship with them and to grow together in the ways of God. But God is faithful and I have found that when we look to Him and trust Him to help us as we continue on in our own walk of faith—loving and obeying Him and genuinely loving others (Matt. 22:37-39)—He honors that faithfulness and helps restore peace and fellowship (1 Sam. 2:30; Prov. 16:7). Eventually, family and friends come to see that we are sincere, that we truly do love them very much and want only the best for them. They begin to respect us. Fellowship is reestablished, and in time, some even open their hearts to the true gospel—the life-giving *commandments of God.*

> *For I am not ashamed of the gospel of Christ: for it is the power of God unto salvation to every one that believes...there is no other name under heaven... given among men, by which we must be saved (Rom. 1:16; Acts 4:12).*

Bible Study Supplement
Chapter 2 — Day 2 — Tradition vs. True Saving Faith - Part Two
To All My Catholic Friends Whom I Love Dearly

The doctrines and practices of the Catholic faith are replete with idolatry and false teaching. It would literally take an entire book—which a number of people have already written—to document all the unbiblical teaching and traditions involved [5]. (For further information, please see End Notes, #5, located at the back of the book just before the appendix). We do not have time here for an in-depth examination of these teachings. However, I have listed in the appendix just a few of the major conflicts between the traditions of the Catholic Church and the Word of God, so you will be more prepared to minister to your Catholic friends. And, if you are a practicing Catholic, I plead with you for the sake of your eternal soul and the souls of your children, ask God to help you keep an open heart and mind as you read the truth regarding the teachings of the Catholic church that are built upon the traditions of man rather than the Word of God. Beware also that practicing unbiblical tradition over a period of time *hardens one's heart.* Tradition always does this because of it's appeal to our flesh. Through the faithful practice of the traditions of the church, it puts us *in control,* not God. It is a natural bent of every fallen nature to want to be "in control", and we stubbornly resist anything that might threaten that *control,* developing a protective "hard heart". This is very serious because whether we recognize it or not, all who practice church traditions that oppose the Word of God are, in reality, relying upon the keeping of church tradition to "save them", which it can never do (Rom. 3:20-28, cf. Eph. 2:8-9; John 14:6; Acts 4:12; Rom. 1:16; 1 John 5:11-13).

Church tradition also involves demonic deception that is very powerful. Only the Word of God can expose and break through that kind of deception. So, please ask the Holy Spirit to soften your heart and make it open and receptive to what He wants to teach you. Please put a bookmark here and after you have finished reading this summary of just a few of the conflicts between the doctrines of the Catholic faith and the Word of God, <u>please return here</u> where we will conclude our study by answering just three questions that will help solidify the truths we have learned today. Please turn now to "Catholic Doctrines vs. the Word of God" in the appendix at the back of the book.

1. Read Rom. 3:20, 23-24, 28.

   Note: The *works of the law* include participation in the sacraments (for the purpose of salvation), repetitive prayers, indulgences and all the other "works" that man performs—including "good deeds" if these are done for the purpose of winning God's favor and obtaining salvation.

   a. How many will be justified in God's sight through "works of the law"? (vs. 20a)

   b. How is one "justified" (made right with God)? (vs. 24)

   c. Fill in the blanks: A man is justified by _____ apart from _____ (vs. 28)

2. Read Eph. 2:1-9.

    a. What were we, before God by His mercy and grace redeemed us? (vs. 1)

    b. What did God do for us? (vs. 4-5a)

    c. How have we been saved? (vs. 8 - fill in the blanks below)

    For it is by _____ you have been saved, through _____ ... it is the _____ of _____ not by (of) _____ so that no one can boast.

    d. What is our salvation? (Circle correct answer) - a) a result of our good works b) a completely free gift of God's grace, received by faith.

3. Read Rom. 1:15-17.

    a. What was Paul eager to do? (vs. 15)

    b. What was Paul not ashamed of... why? (vs. 16)

    c. How do the righteous (those who have truly been born again) live? (vs. 17b).

The redeemed child of God "rests" in the finished work of Christ. He no longer has to *work* to obtain salvation—forgiveness of his sins, a loving, accepted relationship with God, eternal life. He has already received it, by faith in what Jesus did for him. Nor does he have to *work* for the ongoing mercy and grace of God which is an inseparable part of God's "free gift" of salvation to him. Every day he continues to partake of it—freely—by that same faith. There's peace and assurance in *so great a salvation (Heb. 2:3).*

Write out a Bible verse that had special meaning to you today.

Based upon what you have learned today, write a prayer to God expressing the desires of your heart in applying these truths to your life.

Chapter 2 — Day 3
Proofs of Salvation
Examine Yourself — Have You Truly Been Born of the Spirit?

> Test yourselves to see if you are in the faith; examine yourselves! Or do you not recognize this about yourselves, that Jesus Christ is in you—unless indeed you fail the test (2 Cor. 13:5).

In light of what we have just studied regarding salvation deceptions, God's Word urges us to take a test—a salvation test—to make sure we have been "born again" and our faith is truly a genuine *saving faith*. This is the most important test we will ever take, for our eternal destiny is at stake.

Let's review why it is so important that we be "born again" (experience a spiritual rebirth). Because of our inborn "sin nature", we are all born spiritually *dead* (Eph. 2:1)—sinners separated from God because God is holy and "holy" and "sin" cannot fellowship together. We must be "born again" or "born from above" to become spiritually alive and enter into a relationship with God through whom we have eternal life. This "new birth" takes place when we: 1) repent of our sins and 2) place our faith and trust in Jesus' sacrificial death on the cross to pay the penalty for our sins, and in His resurrection, which gives us victory over death, and eternal life with Him in heaven. The moment we *genuinely* do this, a very real miracle of *new birth* takes place. Our "spirit" that has been *dead in trespasses and sins (Eph. 2:1)* now becomes alive. The Holy Spirit comes into our heart and makes us a *new (born again) person in Christ* with a new heart and new desires.

> I will give you a new heart and put a new Spirit within you … and I will put My Spirit within you and cause you to walk in My statutes … therefore, if any man is in Christ, he is a new creature … the old things passed away, new things have come (Ezek. 36:25-28; 2 Cor. 5:17).

Every genuine new birth results in a very real and profound change in the heart/soul. That which was dead comes alive! Just as God breathed into Adam's lifeless form to make him a "living being", the Holy Spirit now enters the dead soul giving it *life*—a life that is now connected to God and able to enjoy personal communion and fellowship with Him. There is, at this moment also, a profound change in desires— from *self*-centered seeking after fleshly lusts, to new God-centered desires for righteousness, holiness, and doing those things that please and honor God.

The Bible clearly instructs that a person is only deceiving himself if he thinks he has been *born again* when there is no change in his attitudes, desires, or behavior.

> … or do you not know that the unrighteous shall not inherit the kingdom of God? Do not be deceived; neither fornicators, nor idolaters, nor adulterers, nor effeminate, nor homosexuals, nor thieves, nor covetous, nor drunkards … shall inherit the kingdom of God (2 Cor. 6:9-10).

The Bible gives specific, clear *proofs of salvation*— proofs that confirm the changes that take place at the time of every genuine new birth. It truly is the most important test we will ever take!

> Test yourselves to see if you are in the faith; examine yourselves! Or do you not recognize this … that Jesus Christ is in you—unless indeed you fail the test (2 Cor. 13:5).

Bible Study Supplement
Chapter 2 — Day 3— Proofs of Salvation
Examine Yourself — Have You Truly Been Born of the Spirit?

1. Read 1 Cor. 6:9–11.

In love, God clearly cautions us in these verses: *Do not be deceived…* He goes on to list specific sins, warning that those who continue on in these sins (habitually practicing them) will not inherit the Kingdom of God.

     a. List the ten specific sins mentioned. (vs. 9-10)

     b. Verse 11 says that many people who come to Jesus were once like this, but what happened? (three things – vs. 11)

This is a very encouraging verse filled with hope because it assures us that in the precious gift of salvation we have not only been washed and cleansed from all past sins, but we have also been *sanctified*—given new desires and the power to overcome all former fleshly (sinful) desires, through the Holy Spirit now resident within us.

It is important to note here also that among the sins listed that will keep people from *inheriting the kingdom of God,* is the sin of idolatry (vs. 9). Idolatry involves loving or worshipping anyone or anything more than we love and worship God. This could mean actual idols of wood and stone, or more commonly, idols of the heart—money, material possessions, fame, (popularity, the praise of man), food, pleasure and a thousand and one other possibilities. We need to be very careful about the sin of idolatry because it is very serious and indicates that we may be deceived—that we have not actually experienced the life changing miracle of the *new birth.* God does not want us to be deceived, so He gives us similar warnings about idolatry in Gal. 5:19–21; Eph. 5:5-6; Rev. 21:8, 22:14-15. God loves us and He wants to protect us from the disillusionment, powerlessness and eventual destruction that idolatry always produces because idols can never help us or give us real, lasting joy and contentment here on earth. And they certainly cannot *save us* or give us *eternal life.*

Ezekiel 36 contains another beautiful picture of all that God, in His grace does for us through the life changing miracle of salvation (redemption, new birth). We won't look it up but please read here God's promise to all who enter into His family through His wonderful gift of salvation.

I will sprinkle clean water on you, and you will be clean; I will cleanse you from all your filthiness and from all your idols. Moreover, I will give you a new heart and… I will put My Spirit within you and (give you a new desire) to walk in My statutes, and you will be careful to observe My ordinances (Ezek. 36:25-27).

2. Read 2 Cor. 5:17.
     a. What happens to every *true* "born again" believer?

   b. Based upon these three texts, (1 Cor. 6:9-11, Ezek. 36:25-28 and 2 Cor. 5:17), is it possible for one to be *born again* and experience no change in his desires, attitudes and actions?

3. Read Eph. 1:13-14.

   a. What does God give us as confirmation that we have truly been born again? (vs. 13b)

4. Read Rom. 8:16.

   a. Who bears witness (testifies) with our spirit? (vs. 16a)

   b. About what does He bear witness/testify? (vs. 16b)

5. Read Rom. 8:9.

   a. Complete this sentence: If anyone does not have the Spirit of Christ, _____

   _____

The central theme of the entire epistle of 1 John is the doctrine of salvation—what it is, how one is saved, and the proofs of salvation that will follow every genuine salvation experience. It's clearly very important to God that we understand these "proofs" and "test ourselves"—verify our salvation.

6. Read 1 John 2:3-4.

   a. What "proof" does John give us here that we have been genuinely *born again?* (vs. 3b)

One of the first things that happens to every born again believer is a new love for and devotion to the Word of God. He loves the Word of God and hungers to know it better so that He can more fully and consistently obey it. By this he proves His love for God and expresses gratitude for His salvation.

7. Read 1 John 3:14-15.

   a. How do we know that we have passed from death into eternal life (been born again)? (vs. 14)

   b. The one who *hates his brother is a* _____. What does he *not* have? (vs. 15).

8. Read 1 John 2:22-23.

   a. Who is a liar? (vs. 22a)

The born again believer has a deep love for and devotion to Jesus, who is not only "the Messiah"—Savior of the world—but also his personal Lord and Savior. He loves to talk about Him and express his gratitude for what He has done for him. He would rather die than deny him. So whenever you hear someone *deny Christ* by not wanting to even talk about Him, or dishonoring Him through irreverence or blasphemous remarks, there ought to be serious concern about his salvation.

9. Read Matt. 7:17–23.

    a. How will other people recognize those who have been born again? (vs. 20)

    b. What will Jesus say to those who *claim* to know Him but have never been genuinely *born again*? (Repented from the heart and received Him as personal Lord and Savior) (vs. 23).

10. Read John 10:27.

    a. What do Jesus' sheep hear/listen to? (vs. 27a)

    b. What do they do? (vs. 27b)

Genuinely *born again* believers will *listen to* Jesus' voice by reading and studying His Word and spending time with Him in prayer. They have a personal relationship with Him—He knows them—and they follow as He leads them. We'll talk more about discernment, making sure that it is Jesus' "voice" that we are hearing and obeying in book three, but for today, note that God's "true sheep" love their Shepherd and have a desire to walk in obedience to Him as He leads them.

The Salvation Test, commanded by God for all who claim to have been *born again (John 3:3),* is undoubtedly, the most important exam we will ever take in our lifetime, for indeed, our eternal destiny and the destiny of those we love, is at stake. We dare not neglect it. I have included a review of the biblical proofs of salvation in the appendix of this study. In light of the eternal consequences involved, it is imperative that we take this examination to see if we have truly been "born again" into God's Kingdom, or if we may be deceived by the *traditions of man* and clinging to these rather than the saving Grace of God that comes to us through our repentance and personal faith in Jesus and what He accomplished for us on the cross and through His resurrection. Please put a bookmark here, then turn to the appendix at the back of the book where you will find "The Salvation Test". Read the instructions carefully, then take the test because truly it is: the most important test you will ever take. After you have finished the test, return here to write out your Bible verse and prayer for today.

Write out a Bible verse that had special meaning to you today.

Based upon what you have learned today, write a prayer to God expressing the desires of your heart in applying these truths to your life.

Chapter 2 — Day 4
Progressive Sanctification
The Holy Image of God — in Restoration

But we should always give thanks to God for you, brethren, beloved by the Lord, because God has chosen you from the beginning for salvation through sanctification by the Spirit and faith in the truth. And it was for this He called you through our gospel, that you may gain the glory of our Lord Jesus Christ (2 Thess. 2:13-14).

I see them all the time—in grocery stores, standing in line at the pharmacy counter, or rushing in stressful stride down airport corridors—lonely, empty, harried faces. But mostly I see them in nursing homes or as homebound invalids in a state of chronic illness of one type or another—listless, devoid of purpose or productivity, and ever so miserable. People who have stubbornly (or because of demonic deception or fear) refused to look to God and pursue *His* good plans for their lives, and they come to the end of their days filled with bitterness and a painful sense of loss, regret and fear. The Bible calls it *kicking against the goad (Acts 9:5).* My heart breaks for each one caught in this oppressive downward spiral. I understand. I lived in that same agonizing emptiness for so many years. And I realize fully, that had it not been for the loving, unmerited grace of God, I would still be there following that same path all the way to my own painful, regretful, plagued-with-fear end. I cannot help but recall one of many of my own personal encounters with that *agonizing emptiness…*

I remember it as if it were yesterday. We were seated in the plush auditorium of the luxury beachfront Fontainebleau Hotel in Miami. A regal, royal blue velvet curtain shimmered in the background of the spacious stage as dozens of spotlights danced across it in anticipation of the special awards soon to be announced by IBM executives. IBM, at that time was a renowned world leader in computer technology, sales and service. Only the sharpest, most energetic applicants were hired so the competition was always intense for it's coveted annual awards. One could only dream…In a few moments, the bright stage lights fell on me as the announcement was made of my being selected as IBM's Eastern Division System Support Specialist of the year. A list of lofty achievements was read as enthusiastic applause echoed through the auditorium. I had dreamed of this recognition since my first awards banquet as the System Support Specialist for our district just one year earlier, and only two years after joining IBM. So quickly had I "climbed the corporate ladder" in achieving this coveted award. It should have been a moment of exhilarating joy and celebration. But even the grand fanfare, spotlights and applause on the outside could not ease the tormenting turmoil inside as my mind churned with plaguing thoughts: how could I top this next year? How many systems would I have to configure/sell? How many overtime hours? How many weekends would I have to sacrifice? I could not enjoy for even a few minutes a sense of real, inner satisfaction, contentment—peace.

I didn't know God then, so I didn't understand that there would be no real or lasting peace or contentment until that situation was remedied, no matter what I achieved. Sadly, many years would pass before I would understand this fundamental truth: All real and lasting peace and contentment begins with peace with God, found in a personal relationship with Him, through faith in Jesus and His redeeming work on our behalf on the cross. But that is only the beginning. God has a beautiful plan for each of our lives and until we are actively involved in the fulfillment of that plan—God's plan—all our dreams and schemes, and even lofty achievements, will be just as the Bible says in James 4:14: *like a vapor that quickly disappears* leaving us empty and ever striving for more, but never finding the true fulfillment and contentment for which we so desperately long and were created to enjoy.

> *But God has chosen you from the beginning for salvation through sanctification by the Spirit and faith in the truth, and it was for this He called you through our gospel, that you may gain the glory of our Lord Jesus Christ (2 Thess. 2:13,14).*

God tells us clearly here that the new birth is but the first step in God's special plan for our lives. The next step is *sanctification*.

Sanctification comes from the Greek word, *hagiasmos*, which means: *Set apart for God's Holy purposes*. It is a glorious ongoing work of God's grace by which the believer is set apart (separated) more and more from sin as he becomes more and more righteous and holy, free of sin's bondages. This is accomplished by the Holy Spirit working through the Word of God (Rom. 8:3-4; John 17:7). In other words, we are, through the redemptive work of Jesus, forgiven of all past sin and guilt, then empowered by the Holy Spirit to live sanctified, righteous lives as we continue in faith and obedience (John 8:31-32). Sanctification is, therefore, an ongoing, progressive, work in which our new "born again" spirit (our new nature), cooperates with the Spirit of God, in conforming us to the image of Jesus, recapturing more and more of that once perfect image of God that was lost in the fall.

It may be helpful to think of it this way: The fall was the image of God, lost. Sanctification is the image of God, regained; or, more specifically, "being regained" through a progressive purification as our love for and obedience to God grows and old sinful habits are *put off* and new righteous ones are *put on (Eph. 4:22-24)*.

Sanctification, therefore is a powerful word of hope for the Christian. He no longer must be a slave to his fleshly lusts and passions that lead always to sin, separation from God, and with that, death to his joy and peace. He is now empowered by the Holy Spirit to trust and obey God as He leads him, in all His good plans…*from glory to glory (Rom. 12:1-2; 2 Cor. 3:18)*.

> *Therefore, having been justified by faith, we have peace with God through our Lord Jesus Christ through whom we have obtained our introduction by faith into this grace in which we stand; (Rom. 5:1-2).*

Sanctification is the second step in the *continuation of grace* in the salvation process: Justification, Sanctification, Glorification.

> *You have been chosen… by the sanctifying work of the Spirit, that you may obey Jesus Christ… I am the vine, you are the branches; he who abides in Me, and I in him, he bears much fruit;… if anyone does not abide in Me, he is thrown away as a branch, and dries up; and they gather them, and cast them into the fire, and they are burned… I chose you, and appointed you, that you should go and bear fruit, and that your fruit should remain (1 Pet. 1:2; John 15:5-6, 16)*

Contrary to popular practice in a tragic number of churches today, God does not save anyone to occupy a pew on Sunday morning, then go out and do his own thing all through the week, come back to church the next Sunday, sit and soak, go back into the world, do his own thing, return and repeat the cycle over and over again until he dies and goes to Heaven, never experiencing any change in his thinking, motivations, or behavior, or bearing any fruit for the kingdom of God. God created all of us to be *set-apart, sanctified, useful vessels, fulfilling His good will and purposes, bearing fruit for Him (2 Tim. 2:21; John 15:8; Rom. 12:1-2; Eph. 2:10; John 13:5–14; John 17:4).*

As obedient children, do not be conformed to the former lusts which were yours in your ignorance, but like the Holy One who called you, be holy yourselves also in all your behavior; because it is written, "You shall be holy, for I am holy" (1 Pet. 1:14–16).

This process of sanctification, (being set apart for God's holy purposes and becoming like Jesus) is that *upward call* in Christ, that leads ultimately to glorification, described by Paul in Philippians 3:

Not that I have already obtained it, or have already become perfect, but I press on in order that I may lay hold of that for which also I was laid hold of by Christ Jesus. Brethren, I do not regard myself as having laid hold of it yet; but one thing I do; forgetting what lies behind and reaching forward to what lies ahead, I press on toward the goal for the prize of the upward call of God in Christ Jesus (Phil. 3:12–14).

What a beautiful example Paul gives us here. He finds great challenge and joy in this sanctification process, ever *pressing on, forgetting what lies behind, reaching forward.* Paul keeps his vision onward and upward in anticipation of what lies ahead: *I press on toward the goal for the prize of the upward call of God in Christ Jesus.* And what is that goal, that prize that Paul keeps ever before him? It is the prize of *glorification*—standing before Christ, in His presence, in sinless, perfect holiness… forever free of all sin, sorrow, sadness, pain, problems, death and dying! And it is the incalculable joy of hearing His Savior say: "Well done, my good and faithful servant. Enter into the joy of your master!" What a goal! What a prize! What joy of anticipation that keeps all who share Paul's onward, upward perspective… *pressing on!*

For we are His workmanship, created in Christ Jesus for good works, which God prepared beforehand, that we should walk in them (Eph. 2:10).

In this beautiful promise, God reminds us that we are **His** workmanship who have become *new creatures in Christ* and, as such, He already *has prepared* a wonderful, meaningful, fulfilling life for each of us. So we no longer have to strive to *find it* or *achieve it*—doing that which would <u>merit</u> God's (and other's) favor as we persistently, through great stress and strain, labor to fulfill every new scheme for success that the tempter puts before us. Such endeavors will never please God, nor will they bring satisfaction to our own lives. God's sanctification plan is so much better! In God's plan, we are simply to remain *in Christ*—in union and fellowship with Him through His Word and prayer—then, in surrendered trust and obedient faith, *walk,* in the power of the Holy Spirit, in God's good plans already *prepared* for us. In other words, according to Eph. 2:10, our responsibility is simply the joy of walking daily in God's already "prepared" *good plans (Rom. 12:1-2)* in the never failing presence of Jesus and power of the Holy Spirit. There's freedom, rest and contentment in that.

Now, may the God of peace Himself sanctify you entirely; and may your spirit and soul and body be preserved complete, without blame until the coming of our Lord Jesus Christ. (1 Thess. 5:23).

Bible Study Supplement
Chapter 2 — Day 4 — Progressive Sanctification

1. Read Eph. 2:10 (Please use the NASB translation below to answer the questions that follow).

   For we are His workmanship, created in Christ Jesus for good works, which God prepared beforehand, that we should walk in them (Eph. 2:10).

   a. Who were we created in (through our new birth)?

   b. For what purpose were we created?...Who prepared these?

   c. What is both our privilege and our joy? (vs. 10b)

Note the important distinction in these verses. We are not saved *by* good works. Jesus already accomplished that impossible task for us on the cross and through His resurrection—forgiveness of sins, salvation, life eternal. In fact, part of our salvation is freedom from striving through good works to earn the approval of God. But that is only the beginning. In God's wonderful plan He also saved us *for* good works—for the glorious privilege of participating with Him in the fulfillment of His good purposes for the redemption and sanctification of mankind.

2. Read Rom. 8:28-29.

   a. To whom do *all things* work together for good? (two qualifications - vs. 28)

   b. What is God's desire (purpose) for all who meet these qualifications? (vs. 29)

3. Read 2 Cor. 5:15,17–21.

   a. What happens to everyone who is truly born again… is now "in Christ"? (three things - vs. 17)

   b. How will he now live? (vs. 15b)

   c. What ministry has God given to all of us? (vs. 18b)

   d. What are we now? (vs. 20a)

   e. What are we "becoming" (living out) – through the ongoing process of sanctification? (vs. 21b)

4. 1 Pet. 2:9-10 is a beautiful picture of our blessed new identity, value and position in Christ as redeemed, sanctified, set apart children of God. Read 1 Pet. 2:9-10.

   a. What are we now that we have been saved and are being sanctified? (four things - vs. 9a)

   b. For what purpose? (vs. 9b)

   c. Who are we now? (vs. 10a)

   d. What have we received? (vs. 10b)

5. Read 2 Thess. 2:13-14.

   a. For what has God chosen/called you? (vs. 13)

   b. How does He accomplish this? (by two means - vs. 13b)

   c. What will be the result if we are obedient to God in pursuing this purpose? (vs. 14b)

6. Read Jer. 29:11–13. (Please use NASB here to answer the questions below).

11. "For I know the plans that I have for you" declares the Lord, "plans for welfare and not for calamity to give you a future and a hope."
12. "Then you will call upon Me and come and pray to Me, and I will listen to you.
13. And you will seek Me and find Me, when you search for Me with all your heart" (Jer. 29:11-13).

   a. What kind of plans does God have for you? (vs. 11)

   b. How can we be sure that we will find God's good plans for our lives? (vs. 13)

Let's conclude today's lesson by giving a summary of biblical sanctification, the 2ⁿᵈ step in the salvation process—justification, sanctification, glorification. That is where you and I are at the moment. According to God's Word, sanctification is:

1. Being set apart for God's holy purposes (2 Thess. 2:13-14).
2. Bringing honor and glory to God and fulfillment and joy to our own lives as we trust and obey Him daily, *walking in* His good plans for our lives (Eph. 2:10; Rom. 12:1-2; Jer. 29:11-13).
3. Becoming conformed to the image of Jesus (Rom. 8:29).
4. Serving as God's ambassadors, sharing His love and truth with others that they, too, might be *born again,* and enter into the sanctification process (2 Cor. 5:15–20).

Write out a Bible verse that had special meaning to you today.

Based upon what you have learned today, write a prayer to God expressing the desires of your heart in applying these truths to your life.

Chapter 2 — Day 5
Man's Wisdom Versus God's Wisdom

> *For it is written, I will destroy the wisdom of the wise; And the cleverness of the clever I will set aside…Where is the wise man? Where is the scribe? Where is the debater of this age? Has not God made foolish the wisdom of the world? (1 Cor. 1:19-20).*
>
> *For the wisdom of this world is foolishness before God (1 Cor. 3:19).*

There are two separate and very distinct kinds of wisdom: 1. God's wisdom, 2. The wisdom of the world. Which wisdom we choose to follow will determine not only the significance, meaning and value of life that is enjoyed—or endured—here on earth, but also our eternal destiny.

As my desire to be pleasing to God in all I did grew in the sanctification process, I was, naturally, drawn into a deeper, more thorough study of the Word of God. One day as I was reading Jesus' warnings to the Pharisees, my heart was struck by a certain verse:

> *You hypocrites, rightly did Isaiah prophesy of you, saying, This people honors Me with their lips, but their heart is far from Me. In vain do they worship Me, teaching as doctrines the precepts of men (Matt. 15:7–9).*

I could see that, having been very much a part of the world system for so many years, I had taken in a cadre of *precepts of men* that I accepted as doctrine. Because I had no solid biblical discernment, I was like the novice prospector, unable to tell the difference between real gold (the ageless, infallible wisdom of God) and fool's gold, (worldly wisdom) that looked like, sounded like, and "felt" very much like the real thing so often (2 Cor. 11:13-15).

I prayed that God would quicken my mind to greater discernment so that I would be able to recognize error and replace it with godly biblical thinking. As the mind of Christ (Biblical truth) began to develop within me, I became more and more aware of the deception that permeates our culture—not only today but in the years when my own personal presuppositions (belief system, assumptions of truth) were being formed.

Man-centered humanism, the present, nearly universally accepted demonic belief system, had already become firmly entrenched and was the predominant philosophy of western culture by the time I reached college. As a conscientious and diligent student (but not yet a Christian), it was impossible for me to escape the influence of this anti-God, anti-biblical philosophy that places man, not God, at the center of the universe. It was everywhere: in the classroom, on television, in the movies, in everyday conversations with other students, family, and friends.

Since man was considered the center of the universe, education, science, and technology were deified, becoming revered *gods*, the source of wisdom and authority to which people flocked for their answers to the problems and "sicknesses" of the world—not God. The more degrees a person could amass, the greater the respect and *esteem* he/she commanded, and the greater was considered his/her wisdom. One's *identity* was often inextricably linked with how much education he had, making the amassing of degrees a very appealing trap into which to fall, just as I did. It is a perilously dangerous trap, however because the modern public education system is in rebellion against God and diametrically opposed to the teachings and authority of Scripture.

As a new Christian, with little true biblical wisdom or discernment, I did not recognize this. And, because I was already struggling with an *identity* problem, I did not want to appear uninformed or intellectually inferior. (My *identity problem*, in reality, was a host of sin problems that I could not see due to the unbiblical psychological indoctrination). So I jumped on the bandwagon with countless others who tried to mesh them together— godly wisdom and worldly wisdom. It was called *integration*. In the case of issues that concerned the "pseuche" (soul)—mind, will, emotions—man-centered, humanistic psychology was *integrated* with the Bible. But it didn't work—not on a long term, permanent basis. It only turned the problem into a vicious cyclical repetition of superficial healing. This kind of "integration" (which, in reality, is adding to the Bible) will never work, because God is holy, and He is building a kingdom of holiness and righteousness, totally free of sinful man's tainted worldly thinking and *self*-centered ambitions— the heart of modern psychology. Whether we recognize it or not, attempting to integrate man-centered psychological counseling with the Bible "distracts believers, dilutes Scripture, dishonors God, develops the flesh, and debilitates spiritual growth."[6]

God is the ruler of the universe and the final authority in all things, no matter how advanced and sophisticated the *wisdom of the world* becomes. It is God's wisdom and God's wisdom alone that has withstood the test of time, remaining unshaken through the ages, and will continue to do so: *Forever, O Lord, your Word is settled… and it will stand… from generation to generation (Ps. 119:89).*

The Bible warns us that *the wisdom of the world is foolishness to God (1 Cor. 3:19)*. But it is a foolishness that, because of demonic deception, appears intellectually sound, unarguably logical, and, as the forbidden fruit, *desirable to make one wise (Gen. 3:6)*. Its tantalizing temptations, which appeal to the natural, unsanctified lusts and desires of our fallen nature, so often make it virtually *humanly* impossible to counteract or resist. <u>Only the Word of God can cut through its seductive lies and give us the discernment we need to stand firm against this kind of powerful demonic deception.</u>

For example: We have all heard the very logical statement: "All 'truth' is 'God's truth'. Is this a true statement or not?

Let's examine it according to God's Word.

Father, sanctify them in truth. Thy Word is truth… the sum of Thy Word is truth, and every one of Thy righteous ordinances is everlasting (John 17:17; Ps. 119:160).

We must always ask: What is the source of the claimed 'truth'? Is it a textbook? Even a "godly" textbook of a seminary course? Is it a quote from a renowned, respected intellect, author, inventor, religious leader? If the *source* is anything/anyone other than the Word of God, the purported 'truth' must be considered suspect until it is held up to the light of Scripture. If it violates Scripture in any way, then it is not *God's truth* and, therefore, not real 'truth' at all. It must be rejected.

God's Word must always be the plumb line against which all 'truth' is judged (Amos 7:7-8).

We must be very careful about this because demonic deception is very powerful and it is easy to fall for subtle misrepresentations of 'truth' – especially when 'real truth' is mixed with error! There is a lot of worldly wisdom coming at us every day, and it is easy to be deceived, because much of the world's wisdom looks very much like 'truth', sounds like 'truth', and everybody and his brother is touting it as 'truth'. But, again, if any part of what is being proclaimed is not in agreement with the Word of

God, then we must take a stand against it, popular or not, because it is the truth alone (God's truth) that sets people free. God will honor our faithfulness and others will be helped.

We must not only know *about* God's truth, we must be continually taking it in—reading it, studying it, meditating upon it—that our minds might be renewed and transformed from worldly thinking to new, righteous thinking and obedience.

> *And do not be conformed to this world, but be transformed by the renewing of your mind, that you may prove what the will of God is, that which is good and acceptable and perfect (Rom.12:2).*

We must *renew our minds* with the truths of God's Word daily because we are creatures of short retention. We forget so easily! A truth learned today can quickly be forgotten "tomorrow" if it is not renewed and reinforced on a regular, ongoing basis.

God wants us to be keenly aware and mentally alert concerning the dangers of "worldly wisdom" deceptions. That's why the Bible is full of warnings concerning such. The best, most concise of these is given to us in God's book of wisdom, Proverbs. We do well to take it to heart and remember it whenever we face decisions that require careful wisdom and discernment, and whenever we are being tempted by something that *appears so right*:

> *There is a way which seems right to a man, but its end is the way of death (Prov. 14:12).*

Most temptations that effectively cause us to stumble (sin) come masked as truth, usually in the form of worldly wisdom that appeals to the natural lusts of our sinful flesh and desires: it "seemeth" so right! Remember Satan's most effective weapon of deception is mixing a little truth with error, to cause the lie to be accepted without question or opposition. There is only one way to protect ourselves from falling for such attractive, very believable and universally accepted 'truths' and to recognize the lies behind them. It is to be so saturated with the Word of God that nothing can come into us that does not pass through the purifying filter of the absolute, incontrovertible truth of God's Word. For only the Word of God provides the needed discernment to cut through—divide, expose, evaluate accurately—the corrupt demonic deception that permeates the wisdom of the world (Heb. 4:12). That is another reason it is important to study and meditate upon God's Word daily so that we have the *sum of God's truth (Ps. 119:160)* within, protecting our hearts and minds from error so that we can stand firm and secure against worldly lies and temptations just as Jesus did (Matt. 4:1–11).

Let's ask God to help us understand the importance of discerning between *worldly wisdom* and *true biblical wisdom*—the wisdom of God—so that we will be quick to recognize and resist destructive demonic deceptions and enticements that come to us in the attractive and very believable cloak of 'truth'.

> *... and no wonder, for even Satan disguises himself as an angel of light, therefore it is not surprising that his servants also disguise themselves as servants of righteousness (2 Cor. 11:14-15).*

Bible Study Supplement
Chapter 2 — Day 5 — Man's Wisdom Versus God's Wisdom

1. Read 1 Cor. 1:18–30.

    a. What is the message of the cross to those who are perishing…being saved? (vs. 18)

    b. What did God say that He would do? (vs. 19) and what has He done? (vs. 20b)

I smile every time I read these verses. I cannot help but think of all the modern, advanced *scientific research* of today that is continually making great, new discoveries, only to have the findings of another *comprehensive research project* just a short time later debunk that *wisdom,* coming to a completely different, often contradictory conclusion. If the *scientifically proven finding* were really true, every test that followed would come to the same conclusion. But they don't, and for those who have put their faith and trust in modern medicine and science, it gets mighty confusing trying to figure out exactly what to believe.

Do you remember that for many years we were told that to have healthy bones and teeth we should drink at least two cups of milk every day? You will still find this recommendation on many official, physician recommended "healthful diet" programs. Several years ago, however, a new study declared that such a habit is very dangerous and causes calcium buildup, kidney stones, and plaque in the arteries. Other *reliable, scientific studies* also revealed that the pasteurization process destroys—renders completely unabsorbable—all nutrients in the milk, including the important mineral, calcium. You must get your calcium from another source—supplements—we were then told. Yet another study declared that all cow's milk was bad for human consumption, destroys the immune system, and causes cancer. So much for two cups of milk a day!

And, as you begin to pay closer attention, you will hear endless additional contradictory statements concerning *scientific discoveries* almost daily. It doesn't take long to observe how truly foolish so much of the world's ever changing wisdom is! But the Word of God does not change. *Forever, O Lord, Thy Word is settled in Heaven (Ps. 119:89-90, cf. Is. 40:8).*

    c. What was God well-pleased to do? (vs. 21b)

    d. What do the Jews demand…and what do the Greeks look for? (vs. 22)

Note: The "Jews" was a term used frequently in the New Testament to refer to the unbelieving within the Jewish community—those who rejected Jesus. The "Greeks" were the intellectual aristocracy within the Greek culture, who considered the mind as "god" and continually sought to expand their (worldly) wisdom and develop superior intellect. These were the skeptics, agnostics and so called "atheists" of that day, just as we have today.

    e. What simple message did Paul preach? What was that to the Jews…the Gentiles? (vs. 23)

  f. Paul emphasizes here the kind of people God called (and still calls) to do His work...most of them were <u>not</u>...(three characteristics - vs. 26)

  g. What kind of people/things has God chosen to carry out His work? (four characteristics – vs. 27-28a).

I find it incredibly encouraging that God so often called—and continues to do so—not the intellectually superior, wealthy or noble—but common, hard working, oft rejected by society's elite, men and women like fishermen, tax collectors, poor widows, prostitutes, humble servants and faithful mothers to be His chosen "vessels of honor" to carry His message.

  h. What has Christ become for us and for all who are "in Him" – all who have received His gift of salvation? (four things - vs. 30)

This is such an important text to help us to get our eyes off of the world with its flawed wisdom and deceptive enticements and back onto Jesus in whom alone is found true wisdom, righteousness, and redemption. It is only in following Him in the good plans God has for us that we are able to avoid the deceptive, destructive foolishness of the world and find real wisdom, fulfillment, peace and joy.

 2. Read 1 Cor. 3:19-20.

  a. What is the *wisdom of this world* in God's eyes? (vs. 19)

 3. Read James 3:13–18.

  a. What will characterize the life of a truly wise person? (two things - vs. 13)

  b. What are the two most common characteristics of worldly wisdom? (two characteristics – vs. 16a)...What does it produce? (two fruits - vs. 16b)

  c. Where does such "wisdom" come from? (vs. 15)

  d. Describe the wisdom that is from above. (eight characteristics - vs. 17)

Please note that wisdom from above is first of all—*PURE*. It is holy, set apart, unstained by the wisdom of the world. It is a clear warning not to mix (attempt to integrate) worldly wisdom with God's wisdom. It does not work and makes a mockery of God's Word. May God help us to be careful to seek *pure* wisdom from above (God's Word) and to conduct our lives according to it, not the tempting, unholy, self-focused—and ultimately destructive—distortions of the world.

Verse 18 tells us that those who live by God's wisdom will walk securely in peace as they *sow seeds of godliness and reap harvests of righteousness.* It's a beautiful picture of the outworkings (fruit) of the wisdom of God in practical day to day living.

4. Read Prov. 2:1-13.

    a. What happens to one who seeks God's wisdom as looking for a treasure? (two things – vs. 5)

    b. Who gives wisdom…and what comes from His mouth? (vs. 6)

    c. To the one who is faithful in His pursuit of wisdom, what does God promise? (four things – vs.10-11)

5. Read Prov. 3:13–17.

    a. Who is blessed? (The man who….two characteristics - vs. 13)

    b. Describe the value of gaining godly wisdom and understanding. (eight benefits – vs. 14-17)

6. Read Prov. 4:18-19.

    a. How is the *path of righteousness* (walking daily in Godly wisdom) described? (vs. 18)

    b. Describe the *way of the wicked.* (two characteristics - vs. 19)

Here we see again the problem of demonic deception that comes to all who refuse to go to the Word of God to seek *godly wisdom*—they live in darkness and do not even recognize what makes them stumble.

May God help us to recognize—and seek—the incalculable value and joy of knowing and living according to the unchanging, sure and secure truths of His infallible Word—wisdom that is *from above.*

Before we conclude today's Bible Study, I just wanted to check with you and see how you are doing in memorizing our theme verse, Isaiah 61:1-3, given at the beginning of chapter 1. I gave you a schedule there for memorizing just a phrase or two every week. If you are keeping up with this schedule, there will be no problem in memorizing the verses by the end of the study, and you will be most blessed to have this beautiful scripture tucked away in your heart to strengthen and encourage you. (In the schedule that I have given, I have taken out a few of the phrases to make it shorter and easier to memorize, but the main points are still there).

Write out a Bible verse that had special meaning to you today.

Based upon what you have learned today, write a prayer to God expressing the desires of your heart in applying these truths to your life.

Chapter 3

Bible Memory Verse: *"If anyone wishes to be my disciple, let him deny himself, and take up his cross daily, and follow Me"* (Luke 9:23).

Bonus Memory Verse: *And Mary said, "Behold, the bondservant of the Lord; be it unto me according to Your Word"* (Luke 1:38).

Day 1

The Psychologization of Sin

Day 2

The Problem of Self-Esteem

Day 3

God's Solution to the Self-Esteem Problem

Day 4

Spiritual Warfare – An Introduction

Be a Good Soldier: Alert, Prepared, Armed

Day 5

The War Within

The Conflict of the Two Natures

Chapter 3 — Day 1
The Psychologization of Sin

> Behold, they have rejected the Word of the Lord, and what kind of wisdom do they have? Lies and not truth prevail in the land; they do not know Me, declares the Lord. And they heal the brokenness of My people superficially, saying, "Peace, peace," but there is no peace (Jer. 8:9, 9:3, 8:11).

God alone knows the pain and devastation through *superficial healing* (above verse) that has already been inflicted upon His people because they have believed the subtle lies of modern man-centered humanistic psychology rather than holding fast to the truths of God's Word.

This is, as you know from reading my testimony, a subject that is of deep, personal concern. Having experienced "psychological" problems from the time I was a child, I naturally sought all the wisdom I could find to help deal with these and have victory over them. Then, as now, psychology was proclaimed by nearly all as having the answer to such problems. Therefore, the study of this subject became paramount in my educational pursuits including post-graduate work and a number of specialized certifications. I ever so faithfully studied every "expert" on the subject, every theory and methodology of dealing with psychological problems found in the textbooks and latest professional journals. After I became a Christian, the Holy Spirit, working through the Word of God, revealed to me the error in this approach to dealing with these kinds of problems, which are, in reality, problems of the soul.

Psychology comes from the Greek word *psyché*, or *pseuche*, which means "soul" and *logia*, "study of." It is, therefore, by its own definition the study of that which affects the soul of man. The soul consists of mind, emotions, and will. Bear in mind that from the beginning of the history of mankind until the late 1800s, when Sigmund Freud came upon the scene,

there was no such thing as "psychology"—study of the soul by man—*apart* from God and His Word. Problems of the *pseuche* (mind, emotions, will) were recognized for what they were—soul problems—and they were dealt with as such. In the earliest days, God Himself addressed issues of the *soul* as He spoke directly to His servants the prophets who then spoke to the people concerning these problems and how they were to solve them. Later, Jesus brought further instruction from God, teaching us many things that would enable us to have and to maintain a strong and healthy soul. After Jesus returned to Heaven, He left us His Word, His Holy Spirit, and His "body", (those who believe in Him), to continue to help us with our soul-related problems.

The solution to all such problems within the Christian community throughout these centuries until the late 1800s, involved identifying related sin issues (inappropriate, unbiblical response to various problems of life), confessing and repenting of these, and replacing them with appropriate godly thinking and behavior. Of course we recognize that because of the fallen nature of man, this did not always happen appropriately, and there were abuses to be sure, but in true Bible believing, preaching, teaching churches, believers dealt with their soul problems—and successfully so—in this manner.

Tragically, because we have allowed the world to set the standards for behavior, sin is so often no longer called sin but a *disease* or *disorder*. This is very sad, because it robs people of the hope for real and lasting help and healing. Throughout my schooling, I was taught that I should never tell my counselees that they could be "healed" (set free) of their soul related problems. That would present to them a false hope. Rather, I was to teach them to accept their *incurable disease* and learn to live with it through the various drug therapies and coping techniques psychology could offer.

This same "psycho" therapy was, naturally, applied to my own personal problems. For many years, I was told that I had an "eating disorder". It was a *disease*, and I was taught various coping techniques—goal setting, visualization and behavioral modification which included a number of rigid rules that could not be violated. That only made the problem worse because I could never keep all the rules. But when I began to study the Word of God, I could see that the disorder was not an *incurable disease* at all but *sin*: gluttony. It involved the seductive, sinful lust for fleshly indulgence and pleasure—a form of idolatry spoken of in Phil 3:18-19, Eph. 4:19, and James 1:14. As I began to confess and sincerely repent of my sin, I soon came to see that, indeed, there is power in the blood of Jesus, in His purifying Word, and in the enabling of the Holy Spirit to redeem and release the sin-sick soul from enslavement to the tormenting cycle of sin and guilt. As opposed to coping techniques, the Word of God offers forgiveness and freedom for all who are willing to confront and confess sin, then genuinely repent and forsake it. What joy to realize that I was no longer a slave to my insatiable fleshly appetite, but rather it now had become a slave to the Lordship of Jesus under whose authority I now rested. (Jesus reigns and rules over all principalities and powers, including the power of the sin of gluttony…and *every other sin*—Eph 1:19–21, 2:6; Rom. 6:4; Eph. 3:16-20 etc.). I'll never forget that glorious day when I awoke and, for the first time in my life, realized that I now had a *choice* regarding my appetite. I no longer had to give in to its seductive temptations, relentless accusations, and badgering demands. I was now free to *choose* to obey the Bible's life-giving command to *eat for strength and not for gluttony (Eccles. 10:17b* - and many other wonderful Scriptures regard-

ing good diet and health practices). And oh, what a difference that made in the well-being of not just my soul, but my body and spirit as well (1 Thess. 5:23).

I could also help other people by taking them to Scripture and showing them what the Bible says about their particular undealt-with sin areas, so that they, too, could repent, *put off* hurtful, sinful thinking and habits and replace these with godly, healthful thoughts and habits (Eph. 4:22-24). As I did this and witnessed, time and time again, the power of the Holy Spirit in setting people free of the tormenting bondage to a never ending cycle of sin and guilt, I no longer wanted to have anything to do with psychology's deceptive *foolishness (1 Cor. 3:19)* that refused to confront sin for what it is: rebellion against God. (Demanding and seeking *my* way, rather than trusting and obeying God). By giving people an excuse for their sin rather than dealing with it biblically, we only tighten the shackles of the sin/guilt cycle, robbing them of the hope of ever being truly free (John 8:31-32, 36).

May God help us all who know the truth and have tasted of the freedom that comes from obeying the truth to stand together in this critical area, ministering hope to those whose lives have been broken by sin's devastating lies and deceptions, that they may be truly set free through the liberating truths of God's Word, not superficially healed by psychology's powerless coping techniques.

> *From the prophet even to the priest, everyone practices deceit. And they heal the brokenness of My people superficially, saying, "peace, peace" … but there is no peace (Jer. 8:10b,11).*

[I've included in the appendix an article that Mel and I wrote for the Psychoheresy Awareness Ministry Newsletter. (Psychoheresy Awareness is a ministry dedicated to exposing the lies and deceptions of modern psychology—especially those that have infiltrated the church). I think this article will be helpful in understanding the far-reaching harmful affects of this problem. Please put a book mark here, turn to the appendix, and read the article, "Psychology, A Biblical Analysis." Then return here (next page) to complete the Bible Study Supplement].

Bible Study Supplement
Chapter 3 — Day 1 — The Psychologization of Sin

If you have not yet read the article, "A Biblical Analysis of Psychology", in the appendix, please turn there now and read this article before completing the questions below.

1. Read Ps. 32:1–5.

   a. Who is blessed? (four characteristics - vs. 1-2)

Please note the last qualification of blessedness: "in whose spirit is no deceit (guile)". True blessedness—freedom, liberation, joy—begins with honesty before God, others and ourselves. It involves taking responsibility for our sins, genuinely confessing and repenting of them, accepting God's total forgiveness and grace, then going on in the Holy Spirit's power to overcome future temptations.

   b. What happened to the psalmist when he kept silent (did not repent of his sin)? (vs. 3, 4b).

Note: "Bones (body) wasting away" refers to basic physical strength and stamina. It's a kind of relentless sapping of energy (life) as deep as the bones.

   c. What did God do when the psalmist confessed his sin? (vs. 5b - Please use NASB below to answer question).

   5. I acknowledged my sin to Thee, and my iniquity I did not hide; I said, "I will confess my transgressions to the Lord"; and Thou didst forgive the guilt of my sin (Ps. 32:5).

Note here that God not only forgave his *sin*, He forgave even the *guilt* that accompanied it. This is so important to recognize. True confession and repentance (where there is no deceit or unbelief) will result in a release from the relentless haunting and accusing guilt that always attaches itself to sin.

2. Read Is. 41:28-29. (Please use NASB below to answer questions).

   28. But when I look there is no one, and there is no counselor among them who, if I ask, can give an answer.

   29. Behold all of them are false. Their works are worthless, their... images are wind and emptiness (Is. 41:28, 29).

   a. For whom was God looking?...Did He find this person? (vs. 28)

   b. What did He find instead? (vs. 29)

God was looking for a true, godly counselor who would minister His righteous, life-giving truth and salvation to His people, but He could find no one. I'm sure that as God looks down upon His Church today, He sees much the same barrenness of true biblical wisdom in ministering His life-giving Word to others, helping them deal effectively with their soul problems. I am so thankful that you are among the precious few who desire to do this. God longs for all of us to answer

His very special call in Is. 41:27b: *I will send a messenger of good news.* So many have been hurt far too long by the devastating effects of the psychologization of sin—which only puts people into deeper bondage to sin and guilt. We can help them by sharing the real, lasting hope and healing found in sincere repentance and knowing and obeying God's Word in the power of the Holy Spirit.

4. Read Jer. 8:8–11.

   a. Why are the *wise men* put to shame? (vs. 9b)

Today, these "wise men" (referred to as "experts") would include counselors, psychologists and psychotherapists, who turn to worldly wisdom to deal with problems of the soul rather than rely upon the truths of God's Word and the Holy Spirit working through these truths. In the next verse we learn that the worldly "wise men/women" who do this are *greedy for gain.* They are, in reality, far more concerned about their pocketbook than the long-term welfare of those who come to them for help. Common rates for one hour of psychotherapy today range from eighty to two hundred dollars!

   b. How do the "wise men" deal with the problems of the people and what is the result? (vs. 11)

5. Read 1 John 1:9.

   a. What will God do every time we come to Him in sincere confession and repentance?

Psalm 38 is a classic "psychological" case study of a man greatly oppressed and weighed down by his own sin and guilt. It was written by David when he was in the quagmire of undealt-with sin—sin concerning which there had been no genuine confession or repentance for some time. It is a very graphic and realistic picture of the awful consequences of unconfesssed sin. I'm so glad the Bible is a book that shows us life as it really is in a fallen world. This honest portrayal of the consequence of an unrepentant heart gives me something with which I can identify, and from which I can move into the encouraging assurance of God's compassionate love, forgiveness, and healing grace (Lam. 3:22-23; 1 John 1:9; 2 Cor. 12: 9-10; Hosea 6:1-2). No wonder God's Word so often urges us to *confess, repent,* and *forsake* all habitual sins which rob us of so much joy and keep us bound in a state of guilt and condemnation. As we, with God's help do this—tearing down sinful strongholds and casting away worthless idols—we will find ourselves enjoying the blessed fruits of true repentance, abounding grace, and peace with God, others, and ourselves.

6. Read Ps. 38:4–15.

   a. What has overwhelmed him (gone over his head)? (vs. 4a) How does it feel? (vs. 4b)

   b. Why do his wounds fester and refuse to be healed? (vs. 5 - Use NIV below to answer).
      5. *My wounds fester and are loathsome because of my sinful folly (Ps. 38:5).*

   c. What are some other physical manifestations of his undealt with sin? (vs. 6-8, 10-11)

   d. To whom does David look (hope in/trust) for the answers to his problems? (vs. 15).

David found hope and healing in God's forgiveness and restorative grace (Ps. 51)…and so will we.

No wonder David wrote after his extended exile from God and long-overdue confession:

> *How blessed is the man whose transgression is forgiven… and in whose spirit there is no deceit. Create within me a pure heart, O God, and renew a steadfast spirit within me…restore to me the joy of your salvation (Ps. 32:1-2, 51:10, 12).*

Write out a Bible verse that had special meaning to you today.

Based upon what you have learned today, write a prayer to God expressing the desires of your heart in applying these truths to your life.

Chapter 3 — Day 2
The Problem of Self-Esteem

> *For the time will come when they will not endure sound doctrine; but wanting to have their ears tickled, they will accumulate for themselves teachers in accordance to their own desires; and will turn away their ears from the truth, and will turn aside to myths (2 Tim. 4:3-4).*

I have prayed long and fervently, and spent countless additional hours in the Word over the past several months seeking God's heart—true biblical wisdom—regarding this subject. I know that the issue of self-esteem is a very sensitive one because of all the attention focused upon it in the past 25 years. In all honesty, I much prefer, like Pilate's wife, to "have nothing to do with it" because of the strong emotion and allegiance connected to it and to the experts who espouse it, several of whom have come to command a near god-like reverence. However, to avoid this topic would clearly be a willful act of disobedience regarding God's call on my life in writing this study. Therefore, I must, in obedience to God, share the burden He has placed upon my heart concerning this subject that has resulted in confusion and bondage for so many.

My people perish for lack of knowledge (true biblical wisdom) (Hosea 4:6).

Of all the factors that played into both the intensity and the duration of those long, agonizing years of mental torment and emotional instability, the one that contributed the most, by far, was believing and applying to my life the very appealing, albeit deceptive and unbiblical teaching of self-esteem. And God alone knows how much pain and suffering others have endured because of the same error. Many families have been destroyed (as ours nearly was),

and inestimable damage has been done to the cause of Christ and to the witness of the Church because God's people have embraced this self-centered (as opposed to God-centered) unbiblical teaching, leaving them weak and absorbed in the pursuit of *self*-esteem (and all that involves!) rather than esteeming Christ and bringing glory to God by honoring, trusting and obeying Him.

For decades now, even as early as grammar school, this unbiblical teaching has influenced how teachers teach and parents parent in the exercising, or lack thereof, of proper biblical discipline. For fear of negatively impacting a child's development, parents were told and teachers were taught that all care must be exercised to avoid damaging fragile Jimmy or tender Suzy's *self-esteem*. Later, as fragile Jimmy and tender Suzy entered high school, then college, the childhood training was reinforced by further teaching that promoted attention to self and "looking out for #1".

When I was in graduate school studying for my master's in counseling, the teaching of self-esteem permeated nearly every psychological methodology and technique I studied. In fact, we were taught that nearly all mental, emotional, and psychological problems were inextricably linked to low self-esteem. The main thrust, therefore, was to use our professional psychological training to build up the counselee's self-esteem until they came to a place where they *felt good about themselves* because only those who *feel good about themselves* are able to take control of their lives and overcome their problems. In my field training and supervised counseling situations, I continually heard: the problem with (now adult) proud, defiant Jimmy and mentally and emotionally unstable Suzy is the result of a lack of attention to their self-esteem as children. The cure was always the same: do whatever it takes to nurture and build up the damaged self-esteem. And so that is what I always tried to do, being totally blind to the fact that I was not helping Suzy at all, but actually playing into the devil's hand to set her upon a course that would lead her deeper into the snare of preoccupation with self and thus farther and farther away from real mental stability, true freedom and peace.

God created us to have a personal relationship with Him, and in and through this relationship to fulfill His good plans for our lives and solve our problems. We are not "in control". God is "in control" and only God has the wisdom, the power and the resources to deal with our problems in a way that brings real victory and lasting peace. It's precisely because we *can't* handle all the problems and heartaches of life in a fallen world—including the temptations that bombard us continually through our own sinful nature—that we don't *feel good about ourselves,* so we need to turn to God in trusting faith and dependence on Him, rather than vainly attempting to pump up our own sinful, weak, inadequate, *self*-esteem. It is, in fact, because of a much too elevated *self*-esteem that most emotional and psychological problems cause so much stress and depression, not a lack of it. But the proud, fearful (of losing control) self does not want to hear that, so it turns away to myths and the doctrines of man in order to avoid dealing with the real underlying problems—pride, selfishness, disobedience, demonic fear, estrangement from God.

For the time will come when they will not endure sound doctrine; but wanting to have their ears tickled, they will accumulate for themselves teachers in accordance to their own desires; and will turn away their ears from the truth, and will turn aside to myths (2 Tim. 4:3, 4).

The concept of self-esteem as a solution to our psychological (pseuche, soul) problems is an unbiblical myth. After I was saved and began seriously studying God's Word in search of *God's* wisdom and solutions to my psychological problems, conviction came to my heart again and again concerning the deceptive fallacies in the *self-esteem* myth. God's Word often, and clearly, instructed me to abandon this pursuit that greatly impeded my growth into true Christlike humility, love for others, and submissive obedience. It was not an easy endeavor. When "self" has ruled for so long, it is not easily dethroned. But I knew that unless Christ truly ruled over my heart, my will and my emotions, there would never be any lasting peace or solution to any of my "psychological" (soul) problems. So I prayed every day that God, through His Holy Spirit would help me to face the sin issues in my life and to deal with them biblically. A new peace and deeper joy came with each victory.

As I witness the continuing erosion of true biblical discipleship in deference to the unholy integration of worldly philosophies—such as the teaching of self-esteem, and a cadre of other unbiblical teachings—my heart breaks. I am still stunned by the degree to which the self-esteem movement has penetrated our Christian institutions of education, from as early as grade school through graduate programs. We see it and hear it everywhere—on Christian radio, in Christian magazines, books, and videos. "Experts" laud it, preachers preach it, retreats and seminars promote it. There are even Bible studies to help build one's *self*-esteem! It has truly become, as Paul so clearly warned against: *another gospel (Gal. 1:6).* No longer are we hearing the clear gospel message of sinners in need of a Savior (repentance, salvation, sanctification). We are hearing instead *another gospel* of "sick" or "wounded" people in need of self-esteem—the *disease model* of excusing sin for sickness.

You too have done evil, even more than your forefathers; for behold, you are each one walking according to the stubbornness of his own evil heart, without listening to Me (Jer. 16:12).

Scripture clearly teaches that man is born with a selfish, proud, stubborn nature, (mind, emotions, will) that is in rebellion against God—refusing to listen to and obey Him. So the more we encourage people to build up their self-esteem, the stronger becomes the selfish, proud nature and the more we will lead them away from God and a loving, submissive, obedient relationship with Him—the only place where true and lasting joy, peace, and fulfillment will ever be found.

It took some time before I was able to see this in my own life, because, as we have studied, sin is very deceptive, and especially in the one who has been bound by it—practicing it daily—many years. We are rarely able to recognize it for what it is, but see it only as it deceptively presents itself to our proud, defiant nature—as something good and desirable. In the case of self-esteem the problem is all the more dangerous because it seductively offers the perfect solution to every demand of our selfish, sinful flesh. The self-esteem argument goes something like this: "The reason you are not happy is because you are not doing enough for *yourself (your "self")* to meet your own personal *needs"*, when in reality what our pampered flesh is demanding is not true *needs* at all, but selfish, sinful lusts originating in our undisciplined, unsanctified, fallen nature. And the longer we believe the self-esteem lies, catering to and pampering our own selfish flesh, the stronger and more resistant to change our heart becomes. And so it was with me. Through all the deceptions of sin, I could easily *justify* every fleshly craving, making them appear as true *needs* rather than fleshly lusts. I *wanted* what I *wanted* and I *deserved* what I *wanted* (another distortion enmeshed in the self-esteem myth) and I was not going to have it any other way! But, in time, as I continued in my studies, the sword of God's truth—God's Word—began to cut through the layers of deception that had hardened my heart through all those years. Little by little, I was able to recognize

the spirit of rebellion (*self*-esteem) in my own heart. I could clearly see that all the self-condemnatory remarks that so often and so bitterly spilled from my lips (that I was told was the manifestation of a poor, low self-esteem), were, in truth, the manifestation of a spirit in rebellion against God, a spirit filled with anger because life had not gone the way *I* had wanted it to go so often. My self-esteem did not need to be built up; it needed to be brought down—broken and put into humble, loving, submission to God, who alone is worthy to be *esteemed*...and who, alone knows what is best for us at all times.

The proof text used as the basis for most self-esteem teaching is Matt. 22:39:

You shall love your neighbor as yourself (Matt. 22:39).

So the argument became that we must love ourselves before we are capable of loving others. But this is clearly <u>not</u> what Jesus meant (as verified over and over throughout the *whole counsel of God's Word - Acts 20:27*). Jesus knew our fallen, sinful hearts were selfish and self-centered to the core. He knew that we always, by nature, love ourselves and look out for our own personal interests (Eph. 5:29; Phil. 2:4). There is plenty of evidence for that throughout the Bible: Adam and Eve, Cain, Lot, Jacob, the rebellious and disobedient children of Israel, Rehoboam, Ahab, Jezebel, Nebuchadnezzar, the Pharisees, Simon the magician, Ananias and Sapphira, the prodigal son, the rich young ruler, Judas, etc., etc. And there is just as much evidence of this same kind of deeply ingrained *self*-centeredness throughout our world today—in our schools, businesses, government, churches, our homes, and in our own hearts. When things don't go your way or you don't get what you want, how do you react? When the pictures come back from the last family reunion, whose face do you look for first? We are self-centered by nature! (Gen. 6:5).

What Jesus was really saying in Matt. 22:39 is that we need to start looking out for our neighbor in the same way that we are ever so careful to look out for ourselves. If we spent as much time thinking about, praying for, and loving our neighbor as we do thinking about, praying for, and loving ourselves, a lot more people would see the love of Jesus shining through our lives. But we don't do that, do we? We are too busy looking after our own self-interests, comfort and "esteem". And what is the result? We lose the very thing we are seeking so hard to gain—meaning, purpose, the joy of being a blessing to others ... *life*.

> *He who has found his life (focused upon developing a strong self-esteem), shall lose it,, and he who has lost his life (abandoned the pursuit of his own self-esteem in service to God and others) shall find it (life, rich with meaning and joy) (Matt. 10:39).*

The more I *lose myself*—by focusing upon God and His love and all that He has done for me (John 3:16; Eph. 1:3-23)—and out of a heart overflowing with gratitude for that, share God's love with others, the more I *find life*, and *that more abundantly (John 10:10).* I can vouch for this and so can you. The times we have set aside (lost) the quest for *self*-esteem, and *self*-gratification and given ourselves to a humble, trusting, obedient walk with Jesus—loving and serving Him and others—have always been the richest, most fulfilling, most joyful and rewarding times of our lives.

> *But Jesus called them to Himself, and said, "You know that the rulers of the Gentiles lord it over them, and their great men (the touted "experts") exercise authority over them. It is not so among you, but whoever wishes to become great among you shall be your servant, and whoever wishes to be first among you shall be your slave; just as the Son of Man did not come to be served, but to serve, and to give His life a ransom for many"* (Matt. 20:25–28).

You just can't find anything here—or anywhere else in the Bible—to support the popular *gospel* of self-esteem. In fact, what is clearly taught throughout the Word of God, is exactly the opposite. We are told that we must *die to self, humble ourselves, think of others more highly than ourselves, serve others, and be obedient to God, even if that means going all the way to the cross as Jesus did (Luke 9:23; James 4:10; Phil. 2:3,7-8; Matt 20:26-28; John 13:4).*

Jesus didn't save us to "feel good about ourselves". He saved us to be holy—to walk daily in a loving, trusting, purifying relationship with Him, bringing Him honor and glory as we gladly with thankful, cheerful hearts follow Him in fulfilling His good plans for our lives and sharing His wonderful love with others. That is where real fulfillment and peace will always be found.

The Bible warns us over and over of God's hatred of pride and selfishness (which are, in reality, at the heart of *self*-esteem), because He knows what destruction these wreak in the lives of His children (James 4:6, 16; Jer. 50:29-32; Ps. 36:11-12; Prov. 6:16-17; Prov. 16:5; Deut. 8:3–14, etc.). God is a loving Father who wants to protect us *from ourselves—our selfish, sinful nature.* In my case—as in the case of others who seek after the very wrong, unbiblical teaching of self-esteem—it led me into a restless, driven, unending quest to satisfy every lust of my insatiable, selfish flesh. But that will never happen, because the fleshly self is never satisfied— *The eyes of a man are (never) satisfied (Prov. 27:20b).* What invariably happens is that the one who allows himself to become caught up in the pursuit of *self*-esteem and *self*-gratification becomes disillusioned and ends up in a joyless, miserable state of chronic discontent, self-pity, and bitterness.

> *I urge you not to ... teach strange doctrines, nor pay attention to myths which give rise to mere speculation rather than furthering (the cause of Christ) ... But the goal of our instruction is love from a pure heart and a good conscience and a sincere faith ... I pray that your love may abound still more and more in real knowledge and all discernment, so that you may approve the things that are excellent, in order to be sincere and blameless until the day of Christ; having been filled with the fruit of righteousness ... to the glory and praise of God (1 Tim. 1:3–5; Phil.1:9–11, sel.).*

Bible Study Supplement
Chapter 3 — Day 2 — The Problem of Self Esteem

1. Read Eph. 5:29a.

   a. What does man *naturally* "not do" and what does he "do" regarding his own body/flesh?

God is saying here that we all, by nature, are concerned about our own bodies, making sure that we feed and take care of them. Those who resort to such things as self-mutilation are not acting "naturally" but are seeking attention through this sinful, selfish (me-centered) act; or they may be demonically possessed (unsaved) or deceived (saved, but still allowing demonic influence— through unbelief or fear—to drive within them a sinful lust for attention) to do this terrible thing that is harmful and clearly forbidden by God. In such cases there has never been true godly sorrow and repentance in this area of their lives. We'll take a more in depth look at this subject concerning why it is so hard for some people to truly repent from the heart and forsake hurtful habits (sins) in book three when we study the lesson entitled, "When You 'Can't' Obey".

2. Read Luke 9:23-24.

   a. What must all who wish to be Jesus' disciple do? (three things – vs. 23)

   b. What will happen to the one who tries to *save his life?...loses his life?* (vs. 24)

3. Read Matt. 20:25–28.

   a. What was the heart attitude of the Gentile leaders/rulers? (vs. 25)

   b. What is the biblical way (God's way) to greatness? (vs. 26)

   c. How do we (God's children) become first? (vs. 27)

Note: Jesus often used the term "slave" to illustrate total love for, allegiance to, and dependence upon one's Master. It indicated a willing, humble submission and obedience. If we truly love God, we will follow Jesus' example and *give our lives* in loving obedient service to God and others. In so doing we will bring blessing (happiness) to their hearts and also to the heart of God as well (Matt. 25:23, 34–40). And we will find, in turn, our own hearts filled to overflowing with joy and satisfaction: *He who waters will himself be watered (Prov. 11:25; cf. Luke 6:38).*

   d. What did Jesus *not* come to do? What did He come to do? (vs. 28)

   e. Since Jesus is our example to follow, what should we be about as His disciples? (vs. 28)

Note: Do you see the clear teaching of Jesus here that is completely antithetical to the psychological self-esteem teaching? People with high *self*-esteem find it incredibly difficult, if not impossible, to be true servants, bondslaves of Jesus (or anyone!). And so they exist in a miserable, empty, rewardless state of self-absorption, bitterness and discontent.

In our study of progressive sanctification last week we studied 1 Pet 2:9-10. Let's take a quick look at these verses again because they are, in a nutshell, the biblical solution to the empty, unbiblical teaching—and practice—of *self-esteem*. (Please use NASB text below).

> *9. But you are a chosen race, a royal priesthood, a holy nation, a people for God's own possession, that you may proclaim the excellencies of Him who has called you out of darkness into His marvelous light;*
>
> *10. for you once were not a people, but now you are the people of God; you had not received mercy, but now you have received mercy (1 Peter 2:9-10).*

Before Christ, we had no real identity or acceptability. We were, as the world often labels us, "nobodies" with no real value, purpose or belongingness. But after receiving Christ as our personal Lord and Savior, we became *children of God—a chosen race, royal priesthood, holy nation*—who continually receive His mercy and grace. And we can't possibly receive any greater value or acceptability (<u>esteem</u>) than that!

4. Read John 12:24–26.

   a. What must first happen before a grain of wheat *bears fruit (seeds)?* (vs. 24)

   b. Contrast what happens to the one who *loves* his fallen, sinful, worldly life with the one who *hates* it. (vs. 25)

   c. What will the Father do for those who choose to love and serve (follow) His Son? (vs. 26b)

I want to close by focusing upon Jesus' life-giving command that we studied earlier in Luke 9:24 (also found in Matt. 10:39):

> *He who has found his life shall lose it, and he who has lost his life for My sake shall find it.*

As we come to God in humble repentance and ask Him to forgive us for our prideful attention to ourselves—satisfying *our* wants, *our* needs, *our* selfish lusts—and ask Him to help us turn away from that kind of *self*-centered absorption and get our eyes back upon Jesus—knowing Him, following Him, obeying Him and sharing His love with others, He begins to pour out His blessings upon us in ways we could not have even hoped or dreamed, and we *find* the fulfilling, rich and rewarding life we have been searching for…*and that more abundantly (John 10:10b).*

Write out a Bible verse that had special meaning to you today.

Based upon what you have learned today, write a prayer to God expressing the desires of your heart in applying these truths to your life.

Chapter 3 — Day 3
God's Solution to the Self-esteem Problem

> *And He was saying to them all, "If anyone wishes to be my disciple, let him deny himself, and take up his cross daily, and follow Me"* (Luke 9:23).
>
> *And Mary said, "Behold, the bondservant of the Lord; be it unto me according to Your Word"* (Luke 1:38).

Thank you so much for your courage in facing this really tough subject so bravely with me. I know that this is not a pleasant or easy topic for any of us. We've all inherited that proud, selfish sin nature that was at the heart of Adam and Eve's rebellion against God. And I'm sure we all get quite weary at times of the battle against it. Satan knows that, too. I see his hand in introducing the wide-spread, very appealing—and nearly universally accepted—teaching of self-esteem. It serves well to justify what we so naturally are. That makes it easier. But we all know that sin is very deceptive and every time we give in to it, we only strengthen its stronghold, causing us to sin further, bringing more pain and heartache as it encroaches determinedly to dominate our life.

That is what self-esteem does. By getting us to continually focus upon ourselves—our wants, our desires, our comfort—we ever so quickly lose sight of what we are really here for: to know, love, and joyfully serve God, to fulfill *His* good purposes for our lives and to share His love and the wonderful good news of salvation with others (John 17:3; Matt. 22:37; Ps. 100:2; 1 Cor. 10:31; Eph. 2:10; Matt. 28:19-20). In so doing, we bring honor and glory to God and we become conformed to the image of Jesus, which is at the heart of all God's good purposes for us (1 Cor. 10:31; Rom. 8:29). Whenever we are not actively involved in this pursuit, everything we

do will be pitifully disappointing at best or lead us to eternal separation from God—Hell—at worst. So yes, it is a huge problem, and the fight will not be easy to dethrone this "god" of self that, for many of us, has dominated our lives for so long. But dethrone him we must if we are to know the real freedom and joy that Jesus gave His life to purchase for us, and in this joy, magnify the awesome beauty and wonder of His goodness, glory and grace all the more. This journey to freedom from the domination of our own sinful *self* is, in reality, a life-long process for *self* will be with us until we are with Jesus. But the good news of the gospel is that it is not only possible, but God's desire that we walk in victory over this enemy day by day as we look to Jesus and obey God's Word in the power of the Holy Spirit (Heb. 12:1-3). God wants to plant seeds of hope in our hearts today that will encourage us and help us in our journey to liberation from the greatest enemy of all—our own sinful *self*. So with open, receptive hearts let us turn our attention off of our petty pursuit of *self*-esteem for a few moments and sit at Jesus' feet once again to hear what He has to tell us that will strengthen us in the battle against this destructive, joy-robbing bane.

> *And He was saying to them all, "If anyone wishes to come after Me, let him deny himself, and take up his cross daily, and follow Me"* (Luke 9:23).

I remember so vividly the first time I came face to face with this verse in a way that clearly tested my faith and level of commitment and obedience. Mel and I were attending a very thorough, in-depth, year long discipleship Bible Study course which had as its central theme, this pivotal verse. I recall just as vividly the very real and very intense pain those words... *let him deny himself*... initially evoked deep in my soul. To *deny self* (also referred to in the Bible as *dying to self*) means to give up every right of my own fleshly, sinful "self"—my desires, my wants, my cravings and lusts. Though I knew it was of utmost importance in my spiritual progress as a disciple of Jesus to obey this command, everything in me recoiled at the sound of it. Deny (die to) the "self" I had worked so hard to "build"... the self I had come to love, cherish and *esteem* so much? The thought nearly paralyzed me in fear as I pondered the reality of it: total surrender and the laying down of the *control* of my life—my well-laid plans, my goals, my selfish (self-centered, self-controlled as opposed to God-centered, God-controlled) ambitions. It could no longer be, "my will be done, and please bless it, God" but rather "Thy will be done"—even if it hurts for the moment as my demanding flesh does battle against relinquishing the control it has claimed so long. It seemed so huge, so all-encompassing, so overwhelming! I felt weak, frightened and totally inadequate for the battle. Yet I knew that God's Word and time had proven that only God knows what is best for us 24/7, and it is only in relinquishing control and walking in humble, surrendered obedience that we experience that never ending, secure and satisfying inner *river of peace and joy* that comes from being in the center of God will (God's best!), day by faithful day (Ps. 46:4-5; John 7:38; John 14:27). So obey Jesus and face this enemy, I must.

Thus began the very difficult, oft painful process—painful, not because I had a low self-esteem, but because, in reality, I had a much too elevated *esteem* of myself and my abilities to manage my own life. I truly believed that I knew better than God the way my life should go and what my goals for the future ought to be. Learning the good spiritual discipline of *denying self* and walking consistently in humble trusting obedience to God is rarely an easy or painless undertaking quickly mastered by any of us, because everything we are by nature—proud and selfish to the core—fights against it. And that battle (spiritual warfare) is continually fueled from the outside by relentless and powerful *self*-promoting propaganda. We see and hear it everywhere—in our schools, on television, in magazines, on billboards. It is clamored from our peers, politicians, psychological practitioners, and sadly, even from the pulpits of many of our churches: "You must love yourself before you can love others; look out for "number one"; take control of your life, do your own thing (as opposed to seeking God's will for your life); you have a right to be happy and healthy, to seek pleasure, to have what you want, so *dream big*, (in your quest to satisfy every inner fleshly craving) and whatever it takes, go for it..."

It is this kind of man-centered inner spirit of rebellion and self-absorption that self-esteem always fosters—an attitude that is already strong and deeply entrenched in most of us. For me, personally, I had no idea at the outset, the intensity of the war into which I had voluntarily entered when I, in obedience to God, decided to do battle against my own cherished, highly-esteemed *self* (2 Tim. 2:3). There were times the conflict became so intense and the inner agonies of the "dying" process so painful, I was sure I could not stay the course. I wanted to quit so badly and resign myself to being a Sunday morning Christian, saved and going to heaven and that was enough. But what would I say to Jesus when I stood before Him with nothing to offer but my one talent that I had buried and failed to use to serve Him and to fulfill His purpose for my life?

Because the self-esteem gospel had ruled over my heart, desires, and goals through all those years and was so deeply entrenched into the very core of my being, progress was slow, and there were far more setbacks and failures than successes in the early years. The old man does not die easily, and the longer it is left in control, the harder the heart becomes and the more resistant to change and to the breaking process, especially when it has been pampered and coddled by the unbiblical teaching of self-esteem over many years. That is why the Bible instructs parents to *bring up their children in the discipline and instruction of the Lord (Eph 6:4)*. Parents are to discipline their children—biblically—and instruct them to be God-centered, not self-centered when they are young and their hearts are yet tender and can be gently and lovingly brought into submission to the Lordship of Jesus, thus sparing them of the much more painful ordeal that comes when *God* must break the resistant, rebellious spirit when it is older, set in its ways—selfish and hardened—and stubbornly resistant to change as mine was.

But God was ever so patient with me, holding me tightly, yet tenderly and mercifully in the grip of his never failing grace (Ps. 37:24). Day by faithful day, He lead me on the path of righteousness and obedience in overcoming the many *self*-centered sin strongholds in my life. And with every victory came greater freedom and deeper joy. As mentioned earlier, there is far too much to share here about all the precious life-giving lessons learned. We'll look at those later, in Book Three. But let me mention briefly here three basic truths that helped so much in those early years of the breaking/restoration process.

The first has to do with the core verse mentioned earlier that is at the heart of God's solution to the self-esteem problem.

> And He was saying to them all, "If anyone wishes to come after Me, let him deny himself, and take up his cross daily, and follow Me" (Luke 9:23).

We've already looked at the meaning of the first part of this verse—*deny self*—but what does it mean to *take up our cross daily,* and *follow Jesus?*

It means first of all to identify completely with Jesus—with His mission and purpose. When Jesus came to earth, He had one goal and one goal only in mind—to *fulfill the will of the Father (John 17:4)*. For Jesus, that was *the redemption of mankind (Matt. 20:28; Luke 19:10)*. Not for one second did He waver from this goal. He followed God's will all

the way to the cross. So anyone who wishes to be a disciple (follower) of Jesus, must also set his heart to have this same attitude—to do the will of the Father wherever He leads him, no matter the cost, and even if it means—a *cross.* But that's not the end of what it means. There's a second part to this *taking up our cross daily.* The cross represents not just the dying and death of Jesus, it is also inseparably linked to His resurrection and His glorious *victory over sin and death.* So if we follow Jesus all the way *to* the cross, we will also follow Him *through* the cross into resurrection glory. Practically speaking, that means that as we come to God each day and in a spirit of humility and sincere contrition, confess our sins, accept God's forgiveness and Christ's righteousness (1 John 1:9), surrender our lives to the control (leading, guiding, infilling power) of the Holy Spirit, we can, and will, go out in the conquering authority of that glorious cross and empty tomb to *be about the Father's business…with JOY* (Luke 2:49, 1:74-75; Eph. 1:18-22, Ps. 100:2).

The second major breakthrough in the journey to liberation from the destructive domination of self, came on a beautiful spring day in April when God took me to a precious promise in Isaiah:

> Is this not the fast (religious practice) that I choose: To loosen the bonds of wickedness, to undo the bands of the yoke, and to let the oppressed go free. Is it not to divide your bread with the hungry, and bring the homeless poor into the house; when you see the naked, to cover him…Then your light will break out like the dawn, and your recovery will speedily spring forth (Is. 58:6–8).

I delightfully discovered that as I set my heart to obey this promise of Is. 58, a beautiful new "light" *broke out like the dawn* and *my recovery began to spring forth.* Looking back on how God worked in doing this, I see so clearly the Holy Spirit's guiding hand. At first, I was too weak and yet far too *selfish (self-*esteemed) to totally and fully *abandon all.* So, under the guidance of the Holy Spirit, I just set aside 2-4 hours per week to reach out with Jesus' love in some special way. Each week I prayed about this and asked the Holy Spirit to guide me, which He always did. Sometimes He led me to visit a widow or shut-in or make a meal for someone who was sick. At other times, He put upon my heart to invite someone who was hurting or lonely into our home for a refreshing lunch or tea. I also prayed, with each occasion, that God would give opportunity to share the gospel. God honored that prayer and several precious souls came to saving faith in Jesus—which always brought overwhelming joy! I soon discovered that every time I practiced this small "dividing of bread", I was energized and joy flowed within as a refreshing stream. It was wonderful and the more I did it, the more I truly *wanted* to do it—more! It was like a blessing that just kept giving... *He who refreshes others will hmself be refreshed! (Prov. 11:25, Niv).*

A third glorious revelation followed adding to the emerging new freedom and joy.

> *I have been crucified with Christ; and it is no longer I who live, but Christ lives in me... Christ in you, the hope of glory (Gal 2:20; Col. 1:27).*

Oh, glorious truth! My identity would never again be linked to how much selfish, trivial *self-*esteem I could muster through my achievements, the strokes of approval I received from others, or all the self-focused pampering I was told I "must do" to build up my self-esteem. I now had a new identity, <u>Christ in me</u>, the hope of glory! (Col. 1:27). As I turned my eyes off of myself and onto Jesus and His perfect love, obedience, sacrifice and all that this meant to me—full forgiveness and complete acceptance with the Father, life eternal and everlasting joy— I realized that I now possessed a priceless *new identity* that was the greatest *identity* any human on earth could ever hope for! I was a dearly beloved child of the God of the Universe, with *Him* living *in me!*—and no man or circumstance could ever again take this glorious identity away from me—ever! It became my greatest joy to share this wonderful *good news* with others. I wanted everyone to have what God had so mercifully, so graciously given to me—a totally new, blood bought, redeemed, forgiven, clothed in the righteousness of Jesus, identity. It would never again be *self-*esteem that made me valuable. It was "Christ-esteem"—Jesus, the *pearl of incalculable worth (Matt. 13:46),* living in me in all His perfection and resurrection glory!—that made me priceless in the eyes of my heavenly Father (Is. 43:4a; 2 Cor. 5:21; Rom. 8:1).

> *I will sing to the Lord as long as I live; I will sing praise to my God while I have my being... As for me, I shall be glad in the Lord... For the Mighty One has done great things for me; And holy is His name. And His mercy is upon generation after generation toward those who fear Him... (they) shall go out with JOY and be lead forth with peace (Ps. 104:33-34; Luke 1:49-50; Is. 55;12).*

Bible Study Supplement
Chapter 3 — Day 3 — God's Solution to the Self-esteem Problem

Isaiah 58:6-11 is one of the most beautiful, practical promises in Scripture concerning overcoming the enemy of "self" and entering into the blessed joys of obedience and sharing God's love with others. Such a life always leads to healing, personal reward and fulfillment. Before we read this text, let's take a moment to review the context in which it was written.

God is speaking to the apostate children of Israel. (Apostate means fallen away from God, from loving Him and obeying His Word). They have been busily engaged in many *religious rituals* like gathering for public worship, fasting, and prayer, but their hearts were far from God and far from what He had instructed them to do. And things weren't going so well for them. So they began to grumble and complain that God was not being fair. After all, they were being good little righteous people, doing all their religious duties like having their own personal "5-minute devotions" each morning, calling on His name freely, (faithfully participating in their various public "prayer rituals"), fasting, etc.—so why wasn't He blessing them? But God told them that they were selfish, spoiled hypocrites who only did these things for attention and to get a blessing from God. But their hearts were not with God or for God. Their hearts were in getting what they wanted, when they wanted it, and as much as they wanted. That's why the blessings had stopped. Then God, being ever so patient and merciful, promised that if they would repent of their sins of selfishness and disobedience, return to Him, and begin to walk once again in humble, loving obedience—sharing His love with others, helping people and befriending the lonely and the poor—then He would hear, heal, and bless them once again.

Verses 6–8 speak of some of the ways God suggested that they could genuinely share His love with others. They could minister to those under the bondage of sin—encourage them, pray *for* and *with* them, and tell them the truths of Scripture that would help them find victory and freedom. They could be hospitable and share their bread with others, or bring someone who had no home or family into their home; they could give clothes to those who were needy. The point is, they had to get past their consuming preoccupation with themselves in order to see the needs of others and respond in obedience to God as He led them. Then God gave them some beautiful promises if they would do this.

1. Read Is. 58:6–11.

   a. What did God say He would do for the people if they repented of their selfishness and began to take a sincere, loving interest in those around them? (four things - vs. 8)

   b. What did He promise to do when they called to Him or cried for help? (two things - vs. 9a)

   c. What other blessings did He promise them? (seven specific blessings - vs. 10b-11)

2. Read Matt. 9:13, using the NASB below.

   But go and learn what this means, "I desire compassion, and not sacrifice" (Math 9:13a).

   a. What does God desire?

Oh, that God would give us all hearts of compassion like Jesus had. God doesn't want all our sacrifices of self-motivated, self-seeking, religious "do-goodism." He just wants our hearts. And if He has our hearts, we will become people of compassion who seek to freely and liberally share His love just as Jesus did. His days were filled with acts of caring compassion as he reached out to people—loving them, healing them, teaching them, encouraging them. Jesus loved people. And so will we as we develop a heart of compassion.

3. Read John 13:3–5, 12–17.

   a. What did Jesus do? (vs. 5)

   b. What has Jesus given us in this beautiful story? (vs. 15)

   c. What promise does He give to all who obey His command to "do as I have done"—minister to and serve others? (vs. 17)

4. Read Prov. 11:25 noting especially 25b.

   Note: "To water" (KJV/NKJV/NASB) means to "refresh." Please use "refresh" in place of "to water" in your answer:

   a. What happens to those who water/refresh others?

Along with Luke 9:23 that we discussed earlier *(denying self, taking up our cross...)*, Phil. 2:3-8 is a pivotal passage in helping us develop a compassionate, disciple's heart. It is, in fact the practical outworking of Luke 9:23 and should always be linked to it as we seek to develop a loving servant spirit. Luke 9:23 tells us *what* a true disciple does—*denies self, takes up cross daily and follows Jesus*—and Phil. 2:3-8 tells us in practical terms *how* to do this.

5. Thoughtfully and prayerfully read Phil. 2:3-8.

   a. What are we *not* to do? (vs. 3a)

Note: Selfish ambition or vain conceit refers to anytime we regard our ambitions and desires as being more important than God's. It is the equivalent of saying: "Not <u>Thy</u> will, but <u>mine</u> be done"—an attitude that a focus upon *self-esteem* always fosters.

   b. What kind of heart and mind attitude are we to have? (Please read vs. 3-4 again, then choose from the two answers below).

      1. Proud, selfish, primarily concerned about "my" needs.

      2. Loving, humble, compassionate, concerned about the needs of others.

   c. How should we regard others? (vs. 3b)

   d. What are we to look out for? (vs. 4b)

   e. What kind of attitude are we to have? (vs. 5)

   f. Describe that attitude. (vs. 7-8)

This beautiful picture of discipleship (being a true follower of Jesus) totally debunks the unbiblical teaching of *self-esteem*. Jesus was God. He had the *right* to all the privileges, the honor, the glory, the true *esteem* of being God (which He was!). Yet, He never tried to grasp this, to claim what was rightfully His. (That would have been *self*-esteem). Instead He *emptied Himself* of all His rights in order to be a humble bondservant of His heavenly Father. It's impossible to find even a trace of *self*-esteem in Jesus' attitude. Are we so proud and so vain to consider ourselves as better than our Master? Or are we willing to follow His beautiful example of humble, faithful, servant obedience?

   g. How far did Jesus go in His commitment to serve the Father in humble obedience? (vs. 8b)

What a beautiful example God has given us in Jesus!

God used these verses in Phil. 2 (along with those we studied in Is. 58) as a real battering ram in bringing down the sinful, selfish, *self*-centered (as opposed to *God*-centered) stronghold (idol) of *self*-esteem that had dominated and controlled my life for so may years. It is a powerful weapon for this purpose. If you are battling a resistant, strong *self*-will that refuses to relinquish control in order to fully love, trust and obey Jesus and reach out to others, you will find that reading, meditating upon, and asking God to help you to obey these verses will do much to bring down that stronghold. I have found this practice of great value in keeping my heart soft, my spirit humble, and my desires pure and sensitive to the Holy Spirit's convictions and leading. In such a state, the spirit of *self-less-ness* (less of self, more of God and others) is liberated, takes wings and flies ever higher and freer.

Write out a Bible verse that had special meaning to you today.

Based upon what you have learned today, write a prayer to God expressing the desires of your heart in applying these truths to your life.

Chapter 3 — Day 4
Spiritual Warfare — An Introduction
Be a Good Soldier: Alert, Prepared, Armed

> *For our struggle is not against flesh and blood, but against the rulers, against the powers, against the world forces of this present darkness, against the spiritual forces of wickedness in the heavenly places (Eph. 6:12).*
>
> *Be of sober spirit, be on the alert. Your adversary, the devil, prowls about like a roaring lion, seeking someone to devour (1 Pet. 5:8).*

Knowledge will increase and many will go back and forth (Dan. 12:4).

We live in a proud, humanistic world of ever increasing knowledge and technological advancement. The whole world is running back and forth, hither and yon, to find the latest answer to—or escape from—their pain and problems. We run to doctors, psychiatrists, intellects, counselors, books, magazines, weekend retreats, training seminars… any and everywhere that promises *the solution* to our problems: everywhere except to God and His Word.

> *But I am afraid lest as the serpent deceived Eve by his craftiness, your minds should be led astray… For our struggle is not against flesh and blood, but against the rulers, against the powers, against the world forces of darkness, against the spiritual forces of wickedness in the heavenly places (2 Cor. 11:3; Eph. 6:12).*

A very effective weapon of deception that Satan has employed since the beginning of time is to make man believe that he (man) is "in control", that he has the intellect and the power to know what is best for him, and is able to solve every problem that surfaces. The more "technologically advanced", a culture

becomes, therefore, the greater the deception. God warns us about this very thing:

> *For the mystery of lawlessness is already at work… with all power and signs and false wonders, and with all the <u>deception of wickedness</u> for those who perish, because they did not receive the love of the truth so as to be saved… but took pleasure in wickedness (2 Thes. 2:7-12, sel.).*

The *mystery of lawlessness,* and the *deception of wickedness* is certainly at work and thriving in our self-centered, pleasure-seeking, consumer-driven age, in which the controlling forces of society— our educational institutions, medical science, our government, the media—refuse to acknowledge anything they cannot *see, touch, test,* and *control.* Therefore, except for diligent students of the Word—or those involved in occult practices—there is a blatant disregard for the spiritual realm: God, Satan, angels, demons, demonic influence, which, in actuality, is <u>far more "real", and far more powerful in affecting our lives than anything we can *see, touch, test* and control.</u>

> *And he sent horses and chariots and a great army there, and they came by night and surrounded the city. Now when the attendant of the man*

of God (Elisha) had risen early and gone out, behold, an army with horses and chariots was circling the city. And his servant (the attendant to Elisha) said to him, "Alas, my master! What shall we do?" So he answered, "Do not fear, for those who are with us are more than those who are with them." Then Elisha prayed and said, "O Lord, I pray, open his eyes that he may see." And the Lord opened the servant's eyes, and he saw; and behold, the mountain was full of horses and chariots of fire all around Elisha (2 Kings 6:14-17).

I pray that God will open our eyes as we study this important lesson today, so that we will *see* the mighty army of God that is standing with us in our daily battles, and in that assurance go forth as confident, well-trained, disciplined soldiers who understand the enemy's deceptive, destructive strategies, stand strong against them, and persevere to the victory.

...for the god of this world has blinded the minds of the unbelieving (2 Cor. 4:4).

As in all things, Satan's best weapon in defeating God's people is deception. And so he has done a masterful job in the area of *spiritual warfare*. Because of his diabolical ploys, there is a very effective deception that permeates the body of Christ today. As a new believer, I fell for this lie. The price I paid—both in personal pain and ineffective service—was incalculable. I pray that by sharing it here, many will become more alert and kept from believing the lie. It went like this:

The devil is a defeated foe...and we who are saved are safe and secure under the protective hand of God who is good, loving and sovereign. Therefore, we ought not even think about the devil or spiritual warfare because that only gives the devil a foothold.

Do you see the demonic deception in the argument? It is filled with truth, but truth that is twisted and distorted and mixed with deadly error leading to very wrong, dangerous and potentially destructive conclusions. Let's look at the deception.

It's true. God is good, loving and sovereign. And because of Christ's work on the cross, Satan *is* a defeated foe and we do have power through the precious blood of Jesus, the Word of God and the Holy Spirit living in us to recognize and overcome his lies and temptations. However, make no mistake, Satan is still very much alive and very much involved in demonic deception, lies, temptations and every other wicked scheme to cause God's people to stumble and fall. To refuse to recognize this or to prepare ourselves to stand firm against his ever so cunning lies and deceptions is unbiblical and very foolish.

Be sober, be vigilant; because your adversary the devil, as a roaring lion, walketh about, seeking whom he may devour (1 Peter 5:8).

...the prince of the power of the air... is now working in the sons of disobedience (Eph.. 2:2).

For our struggle is not against flesh and blood, but against the rulers, against the powers, against the world forces of this darkness, against the spiritual forces of wickedness in the heavenly places (Eph. 6:11-12).

The devil's final defeat in practical terms as we experience day to day living on this earth, will not occur until Jesus returns and finalizes his demise in the War of Armageddon. In fact, the Bible warns us that the intensity of *spiritual warfare* will not lessen, but will increase as the time of Jesus' return nears.

The devil knowing that his time is limited is pouring out his wrath on the people of God (Rev. 12:12b).

Satan may be a *defeated foe,* but he is far from a *dead foe!* For the moment, Satan is very much alive and very active as the diabolical, destructive *god of this world (2 Cor. 4:4).* He is the prince of a very *real,* very *evil* and very *powerful* spirit realm of *rulers, principalities and powers, spiritual forces of wickedness and darkness in this present age (Eph. 6:12, cf. 2 Thess. 2:7-11).*

These *forces*, this *spirit realm*, very much affects your life and mine and those of our children, friends and loved ones every day that we live. Satan's goal is our destruction. His weapon: <u>demonic deception</u>. Worldly wisdom and fleshly strength will never stand against this kind of empowerment. We need *divine weapons* and *divine strength* for that, which God in His mercy and grace has provided for us:

> *For though we walk in the flesh, we do not war according to the flesh, for the weapons of our warfare are not of the flesh, but divinely powerful for the destruction of fortresses. We are destroying speculations and every lofty thing raised up against the knowledge of God, and we are taking every thought captive to the obedience of Christ (2 Cor. 10:3-5).*

And what are these *weapons of warfare* that are not of the flesh, but *divinely powerful* for the destruction of fortresses in the spiritual battles that we face daily? They are clearly described in the most strategic chapter on spiritual warfare in the Bible, Ephesians 6. We do well to examine this chapter carefully, for there is a wealth of information there that will keep us *alert, prepared and armed* for successful warfare.

There are seven weapons and one very clear and all-encompassing battle strategy. Five of the weapons that God gives us are defensive for protection and security (assurance) and two of them are offensive for engaging and defeating our enemies. Our defensive weapons are:

1. The Helmet of Salvation
2. The Breastplate of Righteousness
3. The Belt of Truth.
4. The Sandals of Peace
5. The Shield of Faith

Our offensive weapons are:

6. The Word of God
7. The Indwelling Spirit of God

Our all-encompassing battle strategy that we must employ at all times: Prayer! Steadfast, alert, *in-the-Spirit* prayer. All that we do must be undergirded by a trusting dependence on God through unceasing prayer.

If we allow indifference, laziness or just plain stubborn pride to cause us to become slack in utilizing these weapons of warfare on a daily basis, we can be sure that we will be ill-equipped to stand against the kind of demonic deception and power wielded against us in our spiritual battles. Unprotected and unprepared, we will be overcome by our enemies, forfeiting the very thing Jesus came to give us—victory over sin and the devil's deceptive, lying schemes, (2 Cor. 2:11) and the freedom, peace and joy that such victory always brings (John 10:10b; Rom. 8:37, 14:17).

In earlier lessons, we studied the importance of our two <u>offensive</u> weapons, the Word of God and the indwelling Holy Spirit, but it is important to be reminded that being equipped to stand strong and victorious in spiritual warfare does not mean a casual glance at the Word of God periodically, or even sitting in church and hearing the Word of God on Sunday mornings. It means a consistent, committed, daily personal study of God's Word motivated by a sincere desire to keep our lives pure as we *treasure God's Word in our hearts that we might not sin against Him* (Ps. 119:9, 11). It also means submitting our lives daily to the control and empowerment of the Holy Spirit. This is what it means to be filled with the Holy Spirit. We surrender (give up, empty) ourselves of our own self-rule and self-dependence so that we can be <u>filled</u> with God's Spirit and dependence upon Him—trusting and obeying Him as He leads and empowers us in fulfilling all God's good purposes for our lives day by day (Eph. 2:10, 5:18).

In upcoming chapters, we will examine more closely both the defensive and offensive weapons and the protection, security and power they offer us. We will sharpen our skills in effectively utilizing them to stand firm and victorious in our spiritual battles.

Yes, be sure, the war is real! And it is not going to go away—no matter the wishing or dreaming that it would. And be sure of this also: when you are most committed to doing the will of God, the devil will be the most committed to destroying your every effort to persevere in this. He will do all he can to discourage, distract or confuse you and cause you to want to quit or give up. God knows this also and He has already given us all we need to stand firm and prevail! (Eph. 6:10-18; 2 Cor. 10:3-5).

Of course we should not *dwell* on Satan or spiritual warfare, we should *dwell* on the *Word of God* and upon *the greatness, goodness and sovereign power of God to overcome and to deliver*—come what may! But to say that we should totally ignore the realities of a very real and powerful enemy, or the fact that we are in a battle daily for the kingdom and glory of God—as well as our own well-being and the protection of our loved ones—is indeed, unbiblical and very foolish. How can we keep our minds alert and be properly armed and prepared if we just ignore the reality of spiritual warfare?

I would like to close this introduction to spiritual warfare with one of my favorite "warfare" stories. It is the story of David and the Philistine giant, Goliath. In our daily spiritual battles we need to muster the same confident attitude that David had—a confident attitude that is rooted, not in ourselves or our strength or abilities, but firmly in the faithfulness and power of God. I can almost see David now as he walks boldly onto the battlefield with this war cry for all the world to hear:

Who is this uncircumcised Philistine, that he should taunt the armies of the living God. You come to me with a sword, a spear and a javelin, but I come to you in the Name of the Lord of Hosts, and this day the Lord will deliver you into my hands, and I will strike you down… that all the earth may know that there is a God in Israel for HE will give you into our hands (1 Sam. 17:45-47, sel.).

Bible Study Supplement
Chapter 3 — Day 4 — Spiritual Warfare – An Introduction
Be A Good Soldier: Alert, Prepared, Armed

Eph. 6:10-18 is the classic text on spiritual warfare. With minds alert, let's take a fresh look at this important text.

1. Read Eph. 6:10-14.

   a. In who/what are we to be strong? (two sources of strength - vs. 10)

   b. What is our struggle not against? (vs. 12)

   c. What is it against? (vs. 12)

   d. What are we instructed to do in order to enable us to stand strong and victorious in this kind of warfare? (vs. 13a)

   e. After we have done that, what are we commanded to do? (vs. 13b-14a)

The following verses list the specific spiritual weapons God has given us to be successful in our spiritual battles. We do well to pay close attention and make sure that we are fully armed and protected at all times.

2. Read Eph. 6:14-18.

   a. List the five defensive weapons (spiritual armor) that we must keep securely in place at all times. (vs. 14-17a)

   b. What are our two offensive weapons? (The way this verse is worded in most translations, the "weapons" appear as one, but there are really two. See if you can find them – vs. 17b). [If you are unsure, refer back to today's meditation to check your answer. They are listed there].

   c. What is our all-encompassing *strategy* that we must employ to be successful in our spiritual battles? (vs. 18 – be specific; there are several facets of warfare strategy mentioned here).

3. Read 2 Cor. 10:3-5.

   a. What kind of power do our *weapons of warfare* have? (vs. 4)

   b. What are they able to do? (vs. 4b)

　　c. What do we demolish/destroy? (vs. 5a)

　　d. What do we do with the deceptive, destructive thoughts that come to us? (vs. 5b)

As Satan comes to us with deceptive, destructive, distracting thoughts—through our own sin-ful flesh and his strategic lies—we must immediately *take these thoughts captive to the obedience of Christ.* In other words, we do <u>not</u> believe or act on the lie, but stand firm on the truth of God's Word and act accordingly in the power of the Holy Spirit, just as Jesus did (Matt. 4:4).

　4. Read 1 Sam. 17:45-50.
　　a. Why could David walk out on the battlefield with confidence? (vs. 45, 47)

　　b. What was the result? (vs. 49b, 50)

We, too, can walk out onto the battlefield daily with confidence because the same God who was with David is with us to *fight our battles* and to *give the enemy into our hands (1 Sam. 17:45-46; 2 Chron. 32:8; Deut. 20:1-4)!*

Write out a Bible verse that had special meaning to you today.

Based upon what you have learned today, write a prayer to God expressing the desires of your heart in applying these truths to your life.

Chapter 3 — Day 5
The War Within — The Conflict of the Two Natures

> *For even when we came into Macedonia our flesh had no rest, but we were afflicted on every side: conflicts without, fears within (2 Cor. 7:5).*
>
> *For I know that <u>nothing good</u> dwells in me, that is, in my flesh; for the wishing is present in me, but the doing of the good is not... Wretched man that I am! Who will set me free from the body of this death? Thanks be to God (we have been set free) through Jesus Christ our Lord! (Rom 7:18, 24).*

One of the most difficult things for mature as well as new born Christians to deal with is the conflict of the two natures. New Christians often find themselves confused and questioning: "I am born again. I have truly repented of my sins. I have surrendered my life to Jesus. Jesus is my Lord and Savior. The Holy Spirit lives in me. Why, then, do I keep sinning and why do I keep doing the same things over and over even though I know they are wrong? Why can't I walk in willing, victorious obedient submission to God?...all day, every day? Why can't I <u>not</u> sin anymore?"

> *For that which I am doing, I do not understand; for I am not practicing what I would like to do, but I am doing the very thing I hate… So now, no longer am I the one doing it, but sin which indwells me. For I know that <u>nothing good</u> dwells in me, that is, in my flesh; for the wishing is present in me, but the doing of the good is not. For the good that I wish, I do not do; but I practice the very evil that I do not wish. But if I am doing the very thing I do not wish, I am no longer the one doing it, but sin which dwells in me. I find then the principle that evil is present in me, the one who wishes to do good (Rom. 7:15-21).*

These are the words of the mightily-used-of-God apostle Paul who struggled with the same problem. He has written these verses to help us understand what is really going on in us when we *sin* even though we don't *want* to. He is reminding us that we all have an *innate, inborn <u>sin</u> nature—sin dwells in me*. And all the wishing and hoping it were not so, is not going to change that fact. The only way to deal with the sin nature that resides in our fallen heart/soul, is to put it under that Lordship of Jesus so that *Jesus, through the Holy Spirit now living in us, rules over it* rather than our destructive *sin nature* ruling over us. We must always remember that when we were *born again*, God gave us the Holy Spirit who came into our hearts and gave us a *new nature*. So, in reality, we now have *two natures*. These *natures* are like the control center of our lives. They determine how we will respond to various situations—according to the dictates of our *sin nature* or our new redeemed *righteous* nature. These two natures are continually in conflict, vying for the *control* of our lives. And which *nature* is *in control* will determine how we respond to any situation. The <u>good news</u> is that because of Jesus' victory, we now have the freedom to *choose* who will be in control—our sin nature, which leads to death and destruction every time or our new righteous nature, which always leads to victory, peace and joy. And the even better news is that we are not left alone to *choose,* nor are we left on our own to *obey* our new righteous nature when that is what we *choose.* We now have the Holy Spirit living in us to give us the desire to choose righteousness and the power to live it. So it is a matter of who we *choose* to be *in control.*

This is what Paul meant when he said that he *died daily (1 Cor. 15:31).* He *died* to the ruling *control* of his life by his old sinful flesh, because Paul wisely recognized that *in him, that is in his flesh dwelt no good thing (Rom. 7:18).* If Paul allowed his flesh to be in control, he would sin...and keep on sinning. Sin would separate him from God—from His protection, peace and joy—and he would be most miserable. And that is exactly what will happen to us if we allow the flesh (our sin nature) to be in control, because our natural, fleshly heart is *deceptive, desperately wicked and destructive (Jer. 17:9; John 10:10a).* So Paul dealt head-on with his *fallen sinful nature* by *dying to it* (to its control) and submitting his total being—heart, soul, mind, will, strength—to the control of the Holy Spirit (the Lordship of Jesus). And that is how Paul was able to live such a full, victorious and joyful life. And so can we if we follow Paul's good example.

Scripture is clear that our *profession* of faith must be tested to prove its authenticity and allegiance. To do that, we must be willing to *go to the battlefield* of *the will,* where those decisions of *whom we will serve* are made. That's what Jesus did at Gethsemane. And that's what we must do also if we are to be victorious in the battle of the two wills. We must purify our hearts by the washing of the cleansing blood of Jesus (true confession and repentance) and we must renew our minds (fill them with the truth and righteousness of God's Word), then trustingly walk in this righteousness and truth by the power of the Holy Spirit.

It is inevitable that all Christians encounter the enemy of their own fallen *sinful nature* like never before upon receiving Jesus as their new Master and Savior. Satan who, in reality, controls our sinful nature has lost a subject from his kingdom and he is hell-bent that if he cannot get him back (which he cannot – John 10:28), he will do all he can to tempt, badger, and confuse the new believer in order to keep him from being effective in the work to which God, his new Master, has called him—namely to bring honor and glory to Him, (instead of Satan as he did so well in his previous life), to become conformed to the image of Jesus so that he will now be a holy, victorious warrior against the schemes of Satan, and sharing the good news of the gospel with others so that they can be set free, too. I'll never forget those early days of my own no-holds-barred battle of the will. I walked out upon the battlefield spiritually immature and pitifully unprepared. The lack of biblical wisdom and discernment was at the heart of repeated, painful failures. I did not understand what the Bible teaches about the conflict of the two natures and the enormous problem caused by it. I found myself crying out to God for mercy and grace as failure heaped upon failure. There were many times—so many times!—it *seemed* totally hopeless. I would never see the day of consistent victorious living for the glory of God, though I desired this with all my heart!

The lessons I had to learn did not come easily... or painlessly. It would take years and many tears before I would begin to understand basic biblical principles concerning the conflict of the two natures that would enable me to move from a life of nearly continual defeat and failure to one of progressively strengthening faith, Holy Spirit enabled perseverance, and victory.

Again, however, I do not think that the repeated failures and the painful consequences they inevitably brought had to be that difficult and that extended. Had I understood the Biblical truths that I understand now, I am sure that there would have been far less agonizing heartache and far more gloriously happy days celebrating victories. It is my prayer that by sharing a few of these biblical truths here, I might encourage others who are weighed down with a sense of defeat from repeated failures, sparing them of self-inflicted agonies that came so often in my own journey because of a lack of true biblical understanding (Hos. 4:6). Following are some of the important lessons learned.

1. Get serious about *spiritual warfare* – We live in a world that continually clamors for ease, pleasure and comfort. It is easy to be influenced by this so that our goal becomes "ease, pleasure and comfort" rather than holiness, obedience and the glory of God. Just as we want "life" to be "easy and comfortable", so we want—and expect—our spiritual walk with God to follow this pattern. That is not biblical. Spiritual warfare is real, and it can be, and often is, ruthless. There just isn't room for wishful dreaming or cowardly escaping. We need to get a lot more serious about this thing called *spiritual warfare* in regard to the conflict of the two natures. The "old man", our inborn sinful nature, is not a *nice guy*. It is "sin personified" which *sets itself* (ruthless and mercilessly) *against the new nature and the things of God (Rom. 8:6-8; Gal. 5:17).* That is why there was, and always will be, an ongoing battle for control of our will—the Spirit against the flesh, the flesh against the Spirit (Gal 4:29; 5:17-21). The flesh is strong. It fights hard. It doesn't *die* (relinquish its control) easily and it will <u>never</u> go away. It is here to stay and stay it will until that day when our redemption is complete and we leave behind these corrupt, sin-indwelt bodies to don our *new, glorified,* **sinless** *bodies (1 Cor. 15:20-58).* (Oh, glorious day!) But, in the meantime, our destructive, fallen sin nature does not have to rule over us. It is God's desire for all of us as His redeemed children, through the power of the Holy Spirit, to place Jesus (master of our new nature) upon the ruling throne of our hearts so that <u>He</u> now rules over—and consistently overcomes—our destructive sin nature enabling us to live lives of *victorious righteousness, peace and joy in the Holy Spirit (Rom. 7:25, 14:17; 1 Cor. 15:57-58).*

2. Take responsibility, don't make excuses! – The problem began…*in the beginning*—in the garden. God called out to Adam, "Adam, where are you?…What have you done?" Adam said, "The woman you gave me…" Eve said, "The serpent made me do it." And ever since we've been blaming past circumstances, present problems, our "genes" (I've inherited my dad's bad temper etc.) and everything and everyone else but our own sinful nature for which we are personally responsible. But making excuses will never accomplish what needs to be done—"dying to self", our sinful nature—and giving full control to the Holy Spirit. And that is not a "once for all" experience. It is an on-going life-long process that we do "daily"—and moment by moment as we walk through each day.

> *…for if you are living according to the flesh, you must die; but if by the Spirit you are putting to death the deeds of the body, you will live (Rom. 8:13).*

3. Understand the demonic empowered determination of the "old nature"…and my new redeemed "position in Christ" – How often I asked it, and how often I have heard it asked from other new Christians I have discipled: If I have *died* and *been buried with Christ,* as Rom. 6 tells us, didn't my *old nature* die, too? Isn't it *dead?* How can a *dead* thing cause so many problems?

Here is where careful attention to the Word of God becomes crucial—literally a *life* or *death* matter.

It was *by faith* that I accepted the finished work of Jesus on the cross for my redemption—the forgiveness of my sins—and it is *by faith* that I *live out this victory* in my daily decisions and behavior.

Let's take a moment to really think about what it means to put our faith in Jesus and what He accomplished on our behalf on the cross. It means, first of all, that we move immediately into a new *position.* We are no longer separated from God, as our sin kept us in the past, but we are now mysteriously and inseparably linked to Christ—to the intimate degree that, spiritually, we are <u>in Christ</u> and He, <u>in us</u> (John 14:21, 23; Col. 1:27 etc). All that Jesus did *for me* now becomes a part *of me.*

> *I have been crucified with Christ and it is no longer I who live but Christ lives in me and the life that I now live, I live by faith in the Son of God who loved me and gave Himself up for*

me... Therefore we are buried with him by baptism into death, that like as Christ was raised up from the dead by the glory of the Father, even so we also should walk in newness of life (Gal. 2:20; Rom. 6:4).

Jesus' death becomes my death; His resurrection, my resurrection; and His risen, victorious new life, my risen, victorious new life as well. This position is maintained, just as it began—by faith—as we walk in humble, trusting submission and obedience to Him. The moment we rebel against God and choose to disobey, we step out of the protection, the power, and the joy of this position. We are no longer *in* (submitted to) *Christ* but *in* (submitted to and obeying) *the flesh*. We have, in reality, *died spiritually.* Our sin separates us from God, who is *life* and the source of all *life* in us (John 14:6). Remember what we learned earlier. God is holy, and holy and sin cannot dwell together (Is. 59:2). That is why Jesus lovingly exhorts us many times to *remain/abide in Him (John 8:31, 14:21, 15:5).*

We *abide in Jesus* through reading and studying God's Word, prayer fellowship with Him, maintaining a humble and repentant heart, and surrendering our lives to the Holy Spirit's control, then walking *by faith* in obedience as the Holy Spirit guides us. As we *live by the Spirit*, our *new nature* is in control causing us to say "No" to our old sinful nature and "Yes" to God, bringing honor and glory to Him and joy to our own hearts and to the lives of others (Rom. 8:13; Gal 5:16, 25).

4. Jesus has won the victory over Satan—and my destructive sin nature! We must <u>never forget</u> this truth! We know this, yet I think we all suffer from amnesia often when it comes to living in the power of this profound biblical truth.

> *... knowing this, that our old self <u>was crucified with Him</u>, that our <u>body of sin might be done away with</u>, that we should <u>no longer</u> be <u>slaves to sin</u>;... Even so consider yourselves to be <u>dead to sin</u>, but <u>alive to God in Christ Jesus</u> (Rom. 6:6- 7, 11).*

It is to the degree that we believe and live out this truth—through a life of trusting faith and surrendered obedience to the Holy Spirit—that we will experience the agonies of defeat or the joys of victory in our spiritual pilgrimage. Do I *really* believe that I am "dead to sin" and "alive to God"? The fruit of my life will quickly reveal this. Is my spirit producing love, joy, peace, patience, kindness, confidence ... or fear, worry, doubt, unbelief, bitterness, anger. If it is the latter, I can be sure that I have allowed my *old nature* (my sinful flesh) to be in control and I am *believing* and *obeying* it, which always results in sin, destruction and death. In such moments I need to counsel my heart: "Stop doing this! Stop this fleshly controlled selfish rebellion against God! Stop this sinful attitude, behavior. Repent! And <u>believe God</u> for the victory Jesus won for me on the cross!" It is a matter of life and death for me, the welfare and joy of my loved ones, and the honor and glory of God!

The Bible clearly teaches that as *born again believers,* we no longer sin because we *have* to sin; we sin because we *choose* to sin by surrendering our will to the control of our old sinful nature and obeying it, rather than our *new nature* in the power of the Holy Spirit. The only way that we can break this destructive cycle of sin and defeat and begin to live consistently victorious lives over sin is by remaining *in Christ,* walking *by faith* in humble trusting obedience in the power of the Holy Spirit. As we do so, we can be sure that the victory will be ours, and the glory, God's!

> *Now those who belong to Christ Jesus have crucified the flesh with its passions and desires...For the law of the Spirit of life in Christ has set you free from the law of sin and death (Rom. 8:2; Gal. 5:24). Those who are according to the flesh set their minds on the things of the flesh, but those who are according to the Spirit, the things of the Spirit... The mind set on the flesh is death, but the mind set on the Spirit is life and peace (Rom. 8:5-6).*

Bible Study Supplement
Chapter 3 — Day 5 — The War Within — The Conflict of the Two Natures

As we discussed in today's meditation, one of the main reasons most Christians meet with failure so often in their desire to live a consistent, victorious Christian life is a failure to recognize the *total depravity* of the human heart and the *power of the sinful flesh* that dominates it until it is cleansed (through sincere, fruit bearing repentance), and renewed (through a *renewing of the mind* with the truths of Scripture—what goes into the mind always ends up in the heart) then yielded to the Holy Spirit with a righteous, consecrated desire to trust and obey God. The *flesh*, in reality, is sin personified. Until we recognize that the flesh (sinful nature/heart) is absolutely and totally depraved, set against God, and will always lead us to sin and death (death to our relationship with God...and others - Is. 59:2; Rom. 6:23), we will fail to engage in the serious spiritual warfare that is necessary to consistently render it powerless by wielding a death blow against it—*dying to self,* in order to live in the victory of Jesus by the power of the Holy Spirit.

Romans 6 is the most powerful text in all of Scripture regarding waging successful spiritual warfare against our sinful nature. We do well to read and study it closely…and often.

1. Read Rom. 6:1-9.

    a. Now that we are saved, are we to *continue in sin?*_____ Why or why not? (vs. 2)

    b. What happened to us when we accepted Jesus? (vs. 3-4a)

    c. What does this enable us to do? (vs. 4b)

Verse 4 is a powerful and profound truth. I memorized it long ago and I still repeat it every day at the close of my quiet time to remind me (and Satan) of the powerful reality of what Jesus did for me and who I now am *in Him*. Just as *Christ was raised from the dead through the glory of the Father,* so I (and all who put their faith and trust in Him) have been *raised* to that same kind of victorious overcoming power through the Holy Spirit now living in me and enabling me to walk in this kind of righteous, *newness of life*. This reality fortifies my faith and builds a confidence in my *new,* cleansed heart that girds and upholds me as I go through my day.

    d. What happened to our *old self?* (vs. 6a)

    e. What does this mean to us—in relation to sin and the power it has over us? (vs. 6-7)

When we, by faith, *received* Christ into our hearts, we *received* His finished work on the cross and his triumphant resurrection in defeating sin and the devil. Therefore, the power of sin has been broken and we are now free to love and *serve God*—*not sin and the devil!* Serving God means living righteous, holy lives which always brings blessing and *life*—and abundant life full of love, peace and JOY (John 10:10b, Gal. 5:22-23). Serving sin and the devil results in *death*—conflict, guilt, destruction. So if this is *true,* why do we still, at times, *choose to serve sin?* The key is found in verses 6-8:

Knowing this, that our old self was crucified with Him, that our body of sin might be done away with, that we should no longer be slaves to sin; For he who has died is freed from sin; now if we have died with Christ, we believe that we shall also live with Him (Rom. 6:6-8).

The reason we fail to experience the freedom and JOY of the exchanged life in Christ is because:

A. We don't really *know* this. Either we have never *heard* this wonderful truth (Rom. 6:6-8) or we don't really *believe* that it is actually true. The Word of God tells us here—as well as in several other places—that when we put our faith in Jesus' *finished work on the cross on our behalf,* to purchase our redemption from the penalty (death) and the power (control) of sin, all that happened to Him has already happened to us. We *have been crucified with Him, that our body of sin might be done away with, that we should no longer be slaves to sin; For he who has died is freed from sin!* Now, if we have died with Christ, we believe that we shall also live with Him! *(Rom. 6:6-8).* Praise God that because of Jesus, the power of sin has been broken. We are no longer slaves to sin but fully alive *in Christ* and *His righteous* and *holy resurrection power* over sin now *lives in us through the Holy Spirit.* But how many of us really *believe* this and live our lives accordingly? Far too few, I am afraid. God calls it *unbelief* and it is a deadly sin wreaking havoc wherever it is allowed to reign. We will never experience the blessed freedom and liberty in Christ until we overcome this sin and truly, from the heart, by faith, receive (believe) Christ's finished work on the cross for our *sanctification* just as we did for our salvation. Studying God's Word that we might come to believe God's Word is still, and always will be, God's solution to the unbelief problem…*So then faith comes by hearing and hearing by the Word of God (Rom. 10:17).*

B. We fail to *die* (die to self)—to sincerely repent of our self-rule and relinquish all rights of rule to God, willingly surrendering and placing ourselves under the guidance and control of the Holy Spirit, then walking in obedience to *Him*—not our fallen, *sinful* nature. We must never forget that our fallen sinful (sin full) nature is so *full* of sin that all it *can* and *ever will do* is *sin!* (Rom. 7:14-24).

2. Read Rom. 6:11-18, 22.

   a. What are we to *consider* or *count* (as totally true!)? (two things – vs. 11)

   b. What are we instructed not to do? (two things - vs. 12)

   c. How do we accomplish this? (vs. 13)

   d. What shall no longer be master over us? (vs. 14a)

   e. Why can we as believers be confident of this? (vs. 14b)

   f. What happens to us as a result of whom we *choose* to obey? (vs. 16)

Please note! The Bible clearly warns us here that we will be <u>slaves</u> to what we <u>choose</u> to obey.

    g. Where does being a slave to sin—*choosing* to obey our sinful lust—always lead? (vs. 16b)

    h. What did the believers to whom Paul was writing willingly *choose* to do? (vs. 17)

    i. What was the wonderful result? (two things – vs 18 – notice especially 18a!)

Rom. 6:11-14, 17-18 are excellent verses to memorize. They help us focus upon the power we now have living in us - the power of the Holy Spirit and our *new nature* that enables us to say "no" to sin and "yes" to righteousness…a mighty, glorious power!

Another critical text in understanding how we overcome the lusts of our fallen sin nature is found in Ephesians 4.

  3. Read Eph. 4:17-24.

    a. How are we no longer to walk? (vs. 17)

    b. Describe the "Gentiles"—those who refuse to come to God…to be *born again* into His Kingdom. (Be very specific - 8 characteristics - vs. 18-19)

    c. In reference to our former manner of life what are we to do?…Why? (vs. 22)

    d. What must we do instead? (two things – vs. 23-24a)

    e. Describe this "new self." (vs. 24b)

According to this pivotal Scripture, gaining the victory over the old nature is a matter of *putting off* old habits and practices that are corrupted by the *lusts of our own corrupted, deceitful flesh* and *putting on* new habits that have been created in the likeness of God—righteousness, holiness, and truth.

The more we read, study and obey God's Word, the more our minds will be *renewed* and strengthened in its *life-giving, sin-overcoming* truths. Memorizing key verses brings even more effective benefit. Eph. 4:22-24 is another very powerful scripture that, if tucked in our hearts by memory, will do much towards enabling us to stand firm against *sin* whenever we are tempted.

As you go through the rest of this week take inventory of your habits and practices. Ask yourself: Is this a fleshly practice (from my former manner of life) that does not honor God and conform to the image of Jesus? If it is, confess it as sin (which it is), repent of it and *put it off* by willfully choosing to trust and obey God as He, through the Holy Spirit, leads you in *putting on* a new godly habit. An important caveat here: Do not attempt to *put off* a sinful, evil habit without having sought God about a new desire/practice that He wants you to *put on* in its place. Remember the story of the unclean spirit who goes out from a house that has been swept clean (through confession and repentance). The Bible says: *Now when the unclean spirit goes out of a man, it passes through waterless places, seeking rest, and does not find it. Then it says, "I will return to my house from which I came; and when it comes, it finds it unoccupied, swept and put in order. Then it goes and takes along with it seven other spirits more wicked than itself; and they go in and live there; and the last state of that man becomes worse than the first"* (Matt. 12:43-45). If we leave our newly *clean, swept* houses unoccupied, we can be sure sinful lusts and temptations will quickly return, bringing with them even more sinful thoughts and lusts, take up residence and cause more havoc *than at first.* So ask God to give you good, righteous, holy habits to replace the old ones that you *put off.*

I want to close by giving you an example that illustrates why this is so important. When I was in the most intense battle with my sinful flesh involving the sin of gluttony (bulimia, compulsive eating), before I could effectively *put off these* old sinful habits, I had to develop new, righteous habits. One of my favorite joys in life is reading godly, Christ-centered, edifying books: biographies of godly men and women—how they served the Lord with total commitment and joy, even through extremely difficult trials and difficulties. I also enjoy other instructional Christian books by committed men and women of God regarding how to apply the Word of God to various life situations. So I *put on* this good, godly habit in place of the former sinful, destructive habit—gluttonous eating! When I felt tempted to binge or overeat, I would first pray for strength to resist the temptation, then turn my thoughts immediately to my new godly habit—*fleeing* quickly from the place of temptation to a place where I could get into a good book or biography that would strengthen and build up my faith rather than weaken it and set it up for failure and falling to the temptation. If I was not able to do this immediately because of the circumstances, I would still *set my mind* on godly righteous thoughts through focusing upon scripture that I had memorized while at the same time *looking forward* to getting into a good book that would further edify and build up my godly desires as soon as possible, after the days' activities were completed. This would give me the motivation I needed to stand firm against *(put off)* the temptation. I also posted Bible verses all around the house and in my purse that I could quickly look at to renew and reinforce my mind for those times I was not able to just stop and read a good book. By doing this, there was always something immediately available to fortify the righteous desire within me to overcome the temptation.

Write out a Bible verse that had special meaning to you today.

Based upon what you have learned today, write a prayer to God expressing the desires of your heart in applying these truths to your life.

Chapter 4

Memory Verse: *Now faith is the assurance of things hoped for, the conviction of things not seen (Heb. 11:1).*

Bonus Memory Verse: *But My righteous one shall live by faith; And if he shrinks back, my soul has no pleasure in him. But we are not of those who shrink back to destruction, but of those who have faith to the preserving of the soul (Heb. 10:38-39).*

Day 1

IT TAKES FAITH!

Learning to Walk by Faith—not Sight...or *Feelings*

Day 2:

FAITH THAT PERSEVERES

Pressing on...When Every Fleshly Desire in Me Wants to Quit!

Day 3:

THE OBEDIENCE OF FAITH

The Heart of Faith - OBEDIENCE - Its Blessings and Joys

Day 4:

THE PATIENCE OF FAITH

Wait on the Lord... and Be Blessed

Day 5:

THE INEXHAUSTIBLE SUPPLY OF FAITH - GRACE

Amazing Grace...How Sweet the Sound

Chapter 4 — Day 1
It Takes Faith!
Learning to Walk by Faith, not Sight...or Feelings

> *Now faith is the assurance of things hoped for, the conviction of things not seen (Heb. 11:1).*
>
> *Therefore, being always of good courage...for we walk by faith, not by sight (2 Cor. 5:6-7).*

But My righteous one shall live by faith; and if he shrinks back, My soul has no pleasure in him. But we are not of those who shrink back to destruction, but of those who have faith to the preserving of the soul (Heb. 10:38-39).

*L*iving by true biblical faith is at the heart of who we are as God's redeemed, set apart children. (Hab. 2:4; Rom. 1:17; Heb. 10:38-39). Most of us *know* that. And we are reminded of it at every turn: Preachers preach it, Sunday School teachers teach it, writers write about it, a plethora of seminars and training workshops specialize in showing us how to *get it*, yet so very few practice such a walk consistently. Of all the things that God asks us as His children to do, this one— to *walk by faith not sight* (or feelings!), is among the most challenging. But it's a challenge we must courageously face for indeed the success or failure of our Christian experience and witness rest upon it!

Why is it so hard to develop true *biblical faith* that trusts and believes God, stands strong, and perseveres in righteous and holy obedience...come what may?

It is difficult first of all because we are by nature, stubborn, rebellious *controllers*. We don't like to *submit* to God and simply trust and obey Him as He leads us day by day. We know what we want and we are convinced that what we *want* is always best for us. So we stubbornly and rebelliously push on, pursuing our own fleshly desires—sinning and forfeiting the joys of God's <u>best</u> that can be realized only by consistently walking in trusting obedience...*by faith*.

Secondly, as noted last week, we live in a society obsessed with *self* and driven by *feelings*. We are continually bombarded on every side with the idea that the "first commandment" is "Look out for #1". The unspoken creed of the day has become: *God loves you and wants you to be healthy, happy and pain free.* We are encouraged to pursue this quest and even warned by preachers and teachers who peddle false, unbiblical teaching not to "get all carried away about this righteousness and holiness business. That's legalism. We're under grace... Relax, do your own thing... everything is relative, there are no absolutes, live and let live. If it feels good, do it..."

Because of the two sinful "pulls" upon our soul day after endless day, (the pull of our own selfish, sinful flesh on the inside and the pull of the world with all its lustful enticements and pleasures on the outside), most of us have given in to the temptation to *walk by feelings* rather than *faith* far too often. If I *feel like* doing something, I will do it. But if I don't *feel* like doing it, I will not do it—no matter what anyone says...including God.

That kind of attitude is the antithesis of biblical faith and must be dealt with. The widespread and very powerful demonic deception elevating "self" above all else, has caused many of us to lose our vision of what we are really *here for*. We are not here to have a good time, to do what pleases *me*, or to build *my* self-esteem. We are here to know, love and serve God, to bring glory to His Name, and to be conformed to the image of Jesus...to *become holy for He is holy* (John 17:3; Matt. 22:37-39; 1 Cor. 10:31; Rom. 8:29; 1 Pet. 1:15-16). And the biblical paradox is that once we begin to do this—abandon the pursuit of selfishness and instead, *by faith*, pursue righteousness and holiness for the glory of God— the happiness, the peace and the joy follow in abundant, overflowing measure just as Jesus said: *He who has found his life shall lose it, and he who has lost his life for My sake shall find it (Matt. 10:39, cf. John 10:10; Rom. 14:17)*. Those who make it their goal to "find" a life of comfort and ease, will *lose* the very thing they are truly seeking—real peace and contentment. While on the other hand, those who abandon the search for self—self-esteem, self-gratification, self-aggrandizement—in pursuit of the things of God find not only a rich and fulfilling life, but also with it, that deep *river of joy* that flows in streams of strength, encouragement and peace (Ps. 46:4-5).

But how do we *do* that? How do we break free of the consuming feelings-driven mind set that insists on having it *my* way? There is only one way to do that. It is called FAITH. We must *believe God* and we must *trust* God enough to *do* what He asks us to do—whether we *feel* like it or not.

> *He who comes to God must believe that He is, and that He is a rewarder of those who seek Him... But My righteous one shall live by faith; And if he shrinks back, My soul has no pleasure in him. But we are not of those who shrink back to destruction, but of those who have faith to the preserving of the soul (Heb. 10:38-39).*

True biblical faith always involves a courageous, trusting submission and relinquishment of the will (*my* will) in order to be filled with and controlled by the Holy Spirit to do the will of God...*nevertheless, Lord, not my will, but Thine be done (Matt. 26:39)*. Once our hearts and minds are set on doing the Father's will, those selfish, me-first *feelings* that once dictated our choices will no longer dominate and control us (2 Cor. 5:17). We will have new desires to know and do the *Father's* will, not what we *feel* like doing...or not doing. Ever increasing peace and joy will be ours as we discover that God's reward for trusting obedient faith is always blessing and freedom (John 13:17; 8:31-32; 3:29, 15:11).

The greatest enemy to consistently walking *by faith* for most of us is the *control issue*. Ever since the fall, we have had a driving desire to be *in control*. I remember well those early agonizing, very intense battles with total surrender of my life and will completely to God. It seemed so impossible...so paralyzingly frightening. I was not a "David" by nature who just seemed to be born with a trusting, courageous spirit. I was a selfish, strong-willed, stubborn, rebellious...coward. I didn't like battles and fighting or any such thing like that. I liked peace and comfort and *status quo*. But the more I read God's Word, the more the conviction came. Jesus did not die on the cross to leave me a self-obsessed, self-consuming, bearer of weak, sparse, sickly fruit. He died and rose again that I might be a *good soldier,* an *overcomer* and a *bearer* of *much, lasting fruit* for the kingdom of God (1 Tim. 2:3; Rom. 8:37; John 15:1-8). It is all a part of the *good fight* and I knew that I needed to trust God, get out on the battlefield and fight for the victory. So, *in faith*, I stepped out. "*Son of David, have mercy!... Lord, I believe, help Thou Mine unbelief! (Mark 10:47; Mark 9:24)* became my ongoing, daily battle cry.

It was really difficult at first because the *control factor* was so strong in my life; there were far more defeats than successes. But God was so, so merciful and faithful. He held tightly to my hand so that even when I fell, *I did not fall headlong (Ps. 37:24)*. He lovingly and tenderly picked me up, soothed the wounds, drew me even closer and taught me new truths from His precious Word that gave greater courage and determination to *walk by faith* in obedience to Him (2 Tim. 2:3). And as I did so, I experienced again and again the power of the risen *Christ in me (Col. 1:27)* giving wisdom, strength and victory. And I know that I will continue to do so <u>as long as</u> I *choose* to trust and obey God, walking *by faith,* not feelings...or attempting to be *in control (Rom. 6:11-18; Phil. 1:6; 2 Tim. 1:12).*

We've studied several of the good battle strategies for developing trusting, obedient, victorious *biblical faith*: a daily quiet time with the Lord in His Word and prayer, tucking away encouraging, faith fortifying Scripture in our hearts, and putting on the *full armor of God* each day. We will be looking at more of these in upcoming lessons. But for today, I would like to mention just one more that I have found invaluable:

Now these things happened to them as an example for us, and they were written for our instruction (1 Cor. 10:6, 11).

How much we miss by not looking more closely at the beautiful examples God has given us in His precious Word, *for our instruction.*

There are so many men and women of great faith in the Bible. If only we would take the time to really read and study their lives and *learn* from what they teach us through their example: Abel, Enoch, Noah, Abraham, Joseph, Moses, Joshua, Caleb, Ruth, David, Abigail, Elijah, Elisha, Ezra, Nehemiah, Esther, Mary, Joseph (earthly father of Jesus), John the Baptist, Peter, James, John the Apostle, Paul,

Barnabus, Timothy, Dorcas...and many more! What a treasure of wisdom and encouragement God has given us through these examples. The more I study the lives of these precious men and women of humble, trusting faith and obedience, the more I desire to be like them—to be one who *believes God,* and does not *waver in unbelief (Rom. 4:20).* And <u>God</u> wants that for all of us, His children, even more! That's why He continually urges us to *read the Word (Deut. 17:19; Ps. 119:130); listen carefully as He speaks through His Word (Prov. 8:33-35); study the Word (Acts 17:11; 2 Tim. 2:15, Ps. 1:1-3); love the Word (Ps. 119:97, 140); meditate upon the Word (Ps. 1:2, 119:97); know the Word (Ps. 119:98-99, Ps. 19:7-11); eat His Word* (for spiritual nourishment and strength) *(Ps. 119:103; Jer. 15:16), diligently teach the Word of God to our children (Deut. 6:6, 11:19); hide the Word in our hearts (Ps. 119:11); listen to the Word preached and taught by others (1 Tim. 13-16);* and, most importantly, *obey the Word (Josh. 1:8; John 13:17; Ps. 119:101).*

Now faith is the <u>assurance</u> of things <u>hoped for</u>, the <u>conviction</u> of things <u>not seen</u> (Heb. 11:1).

Yet, with respect to the promise of God, he (Abraham) <u>did not waver in unbelief</u>, but <u>grew strong in faith</u>, giving glory to God; <u>being fully assured</u> that <u>what He promised, He was able also to perform</u> (Rom. 4:20-21).

So then, <u>faith cometh by hearing, and hearing by the Word of God</u> (Rom. 10:17).

Bible Study Supplement
Chapter 4 — Day 1 — It Takes Faith!

Consistently living by true BIBLICAL FAITH is crucial to our Christian walk and witness. It is only as we exude this central character trait—strong, unwavering faith—that we bring honor and glory to God, fulfill His good plans for us and become a light to others that God uses to draw them to Himself (Ps. 34:1-3, 40:1-3; Phil. 2:15). Therefore, it is essential to <u>know</u> the biblical definition of faith that we might confidently and consistently live by it.

The biblical definition of faith is found in Hebrews 11. Because it is at the heart of who we are as God's children, let's take a moment to look at it in several versions.

King James Version (KJV) and New King James Version (NKJV): *Now faith is the substance of things hoped for, the evidence of things not seen.*

New American Standard Bible (NASB): *Now faith is the assurance of things hoped for, the conviction of things not seen.*

New International Version (NIV): *Now faith is being sure of what we hoped for and certain of what we do not see.*

The "things" referred to in all of these definitions are the promises of God found in His Word. Biblical faith is, therefore:

1. The <u>assurance</u> (solid, concrete, not a shred of doubt) that God will bring about those things we "hope for" based upon His promises. (God will do what He has promised!)

2. The <u>conviction</u> (<u>certainty</u>!) of the promises of God not yet seen, i.e. God said it, that settles it! It **will** happen as He has said—even if I have not *yet* "seen" or "experienced" it.

Both of these characteristics involve an absolute, total trust in what God says—every promise He has made in His Word. True biblical faith also involves a hopeful, futuristic view of life and circumstances—an unwavering assurance concerning events that: 1) have not yet happened, 2) have happened but we have not yet personally seen, touched or experienced them, or 3) promises that we cannot fully understand but we accept them as true and act upon them because *God said they are true and we believe God!* It often, therefore, involves present activity based upon an assurance of a future reality. To walk by faith is a *heart attitude* that says that I will walk in obedience to God as He leads me through His Word and Holy Spirit, regardless of what I can see, touch, or feel, or how difficult opposing circumstances may be.

1. The New American Standard definition of faith is simple, concise and accurate. Using the NASB above, write out the biblical definition of faith. Memorize it as soon as you can so it is *hidden in your heart.* This will help you to more consistently walk in true confident, trusting, *biblical faith.*

2. Read Heb. 11:6-10.

   a. What is impossible to do without faith? (vs. 6a)

b. What must the one who comes to God (in faith) believe? (two things - vs. 6b)

c. How did Noah build the ark? (Fill in the blanks - vs. 7a): By_____ Noah, when warned of things to come, in (moved by) _____built an ark to save his family.

d. To what did he become *heir*? (vs. 7b)

e. What did Abraham do *by faith*? (vs. 8)

3. Read and memorize Rom. 10:17 (Use KJV below).

So then faith cometh by hearing, and hearing by the word of God (Rom. 10:17).

a. How do we develop strong *biblical faith*?

Of this we can all be very sure. The strength, purity (accurate biblical wisdom), and power of our faith, will be in direct proportion to the priority we give to God's Word.

In 2 Chronicles we find one of the most encouraging, faith building stories in the Bible for those times when we find ourselves in the middle of a battle against enemies far greater than ourselves and our current resources—those "humanly" impossible situations concerning which there *seems* to be no way of escape from certain defeat and destruction, no way to victory.

4. Read 2 Chron. 20:14-25.

a. What did the Lord command Jehoshaphat **not** to be?... Why? (vs. 15b)

b. In verse 17 God tells the people that they will not have to physically fight this battle themselves. But they <u>are</u> responsible for taking up their positions, and <u>standing firm *in their faith*</u> until the Lord delivered them. Three commands and a promise follow in the latter part of this verse (vs. 17b)... what are they?

c. What must the people do to win in this great battle against enemies far greater and stronger than they? (two things - vs. 20b) (Note: Prophets were men called of God to "speak forth" His Word to the people, so "having faith in God's prophets" meant having faith in what God proclaimed through them).

d. Led by the Spirit of God, (vs. 14) what *battle strategy* did King Jehoshaphat instruct the people to employ? (vs. 21)

e. What was the result? (vs. 22)

f. What was the final outcome of the battle? (24, 25b)

And so will go our battles if we heed the good instructions of God: *Put your trust in the Lord and you will be (victorious). Put your trust in (His Word, what He commands) and you will succeed (2 Chron. 20:20).*

5. Read 1 John 5:4

   a. What brings the victory that overcomes the world? (vs. 4b)

   b. How is that kind of *faith* developed? (Fill in blanks below).
   So then faith cometh by _____ and _____ by the _____
   _____ _____ (Rom. 10:17).

Write out a Bible verse that had special meaning to you today.

Based upon what you have learned today, write a prayer to God expressing the desires of your heart in applying these truths to your life.

Chapter 4 — Day 2
Faith That Perseveres
Pressing on...When Every Fleshly Desire in Me Wants to Quit!

> *Therefore, do not throw away your confidence, which has a great reward. For you have need of endurance, so that when you have done the will of God, you may receive what was promised...But My righteous one shall live by faith; And if he shrinks back, My soul has no pleasure in him. But we are not of those who shrink back to destruction, but of those who have faith to the preserving of the soul (Heb. 10:35-39, sel.).*

Make no mistake about it: the natural drive within every fallen sinner (as we all are), is for sinful selfish, indulgent—and ultimately destructive—pleasure, having it *my* way, and being *in control* at all times. Our flesh (fallen, sinful nature) incessantly insists on walking by *sight* and *feelings*, rather than by *faith* and *obedience*. Allowing our flesh to be in control and dictate our attitude and our actions leads to destruction and death—as sin always does (Rom. 6:23). Walking by faith and obedience to God results in true freedom, joy and blessing (John 15:11; Rom. 14:17; Heb. 10:35-39). There is only one way that those natural, sinful, joy-robbing drives will ever be *taken captive (2 Cor. 10:5)* and their power over us broken. It is called *persevering faith.*

Perseverance: From the Greek word, proskarteresis (pros-kar-ter'-ā-sis); verb - proskartereo: To continue doing a task in spite of difficulties or opposition; Persistent: to be earnest and diligent in accomplishing; to press assiduously toward—regardless of difficulty or length of time involved.

> *Therefore, strengthen the hands that are weak and the knees that are feeble...so that the limb which is lame may... be healed (Heb. 12:12-13).*

We quit too soon!

> *And the seed in the good soil, these are the ones who have heard the Word in an honest and good heart, and hold it fast, and bear fruit with perseverance (Luke 8:15).*

One of the glorious outworkings of our Christian faith when exercised consistently according to the principles of God's Word is a strong, vibrant inner character that perseveres through the hard times, looking to God—to His Word, prayer and the power of the Holy Spirit—for strength and the *faith* to go on. This quality of persistent perseverance is often referred to as "the endurance of the saints."

> *Consider it all joy, my brethren, when you encounter various trials, knowing that the testing of your faith produces endurance. And let endurance have its perfect result, that you may be perfect and complete, lacking in nothing (James 1:2-4).*

Not only will true biblical, persevering faith—built upon the sure and unfailing promises of the Word of God—bring down the most resistant, well-fortified sin strongholds, it will also result in a stronger, healthier, happier person. Trials are no longer seen as enemies that have come to rob and destroy, but as friends sent by a loving Father to strengthen and purify our faith and develop within us true godly character that makes us *perfect and complete, lacking in nothing (James 1:4)*. One who truly walks by persevering faith is able to embrace even the hardest times in life as part of God's loving, perfecting plan. When we look upon the cross of Jesus (<u>all</u> that He suffered and accomplished for us—Matt. 26:36-28:20; Eph. 1:2-21!), when we focus our attention on God's more than 2,000 specific promises found in His Word, when we walk in humble, surrendered obedience empowered by the Holy Spirit, then we are able to *hang on, endure and persevere*—not just "somehow", but triumphantly!

> *Therefore, we … exult in our tribulations…knowing that tribulation brings about perseverance and perseverance, proven character and proven character, hope. And hope does not disappoint because the love of God has been poured out within our hearts through the Holy Spirit (in) us (Rom. 5:3-5).*

Perseverance in times of real suffering—deep, long, hard—suffering builds character, and a hope that cannot be shaken because it is built upon the *love of God poured out in our hearts through the Holy Spirit*. It is this kind of secure, hopeful assurance that enables us to *go on*, regardless of the degree of difficulty or length of the trials, knowing that God's love and grace will always prevail!

> *But He knows the way I take; When He has tried me, I shall come forth as gold (Job 23:10).*

Trials bring out…*the gold!*—that which is beautiful and strong and *useful to the Master (2 Tim. 2:21)*.

But there is one caveat we must heed:

> *Heal me, O Lord, for my bones are dismayed and my soul is greatly dismayed; But Thou, O Lord—how long?…I am weary with my sighing (Ps. 6:2, 6).*

This verse calls our attention to a very real danger we must recognize in this discussion of persevering faith: getting our eyes off of God and onto our circumstances. Rather than focusing upon God—His character and promised faithfulness and goodness, we, like the psalmist here, begin to focus upon our *dismayed bones* (circumstances) and all too quickly *grow weary*. (Thankfully, the psalmist recognized his error and returned to a right view of his circumstances—that they were in the hands of a loving, sovereign, powerful God who had heard his prayers and would answer and overcome his enemies). When we are in the midst of extended testing and trials, when the pain and problems are humanly overwhelming and have gone on *too long*, (according to <u>our</u> sin-tainted evaluations), it is easy to fall into the temptation to question and doubt God's love or wrongly judge His motives for allowing the suffering in our lives. We must ever be on guard against this temptation and steadfastly stand strong against it! We must counsel our heart continually with the truth that God loves us and always has fatherly affection towards us (Ps. 103:8-13, 119:68, 84:11). He cares deeply for us and is—at all times—lovingly, patiently working to strengthen and purify our faith and character so that we are able to *share His holiness* and thus fully partake in the blessed, *peaceful fruit of righteousness (Heb. 12:10-11)*.

> *"For <u>My thoughts</u> are not <u>your thoughts</u>, neither are <u>your ways, My ways</u>," declares the Lord. "For as (high as) the heavens are (from) the earth, so are My ways higher than your ways, and My thoughts than your thoughts"…Oh, the depth of the riches both of the wisdom and knowledge of God! How unsearchable are His judgments and unfathomable His ways! (Is. 55:8,9; Rom. 11:33).*

It is very unproductive—and oft agonizingly painful—to try to get God's ways to *fit* into our finite box of human understanding. God's ways are not our ways. They are *as high as the heavens are from the earth* and as *unsearchable* and *unfathomable* as the vastness of the Universe. They will often <u>not</u> make sense from purely human logic. God's ways are holy and transcend finite, sinful *human reasoning*. That is what *faith* is all about: accepting, believing and living by God's promises because they are true whether my human experience or feelings at the moment verify them or not. Feelings are fickle and tainted by sin and selfishness. They will lead us astray and let us down every time if we allow *them*—rather than faith and obedience to God, through His Word—to govern our lives. The Bible teaches, and our own experiences verify, that if we respond to difficulties and hardships with obedient, persevering faith, we will find that the *feelings* that we truly desire—security, peace and joy—will *follow* the faith and obedience just as the rainbow follows the rain! That's just the way the goodness, mercy and grace of God work! God loves to bless His obedient children—children who walk by *faith*, not *feelings* (Deut. 28; Ezek. 34:26).

Strong, obedient, biblical faith is not a sudden once for all experience. It is a daily "walk". But God gives *joy in the journey* when we keep *His* goal ever before us: that we might *share in His Holiness*… and *His happiness* (Heb.12:10; John 15:11, 17:13). Keeping this perspective will indeed enable us to:

> *Consider it all joy, my brethren, when you encounter various trials, knowing that the testing of your faith produces endurance… and endurance…perfection, <u>that we might be perfect, lacking in nothing</u>. (James 1:2).*

As I have sought to develop the wonderful godly quality of perseverance, I have benefited from the tried and refined biblical wisdom of a fellow sister in the faith, Elizabeth Elliot Gren. Decades of walking with God in faithful, trusting obedience has taught her much which she has generously shared with others through her books and teaching ministry. So often I have been blessed by her very practical counsel for the times we find ourselves in those humanly impossible "Red Sea" situations—an impassable sea of troubles before us and a destructive enemy closing in from

behind—that require an extra dose of *persevering faith*. In instructing her daughter, mother of eight children, she often advised her (not her exact words, but similar): When things become so huge and so overwhelming and it all seems utterly hopeless and impossible, *don't fret*, but instead, *choose to trust God and lean not on your own understanding—or strength (Ps. 34:8b; Prov. 3:5-6; 2 Cor. 12:9-10).* Look to the Holy Spirit for wisdom, guidance and *His* strength; listen as He instructs you, then…<u>*do the next thing*</u>. And when that is done…*do the next thing.* And just keep stretching out the hand of faith, doing the next thing, until you have walked through that "impassible sea", and come safely to the other side. And the next time you experience a similar situation, do the same thing: keep walking, stretching forward with persevering faith…*doing the next thing!*

I heard another testimony once that was also very encouraging in situations like this. Like many of us, the lady sharing her testimony found herself—often—in the midst of back-against-the-wall "Red Sea" situations. So she just kept counseling her own heart similarly: *God has not given us a spirit of (fear), but of power and love and discipline (2 Tim. 1:7). Keep at it, Sherry, keep at it. Fix your eyes on Jesus…trust Him, follow Him…one step at a time… keep at it (Heb. 12:2; 10:35-39).*

And I believe that is what God, through His Holy Spirit whispers in our ear in times of humanly overwhelming trials and difficulties: *Fix your eyes on Jesus (Heb. 12:2);* He is the divider of seas, the mover of mountains, the all-things-possible Savior. Don't fret or shrink back in unbelief…just keep at it; I am with you, I will make a way through; do the next thing, persevere, keep at it.

God is building a holy people (Deut. 7:6). He is raising up His righteous remnant, preparing them to be the *gloriously adorned bride* of His Son! (Jer. 31:7-14; Ps. 45:13-15; Rev. 21;2). Righteous, holy people are strong people: people who endure, standing firm and confident in the hour of testing, bringing honor and glory to God, and shining as beacons of hope and salvation in a dark and troubled world (Is. 25:3; Phil. 2:14-15).

And that's what *persevering faith* is all about: It's about courage and trust and obedience to God; it's about hope and joy and victory; it's about steadfastness and never giving up and finishing well. And it's about sharing the wonderful good news of God's love (John 3:16) with others so they, too, can have hope, victory, and joy. Those who daily, willingly do this—persevering *by faith* in following and obeying God—are those of whom Jesus spoke:

But (there are) a few... who have not soiled their garments; and they will walk with Me in white; for they are worthy... Remember, therefore, what you have... heard; and keep it (Rev. 3:3-4, sel.).

Let us be careful to heed Jesus' good exhortation here: to *remember* what we have *heard (from the Word of God)...and keep it.* Then, in the confidence of all His wonderful promises, let us *press on* in persevering faith as victorious warriors who will not *give up, turn back, wear out, or cave in*—come what may!

His banner over us is love, Our sword the Word of God
We tread the road (that) saints above, With shouts of triumph trod.
By faith they, like a whirlwind's breath, Swept on o'er every field;
The faith by which they conquered death, Is still our shining shield.

To him that overcomes the foe, White raiment shall be given;
Before the angels he shall know, His name confessed in heaven;
Then onward from the hills of light, Our hearts with love aflame,
We'll vanquish all the hosts of night, In Jesus' conquering name.

Faith is the victory! Faith is the victory!
O, glorious victory, that overcomes the world. AMEN.

(John H. Yates, 1837-1900)

Bible Study Supplement
Chapter 4 — Day 2 — Faith that Perseveres
Pressing On...When Every Fleshly Desire in Me Wants to Quit!

1. Read Rom. 5:1-5.

   a. By what have we been justified?...and what does this give us? (vs. 1)

   b. Because of our faith in Jesus, in what do we now "stand"? (vs. 2)

   c. What does tribulation (suffering) produce in the man of faith? (vs. 3)

   d. What does this in turn produce? (vs. 4a)...Then what? (4b)

   e. What will never disappoint? (vs. 5a)...Why? (vs. 5b)

2. Read Heb. 10:35-39.

   a. What are we to be careful not to throw away when trials come? (vs. 35)

   b. Of what do we have need? (vs. 36)

   c. By what will God's *righteous one* live? (vs. 38)

   d. What happens if he shrinks back? (vs. 38b)

   e. What kind of people are we <u>not</u> to be...to be? (vs. 39)

3. Read 1 Pet. 5:7-10.

   a. What are we to do with our anxieties and cares?...Why? (vs. 7)

   b. How can we resist the devil? (vs. 9a)

   c. When we are experiencing suffering, what can we be sure is happening to others? (vs. 9b)

   d. What will God do if we trustingly persevere through our sufferings? (four things - vs. 10b)

4. Read 1 Pet. 2:19-25

   a. What finds favor with (is commended by) God ? (vs. 19, 20b)

b. What has Jesus done for us? (two things - vs. 21).

c. How did Jesus respond to His suffering? (vs. 23) How was He able to do this? (vs. 23b)

In these verses written about Jesus' terrible, unjust persecution and suffering, we are given the most beautiful example for handling our pain and suffering: *And while being reviled, He did not revile in return; while suffering, He uttered no threats, but kept entrusting Himself to Him who judges righteously (1 Pet. 2:23).* What a beautiful picture of faith and perseverance. Jesus understood His mission. He *knew* the love and faithfulness of His Father, and He kept ever before Him the Joy—in all its eternal glory—that awaited Him on the other side! (Heb. 12:2; Phil. 2:8-10). We can endure whatever befalls us as well, if we follow Jesus' example—*entrusting ourselves to our faithful, loving Father* who is a rewarder of all who persevere in steadfast, trusting *faith* (1 Pet. 2:23; Rev. 22:12).

5. Read James 1:2-4.

a. What are we to do when we encounter various trials? (vs. 2)

b. What is the purpose of our trials? (two things - vs. 3)

c. What will be the final result? (vs. 4)

A beautiful story of the importance of faith and trust in God is found in Is. 7:1-9. In this historic account, Rezin, King of Aram, (the Arameans) and Pekah, King of Israel, had *gone up against Jerusalem to wage war against it and to destroy it.* Ahaz was the ruling King of Judah (Jerusalem was the capital of the land of Judah). The joint army of the Arameans and the Israelites was so massive and so intimidating that the Bible says: *(King Ahaz's) heart and the heart of his people shook as the trees of the forest shake with the wind.* In His deep love and care for His frightened children, God intervened. He sent the prophet Isaiah to King Ahaz to encourage him: *Take care and be calm, have no fear and do not be fainthearted because of these two stubs of smoldering firebrands...this plan of theirs shall not stand; it shall not come to pass.* He then gives King Ahaz one of the most concise, dynamic statements of faith in all the Bible:

If you do not stand firm in your faith, you will not stand at all (Is. 7:9b, Niv).

What a great exhortation this is to all of us when we face trials of various kinds. May God help us to recognize the importance of *faith* that is rooted and grounded in the immutable, infallible truths of God's Word so that we will *stand firm in our faith*... come what may!

He (Jesus), who for the joy set before Him, endured...and having been made perfect, He became to all those who obey Him the source of eternal salvation (Heb. 12:2; Heb. 5:9).

Write out a Bible verse that had special meaning to you today.

Based upon what you have learned today, write a prayer to God expressing the desires of your heart in applying these truths to your life.

Chapter 4 — Day 3
The Obedience of Faith
The Heart of Faith – Obedience – Its Blessings and Joys

> *Although He was a Son He learned obedience from the things which He suffered (Heb. 5:8).*
>
> *Now it shall be, if you will diligently obey the Lord your God being careful to do His commandments, blessings shall come upon you and overtake you (Deut. 28:1-2).*

After nearly three decades of walking with the Lord and studying the Bible faithfully, I am convinced that at the heart of it all in terms of our relationship with God, growing our faith, and experiencing the truly *abundant life* of *righteousness, peace, and joy in the Holy Spirit* that Jesus came to give us (John 10:10b; Rom. 14:17), is one word – OBEDIENCE. When I follow Jesus' example and set my heart upon *pleasing God*, by *obeying God*, heaven smiles down, the blessings flow, and joy fills my soul (Deut. 28:1-14; John 17:4, 15:13).

Because this wonderful topic of obedience truly is at the *heart of faith*, it will take a good deal more time than we have today to adequately study it. In book three we will look more closely at various aspects of obedience that will strengthen our faith even more and move us deeper into its joy and blessings. Specific topics will include: "Learning to Discern" – how can we discern God's voice from all the other conflicting voices that vie for our attention and sound very much like "God" so that we can *know His will* in order to *obey* His will; "What to do When we 'Can't' Obey" – dealing with strongholds that keep us from hearing/obeying God's voice; "These Things are Given as Examples for You" – taking a look at Biblical characters who demonstrate God's faithfulness to His children

who chose to *trust and obey*. Studying this subject of biblical obedience in depth was truly one of the most strengthening and liberating joys of writing this Bible Study. And I feel quite sure that it will be for you as well. So let's get started today with this introduction to the *heart of faith:* OBEDIENCE.

> *For the time will come when they will not endure sound doctrine; but wanting to have their ears tickled, they will accumulate for themselves teachers in accordance to their own desires; and will turn away their ears from the truth, and will turn aside to myths (2 Tim. 4:3-4).*

We've already talked about a number of *myths* that have, through demonic deception, made their way into the Church today. There is another very dangerous myth that threatens to destroy the joy of obedience for many of God's children. It is the modern, "easy believism, prosperity gospel" which teaches that all who are saved are now children of the King and have a *right* to health, wealth and happiness at all times. They are entitled to *get* whatever their heart desires by *naming it* and *claiming it*. And how is one *saved*? It's easy: just *confess Christ*—say you love Jesus—with no solid instruction or understanding of what biblical salvation really is: true repentance, complete faith and trust in Christ's atoning work on the cross and His victory over sin and death through His resurrection, then making Jesus one's personal *Savior and Lord*. Making Jesus Lord means becoming a disciple—following Him in a willing, glad surrender that produces a *new life* of faith and obedience. True *saving faith* always results in a changed heart that produces a changed life (2 Cor. 5:15, 17).

> *For certain persons have crept in unnoticed… ungodly persons who turn the grace of our God into licentiousness and deny our only Master and Lord, Jesus Christ (Jude 1:4).*

The "easy believism" preachers and teachers encourage licentiousness, making a mockery of God's precious grace, proclaiming that because all believers are *under grace*, they are basically free to do whatever they want, ask forgiveness if they "mess up", and just carry on—continuing to pursue and enjoy every worldly (sinful) lust and pleasure. This unbiblical ear-tickling promotes fleshly indulgence and runs contrary to the teachings of God's Word just as Paul warned against in *Rom. 6:1-2: What shall we say then? Are we to continue in sin that grace might increase? May it never be! How can we who died to sin (continue) in it?*

How careful we must be! For, under the influence of demonic deception, the highly popular preachers and teachers of the "easy believism, prosperity gospel" are incredibly adept at "picking and choosing" Scripture that *proves* what they are saying. These "proof texts" come directly from the Word of God, so they are incredibly effective in deceiving vulnerable sheep who may not yet be grounded in a thorough knowledge of *the whole counsel of God's Word (Acts 20:27)*. Did not Satan use this same strategy in his diabolical temptation of Jesus—actually quoting Scripture (Matt. 4:6)? His use of Scripture was out of context and twisted in application, inferring something that it did not mean at all, but nonetheless, it would surely have proven effective had Jesus not been alert, saturated with a thorough knowledge of God's Word, and totally committed to obeying His heavenly Father. That is what enabled Him to recognize and stand

firm against the deception. And so must we be if we are to *recognize* and *stand firm* against the deceptions of the *pick and choose, easy believism, propriety gospel*—and a host of other false teaching. Here are just a few examples of the texts often quoted:

> *Ask and it shall be given to you (Math. 7:7); whatever you ask in My Name, that I will do (John 14:13); you have not because you ask not (James 4:2); therefore, I say to you, all things for which you ask, believe that you have received them, and they shall be granted you (Mark 11:24) etc.*

But they leave out verses like:

> *If anyone wishes to come after Me, let him deny himself, take up his cross daily, and follow Me…. whoever wishes to become great among you shall be your servant, and whoever wishes to be first among you shall be your slave; just as the Son of Man did not come to be served, but to serve, and to give His life a ransom for many… Although He was a Son, He learned obedience from the things which He suffered…the slave is not greater than his Master (Luke 9:23; Matthew 20:26-28; Heb. 5:8; John 15:20).*

The prosperity gospel is very appealing to our natural selfish, proud flesh that does not like to hear about things like *denying self, taking up our cross, being a slave* or *learning obedience through suffering*. Sinful, self-centered man demands—the *crown* without the *cross*, the *rewards* without the *labor*, the *blessings* without the *obedience*.

But that is not truth and that is not *God's way*. It is a false, rebellious and sinful way. If we allow such attitudes to take root in our hearts we can be sure that they will dominate our lives, lead us away from God and into sin, which in turn results in death—either temporary (death to our joy, peace, relationships) or eternally (Hell)—as sin always does (Rom. 6:23). God has a purpose for our lives—a good, meaningful and fulfilling purpose (Jer. 29:11-14). Remaining in a comfortable, self-centered, pleasure-focused lifestyle—ever seeking to make it *more* comfortable and pleasurable as our selfish flesh demands and the prosperity gospel promotes—is not it. Obeying God as He leads us in fulfilling His good plans for our lives, is. Christlike obedience requires commitment and perseverance, spiritual growth and perfecting of character, holiness and righteousness—the things that bring real and lasting joy. These good character qualities will only be developed by following Jesus' example:

> *Have this attitude in yourselves which was also in Christ Jesus, who, although He existed in the form of God, did not regard equality with God a thing to be grasped, but emptied Himself, taking the form of a bond-servant, and being made in the likeness of men… He humbled Himself by becoming obedient to the point of death, even death on a cross (Phil. 2:5-8).*

> *I glorified Thee on the earth, having accomplished the work Thou hast given Me to do (John 17:4).*

> *…fixing our eyes on Jesus, the author and perfecter of faith, who for the joy set before Him endured the cross… and has sat down at the right hand of the throne of God (Heb. 12:2).*

> *Although He was a Son He <u>learned obedience</u> from the <u>things which He suffered</u> (Heb. 5:8).*

What a contrast to the lies that pervade our materialistic, pleasure-seeking/saturated western culture. The devil is having a hey day deceiving people into believing that such a preoccupation—with pleasure and materialism—will bring real, lasting peace and joy. It does not. It can not. It never has, and it never will!

Sadly, I fear that we've all gotten caught up in the pleasure seeking lie to some degree. We've allowed this obsessive quest to affect our own attitudes and motivations. We've even listened to the lies that denigrate obedience as something negative and joy-robbing and thus to be shunned and avoided, rather than embraced and sought after for the true joy and blessing it brings. Isn't that just like Satan—to make

evil *appear* as good and desirable, and that which God has made *good* as something that is bad and undesirable. So he has masterfully done with the good biblical discipline of obedience. But a look into God's Word tells us the truth, dispelling the deceptive lies. <u>In the Word of God, obedience is always linked with blessing and joy—always!</u>

So, for the remainder of our time today, let's turn our ears away from the ear-tickling myths and lies of Satan and our pleasure-obsessed world and return to the Bible to see what God has to say about the blessings of obedience and the deep, abiding *peace and joy* it always brings.

> *How blessed are those whose way is blameless, who walk in the law of the Lord. How blessed are those who observe His testimonies, who seek Him with all their heart. They also do no unrighteousness; they walk in His ways; (they) give thanks to God with uprightness of heart (Ps. 119:1-3, 7).*

Blessedness is another word for happiness. Happy, therefore, are those who *seek God and walk in His ways*—in glad, surrendered obedience. Their hearts will be filled with joy and thanksgiving.

> *O how I love Thy law! It is my meditation all the day. Thy commandments make me wiser than my enemies… I have more insight than all my teachers… I understand more than the aged, because I have observed Thy precepts. I restrain my feet from every evil way, that I may keep Thy word… How sweet are Thy words to my taste! Yes, sweeter than honey to my mouth! (Ps. 119:97-103, sel.).*

Obedience not only fills our heart with joy and thanksgiving, but also with the sweetness of godly wisdom and insight (discernment), and the strength we need to withstand temptation.

> *How blessed is the man who does not walk in the counsel of the wicked, nor stand in the path of sinners, nor sit in the seat of scoffers! But his delight is in the law of the Lord, and in His law he meditates day and night. And he will be like a tree firmly planted by streams of water, which*

yields its fruit in its season, and its leaf does not wither (Ps. 1:1-3).

Obedience always leads to a fear-dispelling security and endurance in times of difficulties. It also results in the blessed joys of kingdom-advancing productivity and fruitfulness.

How blessed is the man who fears the Lord, who greatly delights in His commandments…wealth and riches are in his house, and his righteousness endures forever. Light arises in the darkness for the upright; he will never be shaken; he will not fear evil tidings; his heart is steadfast, trusting in the Lord. His righteousness endures forever; (he) will be exalted in honor (Ps. 112:1-9, sel.).

Real wealth and lasting riches will be found in the heart and home of the righteous man who *greatly delights in God's commandments.*

If you know these things, you are blessed if you do them (John 13:17).

It is not enough to *know* what God says in His Word. The joy comes in doing it—OBEDIENCE.

Now it shall be, if you will diligently obey the Lord your God, being careful to do His commandments…all these blessings shall come upon you and overtake you….Blessed shall you be when you come in, and blessed shall you be when you go out…the Lord will drive out all (your enemies) from before you, and you will dispossess those greater and mightier than you… You shall possess and live in the (good land) to

which He is taking you. The Lord will open for you His storehouse, the heavens…to bless all the work of your hand (Deut. 28:1-7, 12, 11:23, sel.).

God cannot lie (Titus 1:2). If God said that He will bless the one who *diligently listens to* and *obeys Him* you can be sure He will. Ask those who have chosen to *believe* this promise and have set their hearts on trusting and obeying Him. I am certain that every one of them will tell you that they have been blessed beyond anything they could have imagined and their only regret is that they did not *believe God* sooner! (Ps. 40:2-4).

See, I have set before you life and death, the blessing and the curse. So <u>choose life</u> in order that you may live, you and your descendants, by loving the Lord your God, by obeying His voice, and by holding fast to Him; for this is your life (Deut. 30:15, 19-20, sel.).

The degree to which we experience *life* as God intended and Jesus came to give us—abundant and full of real and lasting joy and blessing—will always be in direct proportion to our love for God and how carefully we *listen to His voice, hold fast to Him,* and *walk in humble, trusting obedience.*

How blessed are those whose way is blameless, who walk in the law of the Lord… who seek Him with all their hearts…How blessed is the man who greatly delights in His commandments…he will never be shaken; his heart is steadfast, trusting in the Lord (Ps. 119:1-2, 112:1-2, 6-7).

Bible Study Supplement
Chapter 4 — Day 3 — The Obedience of Faith
The Heart of Faith – Obedience – Its Blessings and Joys

Deuteronomy 28-30 is a classic text for studying God's heart concerning the path of obedience and the importance He ascribes to it. Though we won't have time to examine this text in its entirety, I encourage you to keep it in mind, and when you find yourself in a battle with your own flesh that refuses to obey God in a certain area, go to Deuteronomy 28-30 and read through these chapters in one sitting. It will do much to strengthen your resolve to choose the path of obedience, and with it, blessings, joy and peace.

1. Read Deut. 28:1-14.

   a. What does God promise to those who diligently obey Him? (vs. 6)

   b. What else will He do? (vs. 9a, 12)

2. Read Deut. 30:15-20.

   a. What does God *set before* His children each and every brand new day? (vs. 15)

   b. What will God do for all who follow His good instructions to love and obey Him? (Fill in the blank - vs. 16b)

      …the Lord your God will _____ you in the land you are entering to possess.

   c. What will happen if His children rebel against God's good commands and *turn away* to seek after other "gods"? (vs. 17-18)

   d. God reiterates and emphasizes even more strongly the choice He gives us in verse 19. Describe this choice. (vs. 19 – middle of verse – two pairs of choices)

   e. How can we *choose life* (blessings and joy) for us and for our children? (by doing three things – vs. 20a)

In these very important verses, Deut. 30:15-20, we see the inseparable link between love for God and faithful, trusting obedience, to protection, provision and blessing. But we cannot *obey* what we do not *know*. Nor can we love someone with whom we never spend any time. That is why it is so important to spend time with God every day—in His Word and prayer—so that our love for Him grows ever stronger, purer and deeper as we *listen to His voice and hold fast to Him (Deut. 30:20)*.

3. Read 1 John 5:3-4.

   a. How is love for God demonstrated? (vs. 3a)

b. Complete this sentence: God's commands are <u>not</u> _____ (vs. 3b).

How often we have read this verse. But have we really taken to heart what it says? <u>*God's command-ments are not burdensome*</u>*! (1 John 5:3).* When we are walking in humble, trusting obedience to God, He *is with us, a victorious warrior who fights for us, delivers us from all our troubles and enemies, and supplies all our needs according to His riches in glory in Christ Jesus (Ps. 46:1; Zeph. 3:17; Ps. 34:19; Ps. 35:10; Phil. 4:19).* It is only when we step outside God's good, protective boundaries—through stubborn, willful acts of disobedience (or fear and unbelief)—that life become *burdensome:* heavy with sin and its inevitable guilt, anxiety, fear…and other painful consequences. Such heaviness destroys our joy and, if not dealt with through sincere repentance, leads to a sense of chronic oppression as sin piles upon sin adding to the burden.

c. What <u>overcomes</u> *the world?* (which includes the schemes and enticement of the devil, the world, and our own sinful flesh that lead to sin's burdensome bondages - vs. 4b).

And we know that *faith comes by hearing and hearing by the Word of God (Rom. 10:17).* The more we "hear"—listening attentively—as God speaks to us through His Word, the purer and stronger becomes our faith, our trust, our obedience…and our joy.

Write out a Bible verse that had special meaning to you today.

Based upon what you have learned today, write a prayer to God expressing the desires of your heart in applying these truths to your life.

Chapter 4 — Day 4
The Patience of Faith

Wait on the Lord…and be Blessed!

> *Be patient, therefore, brethren, until the coming of the Lord (James 5:7).*

We live in a materialistic, pleasure-seeking society that by specific demonic design has programmed minds to seek and to expect a life of comfort, convenience and immediate gratification. We have instant coffee, instant breakfast foods, pre-packaged quick and easy diet formulas, *fast food* restaurants with drive through windows, packaged, prepared foods that we can pop into the microwave for a quick and easy "instant meal", cellphones so we are always "connected", satellite hookups for instant viewing of any event in any part of the world, and remote controls so we don't even have to get up from our easy chairs to change the channel.

But the Bible teaches that this obsession with comfort, convenience and immediate gratification is *not of the Father, but of the world (1 John 2:16).* We are rather to be occupied with *purifying our hearts, transforming our minds, strengthening weak places,* and *diligently being about the Father's business.* We are to be in a continual cooperative venture with the Holy Spirit as He works to conform the inner, fallen, sinful nature of man into Christlike qualities of character, righteousness, and holiness. To develop these godly character qualities takes faith, obedience, perseverance…<u>and</u> patience.

Be patient, therefore, brethren, until the coming of the Lord. Behold, the farmer waits for the

precious produce of the soil being patient about it, until it gets the early and late rains. You too be patient; strengthen your hearts (James 5:7-8).

God's ultimate goal for each of us is holiness— the forming of the very nature and character of Christ in us. That is not an immediate or instant undertaking. In fact it is a lifelong process. But there is joy in the journey as we look to God, resting daily in the loving, peaceful patience of the Holy Spirit.

And the fruit of the Spirit is love, joy, peace, <u>patience</u>…(Gal. 5:22).

A surrendered, Spirit-filled life is a full and abundant life lived in the calm assurance of God's presence and "all things good" provision (Ps. 73:1, 84:11, 119:68; Phil. 4:19 etc.).

To whom would He teach knowledge?…for He says, line on line, precept on precept, a little here, a little there…Here is rest… I will not drive them out before you in a single year, that the land become…desolate, and the beasts of the field become too numerous for you. (Is. 28:9-10; Ex. 23:29-30).

God in His infinite wisdom, knew that we would, in our fallen state, be frail, fragile and easily discouraged (Ps. 103:14;1 Kings 19:4). We simply could not handle a massive purging of all that is unholy and ungodly within. We would become frightened, overwhelmed, defeated—to the point of despair. We would give up! Therefore, God's good plan involves learning and growing and being transformed slowly, steadfastly, patiently. It is the beautiful process of progressive sanctification that we learned about earlier. God's plan works because it builds into us character, strength and stability so that we do not cower and shrink back in fear and faith failure when temptation or the winds of adversity strike (Math. 7:24-27). Rather, we stand confident, firm in our faith, resisting temptations (to quit), patiently persevering through the hard times (Phil. 3:12-14).

> *I will drive them out before you little by little, until you become fruitful and take possession of the land...but they would not listen...so they will stumble backward, be broken, snared and taken captive...and the Word of the Lord... will* (have to be) *repeated* (over and over again) (Is. 28:12b,13).

Every time we cower in fear, throw up our hands in defeat, or fail to obey God because of unbelief and lack of persevering, obedient faith, we have to repeat the lesson and we can get very stuck in a pattern of *getting snared, falling back, being taken captive...repenting, getting snared, falling back, being taken captive.* Instead of moving forward in our faith we bog down in a fruitless, non-productive cycle of failure and defeat. Why? Because we refuse to really *listen* with an obedient heart and will. We need to heed the warning here and *listen more closely* and *obey more carefully.*

Another reason we get stuck sometimes and fail to grow and mature in our faith and trust in God is similar: we fail to *wait on God.*

> *I would have despaired unless I had believed that I would see the goodness of the Lord in the land of the living. Wait for the Lord; Be strong, and let your heart take courage; Yes, wait for the Lord... Those who wait on the Lord will renew their strength; they will mount up with wings like eagles. They will run and not be tired; they will walk and not faint (Psalm 27:13-14; Is. 40:31).*

This principle of *waiting on the Lord* is one of the most valuable commands of Scripture. God's Word says that we are to *let the peace of Christ rule in our hearts (Col. 3:16).* Therefore, when there is anxiety, turmoil or a lack of peace, it is time to practice patience and *wait on the Lord.* We must *be still (Ps. 46:10)*...and wait for further direction from God. This does not mean that we just go to bed, pull the covers over our head and stay there until "God speaks to us from heaven". Biblical waiting is <u>not</u> an inactive, do-nothing state. It is a patient, trusting, active obedience to the will of God—<u>doing</u> what we already <u>know to do</u> (John 13:17), while at the same time trusting God for His continued direction in the future through fervent, expectant prayer (Matt. 7:8). It is very dangerous to lag behind when God is clearly asking us to move forward. It is potentially even more dangerous, however, to move ahead of God—to go out without His guiding presence and accompanying peace. I have a little rule that I practice that has saved me untold agonies from the defeat and regret that always follow *not listening to God,* or *getting ahead of God.* It is based on Col. 3:16: *Let the peace of Christ rule in your hearts.* The principle I follow is simply this: "No peace; no pursuit; or "When in doubt, don't". Keep on praying...and waiting...seeking God until the guidance <u>and</u> the peace comes. Whenever I fail to follow this good discipline, *going out in haste,* I experience disappointment, failure, and a painful sense of loss and regret just as the Bible warns (Prov. 21:5).

> *He gives strength to the weary, and to him who lacks might He increases power...do not fear, for I am with you; do not anxiously look about you, for I am your God. I will strengthen you, I will help you, surely I will uphold you with My righteous right hand...Wait for the Lord; Be strong, and let your heart take courage; Yes, wait for the Lord (Is. 40:29, 41:10,13; Ps. 27:14).*

What a beautiful promise for all who choose to trust in God and *wait patiently for Him.*

Bible Study Supplement
Chapter 4 — Day 4 — The Patience of Faith
Wait on the Lord…and Be Blessed

1. Read Ps. 27:13-14. (Please use NASB below to answer the questions).

   13. I would have despaired unless I had believed that I would see the goodness of the Lord in the land of the living.
   14. Wait for the Lord; Be strong, and let your heart take courage; Yes, wait for the Lord (Ps. 27:13-14).

   a. What would have happened had the Psalmist not <u>believed</u> (had faith) that he would see *the goodness of the Lord in the land of the living* (while he was still alive)? (vs. 13)

   b. What good counsel do we find in verse 14? (three things).

2. Read Joshua 1:5-9.
   a. What did God command Joshua to do (to be)? (two things - vs. 7a)

   b. What else was he to do? (two specific things - vs. 8, middle of verse)

   c. What did God promise Joshua if he obeyed this command? (vs. 8b)

3. Read Joshua 11:15-18, 23.
   a. How did Joshua respond to God's commands? (vs. 15)

   b. How long did Joshua *wage war against all the kings?* (vs. 18)

I love verses 15 and 18: *Just as the Lord had commanded Moses his servant, so Moses commanded Joshua, and so <u>Joshua did; he left nothing undone of all that the Lord had commanded</u>…*And Joshua *waged war for a long time against all these kings (vs. 15, 18).* And so will most of us as we approach Jordan to *enter in* – to possess our possessions. We will face enemy kings (demonic strongholds) skilled in combat and destruction. But we must, like Joshua be <u>*very*</u> brave and <u>*very*</u> courageous—determined to *fight for the victory.* We must boldly face every enemy and we must fight until they are *utterly destroyed (Josh. 11:12).* I long to live my life after this exemplary model of faith, obedience, perseverance and patience! By the way, did you know that Joshua is the Hebrew name for Jesus?

   c. What was the result of Joshua's careful, persevering obedience? (vs. 23b)

4. Read Ps. 37:7-9.
   a. What good counsel does the Psalmist give us? (two things – vs . 7a)

   b. What does he warn us <u>not</u> to do? (vs. 8b)

What a simple but profound command: <u>*Don't fret*</u>. *It leads only to evil doing,* Would that we all would heed this wise instruction. We'd save ourselves and every one around us a lot of frustration and hurt since fretting nearly always leads to outbursts of anger and harsh, unkind words.

   c. What will happen to those who obey the command to *hope in/wait on the Lord*? (vs. 9b)

5. Read Ps. 62:5-8.
   a. What did the wise psalmist instruct his soul to do? (vs. 5a) Why? (vs. 5b)

   b. What was God to him? (three things - vs. 6) Because of that, how was his confidence? (vs. 6b)

   c. What did he recognize as far as his salvation and honor/glory were concerned? (vs. 7a).

   d. What else was God to him? (vs. 7b)

   e. What further wise counsel does he give? (two things - vs. 8)

6. Read Lam. 3:25-26.
   Complete the following sentences:
   a. The Lord is good to _____, to the one who _____ (vs. 25)
   b. It is good to_____ (vs. 26)

7. Read Hosea 12:6 (Please use NASB below).

   Therefore, return to your God, observe kindness and justice, and wait for your God continually.

   a. How often/long should we wait for God?

8. Read James 5:7-8.
   a. How are we to be as we go through life? (vs. 7a)

   b. To whom does James compare this kind of godly patience? Describe it. (vs. 7)

Proverbs 19:11 says: *A man's wisdom gives him patience.* The more we study God's Word, the more wisdom we have. And the more wisdom we have the more *patience* we will develop to *wait on, trust and obey* God. Then we will *make our way prosperous and have success wherever we go (Josh. 1:8)*.

Write out a Bible verse that had special meaning to you today:

Based upon what you have learned today, write a prayer to God expressing the desires of your heart in applying these truths to your life.

Chapter 4 — Day 5
The Inexhaustible Supply of Faith — Grace

> And He has said to me, "My grace is sufficient for you, for (My) power is perfected in (your) weakness." Most gladly, therefore, I will rather boast about my weaknesses, that the power of Christ may dwell in me (2 Cor. 12:9).

AMAZING GRACE... How Sweet the Sound

As we have been studying throughout this series, and as we have all experienced, sin has played havoc upon our world. Our fight against sin is what the Bible refers to as *the good fight* (*1 Tim. 6:12*). In describing this spiritual warfare, the Bible warns us that Satan (the source and perpetuator of sin) and our own indwelling sin nature, is too strong and too deceptive for us to fight alone, or in our own strength (Ps. 35:10; 2 Cor. 11:3, 14; Eph. 6:12). We need the power of the Holy Spirit as we studied earlier...and we need the ongoing, always sufficient and inexhaustible supply of GRACE.

GRACE: The undeserved, unmerited favor of God.

Nelson's Illustrated Bible Dictionaray defines grace as: "kindness and favor shown without regard to the worth or merit of the one who receives it and in spite of what that person deserves." The grace of God is a central theme throughout in the Bible and one of God's key attributes. Inseparably linked to the attribute of GRACE is God's mercy or lovingkindness. GRACE is getting what we <u>don't deserve</u>; mercy is <u>not getting</u> what we do! *The Lord God (is) compassionate and gracious, slow to anger, and abounding in lovingkindness (Ex. 34:6).*

God knew, long before the foundations of the world that the man and woman He created with a volitional free will would reject His love, rebel, and thus sin and be separated from Him, as <u>God is holy</u>, and <u>holy and unholy cannot dwell and fellowship together</u>. That is exactly what happened. Adam and Eve did rebel against God, sinned and were separated from God. (Just as the Bible tells us we all would have done...and in fact, continue to do – Rom. 3:23; Ps. 14:1-3, 53:3). Therefore, Adam and Eve and all their prodigy that followed would be separated from God and His love. They would remain under the *curse of sin*—experiencing guilt, inner turmoil and fear throughout their lives—then they would die, and go to Hell where all sinners go to receive the punishment sin requires (Rom. 6:23; Rev. 20:11-15). Unless...

God intervened.

But...*thanks be to God...while we were yet sinners* (helpless and estranged from God), *Christ died for us! (Rom. 7:25, 5:8).* On the very day that Adam and Eve sinned, God, out of His great love and unmerited GRACE, promised them a Savior (Gen 3:15) who would redeem them—pay the penalty for their sins (death – Rom. 6:23)—and restore them to a loving, forgiven relationship with Him. And God kept that promise!

The Lord your God has chosen you to be a people for His own possession out of all the peoples who are on the face of the earth. The Lord did not set His love on you nor choose you because (of any merit of your own)...but because the Lord loved you;... the Lord brought you out by a mighty hand, and redeemed you from the house of slavery... Know, therefore, that the Lord, your God, He is God, the faithful God, who keeps His covenant and His lovingkindness to the thousandth generation with those who love Him.... You shall not (be afraid), for the Lord your God is in your midst, a great and awesome God. And the Lord your God will clear away (your enemies) before you...and shall deliver... you (Deut. 7:6-11, 17-23, 8:19-20, sel.).

Thus God did for the children of Israel. God continued that GRACE with His people until the *fullness of time (Gal. 4:4)*, when God's GRACE was fully expressed in the person and redemptive work of Jesus.

BUT GOD

...being rich in mercy and GRACE sent Jesus to be the propitiation (payment) for our sin...He who knew no sin became sin for us, that we might become the righteousness (holiness) of God in Him (Rom. 5:8; 1 John 2:2; 2 Cor. 5:21).

G – R – A – C – E
GOD 'S RICHES AT CHRIST'S EXPENSE

Because of Jesus, because of GRACE, we no longer have to be separated from God, live under sin's curse, die, and go to Hell. We can repent, be united with God, experience loving fellowship with Him and one another now—and enjoy the glories of heaven for all eternity!

Jesus, the spotless, sinless lamb of God went to the cross on the behalf of every sin-cursed child who would ever come into the world (John 3:16). In perfect, sinless, divine love—the magnitude of which none of us can fully comprehend—Jesus took upon Himself the wrath that our blatant, defiant rebellion against the love of God deserved; He bore in His own body, the punishment (wrath/death) for every sin ever committed by every person from

the beginning of time until its end. It was the most hellish battle, the most gruesome, unjust death the world would ever witness. But Jesus prevailed in that battle against sin and the devil; He *paid in full* the sin debt of us all (Rom. 6:23; 2 Cor. 5:21). Then, on the 3rd day, Jesus rose victoriously from the grave, procuring victory over sin and death forever! (Luke 24:4-7). As we repent of our sins and, *by faith*, receive the GRACE of God (Christ's payment for our sins through His death and victory over sin through His resurrection), His payment and His victory, becomes "ours"—our blessed inheritance in Christ. By GRACE, God enables us to *live and move and have our being... in Him*—in the fullness of Christ's victory, and all this means for us (Acts 17:28; Eph. 1:2-21; Col. 2:9-10). That is what GRACE is all about. Instead of wrath and punishment from God, we receive forgiveness and favor; instead of rejection and separation, we receive acceptance and fellowship; instead of conflict and strife, we receive mercy and peace with God; instead of the death and eternal punishment in Hell that our sins deserve, we receive life and eternity in the glories of Heaven!

But this wonderful gift can only be enjoyed within the Covenant. We enter God's Covenant of eternal love through repentance and faith. And we continue to enjoy the boundless blessings of God's unmerited favor—GRACE—by the same means: *faith!* We must believe that *God is good and a rewarder of those who seek Him (Heb. 11:6; Ps. 84:11).*

There can be no more beautiful example of one who understood—and lived by—the magnitude and power of God's GRACE in all the Bible than the Apostle Paul. Having experienced the richness of God's GRACE through his own conversion, Paul continually committed Himself to the *unfailing mercies and lovingkindness of God* believing that He, through His inexhaustible GRACE, would *supply all His needs according to His riches in glory in Christ Jesus (2 Cor. 12:9-10; Phil. 4:19).*

And working together with Him, (I) urge you not to receive the GRACE of God in vain....but in everything (be) servants of God—in much endurance, in afflictions, in hardships, in distresses… in sleeplessness… in patience, in kindness, in genuine love, in the Word of truth, in the power of God (through the Holy Spirit) by the weapons of righteousness… always rejoicing… making many (spiritually) rich (2 Cor. 6:1-10, sel.).

Paul unwaveringly conducted his life—moment by moment, day by day—in the confidence and joy of what it meant to be a redeemed, sanctified, Grace-kept child of God.

Five times I received from the Jews thirty-nine lashes. Three times I was beaten with rods, once I was stoned, three times I was shipwrecked, a night and a day I spent in the deep. I have been on frequent journeys; in dangers from rivers, dangers from robbers, dangers from my countrymen, danger from the Gentiles, dangers in the city, dangers in the wilderness, dangers on the sea, dangers among false brethren; I have been in labor and hardship, through many sleepless nights, in hunger and thirst, often without food, in cold and exposure (2 Cor. 11:24-27).

Yet, in spite of all these things, this man of God says confidently: *I rejoice; yes, and I will rejoice…and I urge you, make my joy complete by being of the same mind; for it is God who is at work in you… He who did not spare His own Son, but delivered Him up for us all, how will He not also with Him freely give us all things. Therefore… I rejoice and share my joy with you. And you, too… rejoice in the same way and share your joy with me! Rejoice in the Lord always; and again I say, rejoice! (Phil. 1:18, 2:18, 2, 13; Rom. 8:32; Phil. 4:4).*

How could Paul maintain such a confident, joyful spirit in the midst of nearly continuous, humanly overwhelming hardships and difficulties? He could do this because He believed Jesus, who said:

"My Grace is sufficient for you, for (My) power is perfected in (your) weakness (times of hardships, trials and human suffering). Most gladly,

therefore, I will rather boast about my weaknesses, that the power of Christ may dwell in me. Therefore, I am well content with weaknesses, with insults, with distresses, with persecution, with difficulties, for Christ's sake; for when I am weak, then I am strong (in Christ's strength that now dwells in me) (2 Cor. 12:9-10).

Paul had learned the secret of the victorious Grace-empowered "exchanged life". By faith, Paul received the victory of Christ. And the *all-sufficient, overcoming power* of that victory became Paul's victory…*in whatever circumstance He was in (Phil. 4:11-12).* Because Paul knew that the victory had already been won, it really didn't matter what happened to him on the outside. God would cause everything to *work together for good* through the power of His Grace—even His weaknesses, his hardships, his failures, his disappointments—everything!

What an example Paul is for all of us! We need to ask God each and every day to enable us, through the Holy Spirit—who is now the power of Christ in us (Col. 1:27; John 14:16)—to live our lives, as Paul consistently did, *by faith,* in confident assurance of God's glorious, all-sufficient, joy-producing Grace: when I'm weak, He is strong; when I am discouraged, He is my encouragement; when I am sad, He is my joy; when I think I just can't go on, He lifts me and carries me (2 Cor. 12:9-10; Deut. 31:7; 2 Chron. 32:7-8; John 7:38, 17:13; Is. 46:3-4). As we manifest this kind of trusting confidence, the world receives a powerful witness and we become a lot happier people—less apt to grumble and complain and a lot more eager to *rejoice always (Phil.2:14, 4:4).*

What then shall we say?…If God is for us, who (can be) against us? He who did not spare His own Son, but delivered Him up for us all, how will He not also with Him freely give us all things (Rom. 8:31-32).

That is what grace is all about; it is the undeserved, unmerited favor of God that gives and gives and gives…and gives again. GRACE is divinely powerful and inexhaustible to the one who receives it *by faith,* sincerely placing His trust in Jesus, then walking in that same trusting faith and overcoming power day by day (2 Cor. 10:4; 2 Pet. 1:4).

Who shall separate us from the love of Christ?… Shall tribulation, or distress, or persecution, or famine… or peril, or sword?…But in all these things we overwhelmingly conquer through Him who loved us, and gave Himself up for us (Rom. 8:31-37, sel.; Eph. 5:2).

Amazing GRACE! How sweet the sound, that saved a wretch like me!
I once was lost, but now am found, was blind, but now I see.

Through many dangers, toils and snares, I have already come;
'Tis GRACE hath brought me safe thus far, and GRACE will lead me home.

The Lord has promised good to me; His Word my hope secures
He will my shield and portion be, as long as life endures.

When we've been there ten thousand years, bright shining as the sun,
We've no less days to sing God's praise, than when we first begun.

John Newton (1725-1807)

Bible Study Supplement
Chapter 4 — Day 5 — The Inexhaustible Supply of Faith – Grace
Amazing Grace, How Sweet the Sound.

One of the most precious attributes of God for all of us who struggle with weaknesses and failure is His unconditional, unmerited, inexhaustible *Grace.*

Note: In the Old Testament, Grace is referred to as God's *unmerited favor, goodness, compassion, lovingkindness, and tender mercies.*

1. Read Lam.3:22-23.

    a. What is "great"/never ceases? (vs. 22a)

    b. What is new and fresh every morning? (vs. 22b, 23a)

    c. What else is "great"? (vs. 23b)

2. Read Rom. 5:1-2.

    a. What do we have since we have been justified by faith? (vs. 1)

    b. Based upon verse 2, fill in the blanks in the following sentence:
    Through (Jesus), we have gained access (our introduction) _____ _____ *into the* _____ *in which we now stand.*

3. Read Ps. 103:8-18.

    a. List four core attributes of the Lord. (vs. 8)

    b. How has He <u>not</u> dealt with us? (vs. 10)

    c. How great is the Lord's lovingkindness...and to <u>whom</u> is it freely extended? (vs. 11)

    d. How does God treat those who fear Him? (vs. 13a)

    e. Of what is God mindful? (vs. 14b)

    f. How long does the lovingkindness of the Lord last? (vs. 17a)

    g. To whom is this promise given? (to those who…three characteristics - vs. 17-18)

4. Read 2 Cor. 12:9-10.

a. What can we be assured will <u>always</u> be sufficient for us? (vs. 9)

b. What is made perfect in weakness?... Whose power is this? (note: God is speaking - vs. 9)

c. Therefore with what can we, like Paul, be content (delight in) and why? (vs. 10)

5. Read James 4:6.
   a. To what/whom is God opposed?

   b. To whom does he give GRACE?

Here we find the heart of the message of God's GRACE: *God <u>opposes the proud</u>, but .<u>gives GRACE to the humble</u>.* Jesus, Himself, reiterated this precious truth in the Sermon on the Mount: *Blessed are the meek (humble), for they shall inherit the earth (Math. 5:5).* Throughout Scripture this truth is proclaimed: God gives GRACE to those who realize that they are poor, sinful, needy people who cannot make it in this world without Him—without salvation, without the truths and promises of His precious Word and without the power of His Spirit working in them through God's manifold GRACE.

6. Read John 1:14-16.
   a. Of what was the Word (Jesus) full? (vs. 14b)

   b. What have we received? (vs. 16b) From where have these wonderful gifts come? (vs. 16a)

A favorite scripture of mine regarding this wonderful, matchless gift of GRACE is found in Rom. 5.

7. Read Rom. 5:20.
   a. According to God's wonderful economy of GRACE, what happens when sin increases?

What a beautiful promise! What love, what mercy, what riches…What GRACE!

G - R - A - C - E: What does it mean? _____ _____ _____ _____
_____

Thank God today for His AMAZING GRACE!

Write out a Bible verse that had special meaning to you today.

Based upon what you have learned today, write a prayer to God expressing the desires of your heart in applying these truths to your life.

Chapter 5

Bible Memory Verse: *Watch over your heart with all diligence for from it flows the wellsprings of life (Prov. 4:23).*

Bonus Memory Verse: *Do not be conformed to this world, but be transformed by the renewing of your mind (Rom. 12:2a).*

Day 1

The Heart/Mind Connection

Watch over your Heart – Renew Your Mind

Day 2

The Problem of Pride/The Joy of Discipline

Day 3

Holy, Holy, Holy

Day 4

The Surprising Side of Holy Love

God's Righteous Wrath

Day 5

Remnant Blessings!

God Always Has His Remnant...

Chapter 5 — Day 1
The Heart/Mind Connection

Watch over your heart with all diligence for from it flows the wellsprings of life (Prov. 4:23).

I urge you therefore, brethren, by the mercies of God, to present your bodies a living and holy sacrifice, acceptable to God, which is your spiritual service of worship; and do not be conformed to this world, but be <u>transformed</u> by the <u>renewing</u> <u>of your mind</u>, that you may prove what the will of God is, that which is good and acceptable and perfect (Rom. 12:1-2).

The Lord said to Samuel, "Do not look at his appearance or the height of his stature... for God sees not as man sees, for man looks at the outward appearance, but the Lord looks at the heart" (1 Sam. 16:7).

I'm so thankful that God looks at the heart and not at the outward appearance, aren't you? But I think we forget that so often and we spend far more time and energy being concerned about how we appear on the outside while neglecting that part of us that is of far greater value—having the potential to bring joy and peace, or conflict and turmoil to our lives—our heart. For truly, just as the Word says, from our heart flows the *wellsprings of life (Prov. 4:23)*. If the heart is pure—through genuine confession and repentance (2 Cor. 7:10)—then filled with godly wisdom and truth from God's Word, and yielded to the Holy Spirit's control and empowerment, even in times of physical, mental, or emotional trials and difficulties the *good treasure* that has been stored away will flow through us and out of us.

...how can you, being evil, speak what is good? For the mouth speaks out of that which fills the heart. The good man out of his good treasure brings forth what is good; and the evil man out of his evil treasure brings forth what is evil (Matt. 12:34-35).

What fills our hearts will spill out into lives through the words we say, the way we treat others

and the way we respond to various life situations, including trials and difficulties. It is God's desire that our hearts be a continual flow of "good treasures"—both within and without. That is why He urges:

Watch over your heart with all diligence, for from it flow the wellsprings of life (Prov. 4:23).

Early in my Christian walk, I memorized this verse and I asked God to help me do this every day: to keep my heart cleansed and pure, filled with godly wisdom and truth, and yielded to the Holy Spirit's control. By doing so I would be prepared and empowered to walk through my day in faithful, trusting obedience. I soon learned that having a cleansed and purified heart is especially important when I am tired, having a really difficult, painful day or feeling overwhelmed from pressing needs and responsibilities. These times of weakness and stress make me all the more vulnerable to the lies and deceptions of Satan, and also to my own sinful, fleshly lusts. God knew there would be *days like that.* That's why He further encourages us:

We shall know by this that we are of the truth, and shall assure our heart before Him, in whatever our heart condemns us; for <u>God is greater than our heart, and knows all things</u>. Beloved, if our heart does not condemn us, we have confidence before God (1 John 3:19-21).

This verse was especially precious to me as a young, fledgling Christian when my own stubborn selfish desires and fleshly lusts kept me so often from obeying God in a totally surrendered way, and, consequently, the failures came much more frequently than the victories. But I was comforted (and continue to be) by this verse. I did love God and I was trying to be a faithful, trusting child, walking in obedience to the Holy Spirit as He led me in fulfilling God's good plans for my life each day. So on those difficult days when I didn't get it right, fell and sinned, I felt the comfort of this promise: *God knows my heart.* As I sincerely repented of my sin, the assurance of God's forgiveness and inexhaustible mercy and grace flowed into my languishing heart bringing a renewed sense of purity, peace, and joy.

> *From the same mouth come both blessing and cursing. My brethren, these things ought not to be. Does a fountain send out from the same opening both fresh and bitter water? Can a fig tree produce olives, or a vine produce figs? Neither can salt water produce fresh (James 3:10-12).*

Here, God gives us another verse that graphically reminds us that our tongues will always reveal what is in our hearts. If blessing and cursing are coming out of the same mouth, we need to pay attention and realize that we have a very serious *heart* problem. We need to seek all the more diligently the Holy Spirit's enlightenment and conviction that will lead to genuine repentance, so that our hearts will be filled with fresh, sweet water that glorifies God and encourages and builds up others.

One day as I was praying about this, asking God how I could better *watch over my heart,* the Holy Spirit began to bring to mind a number of verses about the importance of *renewing the mind* daily with the truths of Scripture. I began to see the inseparable link between the heart and the mind. The Bible actually uses the heart and mind interchangeably often because what goes into our minds invariably makes its way quickly into the heart, so if we are to obey the command to *watch over our hearts,* we must first *watch over our minds,* being very careful what we put into them.

> *For as a man <u>thinks</u> within himself, <u>so is he</u> (Prov. 23:7)*

God's Word warns us here that we will *become* what we *think about*—what we allow our minds to *dwell upon.* So we need to heed God's good exhortation in Romans 12 carefully:

> *I urge you therefore, brethren, by the mercies of God, to present your bodies a living and holy sacrifice, acceptable to God, which is your spiritual service of worship. <u>And do not be conformed to this world,</u> but <u>be transformed</u> by the <u>renewing of your mind,</u> that you may prove what the will of God is, that which is good and acceptable and perfect (Rom. 12:1-2).*

The Greek Word translated *conformed* here is *suschematizo* and actually means to *squeeze into a mold.* In other words, we must not allow the world to squeeze us into its mold of corrupt, lustful, ungodly thinking and practices, but rather *be transformed* by the *renewing of our minds* according to the truths of Scripture so that our heart and behavior will reflect the righteousnesss of Jesus. When we set our hearts upon doing this, God promises that we will know and we will *do* the will of God—proving that His will is always <u>good and perfect</u>.

So how can we do this? How can we continually *renew our minds* so that our hearts will remain pure and righteous and we will begin to much more consistently resist the temptations of *the devil, the world and our own sinful flesh,* bringing ever more glory to God, and joy to our own hearts and to the lives of others (John 15:11)?

> *Finally, brethren, whatever is true, whatever is honorable, whatever is right, whatever is pure, whatever is lovely, whatever is of good repute, if there is any excellence, and if anything worthy of praise, <u>let your mind dwell on these things</u>. The things that you have learned and heard and seen in me, practice these things; and the God of peace shall be with you (Phil. 4:8-9).*

I was greatly convicted after several readings of these verses, so I went through my house taking inventory of my collection of books, magazine subscriptions, and teaching tapes. I held each one up to the Phil. 4:8 test. Are the contents of this book, magazine, teaching tape *true, honorable, right, pure (undefiled by worldly thinking/philosophies), lovely… excellent, and worthy of praise?*

> *And many… brought their books together and began burning them in the sight of all; and… the price of them (was) fifty thousand pieces of silver (Acts 19:19).*

Following the good example of these faithful, committed new Christians in Ephesus, I actually gathered and burned a number of books that were tainted with worldly thinking and deception. I was especially concerned with those books that stood blatantly against the *authority* and *sufficiency* of God's Word—adding to it, or taking away from it. I did not want anything to do with them and I did not want them in my house defiling it with *unbiblical worthlessness (Ps. 101:3).* So that got rid of a lot of material that was a great distraction and a barrier to my developing *the mind of Christ* and a pure and holy heart.

NOTE! I am not saying here that everyone must burn books in order to be in God's will regarding renewing the mind. God doesn't bring the same convictions to every person's heart. I only mention this example to show the importance of <u>obedience</u> in our fight against sin. Only God knows what is best for each of us and what we need to do to rid our lives of those things that ensnare us, keep us from fulfilling God's good purposes, and from experiencing the freedom and joy Jesus came to give us (Gal. 5:1; John 15:11). So we need to be careful to *listen* and *obey* as the Holy Spirit leads us.

Another thing that I did (and continue to do) to insure that my mind is ever thinking on the things of God, was to listen to good Bible-teaching tapes as I prepared meals, ironed, did my housework, or traveled by car. I literally did not let anything *enter my mind* that did not pass the Phil. 4:8 test.

At the close of the day, just before our evening Bible reading and prayer, as often as I could, I also read biographies of great men and women of faith or other excellent books on Christian life and ministry. This good practice continues as an excellent source of renewing my mind and increasing my desire for holiness.

When I think of this important matter of *guarding our heart/mind* at all times, I am drawn to the encouraging example of David in the Bible. Even though David, at one sad, tragic point in his life, left the path of righteousness in pursuit of his own fleshly lusts and became an adulterer, a liar and a murderer, yet God calls him: *a man after (My) own heart, who will do My will (Acts 13:22; 1 Sam. 13:14).* David sincerely repented of his terrible sins and from that point on, He remained loyal to God, intent at all times on knowing and doing the will of God. Consequently, God often lifted David up as a godly example, praising him: *And I, the Lord, will be their God, and My servant David will be prince among them (Ezek. 34:24).* Whenever we go to the psalms we get a glimpse of David's sincere *heart for God.* David was keenly aware at all times of the fact that he, like all of us, had a fallen sinful heart and that he was, therefore, ever dependent upon the cleansing, purifying mercy and grace of God. He maintained a spirit of humble contrition, teachableness, and obedience. I believe that this is the kind of *heart* God loves to see—and bless—in His children.

Listen for just a moment to David's God-centered, dependent, trusting heart:

> *The Lord is my shepherd, I shall not want. He makes me lie down in green pasture; He leads me beside still waters. He restoreth my soul; He leads me in the paths of righteousness for His Name's sake (Ps. 23:1-3, KJV).*

> *I will walk within my house in the integrity of my heart. I will set no worthless thing before my eyes (Ps. 101:2-3).*

> *…one thing I have asked, from the Lord that <u>I will seek</u>; That I may <u>dwell in the house of the Lord</u>* (in an ongoing awareness of His loving, holy presence), *all the days of my life, to behold the beauty of the Lord, and to meditate in His Holy temple; for in the day of trouble He will conceal me in the secret place of His tent;… He will lift me up on a rock. And my head will be lifted above my enemies around me; And I will offer in His tent sacrifices with shouts of joy; I will sing, yes, I will sing praises to the Lord (Ps. 27:4-6).*

Bible Study Supplement
Chapter 5 — Day 1 — The Heart/Mind Connection
Watch Over Your Heart - Renew Your Mind

1. Read Prov. 4:20-27.

   a. To what are we to give attention? (vs. 20)

   b. What are we to do with the truths of God's Word? (two things - vs. 21)

   c. What will God's precious truths and promises provide? (two things - vs. 22)

   d. What are we to do above all else (with all diligence)—and why? (vs. 23)

   e. What are we to be careful <u>to do</u> and <u>not</u> to do with our "feet"? (vs. 26-27)

2. Read 1 Chron. 22:19a.

   a. What did David instruct the people to do? (19a)

3. Read 1 Chron. 29:16-18.

   a. From whom did "all this abundance" come to build a temple for God? (vs. 16)

   b. What did David <u>know</u>? (two things - vs. 17a)

   c. What kind of attitude did David/the people have regarding giving to the Lord? (vs. 17b)

   d. What did David pray that the Lord would do in the hearts of the people? (vs. 18b – very last part of verse).

It's a good prayer for us also as we begin each new day: "Keep our hearts loyal/directed to Thee".

4. Read Luke 6:43-45.

   a. What can a bad tree (bad heart) not produce? (vs. 43b)

   b. How will each tree (man) be known? (vs. 44a)

   c. From where does the *good man* bring forth *good fruit?*...and the *evil man, bad fruit?* (vs. 45)

   d. Note again the importance of what we put into our hearts. From what do our mouths speak? (vs. 45b)

In Proverbs 16:2 we are told that God *weighs the motives* of our hearts. God is much more concerned about *why* we do what we do than merely *what* we do. God is always looking for a tender heart that loves Him and desires to live in a manner pleasing to Him. Such a person will faithfully <u>do</u> what is right because his heart is right. He has yielded His heart to the Holy Spirit's control who now "fills" Him with God's wisdom and truth and enables him to walk in a righteous, godly way.

The Bible clearly teaches the importance of *guarding* our *heart and mind.* This means that we are to be careful about what we allow to <u>enter</u> our mind and also what we choose to <u>dwell upon</u>.

5. Read Rom. 8:5-6.

    a. What do those who are living according to the flesh *set their minds on?* (vs. 5a)

    b. What do those who are living according to the Spirit *set their minds on?* (vs. 5b)

    c. What will be the result for the one whose mind is *set on the flesh?* (vs. 6a)

    d. What will be the result for the one whose mind is *set on* (controlled by) *the Spirit?* (vs. 6b)

Some of the most practical and powerful verses in all the Word of God that will help us focus upon the things of the Spirit and not the things of the flesh are found in the fourth chapter of Philippians.

6. Read Phil. 4:8-9.

    a. What are we to think on (dwell on)? (eight characteristics – vs. 8)

    b. If we faithfully <u>practice</u> this, what does Paul say will happen? (vs. 9b)

7. Read Ps. 101:2-3a.

    a. How does David walk in his house? (vs. 2b)

    b. What does he purposely decide that he will <u>not</u> do? (vs. 3a)

It is wise to periodically take inventory of our homes...and our hearts. Are there *worthless/vile* books, tapes, magazines, television programs that would never pass the Phil. 4:8 and Rom. 8:5-6 test? Things that will dull our sense of godly wisdom and discernment and our pursuit of holiness, making our hearts and minds vulnerable to the devil's lies and deceptions? I know that you, like me, want to have the *mind of Christ,* that we might have the *heart of Christ* that faithfully produces the *good fruits of Christ.* In so doing, we bring honor and glory to Him and joy and peace to our own lives, spilling over into the lives of others.

Write out a Bible verse that had special meaning to you today.

Based upon what you have learned today, write a prayer to God expressing the desires of your heart in applying these truths to your life.

Chapter 5 — Day 2
The Problem of Pride/The Joy of Discipline

> *My son, do not regard lightly the discipline of the Lord, nor faint when you are reproved by Him, for whom the Lord loves, He disciplines (Heb. 12:5-6).*

iscipline. For most of us, the word conjures up less than happy thoughts. We want the love of God. We want the blessings of God. We want the peace and joy of God. But we don't want the discipline of God. That is really sad, because without godly discipline, there would be no change, no victory over our sinful nature, and thus, no real or lasting love, peace or joy. We would continue on in the same destructive, rebellious sinful state into which we were born, suffering the inevitable, agonizing consequences. And God loves us too much to allow that to happen.

All discipline for the moment seems not to be joyful, but sorrowful; yet to those who have been trained by it, afterwards it yields the peaceful fruit of righteousness (Heb. 12:11).

As I was preparing this lesson on godly discipline, I was reminded once again of those early years of my Christian walk in which stubbornness and rebellion ruled my heart with an iron fist. The rebellion was so strong that I often refused the chastening hand of God when it was lovingly necessary to bring me to a place of obedience that I might begin to experience and reflect those blessed *fruits of righteousness and peace (Heb. 12:11; Gal. 5:22).* As we have learned throughout this study, sin—especially habitual sin—always results in a hardening of the heart to the things of God. And

hardness of heart causes spiritual blindness. I could not recognize the selfishness and pride in my heart that fostered the rebellious spirit and caused me to lash out in vehement protest against the discipline of God. I hated it, as was documented in my quiet time journals in which the letters of my seething, daily railings against God's *injustice* were often expressed in angry, inch-high letters, scribbled heavily and nearly illegibly. And the saddest part of it all was that the stubborn, resistant pride drove me to spend more time and energy *fighting the discipline of God than fighting the awful sin in my life that necessitated it!* That serious, tragic error resulted in years of incalculable pain and suffering that I brought upon myself and those I cared about the most, not to mention the irreverence and reproach to God's holy Name it caused. So many wasted years...and tears! Oh, the price we pay for rebellion against God's loving hand of discipline!

At the core of any hard heart that is resistant to divine discipline is an arrogant self-centered PRIDE. Like Lucifer of old, it is a pride that *raises itself above the Throne of God* proclaiming, "I know what I want, and I will have what I want, when I want it, and as much as I want! I will be my own 'god'. I will be *in control.*" The Bible is full of warnings against pride because it always fosters a selfish, rebellious spirit and will—nevertheless Lord, not <u>Thy</u> will but <u>mine</u> be done! It was selfish pride that led to the downfall of the first man and woman and it is that same pride today that is at the heart of so much of our destructive sinful habits.

> *What is the source of quarrels and conflicts among you? Is not the source your pleasures that wage war? You lust and do not have; so you commit murder* (lashing out at others, causing them pain and destroying your relationship with them...and God). *And you are envious and cannot obtain; so you fight and quarrel. You ask and do not receive, because you ask with wrong motives, so that you may spend it on your pleasures (James 4:1-3).*

Only the discipline of God can break such a resistant, selfish spirit. We do well to heed the Bible's good instruction about this often neglected subject. God knows what selfish pride leads to every time and He loves us too much to allow it to continue to destroy us and those we love.

> *God is opposed to the proud, but gives grace to the humble. Submit therefore to God. Resist the <u>devil</u>* (not the good discipline of God)... *Draw near to God and He will draw near to you. Cleanse your hands, you sinners; and purify your hearts, you double minded...humble yourselves in the presence of the Lord and He will exalt you (James 4:6-10 sel.).*

The purpose of godly discipline is to humble us, that we might yield our heart, our mind and our will completely to the Holy Spirit's control. And in so doing, be strengthened in our new, godly nature. When the Holy Spirit is in control of our thoughts and will, we will begin to have godly thoughts and walk in victory over our destructive sinful nature.

> *...that you might become partakers of the divine nature, having escaped the corruption that is in the world by lust (2 Pet. 1:4).*

Only those who consistently master the flesh with its sinful lusts and passions through humbly yielding to godly discipline when needed *(learning obedience – Heb. 5:8)* can enter such a blessed state.

> *Behold, how happy is the man whom God reproves, so do not despise the discipline of the Almighty...(for) you have not yet resisted to the point of shedding blood in your striving against sin; and have you forgotten the exhortation which is addressed to you as sons, My son, do not regard lightly the discipline of the Lord, nor faint* (or rebel) *when you are reproved by Him; for... whom the Lord loves He disciplines (Job 5:17; Heb.12:4-6).*

> *It is for discipline that you endure; God deals with you as with sons; for what son is there whom his father does not discipline? But if you are without discipline, of which all have become partakers, then you are illegitimate children and not sons (Heb. 12:7-8).*

Godly discipline is proof of our *sonship.* We should never resist it, but welcome it with a thankful and grateful heart that we are God's children and He *loves us enough to discipline us* so that we will learn to resist the devil and the sinful lusts in our heart that lead only to pain, destruction, and death.

> *Furthermore, we had earthly fathers to discipline us, and we respected them; shall we not much rather be subject to the Father... and live? For they disciplined us for a short time as seemed best to them, but He disciplines us <u>for our good</u>, that we may <u>share His holiness</u> (Heb. 12:9-10).*

> *All discipline for the moment seems not to be joyful, but sorrowful; yet to those who have been trained by it, afterwards it yields the peaceful fruit of righteousness. Therefore, strengthen the hands that are weak and the knees that are feeble (Heb. 12:11-12).*

Bible Study Supplement
Chapter 5 — Day 2 — The Problem of Pride/The JOY of Discipline

1. Read Deut. 8:1-6.

   a. What are the people to remember? (vs. 2a)

   b. What was God's purpose in leading them to/through the wilderness/desert? (four things - 2b)

   c. What else did God want them to learn/understand? (vs. 3b)

   d. What are the people to know in their hearts? (vs. 5)

   e. What was God's purpose in His loving discipline? (that they might…three things - vs. 6)

God goes on to explain in verses 7-9, that if they will be careful to do these things—*observe the commands of the Lord, walk in His ways and reverence Him*—He will lead them into a *good land of springs in the valley and hills… a land of wheat and barley, vines and figs… a land flowing with olive oil and honey… where their bread will never be scarce* and they will *lack nothing.* Such is His promise in the New Testament also for every redeemed child who, through godly discipline, gladly and joyfully *obeys the commands of the Lord, walks in His ways and reverences Him (Phil. 4:19; Eph. 1:18-21, 3:20; John 7:38).*

2. Read Ps. 94:12-14, 18-19.

   a. Who is blessed? (two qualities - vs. 12)

   b. What will be his reward? (vs. 13a)

   c. What does God promise never to do? (two things - vs. 14)

   d. What upheld the psalmist even when his foot slipped? (vs. 18)

   e. What delights his soul (brings joy) even when anxious thoughts threaten to undo him? (vs. 19)

The psalmist is saying that he knows that God is with him at all times through the precious peace and comfort (consolation) He gives him. He remembers that God has always been faithful to His promises in the past, bringing him through every trial and difficulty victoriously. He also recalls the good discipline God worked in him through the trials that have made him stronger, purer, and more secure. Because of all these things, there is comfort and joy deep within his soul—regardless of his outward circumstances.

3. Read Prov. 23:12-14.

   a. To what are we to apply our heart…our ears? (vs. 12)

b. What are we not to withhold from our children? (vs. 13)

c. Why? (vs. 14b)

The Bible has much to say about the discipline of children. We, as parents and grandparents, do well to heed this—for the sake of their happiness and security here on earth as well as for the eternal destiny of their precious souls.

4. Read Heb. 2:10 and Heb. 5:8.

a. How did Jesus, the Son of God, *learn* obedience?

If it was necessary for Jesus to *learn obedience* through suffering (hardships and godly discipline), how much more we rebellious, sinful mortals!

The Bible clearly teaches that discipline always yields sweet, blessed rewards—<u>if</u> we embrace it with thanksgiving and allow it to achieve God's good purifying, fortifying purposes in us.

5. Read 1 Tim. 4:7-8.

a. For what purpose are we to discipline/train ourselves? (vs. 7b)

b. Which is more profitable – bodily discipline or godly discipline? Why? (vs. 8)

The Bible gives clear warnings against those who spurn the discipline of the Lord. In Zeph. 3, we are given a classic example of a rebellious spirit that refuses to accept the discipline of God.

6. Read Zeph. 3:1-2 in the NSAB below:

1. Woe to her who is rebellious and defiled…

2. She heeded no voice; She accepted no instruction. She did not trust in the Lord; She did not draw near to her God (Zeph. 3:1-2).

a.   List four characteristics of those who choose a path of rebellion, rejecting God's good discipline. (vs. 2)

7. Read Jer. 5:2-3.

a. What did the rebellious people refuse to do? (three things – vs. 3b)

As we are reminded here once again, whenever we spurn or rebel against the good discipline of the Lord, our hearts become hard and all the more stubborn and resistant to godly change in the future. This is a very dangerous condition, because hard hearts cut off communication and instruction from God, leaving us separated from Him and in the hands and power of the devil. May God help us to keep our hearts tender and teachable, gladly embracing His loving hand of discipline when needed, that we might *grow up*, becoming strong, steadfast men and women of God who radiate and reflect the *beauty of holiness (Heb. 12:10; Ps. 29:2, KJV).*

8. Read Prov. 3:11-12.

    a. What are we warned not to despise (reject), or resent? (vs. 11a)

    b. What does the Lord do for those he loves?…To what/whom is God likened here? (vs. 12)

Though we won't have time to look it up today, there is another beautiful promise in Is. 29:17-24 that tells of the reward of blessing and joy after discipline. It states that, *in a little while,* all those who embrace God's loving hand of discipline and learn the valuable lessons He teaches them through it…*will be given wisdom and discernment* and *will no longer err in mind* because they will *know the truth* and will continue to have a teachable spirit, accepting instruction and growing in purity, strength and godliness.

The classic Scripture dealing with the high value God places upon godly discipline is found in Hebrews 12. We will review it briefly here today, but it would be of tremendous benefit to return to this text often in the future. It will greatly encourage and fill our hearts with joy in knowing the *good fruit* that times of testing and godly discipline produce.

  9. Read Heb. 12:4-13.

    a. What warning is given here to those who never experience God's discipline? (vs. 8)

    b. Why does God discipline us? (vs. 10b)

    c. What does godly discipline produce in those who gladly accept it and learn from it? (11b)

Note: The *peaceful fruit of righteousness* includes all the precious *fruit of the Spirit*—love, joy, peace, patience, kindness, goodness, faithfulness, self-control.

    d. In light of all these things, what are we to do? (vs. 12)

It has been accurately said that the adversity of discipline will do one of two things, depending upon the attitude of the heart. It will make us bitter…or better. If we rebel against it, it will harden our hearts further, making them even more resistant to the voice of God—His guidance and instruction. If, on the other hand, we welcome it and embrace it for the good God wants to produce in us through it, it will break the pride and stubbornness within our hearts and make us humble, gentle and malleable in the hands of the Holy Spirit to do His perfecting work in us. As a result we will become much more stable, fruitful, happy people whose hearts are pure and at peace. I pray that God will help all of us to keep an open and teachable spirit that gladly welcomes the discipline of God, cooperating with the Holy Spirit as He accomplishes God's good and holy purposes through it.

Write out a Bible verse that had special meaning to you today.

Based upon what you have learned today, write a prayer to God expressing the desires of your heart in applying these truths to your life.

Chapter 5 — Day 3
Holy, Holy, Holy

Holy, Holy, Holy, is the Lord God Almighty, who was and is and is to come...the whole earth is full of His glory...The Lord is high above all nations; His glory is above the heavens...Worthy art Thou O, Lord, our God, to receive glory and honor and power for Thou hast created all things...when I consider Thy heavens, the work of Thy fingers, the moon and the stars, which Thou has ordained; what is man, that Thou dost take thought of him? (Rev. 4:8; Is. 6:3; Ps. 113:4; Rev. 4:11; Ps. 8:3).

One of the most tragic results of our modern cheap grace, easy believism Christianity with its laissez-faire, worldly tolerance-driven "gospel", is a blatant disregard for the flawless righteous, sin-hating, wickedness-consuming holiness of God. Such a disregard inevitably results in an idolatrous worship of a false image of God—a "god" (and usually many "gods") of our own making, not the God of the Bible. Any such "god" is powerless and cannot save. The reality of this is confirmed by the sad condition of the body of Christ today: broken hearts, broken homes, broken churches. Surveys indicate that the divorce rate among those who profess to be Christians is actually slightly higher than that of the general public who make no claim to Christianity. *My brethren, these things ought not to be! (James 3:10b).* Even more grievous is the broken witness and reproach such a sad state of affairs brings to the precious name of God—His mercy, grace, saving/keeping power... and *holiness.*

May God help us to recognize the seriousness of this problem, that we might seek to know this aspect of God's nature—His holiness—just as we have come to know His love, mercy and grace. For if we fail to do this, it is inevitable that we will drift away from the one and only true God (Is. 43:10-11), and begin to worship false "gods" that cannot help, save, or keep us from sin and its deadly, destructive consequences.

What does it mean that God is Holy?

"Holy" comes from the Greek word "hagios" which means transcendent, unique, totally and utterly separated from sin; morally and spiritually perfect; flawlessly righteous; sacred.

The glory of God is the ultimate expression of perfect, transcendent holiness. God's holiness is also expressed through His perfect love and perfect justice. Sin marred that expression bringing with it destruction and death. *God is love (1 John 4:8).* Holy, perfect love cannot embrace that which destroys—as sin always does! That is why holiness cannot look upon sin with impunity. In jealous protection, holy love must bring judgment against that which is unholy—that which destroys. Failure to do so would result in the defilement of the pure, the holy. Such corruption would continue to spread and eventually destroy all that is good. That is what the cross is all about. Through His sacrificial death, Jesus stopped that encroachment of sin by taking upon Himself the judgment (payment) that sin required (death). Then, through His resurrection, Jesus rose victoriously over sin, defeating it's destructive power and making a way for all who put their faith in Him to be restored to righteousness... to *be holy*—sins forgiven and clothed in the perfect, holy righteousness of Jesus (2 Cor. 5:21). If we are to walk in the full blessing of who we are *in Christ*—holy, victorious over sin's destructive power—we must keep in mind these facts:

1. God is holy. God's holiness manifests itself in perfect love. Holy, perfect love cannot embrace or fellowship with that which is unholy—defiled by sin, destructive.

2. *Sin* brings suffering and death. *The wages of sin is death (Rom. 6:23).* Sin—rebellion against God and His holy, protective law—always results in death: death to our innocence (guilt), death to our joy, death in our relationships with others, and, most tragically, separation from God (Is. 59:2). Sin cost Adam and Eve rejection from the glorious paradise of Eden. It also cost them their physical lives. Even more grievous, *sin cost God the death of His only, beloved (holy) Son (John 3:16).*

3. *Sin,* through it's various means of deception—satanic lies and our own sin-corrupted fallen nature—continues to wreak havoc upon the world and sadly, upon far too many of God's children, robbing them of the blessings and joy of righteous, holy living. Those who practice habitual sin forfeit the intimate fellowship with God and one another that God created them to enjoy.

4. *But God demonstrates His own love toward us, in that while we were yet sinners, Christ died for us (Rom. 5:8).* Into the darkness of this bad news of sin and it's terrible consequences comes the light of the *good news* of the Gospel. God has given us the remedy for the devastating problem of sin. That remedy is repentance and faith in Jesus' sacrificial death on the cross and victorious resurrection from the dead; then, *by faith,* living out Jesus' victory as a redeemed, set-free child of God.

5. True repentance, and victorious living thereafter, always involve a faithful devotion to the Word of God, for it is only God's holy, undefiled Word that is able to cut through the deception of sin's allurements and expose them for what they are—destructive lies—then give us the wisdom and the power, through the Holy Spirit, to overcome them!

Everyone who practices sin, practices lawlessness; and sin is lawlessness. And you know that He appeared in order to take away sins; and in Him there is no sin. No one who abides in Him sins (habitually); no one who (habitually) sins has seen Him or knows Him. Little children, let no one deceive you; the one who practices sin is of the devil; for the devil has sinned from the beginning. The Son of God appeared for this purpose, that He might destroy the works of the devil. No one who is born of God practices sin because His seed abides in him; and he cannot (continue on in habitual) sin, because he is born of God. By this the children of God and the children of the devil are obvious; anyone who does not practice righteousness is not of God (1 John 3:4-10a).

Do you hear what God is saying to us here? He is saying that a brand new, redeemed, sanctified seed of Jesus' *holiness* was planted in our hearts the very moment we accepted Him as our Lord and Savior. It is that seed that God nurtures and grows and brings to fruition as we come to know Him and love Him through the truths of His Word and prayer. It is also through this process that we become *partakers of His divine nature (2 Pet. 1:4).*

Seeing that His divine power has granted to us <u>everything</u> pertaining to life and godliness, <u>through the true knowledge of Him</u> who called us by His own glory and excellence. For by these (the divine power of the Holy Spirit within us and the truths of the Word of God) He has granted to us His precious and magnificent promises, in order that by them you might become partakers of the divine nature, having escaped the corruption that is in the world by lust … Therefore, gird your minds for action, keep sober in spirit… As obedient children, do not be conformed to the former lusts which were yours in your ignorance, but like the Holy One who called you, be holy yourselves also in all your behavior; for it is written, "You shall be holy, for I am holy" (2 Pet. 1:3-4; 1 Pet. 1:13-16, sel.).

More good news! God promises us in these verses that He has given all that we need—through the truths of His Word and the power of the Holy Spirit within us—to become *partakers of Jesus' divine nature*—holy and victorious over sin. We no longer sin because we *have to*. We sin because we *choose to*, through willful rebellion. He goes on in this passage, and many other related passages, to assure us that it is God's will that His children be *more than conquerors* over sin and its destructive consequences (Rom. 8:37). As we place our trust in God and His grace to help us each day, then walk in obedience as He leads us—through His Word and the Holy Spirit in us—we are given the wisdom and power we need to stand strong against sin, overcoming its temptations and trials in our lives. And we, and our loved ones, enjoy the blessed fruit of *righteousness, peace and joy in the Holy Spirit (Rom. 14:17).*

> *For whatever is born of God overcomes the world (the worldly temptations and enticements of sin) (1 John 5:4).*

Here is yet another wonderful promise that confirms what we have just studied. In this verse, we are told that all redeemed children of God have already been given the power to confidently and consistently overcome sin. I long for that! Don't you?

If God wants that, and we want that, and God says that He has already given us the power to consistently *do it*, why do we still so often lead lives of failure and quiet desperation? Why can we not bring down the *sin strongholds* that yet reign over our lives? Why can we not *put off* those obsessions, addictions and all forms of habitual sinning?

> *...and this is the victory that has overcome the world... our faith. So then faith comes by hearing and hearing by the Word of God (1 John 5:5; Rom. 10:17).*

We will only have as much *victory* as we have *faith*. And we will only have as much *faith* as we have *Word of God* abiding in us and being lived out through us in a life of trusting faith and obedience (James 1:22, 25; John 13:17).

> *To you it was shown that you might know that the Lord, He is God; there is no other besides Him. Out of the heavens He let you hear His voice… He personally brought you out of Egypt (bondage) by His great power… Know, therefore, that the Lord, He is God in heaven above and on earth below; there is no other...So you shall keep His statutes and His commandments… that it may go well with you and with your children (Deut. 4:35-40).*

> *Oh that they had such a heart in them, that they would fear Me, and keep My commandments ...that it may be well with them, and with their sons forever! (Deut 5:29).*

One of the most precious passages on the beauty and power of holiness in all the Bible is found in Isaiah 6.

> *In the year of King Uzziah's death, I saw the Lord sitting on a throne, lofty and exalted, with the train of His robe filling the temple. Seraphim stood above Him...And one called out to another and said, "Holy, Holy, Holy, is the Lord of hosts; the whole earth is full of His glory" (Is. 6:1-3).*

Like Isaiah, we, too, can gaze upon the beauty of God's holiness whenever we open His Word or commune with Him in prayer. And the more we do that—gaze upon His holiness as revealed to us in His Word—the more His majestic, holy glory will purge us of our sinful desires, and we will join the heavenly hosts in unrestrained worship and praise:

> *Holy, holy, holy, is the Lord God Almighty, who was and who is and who is to come... the whole earth is full of His glory…Worthy art Thou, our Lord and our God, to receive glory and honor and power; for Thou didst create all things (Rev. 4:8, 11; Is. 6:3).*

As amazing as it is, the Bible clearly teaches that this great, majestic and holy God, who created this vast, incomprehensible universe in which we live, desires to have a personal, loving, interactive relationship with us! He desires to *dwell among us* and fill our lives with the joy of His presence, peace and blessing. But He is holy. He can't dwell among the unholy—the stubborn and rebellious who *choose* to ignore or reject His loving, protective commands.

> *…what agreement has the temple of God with idols? For we are the temple of the living God, just as God said, "I will dwell in them and walk among them; And I will be their God, and they shall be My people…Therefore, come out from their midst and be separate," says the Lord. "And do not touch what is unclean; And I will welcome you. And I will be a Father to you, and you shall be sons and daughters to Me," says the Lord Almighty (2 Cor. 6:16-18).*

I cannot think of a more precious invitation!

> *The heavens are telling of the glory of God; And their expanse is declaring the work of His hands. Day to day pours forth speech, and night to night reveals knowledge (Ps. 19:2).*

To encourage us as we press on in this glorious journey of holiness that leads to ever increasing righteousness, peace and joy in the Holy Spirit (Rom. 14:17), God gives us glimpses of His majestic, holy glory (that we will enjoy in all its fullness in Heaven one day!), through the *work of His hands:* the splash of color and exquisite beauty of an awe-inspiring sunrise or sunset; a glistening pastel rainbow that stretches across the broad expanse of the sky; the romantic enchantment of a star-studded night; the winsome flight of a brigade of butterflies; the breathtaking glory of a field of wildflowers; a thundering summer storm; a gentle, cascading brook.

When we begin to see God for Who He truly is—*majestic in holiness, awesome in praises, working wonders (Ex. 15:11),* the *things of this world grow strangely dim, in the light of His glory and grace."*[4] And our ridiculous graven idols that we ran to so often, show themselves for what they really are: lifeless, impotent, "gods" who cannot save, deliver, or bring any real, lasting peace or joy (Is. 45:20).

> *But we all, with unveiled face beholding as in a mirror the glory (holiness) of the Lord, are being transformed into the same image from glory to glory (2 Cor. 3:18).*

Bible Study Supplement
Chapter 5 — Day 3 — Holy, Holy, Holy

1. Read Is. 6:1-8.

   a. Describe in detail what Isaiah saw. (vs. 1)

   b. What did the Seraphim cry out to one another? (two things - vs. 3)

   c. Isaiah's first response to seeing God's awesome holiness was one of fear and guilt. He cried: "Woe is me…I am _____". (vs. 5a)

   d. Why? What did Isaiah recognize about himself/his situation? (two things - vs. 5 – middle of verse)

God's loving response to Isaiah's repentance—acknowledgement of his sin and unworthiness before a holy God—was to send the angel of His mercy to touch his lips with a purifying coal of his righteous holiness.

   e. What was the result? (vs. 7b)

Do you see the beautiful symbolism here? The burning coal represents God's purifying holiness which purged Isaiah of his sin. This is exactly what happens when we sincerely confess and repent of our sins: God forgives us and clothes us in the righteousness of Jesus. Just as God, through His mercy and grace declared Isaiah forgiven and released from his sin and guilt, so He also declares us forgiven and released from our sin and guilt every time we come to Him in sincere repentance, *believing* that Jesus' redemptive death on the cross has made atonement—paid the penalty—for our sins, and His glorious resurrection (victory over sin and its power), has raised us up to new life, clothed in the righteousness of Jesus (1 John 1:9; 2 Cor. 5:21).

What a beautiful picture of the <u>holiness</u> and <u>mercy</u> of God. God is so awesome that the manifestation of His shekinah glory (holiness) flowed as a radiant white robe throughout the throne room, *filling it with smoke and causing the foundations to tremble.* Yet, when Isaiah recognized his sinful condition, and repented of his sin, God touched him with the purifying coal of His righteous holiness, cleansing him of His sin and guilt—just as he does for us whenever we come to him in sincere, humble repentance (1 John 1:9). After so great a miracle of forgiveness and restoration, Isaiah gladly and eagerly exclaims: *Here am I, send me, send me.* And so will we after we have gazed upon the awesome majesty and glory of God's holiness…then experienced His unfathomable love and mercy at the cross of Jesus.

There are two key Scriptures that we must always keep in mind whenever we study this crucial subject—the pure, undefiled, transcendent holiness of God. Let's take a look at these.

2. Read: 2 Sam. 6:1-7.

   a. What did Uzza do? (vs. 6)

   b. What did God do? (vs. 7b)

　　c. What specifically was Uzza's sin that warranted death? (vs. 7a)

The Ark of the Covenant represented God's presence and transcendent holiness. God had given clear instructions (Ex. 25:10-15; Num. 4:15) that any time the Ark of the Covenant was moved, it was to be carried by the priests on poles that fit through loops attached to its sides. The men, themselves were never to physically touch the Ark...*or they would die (Num. 4:15)*. God was establishing here the divine principle that transcendent holiness is like a consuming fire that, because of its very nature cannot tolerate that which is unholy. It must "consume"—devour—it. Failure to do so would result in defilement of the holy. The only protection from that kind of purifying purging was a "holy" reverence for God. Later Jesus would offer His holiness as protection that would enable us to enter into God's presence without fear, having been declared *holy* by His purifying, sanctifying blood. But in both cases, we see that humble, holy awe, (reverence) and repentance bridges the gap between God's transcendent holiness and man's corrupt, sinful unholiness. By carrying the Ark the priests would also safeguard against its being damaged as might happen if placed upon an unstable oxcart. Do you see the subtle yet tragic deceptiveness of sin here? What the priests and Uzza did *seemed* so innocuous and innocent. It even *seemed* "right"—like a better plan than God's. It would be much faster and easier to place the Ark upon the oxcart and carry it that way. This is such a graphic picture of the deception and power of sin—it always *seemeth so right (Prov. 14:12)*. Only God's Word can cut through that kind of deception and reveal the sin for what it is—wrong, and powerfully destructive. God's way, as revealed to us in His Word, is not only the best way, it is the only way to avoid the deception of sin and thus to be spared the awful consequences it always brings.

　3. Read Num. 20:7-13.

　　a. What was Moses' overt (outward) sin? (note God's specific command regarding the rock and how Moses responded – vs. 8, middle of verse, 11a)

　　b. What was his inner (heart) sin that caused him to disobey God? (vs. 12a)

　　c. What did it cost him? (vs. 12b)

I hope that we will heed God's loving warnings here and learn (1 Cor. 10:6, 10) from these two tragic examples, the crucial importance of reverencing the *holiness* of God through a life of trusting faith and obedience. Failure to do so cost Uzza his life. It cost Moses the wonderful joy of leading the children of Israel into the promised land for which he had worked so long and so diligently. Every time I study these two passages I am first of all overwhelmed with God's mercy and grace in my life to have spared me so often from the punishment I deserved because of my irreverent stubborn and rebellious disobedience. I fall on my knees in humble gratitude, praise, and thanksgiving. Beyond this, I cannot help but wonder how much needless suffering and disappointment we bring upon ourselves—and upon those we love the most!—and how many of God's blessings we forfeit because we fail to obey God's good command to *reverence Him as holy* by listening to Him, believing Him, trusting and obeying Him (Num. 20:12).

Have you ever thought about why the Word of God is called the Holy Bible? It is because God is holy and the Bible is God's revelation of Himself and His desire for His children to *share in His holiness*...to become *holy for He is holy* (Heb. 12:10), avoiding the painful pitfalls of sin and entering into the joys of righteous, holy living. Whenever we fail to give attention to God's Holy Word, we easily forget His clear instructions (just as both Moses and Uzza did) and begin to do things our way instead of obeying God. Following our own sinful, fleshly lusts rather than the Word of God, we begin to erroneously rationalize: "This *sin* isn't any big deal. I'm sure God doesn't really care about such an insignificant thing as this. So it doesn't really matter if I … don't read and study His Word so that I can obey His Word; keep that little pet idol in my life that I love and cherish and 'cling to' more than God; cheat on my income tax; tell a little white lie; don't go to church because I'm too weak and too sick (when I can go to other places that I *want* to go…"). But it does matter! <u>There is no such thing as an *innocuous, innocent sin.*</u> *The wages of sin is death (Rom. 6:23)*—death to our innocence, (and it's inevitable consequence, a badgering, gnawing guilt), death to our joy, death in our relationships with others, separation from God (Is. 59:2). God loves us. He wants to spare us of this kind of pain and suffering. That's why He has given us His precious Word—to light our way and keep us on His path of righteousness, thus avoiding the agonizing pitfalls of sin. May God help us to remember that it is **sin**—failure to reverence Him as holy by rebelling against His clear instructions in His Word (disobedience)—that always results in painful loss and destruction in our lives.

At the same time, we must remember also that God always extends mercy and grace to the one who comes to Him in genuine *godly sorrow (repentance - 2 Cor. 7:9-10)*, and asks for His forgiveness and restoration: *To this one I will look; to him who is humble and contrite of spirit and who trembles at My Word … for as high as the heavens are above the earth, so great is His lovingkindness toward those who fear Him. As far as the east is from the west, so far has He removed our transgressions from us. Just as a father has compassion on his children, so the Lord has compassion on those who fear Him (Is. 66:2; Ps. 103:11-13; cf., 1 John 1:9; Is. 1:18-20).*

> Holy, Holy, Holy! Lord God Almighty! Early in the morning our song shall rise to Thee;
> Holy, Holy, Holy! Merciful and mighty; God in three persons, blessed Trinity!
>
> Holy, Holy, Holy! Though the darkness hide Thee;
> Though the eye of sinful man, Thy Glory may not see.
> Only Thou art Holy; there is none beside Thee; Perfect in power, in love, and purity.
>
> Holy, Holy, Holy! Lord God Almighty!
> All Thy works shall praise Thy Name; In earth and sky and sea;
> Holy, Holy, Holy! Merciful and mighty; God in three persons, blessed Trinity!
>
> Reginald Heber, 1783-1826

Write out a Bible verse that had special meaning to you today.

Based upon what you have learned today, write a prayer to God expressing the desires of your heart in applying these truths to your life.

Chapter 5 — Day 4
The Surprising Side of Holy Love

> *Let no one deceive you with empty words, for because of these things (immorality, impurity, idolatry, etc.) the wrath of God comes upon the sons of disobedience (Eph. 5:6).*
>
> *For the Lord your God is a consuming fire, a jealous God (Deut. 4:24).*

God's Loving Righteous Wrath

Therefore, thus says the Lord God, "Because you have not…walked in My statutes, nor observed My ordinances… And because of all your abominations, I will…execute judgments on you… "So as I live," declares the Lord God, "surely, because you have defiled My sanctuary with all your detestable idols and with all your abominations, therefore, I shall judge you according to your ways, and I shall bring all your abominations upon you... then you will know that I am the Lord!" (Ezek. 5:7-15, 7:3-4, sel.).

When is the last time you read a book, attended a small group Bible study, or heard a sermon on the wrath of God? For most, the answer would be, "I have never read a book, done a Bible Study, or heard a sermon on the wrath of God." And then, if we were honest, we would say, "and that is quite fine with me! I don't want to hear about that. There is enough trouble in this world. I can open the newspaper and read about that. When I go to church, I want to hear about God's love and grace, prosperity and blessings."

I used to feel exactly this way…until I read the Bible through several times. Then I realized how dangerous it is to "pick and choose" the parts of the Bible that we will read and focus upon at the neglect of *the whole counsel of God's Word (Acts 20:27)*. It is dangerous because what happens is that, in our quest to be "positive", we create a warped, unbiblical view of God. And a warped view of God results in deception, idolatry and sinfulness. We have made God into an "image" that we wish Him to be, rather than who He really is, as He has revealed Himself to us in His Word. But "idols" can't save. And *those who put their trust in them will become like them (weak, impotent, powerless) (Ps. 135:18)*. I can testify to the tragic results of this in my own life. As long as I clung to the *image* of God that I had set up in my own mind—totally loving, accepting, tolerant of all my sins and rebellion, I *became* like the idol I had created—weak and continuously badgered, bruised and defeated by Satan and my own sinful flesh. There was little joy in my life because of the painful consequences I brought upon myself through my habitual, rebellious sinning against God. I was an idolater who did not really *know* God as He truly is: Pure, undefiled, holy. Being such, God could never look upon sin with impunity, because sin destroys and holy love cannot embrace that which destroys. It must be dealt with, lest it consume those for whom His Son *gave His life* to redeem—you and me!

God wants to deliver us from bondage to false "images" that will never be able to save us. God is so much greater—more powerful, more awesome, more <u>holy</u>—than the weak, faulty *images* we create in our own sinful, selfish hearts. That is why we need to be in His Word daily. For it is there that God reveals Himself for who He really is…*majestic in holiness…working wonders (Ex. 15:11)*.

Pink is my favorite color. I like to wear pink blouses, pink skirts, pink jackets, and pink-tinted glasses. I am also very nostalgic. I like to look at old pictures and old movies and T.V. shows like "Happy Days", "Little House on the Prairie", and "Andy Griffith"; I love family gatherings—especially Thanksgiving and Christmas—and remembering the "good old days". I miss my dad, my grandmas and my grandpas (who are in heaven). I am, by nature, tender-hearted and emotional. I *feel* life more deeply than most, so hard times, suffering and adversity (including dealing with sin in my life!) were especially difficult—painful—for me. In order to protect myself from such, I would often withdraw, hide, or do anything and everything I could to avoid any such adversity, including running to one of the many idols I had created to give comfort and ease the pain (like food, drugs, sleep…or a "happy" movie). But God, through His Word, showed me the danger in this. By not facing my problems—and my sins!—I was only giving the devil a stronghold and delaying the joy of victory over them (John 10:10b). So I asked God to help me to view adversity as opportunity—opportunity to strengthen and purify my faith, and to purge my life of worthless idols and false "images" of God (and other sins). With God's help and wisdom from His Word, I began to recognize previously hidden sins (sins "hidden" by the deceptions of my own fallen heart – Jer. 17:9). I was then able to sincerely repent of them—*put them off,* and *put on* new godly habits (Eph. 4:22-24). Strongholds began coming down. This wonderful, liberating process continues, and I thank God for each victory thus far that has enabled me to become a stronger, more stable, hopeful, and happier person. And I thank Him for the ones yet to come!

> *And this is eternal life, that they may* <u>*know*</u> *Thee, the only true God, and Jesus Christ whom Thou hast sent (John 17:3).*

The primary way God works to destroy false images we have of Him—which always results in idolatry and creating "gods" to which we cling that cannot save, help or deliver us—is by *knowing Him (John 17:3).* As we come to truly *know Him* for who He really is, the light of His holy glory and grace exposes the false images and shows them for what they are— false "gods" with no power to save. The best way that we can come to truly *know God* is by going to the source of His own revelation of Himself to us—His Word. And that is where God led me a number of years ago, after living a fruitless, joyless defeated life far too long. He led me to read the Bible through from Genesis to Revelations with a very deep and intentional desire to really come to *know* my heavenly Father, my Lord and Savior, Jesus, and my counselor and comforter, the Holy Spirit. Who are these three "persons" of the Godhead who function at all times as "one God"? What is the true nature and character of this "Godhead"—Father, Son, and Spirit? What makes them happy? What makes them sad? What brings them pleasure? What provokes them to anger? At first it was hard and a little scary. There seemed to be a lot of devastatingly painful and sad things happening in those early books of the Bible— willful rebellion, blatant sin and wickedness, judgment, war, bloodshed. It did not seem to me to be a happy "good news" story. I actually thought of quitting a number of times. But I knew that God wanted me to persevere and that I would "understand" a lot of what I was not, at that point able to comprehend, by the time I finished. And so I did persevere and I completed the entire Bible.

It was definitely a significant turning point in my life and in my relationship with God. Never before had I been able to grasp even a small glimmer of the magnificent magnitude of God's love, mercy and grace. I saw God in a whole new light. He was no longer *only* the great, awesome, transcendent Creator and Master of the Universe, he was also now my personal loving, caring, and *protective* Father. And the security of that love and protection freed me to grow and gave me the courage to face and defeat enemies that I could never before have faced. I could only run and hide and live a weak, fear-dominated, defeated life. How thankful I am for the deeper, sweeter, more intimate relationship with God that began—and continues to grow—as a result of that first "read-through" of the Bible.[8]

It is only in *knowing God* as He really is—as He has revealed Himself in His Word—and in knowing and living out His good plans for our lives (also revealed in His Word) that we experience real *life, and that more abundantly (John 10:10)*—a life of meaning and purpose, victory over our enemies, and an ever deepening peace and joy. We've already talked about God's attributes of love, mercy, grace and holiness. But what about His justice, judgment and divine wrath? What do we need to know about these that will help us know and love, follow and obey Him more closely? Once again we return to God's Word for the answers.

1. God is slow to anger.

   Then the Lord passed by in front of him and proclaimed, "The Lord, the Lord God, compassionate and gracious, <u>slow to anger</u>, and <u>abounding in loving kindness</u> and truth; who keeps lovingkindness for thousands, who forgives iniquity, transgression and sin (Ex. 34:6-7, cf. Ps. 103:8).

   And He rained down manna upon them to eat, and gave them food from heaven… He sent them food in abundance… then He rained meat upon them… He let (quail) fall in the midst of their camp, round about their dwellings. So they ate and were well filled; and their desire He gave to them… In spite of all this they still sinned, and did not believe in His wonderful works... their heart was not steadfast toward Him, nor were they faithful in His covenant… and <u>often He restrained His anger, and did not arouse His wrath</u> (Ps. 78:24-29, 38 sel.).

2. God's anger/wrath is always justified and always provoked by <u>willful</u> and <u>repeated</u> acts of rebellion and disobedience.

   How <u>often</u> they rebelled against Him… and grieved Him in the desert! And <u>again and again</u> they tempted God and pained the Holy One of Israel. They did not remember His power… when He redeemed them from the adversary, when He performed His signs in Egypt…

   they <u>provoked Him</u> with their high places and aroused His jealousy with their graven images… (<u>Finally</u>), God… was filled with wrath… so He gave (them) up to captivity… to the sword (Ps. 78:40-43, 58-62, sel.).

   They rebelled by the sea; they quickly forgot His works; they did not wait for His counsel, but craved intensely in the wilderness, and tempted God in the desert...they forgot God their Savior, who had done great things in Egypt… and awesome things by the Red Sea...they did not believe in His Word, but grumbled in their tents; they did not listen to the voice of the Lord… they joined themselves also to Baal-peor, (an idol) and (committed abominable acts—prostitution, idolatry, child abuse, murder)… thus they <u>provoked</u> Him to anger <u>with their deeds</u>; and the plague broke out among them… they also <u>provoked</u> Him to wrath at the waters of Meribah; they were rebellious against His Spirit… they mingled with the nations, (which God had strictly forbidden them to do – Deut. 7:5-6; Is. 30:22; Jer. 32:30–35), and learned their practices, and served their idols, which became a snare to them. They even sacrificed their sons and their daughters… and shed innocent blood (abortion/infanticide), and the land was polluted with the blood. Thus they became unclean in their practices…Therefore the anger of the Lord was kindled against His people… He gave them into the hand of the nations; and those who hated them ruled over them. Their enemies also oppressed them… <u>Many times</u> He would deliver them; they, however, were rebellious in their counsel, and so sank down in their iniquity (Ps. 106:7-43, sel.).

God always clearly instructs His people what to do and also clearly communicates the consequences of disobedience. He then does only what He has said He will do… blesses the obedient, brings judgment against the rebellious disobedient. Those who experience God's wrath do so because they *choose* to rebel, rejecting His love and protective commands.

3. God often restrains His anger. He does not deal with us as our sins deserve.

The Lord is compassionate and gracious, slow to anger and abounding in lovingkindness... He has not dealt with us according to our sins, nor rewarded us according to our iniquities. For as high as the heavens are above the earth, so great is His lovingkindness toward those who fear Him. As far as the east is from the west, so far has He removed our transgressions from us (Ps. 103:8-12, sel.).

Thank God He does not deal with us *according to our sins!* Truly, He is *compassionate and gracious, slow to anger and abounding in lovingkindness.*

4. God's anger is turned away when we repent.

"Come now, and let us reason together," says the Lord., "Though your sins are as scarlet, they will be as white as snow; though they are red like crimson, they will be like wool. If you consent and obey, you will eat the best of the land; But if you refuse and rebel, you will be devoured by the sword." Truly, the mouth of the Lord has spoken (Is. 1:18-20).

5. God's anger lasts only as long as necessary to accomplish its purpose. Repentance and obedience dispel God's anger and bring restoration. Continued rebellion and disobedience prolong it.

The anger of the Lord will not turn back until He has... carried out the purposes of His heart; (in days to come), you will clearly understand it (Jer. 23:20).

6. God must pour out His anger and wrath *for His Name's sake*—to establish His Name among the nations, to prove His sovereignty and to establish love and holiness as His reigning rule.

Son of man, when the house of Israel was living in their own land, they defiled it by their ways and their deeds;... Therefore, I poured out My wrath on them for the blood which they had

shed on the land, because they had defiled it with their idols... <u>According to their ways and their deeds</u> I judged them. When they came to the nations where they went, they profaned My holy name... But I had concern for My holy name, which the house of Israel had profaned among the nations where they went. Therefore, say to the house of Israel; thus says the Lord God, "It is not for your sake... that I am about to act, but for My holy name, which you have profaned among the nations where you went. And I will vindicate the holiness of My great name... Then the nations will know that I am the Lord... when I prove Myself holy among you in their sight" (Ezek. 36:17-23, sel.).

God is love. God is holy. God is just. Sin robs and kills and destroys. Perfect love, transcendent holiness, and divine justice cannot look upon sin with impunity. If God did not deal with sin, what kind of a world would we have and what kind of "heaven" could we look forward to? The world would be total chaos (which it is quickly becoming as God patiently endures, holding back His hand of judgment) and there would be no heaven because every evil that now plagues our world with death and destruction would also find its way to heaven. Can you imagine living *forever* in a place like that? I would rather be eternally annihilated than to live in a "heaven" contaminated with sin and its painful, destructive consequences. But, thank God, there will be no sin, destruction or death in heaven. God is dealing with that now as He exercises divine, holy wrath, and He will complete His purifying work in His final judgment when Jesus returns.

The fact that we will never again have to face the enemy of sin and all of its destructive, painful consequences on that glorious day when God brings us to his holy Heaven ought to send us to our knees in grateful thanksgiving morning by morning... and all through the day!

However, for those who reject God, the future is not so bright. In fact, it is the saddest reality of all. Everyone who rejects Jesus as their Savior will spend an eternity separated from God and His love, living with the consequences of that rejection, the ultimate expression of divine holy wrath—Hell's tormenting fires. My heart is grieved for all who *choose* such a destiny. I earnestly pray for those I know and love dearly who are in such a state, asking God to be merciful and to open hard hearts and deaf ears to *hear, receive, and believe* His wonderful *good news* of salvation, so that they may be spared an eternity in that unimaginable place of separation from God *where their torment goes up forever and ever; (they) never die…the fire is not quenched and they have no rest day and night (Rev. 14:11; Mark 9:46).*

As I think on all these things and remember God's great mercy in saving my soul and making me His child so that I will never again be separated from Him and His love (Rom. 8:38-39), or have to experience His wrath—not now, not tomorrow, not ever! (1 Thess. 5:9)—my heart wells up with songs of praise and thanksgiving, and I am all the more eager to *press on* to a life of ever greater *righteousness, peace and joy in the Holy Spirit (Phil. 3:12; Rom. 14:17).*

For God has not destined us for wrath, but for obtaining salvation through our Lord Jesus Christ… Therefore, encourage one another… encourage the exhausted, and strengthen the feeble. Say to those with anxious heart, "Fear not, take courage…do not be afraid; do not let your hands fall limp. The Lord your God is in your midst…(you) shall not be moved" (1 Thess. 5:9, 11; Is. 35:3-4; Zeph. 3:16-17; Ps. 46:5, sel.).

Bible Study Supplement
Chapter 5 — Day 4 — The Surprising Side of Holy Love
God's Loving, Righteous Wrath

Thank you for your diligence in studying this difficult, but ever so necessary subject, in order to have a clearer, more accurate view of the nature and character of God. Because our meditation today was longer than usual, we will look at only two additional Scriptures in our Bible Study Supplement.

1. Read Ps. 78:1, 5-22.

    a. What did He command our forefathers to do? (vs. 5b)

    b. Why were they to do this? (three reasons - vs. 7)

    c. Describe our forefathers (three characteristics – vs. 8)

Note: "Ephraim" was the second son of Joseph. He was adopted by the aged patriarch Jacob upon Jacob's arrival in Egypt. At the end of his life, when Jacob "blessed" the sons of Joseph (Gen. 48:1-6, 12-20), Ephraim received his blessing as the "first born". (Though this blessing rightfully belonged to Ephraim's older brother Manassah. Ordained of God, Jacob crossed his arms and placed his right hand upon the head of Ephraim and his left hand upon the head of Manassah). Following the revolt of the ten tribes after the rule of Solomon, the tribe of Ephraim became a prominent leader in the northern kingdom (Israel) and the name "Ephraim" became synonymous with the northern kingdom. So when "Ephraim" is mentioned in the Bible it is often referring to "Israel".

    d. What did the men of Ephraim do? (four things - vs. 10-11)

    e. What did God do for the people? (vs. 12a) (Note "wonders" is another word for "miracles")

    f. List four of these. (vs. 13-15)

    g. What was the response of the people after all these demonstrations of God's loving care? (vs. 17)

In spite of all He has done for them, the children of Israel continued to grumble and complain and "put God to the test" by their endless ingratitude, selfish whining and demands.

    h. Finally after months of enduring this kind of blatant rebellion, what happened? (vs. 21)

    i. Why was God's wrath aroused? (two reasons – vs. 22)

We won't read the rest now, but as soon as you have a chance, it would be good to return to this scripture and finish reading the chapter. You will be amazed at the magnitude of God's love, mercy and grace towards His obstinate, ungrateful, rebellious children. It is the same compassion and mercy God shows us day by day. God is so patient and longsuffering! Similar accounts of the people's blatant rebellion, in spite of God's endless expressions of love and provision, are found in Ps. 106 and Neh. 9:29-37. I return to these scriptures often when I am tempted to have a "pity party", and I am reminded once again of my own repeated stubbornness and rebellion and God's longsuffering patience, and bountiful, undeserved grace in my life.

  2. Read Eph. 5:1-8.

      a. Upon whom does the wrath of God fall? (vs. 6b)

      b. What does God's Word lovingly exhort us to do so that we never have to experience God's wrath? (vs. 8b).

Write out a Bible verse that had special meaning to you today.

Based upon what you have learned today, write a prayer to God expressing the desires of your heart in applying these truths to your life.

Chapter 5 — Day 5
God's Blessed Remnant

And they shall come and shout for joy on the height of Zion, and they shall be radiant over the bounty of the Lord—over the grain, and the new wine, and the oil…and their life shall be like a watered garden, and they shall never languish again (Jer. 31:12).

Thus says the Lord, "The people who survived the sword found grace in the wilderness…I have loved you with an everlasting love; therefore I have drawn you with lovingkindness. Again I will build you, and you shall be rebuilt… again you shall take up your tambourines… and go forth to the dances of the merrymakers. Sing aloud with gladness…And shout among the…nations; Proclaim, give praise, and say, 'O Lord, save Thy people, the <u>remnant</u> of Israel… For the Lord has ransomed Jacob, and redeemed him from the hand of him who was stronger than he. And they shall come and shout for joy on the height of Zion…For I will turn their mourning into joy, and will comfort them, and give them joy for their sorrow. And My people shall be satisfied with My goodness… and I will be their God and they shall be My people… and I will be a father to (them) and (they) shall be sons and daughters to Me" declares the Lord (Jer. 31:2-14, sel.; 2 Cor. 6:16b-18, sel.).

God's Faithful, Obedient Remnant

One of the most precious doctrines in the Bible is the doctrine of the remnant. The Bible clearly teaches that God has always had, and He always will have His blessed remnant to whom He is totally committed as a loving, merciful Father and who, in turn, remain faithful and loyal to Him as trusting obedient children. If you have passed the salvation test and are a true believer and faithful disciple, then you are among this blessed remnant—the "called out", saved and sanctified ones—and God has special *precious and magnificent promises* reserved just for you! (2 Pet. 1:4). They are promises for His personal, unconditional love, presence, and limitless mercy, grace, and overcoming, victorious deliverance in the midst of every trouble, trial, or tribulation that will ever come your way! (Heb. 13:6; Jer. 33:3; Is. 41:10, 43:1-4a; Ps. 34:19; John 16:33; Eph. 1:18-21, 3:16-20).

This is such a precious faith-fortifying, hope-building truth regarding our blessed inheritance in Christ, I don't want to cloud or diminish it in any way with a lot of my own thoughts. I want you to hear some of the beautiful promises directly from God Himself, who is our great *Savior and Shepherd of our souls*—provider and protector of His remnant (1 Pet. 2:25; 2 Pet. 1:2-4).

Look, listen, believe, and be blessed.…

Bible Study Supplement
Chapter 5 — Day 5 — God's Blessed Remnant

Just a quick note of explanation before we begin looking at "remnant blessing" verses. A strong and consistent characteristic of Scripture is its use of "types" and "patterns" that point to future event realities. Abraham gives us a "pattern" of new testament righteousness and faith; Isaac was a "type" of Jesus (Abraham's willingness to give up His son and Isaac's willingness to be sacrificed on Mt. Moriah pointed us to Jesus and the time God would again supply a perfect, spotless lamb). The exodus is a "pattern" of our deliverance from the bondage of sin, and there are many other such types and patterns from which we gain insight. From Genesis to Revelation we are repeatedly pointed forward as God's eternal plans are unfolded, and His love is expressed in ever greater measure. It is faith that links it all together—the past, the present, the future, and eternal glories. So, as we read God's Word, promises that He has made that will have their full revelation and fulfillment in the future can, by faith, be ours to enjoy, as a foreshadow of things to come.

Jeremiah 31 speaks of the coming restoration of the nation of Israel when her exiled people would be brought back into their own land to enjoy once again the rich blessings of their inheritance. It casts a forward glance also to the consummation of the deliverance of all God's people at the return if Christ. As a part of God's blessed remnant now, however, we can appropriate its promises because God is the same *yesterday, today and forever (Heb. 13:6),* and what is going to *be* in its perfection, already *is* in its glorious "remnant blessing" foreshadow (Prov. 4:18).

1. Read Jer. 31:2-4.
   a. What did the people who survived the sword find in the wilderness/desert? (vs. 2)

Note: Similar to the present/future illustrations in the Bible as explained above is another related biblical pattern. Throughout His Word, God also uses real, physical situations to teach us deeper spiritual truths. Here, "the sword" is referring not only to the very real enemies of Israel that came against them to destroy them, it is referring also to the "the sword" of the enemies of our souls—the devil, the world, and our own sinful flesh—that come to defeat us and turn our hearts away from God. Through Christ's redemption and the indwelling presence of the Holy Spirit within us, we are given the power to "survive the sword" and to live in the blessed "promised land" of God's favor and rest—even in the "desert" of a fallen world.

   b. Describe God's love for His special chosen, redeemed (remnant) people. (vs. 3)

   c. What does He promise to do for them? (vs. 4a)

   d. What will they again do? (vs. 4b)

2. Read Jer. 31:6-14.
   a. What will the watchmen on the hills of Ephraim (Israel) call out? (vs. 6b)

    b. What is God's blessed remnant instructed to do? (vs. 7)

    c. What type of people will be among this precious remnant? (vs. 8b)

    d. In verses 8 and 9 God promises to gather this faithful remnant *from the north and from the ends of the earth.* How will they come? (vs. 9a)

Note: The tears are tears of recognition of their own sinful unworthiness mingled with tears of deep gratitude, praise and joy for what God has done for them.

    e. How does He lead them? (vs. 9b)

    f. How will He watch over/keep them? (vs. 10b)

    g. From whom will the Lord redeem His remnant? (vs. 11b)

    h. What will be the result? (they will do two things – vs.12a)

    i. What will their lives be like? (two characteristics - vs. 12b)

    j. What does God promise to do for them? (two things - vs. 13b)

    k. With what will God's people—His blessed remnant—be filled/satisfied? (vs. 14b).

3. Read Jer. 50:20.
    a. What will God do for His precious remnant that He spares? (vs. 20)

4. Read Is. 65:13-14.
    a. Contrast God's promises for His redeemed, faithful, obedient remnant ("My servants") with those of the rebellious and disobedient ("You"): (four contrasts).

       "My servant" (Faithful Remnant)   "You" (The Disobedient)

5. Read. 2 Cor. 6:16-18.

    a. What does God command His redeemed (remnant) children to do? (two things - vs. 17)

    b. What does He promise if they do this? (vs. 16b, 18)

6. Read Ex. 10:22-23.

    a. What covered all the land and every Egyptian home for three days and how bad was it? (vs. 22b-23a)

    b. What did the Israelites (God's chosen remnant) have in their homes? (vs. 23b)

7. Read Ex. 13:21-22.

    a. What did the Lord do for His remnant by day…by night? (vs. 21)

    b. Therefore, what could they do? (vs. 21b)

    c. Did the cloud or pillar of fire ever abandon them or leave them alone? (vs. 22)

8. Read Zeph. 3:12-17.

    a. What/who is God going to leave among His people? (three characteristics - vs. 12)

    b. What will this remnant do/not do? (three things - vs. 13a)

    c. What will be the result? (vs. 13b)

    d. What has the Lord taken away…and what has He cleared away/turned back? (vs. 15a)

    e. What will His remnant never again fear? (vs. 15b)

    f. Who is ever with (in the midst of) the remnant…and what is He? (vs. 17a)

    g. What will He do? (three things – 17b)

As mentioned at the beginning of today's Bible Study Supplement, we have not yet experienced our full redemption. Therefore, all these blessings that are ours as God's remnant children, wonderful as they are, are but a foreshadow of the far more glorious "eye-hath-not-seen" splendor and rewards yet to come! (1 Cor. 2:9; 2 Tim. 4:8). But, *by faith,* we can take hold of them and live in the magnificent reality of these "remnant blessings" already "at work" in our lives day by day. What encouragement this should bring our hearts—to realize that we are among those blessed few, for whom God is our mighty warrior *fighting for our victory in all our battles (Zeph. 3:17; 2 Chron. 20:15-25),* as well as our loving heavenly Father who protects us and cares for us with an *everlasting love (Jer. 31:3).* These assurances give us plenty of reason to *rejoice and exult with all our hearts (Zeph. 3:14).* That's why for all God's *blessed remnant:*

> *There is a river whose streams make glad the city of God, (where God lives among His blessed remnant), the holy dwelling places of the Most High. God is in the midst of her, she will not be moved; God will help her when morning dawns (every morning God will faithfully "be there" to help us)... The Lord of hosts is with us; the God of Jacob is our stronghold (Ps. 46:4-7, sel.).*

Write out a Bible verse that had special meaning to you today.

Based upon what you have learned today, write a prayer to God expressing the desires of your heart in applying these truths to your life.

Chapter 6

Memory Verse: *There remains, therefore a Sabbath rest for the people of God. Let us therefore be diligent to enter that rest (Heb. 4:9, 11).*

Bonus Memory Verse: Devote yourselves to prayer, keeping alert in it with an attitude of thanksgiving (Col. 4:2).

Day 1

Possessing Our Possessions

The Believer's Rest

Day 2

As Sparks Fly Upward

Biblical Reality Therapy

It's Not Supposed to be <u>Easy</u>…Just Blessed, Victorious and Laced with Grace!

Day 3

You Have Need of Endurance

Fighting the Good Fight - Finishing Well

Day 4

Sweet Hour of Prayer – Part One

Day 5

Sweet Hour of Prayer – Part Two

Chapter 6 — Day 1
Possessing Our Possessions
The Believer's Rest

> *I pray that the eyes of your heart may be enlightened, so that you may know what are the riches of the glory of His inheritance in the saints… for your own eyes have seen all the great work of the Lord which He did. You shall, therefore…be strong and go in and <u>possess the land</u> into which you are about to cross to possess it (Eph. 1:18; Deut 11:1, 7-8).*

There is a very real spiritual dwelling place—*a promised land*—into which God desires all of His redeemed, sanctified children to enter and live. This peaceful, secure *dwelling place* is called the kingdom of God and is described in Rom. 14:17: *for the kingdom of God is not eating and drinking, but righteousness and peace and joy in the Holy Spirit.* In Hebrews 4 this beautiful kingdom is referred to as *the believer's rest* (*Heb. 4:9*).

Blessed be the God and Father of our Lord Jesus Christ, who has blessed us with every spiritual blessing in the heavenly places in Christ, just as He chose us in Him before the foundation of the world, that we should be holy and blameless before Him. In love, He predestined us to adoption as sons through Jesus Christ to Himself, according to the kind intention of His will, to the praise of the glory of His grace, which He freely bestowed on us in the Beloved. In Him we have redemption through His blood, the forgiveness of our sins, according to the riches of His grace, which He lavished upon us… in Him also <u>we have obtained an inheritance</u>…that we who hope in Christ should be to the praise of His glory (Eph. 1:3-12, sel.).

In this beautiful promise we are told that all who are *in Christ Jesus* (have been born again) have already obtained a rich inheritance as God's children. A precious part of that inheritance is *the believer's rest.* How, then can we *possess* what is rightfully ours as God's redeemed children—not just so we can live like kids of the King, but all the more importantly, so that God is glorified in our lives and others *see and believe?* (*Eph. 1:12; Ps. 40:3*).

Therefore, let us fear lest, while a promise remains of entering His rest, any one of you should … come short of it. For indeed we have had good news preached to us, just as they (the rebellious, disobedient children of Israel) also; but the word they heard did not profit them, because it was not <u>united by faith</u> in those who heard. For we who <u>have believed</u> enter that rest (Heb. 4:1-3).

The Bible is clear, and our own experience confirms, that the reason most of us do not experience the wonderful blessing of dwelling in God's promised land of *righteousness, peace, joy, and <u>rest</u> in the Holy Spirit* is the result of one simple, but powerfully destructive word: Unbelief.

Adam and Eve did not really *believe* that God knew what was best for them. They did not *believe*

God when He said, *but from the tree of the knowledge of good and evil you shall not eat, <u>for in the day that you eat from it you shall surely die</u> (Gen. 2:17).* In arrogant pride and selfishness, they were convinced they knew what was best for them: *When the woman saw that the tree was good for food, and that it was a delight to the eyes, and that the tree was desirable to make one wise, she took from its fruit and ate; and she gave also to her husband with her, and he ate (Gen. 3:6).*

So Adam and Eve, in prideful selfishness and unbelief rebelled against God, disobeying His clear command and the result was exactly as the Lord had said—*death (Gen. 2:17, 3:7-19, 24, 5:5).*

As *death* came to Adam and Eve through their *unbelief*—and to all their progeny since—so we must enter into a new, redeemed *living* relationship with God through *belief*—*faith.* We must, with trusting faith, *believe* that Jesus is the Son of God, that He came down from heaven, was incarnate in human form, lived a perfect life, then took upon Himself the wrath and punishment for our sins—death. He then rose from the dead giving us forgiveness of our sins and power to live a victorious life over sin and the devil in this life, and thereafter, to enjoy with Him the glories of heaven forever.

But that's just the beginning of our "salvation". Christ's resurrection from the dead also obtained for us a *blessed inheritance* that only people who *continue* in a trusting, obedient relationship with Him can enjoy. This wonderful inheritance, like our personal, totally forgiven, unconditional love relationship with God, can only be *possessed* by *faith.* So what exactly are our rightful possessions as believers in Christ? What is our *blessed inheritance?*

It is all the *precious and magnificent promises (2 Pet. 1:4)* of God found in His Word. Promises like:

"For I know the plans that I have for you" declares the Lord, *"plans for welfare and not for calamity to give you a future and a hope. Then you will call upon Me and come and pray to Me, and I will listen to you. And you will seek Me and find Me, when you search for Me with all your heart … and I will restore your fortunes" (Jer. 29:11-14, sel.).*

No temptation has overtaken you but such as is common to man; and God is faithful, who will not allow you to be tempted beyond what you are able, but with the temptation will provide the way of escape also, that you may be able to endure it (1 Cor. 10:13).

What then shall we say to these things? If God is for us, who (can be) against us? He who did not spare His own Son, but delivered Him up for us all, how will He not also with Him freely give us all things? (Rom. 8:31-32).

Who shall separate us from the love of Christ? Shall tribulation, or distress, or persecution, or famine, or… peril, or sword… But in all these things we overwhelmingly conquer through Him who loved us… I can do all things through Christ who strengthens me (Rom.8:35, 37; Phil. 4:12).

God is good… and does good… And we know that God causes all things to work together for good to those who love God, to those who are called according to His purpose… no good thing does He withhold from those who walk uprightly (Ps. 73:1, 119:68; Rom. 8:28; Ps. 84:11).

The joy of the Lord is your strength…He who believes in me, from his innermost being shall flow rivers of living water… These things I have spoken that My joy may be in you and your joy may be full (Neh. 8:10; John 7:38; John 15:11).

For you will go out with joy, and be led forth with peace; the mountains and the hills will break forth into shouts of joy before you, and all the trees of the field will clap their hands (Is.55:12).

…along with more than 2000 other promises that are *yes and amen in Christ Jesus (2 Cor. 1:20)…* to *all who believe.*

So then whether we actually *possess*—experience—all these promises or merely gaze at them from afar and *wish* that they were ours, is based upon the strength—or weakness—of our faith in *every word that proceeds from the mouth of God (Matt. 4:4)*. Little faith, little inheritance. Big faith, big inheritance.

We will be looking more closely at a number of the *precious and magnificent promises (2 Pet. 1:4)* that are a part of the blessed inheritance of all who are *in Christ* (genuinely born again) in upcoming lessons. For today, however, I want to focus upon just one—the *believer's rest*—that we spoke of earlier. We must remember always that God's promises are all based upon living and active *faith*—faith that not only *believes* what God has said, but acts upon it (obedience). The Bible tells us that the children of Israel did not *profit from* the promises of God because *they were not united with faith*—believing, trusting, obedient faith (Heb. 4:2). The absence of faith is *unbelief*. Unbelief invariably leads to disobedience. Disobedience is sin. Sin separates us from God and destroys that blessed "rest" of *righteousness and peace and joy in the Holy Spirit (Rom. 14:17)*.

<u>God's solution to the sin problem of unbelief is, and always has been, the same: Faith.</u>

But faith, as we studied in week four, is not something that automatically "happens". It must be exercised (obedience), purified, strengthened and perfected. This can only be accomplished by an ongoing attention to the Word of God as we seek to *know it, believe it and obey it* ever more carefully.

> *So then faith cometh by hearing, and hearing by the Word of God (Rom. 10:17, KJV).*

It is impossible to grow, strengthen, perfect and purify our faith apart from a diligent study of the Word of God. Any attempt to do so will result in a weak, faulty faith that will fail us in those especially difficult times of oft complex, prolonged, *humanly* overwhelming trials. It will fail us because it is not strong enough to <u>trust God</u> to deliver us from, or sustain and carry us through such times.

> *But we are not of those who shrink back to destruction, but of those who have faith to the preserving of the soul (Heb. 10:39).*

As we nurture our faith by giving attention to the Word of God—reading it, studying it, obeying it—our faith grows and as our faith grows, so grows our confidence, joy and capacity to truly *rest* in all God's wonderful *precious and magnificent promises (2 Pet. 3:18).*

> *For we who have believed enter that rest...There remains therefore a Sabbath rest for the people of God...let us, therefore, be diligent to enter that rest (Heb. 4:3, 9, 11).*

Bible Study Supplement
Chapter 6 — Day 1 — Possessing Our Possessions — The Believer's Rest

1. Read Deut. 11:7-17

    a. Why is it important to set our hearts on obedience to God's good commands? (vs. 8)

    b. Describe the land to which God is taking His children? (vs. 9b, 11-12)

    c. What does He promise in verse 15b?

Note: The word translated "filled" in some translations more accurately means "satisfied". I can certainly attest to the truth of this promise. For ever since I got serious about <u>knowing</u> God's promises and <u>obeying</u> God's promises, I began to experience a contentment and satisfaction I never dreamed possible—even in my eating. I could, for the first time actually sit down to a meal, eat to the nourishment of my body, and leave the table completely satisfied. That was nothing short of a major miracle! All praise to God!

    d. What loving and *clear* warning does God give us in verse 16?

    e. What would happen if they disobeyed God—turned away and served other gods? (vs. 17)

Every time I read these verses, I cannot help but wonder how often we *shut up the heavens* and *quickly perish from the good land* through our own unbelief and selfish rebellion against God's loving—*not burdensome (1 John 5:3)*—commands.

The book of Joshua tells the story of the children of Israel entering into and, under the capable and faithful leadership of Joshua taking possession of the "promised land"—the land that God had promised to Abraham *and to his descendants forever (Gen. 12:7, 13:14-15, 15:18)*. When the children of Israel arrived at this land of promise, they found it occupied by pagan kings and their subjects who were enemies of God. God had already warned Moses of this situation, instructing him to commission Joshua to lead the fighting men of Israel to take back this land from enemy occupation and to give it to the children of Israel (God's chosen people) to whom it rightfully belonged.

2. Read Joshua 11:12, 23.

    a. What did Joshua do to all the (pagan, God-hating) cities and their kings? (vs. 12)

    b. What was the result of Joshua's careful and thorough obedience? (vs. 23b)

Many people get very upset (I among them, until only recently) when they read Joshua, Judges, 1st and 2nd Kings, and Chronicles. They just can't understand how a *loving God* would allow—and even demand—so much warfare and bloodshed. Sadly, they have failed to understand the deep, deep <u>love</u> of God for His people in what He did. We must remember that the kings and inhabitants of these lands were enemies of God and His people. They were emissaries of Satan. They had one goal in mind and one goal only—the complete annihilation of the people of God. (So Satan could take over God's kingdom). God understood Satan's diabolical plans. And, through his trusting faith in God,

Joshua understood it, too. He knew that it was critically important that he obey God completely in order to save His people from annihilation from these wicked, Satan-controlled people. Remember also that it was never in the heart of God to destroy the *people,* but the <u>sin</u> of these wicked people that was encroaching upon and destroying <u>His</u> people. Had the sinful, rebellious people repented of their sins and turned to God, <u>He would have spared them</u>, just as He did wicked Nineveh – (Jonah 3:10). Think about it. The *promised land* was the land that God had set aside for His people to possess (Gen. 12:1-2, 15:18). He had *promised* this land *to Abraham...and to his descendants forever.* God's Word was at stake here: *The counsel of the Lord stands forever, the plans of His heart from generation to generation – Ps. 33:11).* Had Joshua not carried out God's plans, you and I would not be here, because there would have been no *promised land* and no *children of God* to possess it.

Just as Joshua courageously faced and defeated the enemies of God that His people might *possess* their *possessions,* so we must get serious about defeating the enemies of our soul—pride, rebellion, selfishness, greed, fear, worry, anxiety, doubt, unbelief, etc.—that keep us from *possessing our possessions,* our glorious *inheritance in Christ.* For if we do not, there will never be a *promised land of rest and peace* for us or for our children and, even more tragically, we will have no witness to the world through which souls are brought into the kingdom of God—*the promised land of God's loving righteous rule, provision, protection...and blessing.*

One of my favorite scriptures in all the Bible that has fortified my faith so often and kept me hopeful and pressing on with courage in my own most difficult and trying times is found in Deut. 20. I pray that it will be a special encouragement to you today...and in the days to come.

3. Read: Deut. 20:1-4.

   a. What are we <u>not</u> to do when we go out to battle against our enemies who are *greater than we are?* (vs. 1)

   b. Why not? (vs. 1b)

   c. What four things does God specifically instruct us **not** to do when we approach any battle? (vs. 3b)

   d. Why? (3 reasons - vs. 4) (Do you <u>really</u> *believe* this? You can be sure that the outcome of your big—and small—battles is dependent upon how you answer this question).

The book of Habakkuk is one of the most profound and powerful books in all the Bible for helping us face and overcome fear that we might be able to truly *possess the possessions* that are rightfully ours as children of God—*confidence, peace, joy, victory*—regardless of our outward circumstances. It is the intriguing story of the prophet Habakkuk's journey from depressing, joy robbing *fear* to a vibrant, victorious *faith.* This journey—from *worry to worship*—is so full of wise counsel that we will devote several days to studying it in book three. But for today, let's take a brief look at the most important lesson that Habakkuk learned through his meetings with God and all that God revealed and taught him during these valuable times.

Before we read this scripture, we must take a moment to understand the background concerning the situation in the land of Judah where Habakkuk lived and prophesied. Habakkuk wrote his book well into the northern kingdom's captivity and exile by the Assyrians. As if that were not bad enough, in the opening chapter, God warns Habakkuk that He is about to call up the Chaldeans (Babylonians) to march against Judah (the southern kingdom) to render judgment against it for the people's blatant and repeated idolatry, blasphemy and apostasy. The situation does not look good for the people of Judah, or for Habakkuk personally. In fact it *appears* rather disastrous and hopeless. Habakkuk wisely recognizes that the only source of help and deliverance that the people have is God! So, rather than cower in unbelief and defeat, Habakkuk cries out to God for His unmerited mercy, grace and deliverance from the impending, devastating judgment. Then, in a step of bold, trusting faith, he relinquishes the outcome completely to God and *rests* in God's proven faithfulness and goodness. He *believes God* for His provision and deliverance...*come what may*. And that is what we must do also, if we are to fully *possess our possessions* and live in the land of the *believer's rest* in which we are secure, having at all times the assurance of God's loving presence with us, along with His never failing promises of protection, provision, and blessing for all who *trust and obey* (Heb. 13:5; Ps. 46:1; Deut. 11:1-31).

4. Read Habakkuk 3:17-19.

   a. In the first column, list the circumstances that this courageous, godly man was willing to face with unwavering, trusting faith in the goodness and faithfulness of God. Then, next to these, list several difficult situations that you might face (or are currently facing) in your own life. (vs. 17)

What Habakkuk would possibly face:	What I may face (or am currently facing):

   b. Even if all these things happened, what does Habakkuk determine in his heart to do? (two things - vs. 18)

   c. How could he do this? (vs. 19a)

By the way, in the days that followed, God did watch over, protect and provide in miraculous ways for His faithful, trusting remnant who *chose* to *trust and obey*.

We, too, can *choose* the same kind of courageous response to our difficulties and trials as Habakkuk did: In sickness, in health, in trials and tribulations, in pain and in problems...*I will exalt in the Lord. I will rejoice in the God of my salvation. The Lord God is my strength* (Hab. 3:18).

Write out a Bible verse that had special meaning to you today.

Based upon what you have learned today, write a prayer to God expressing the desires of your heart in applying these truths to your life.

Chapter 6 — Day 2
As Sparks Fly Upward

These things I have spoken to you, that in Me you may have peace. In the world you shall have tribulation, but be of good cheer; I have overcome the world (John 16:33 NASB/KJV).

For man is born for trouble, as sparks fly upward (Job 5:7).

Biblical Reality Therapy

It's Not Supposed to be <u>Easy</u>... Just Blessed, Victorious and Laced with Grace!

A number of years ago when I was in the crucible of another protracted time of relentless, excruciating physical, mental and emotional pain which manifested in suicidal depression, at the pleading of my husband and medical doctor, I ended up where I had been so often before: in the plush office of a highly respected "Christian" psychotherapist who specialized in dealing with severe cases of clinical depression/bipolar disorder. The main focus of my therapy on this occasion was an assignment to read a book entitled *Reality Therapy*. I was told that if I applied the principles in this book, I would be able to *cope* successfully with the deep, joyless, helplessly-hopeless depression that now engulfed me. This, in itself was depressing to me as I had, in the past, so often thrown myself into literally hundreds of behavioral modification and other psychological *coping techniques* which, in reality, contributed nothing of lasting value in ameliorating the pain and problems of the depression but only moved me deeper into an ever darkening pit from which there seemed to be no escape. I had not come to this doctor seeking another technique to help me *cope*. I had come seeking healing—real, lasting, freedom and joy-producing healing. But, I was, at this point more utterly desperate than I had

ever been, realizing that if I did not get serious help soon, there would be no hope of stopping the destructive spiral hurtling me ever downward into a weaker, more dysfunctional state. Death seemed imminent, for by this time I had nearly destroyed my body through the overmedication of psychotropic drugs, along with poor eating and sleeping habits that invariably accompanied the complicated side-effects of the drugs. An overwhelming sense of hopelessness and despair had driven me to attempt suicide several times and my thoughts now turned more and more often to it.

So I read the book. Like so many that I had read before, it *sounded* great. A confident message of promised success permeated every chapter of the "new and improved" coping technique. The main idea of this particular psychological therapy was that life could be rough at times, but if one just accepted this fact, *believed in himself,* faced his problems realistically, then with great determination exerted the *power from within* to overcome them, he would rise above his problems and life would be one grand succession of confident victory after another. And so I tried—with more fervor than ever to make it work. Even though I could *understand* everything the book said, that mysterious, ethereal *power within* was no match against the diabolical, demonic hold of the depression over my *soul*—mind, emotions, will (Rom. 7).

It was at this darkest point in my life—locked in the grips of suicidal depression—that God, by His matchless grace saved my war-torn soul and gave me a *new heart* and a *new Life*. He also placed within my spirit a brand new "therapy"—*Biblical Reality Therapy*—the application of the pure, unadulterated, undiluted truths of the Word of God to my problems, both those *within* and those *without (2 Cor. 7:5)*. For the first time in my life I knew that the answers to the unconquerable depression—along with all the other related life-dominating obsessions, addictions and debilitating *fears* that had destructively ruled over my life since I could remember—were in this precious Book. Its words and wisdom were so different from the ever changing, ineffective theories of fallible, sinful man. They carried the authority and power of the never failing, never changing, omnipotent God of the Universe whose mouth *breathed them—full of life—onto the pages (2 Tim. 3:16)*. Like a spring in the desert, hope burst forth onto the parched, barren soil of my heart bringing nourishment to sustain and "grow" the seeds of new life that had been planted within. I discovered again and again the power of God's Word—not merely to help me *cope*—but power to change, liberate, and truly heal.

> He sent His Word and healed them (Ps. 107:20).

I quickly saw the fallacy in the book I had been given to read—and in every other book about life and its problems written from a purely man-centered, humanistic perspective, which intentionally leaves God and the reality of sin and its destructive power, out of the *coping technique* formula. I also saw the fallacy of refusing to acknowledge the 3rd dimension of life—the *spirit realm*—which, in reality affects our world far, far more than anything we can see, touch or feel. Any therapy or counseling that excludes the realities of our unseen world—God, the devil, sin, guilt, forgiveness, spiritual warfare—and all the other related truths taught in the Bible, will never work; not in a lasting way! It will only deceive and disappoint and lead into further defeat...and depression.

Earlier in this study, we established the foundation of the only true *Reality Therapy* that will work and that is: there is a sovereign God of the Universe who created us to have a loving, growing relationship with Him, to bring honor and glory to Him as we fulfill His good plans for our lives, and to become conformed to the image of His Son. We learned also that there is a complex and powerful, deceptively wicked spirit world led by Satan who is in rebellion against God, seeking to usurp God's power and authority and destroy His Kingdom along with every man, woman and child in it.

Therefore, any *therapy* that does not approach life's problems from a biblical perspective is not *reality* at all and will only lead down a path of demonic deception and further bondage.

Dealing with our problems biblically works because it confronts the real issues of life from a God centered, biblical perspective. Through the power of the Holy Spirit who now lives in us (if we are truly born again), we are able to search out and *apply* (obey) the life-giving truths of God's Word in resolving our problems. The Bible tells us that God has given us all that we need for life and for godliness through *His Word* and *the power of His Holy Spirit living and working in us (2 Pet. 1:3; John 14:16-17, cf. 16:7-15)*.

Even though I knew this, I confess that living these truths out—*doing life* according to the principals of the Bible—was not an easy assignment for me. (Because of the sinful nature that we all are born with, it's not *easy* for anyone...but for some of us it is an even greater challenge). Why? Because, as I have shared, I am, by nature, very stubborn and rebellious with a nearly insatiable need to *control*. I could not see it then, but now realize that this control factor was fed and fortified by a very real and powerful demonic *fear* that dominated my life for many years. Because I did not know God and had never experienced His unconditional love, forgiveness and acceptance, my whole life revolved around what I could *achieve* in order to win the approval and acceptance of man. And no matter how hard I tried, I never was able to reach that proverbial "top" where I could rest on my laurels and receive the continual accolades that my attention-seeking fallen flesh demanded. The fear of failure drove me into a ceaseless, ever more maddening, joyless, striving for the approval of man to succeed. We will talk more about the power of such a stronghold in one's life in book three, but for now, I just want to mention that demonic strongholds are a very real part of the battles of life and we dare not disregard them or fail to do serious spiritual warfare against them, lest we be consumed by them.

Because I had been enmeshed for so long in the world's man-centered thinking, many sin patterns had developed into well fortified strongholds by the time I became a Christian and strongholds rarely come down with ease or free of pain. Conquering these is one of the most challenging aspects of the *good fight.* How patient and faithful God always was in my own battles! He understood my particular "personality weaknesses" (sin-bents) and He mercifully, graciously gave me the strength through His Holy Spirit to face and begin to deal with each one as they were revealed. Though that process is far from complete, there is joy in the journey as I press on with the goal in mind of that blessed day when it *will* be finished and these days of *fighting the good fight* will have ended. My sanctification will cease and *glorification* will commence—in the presence of Jesus. Oh, glorious day!

There was another aspect of my sin-tainted "personality" that was so often a huge stumbling block to my progress in overcoming the strong stubborn domination of the sinful nature. I often thought that I must have inherited Joseph's *genes.* I am a dreamer! I did not want to wait until I actually got to *heaven* to *experience heaven*! I wanted to experience heaven with all its sin-free and problem-free perfection and glory now! And so often I thought that if I just worked a little harder at it, I could somehow make that happen! But it didn't happen; and it's not going to happen. Because this is

not heaven and all the dreaming and valiant efforts by the most determined of souls will not change that! But, again, the relinquishment and acceptance of that which I cannot change has never come easy for me. I can't tell you how many times, when things were especially difficult that I lamented: It's not supposed to be *this hard!* And I often got intensely frustrated and even angry with God that the battle had to go on *this* long and be *this* painful! I knew such an attitude was sinful and displeasing to God (Num. 11:1), so I confessed this sin. God lovingly forgave (as He always does – 1 John 1:9), and by His mercy and grace I soon came to realize that God always knows what is best. Every battle has a purpose that works for good and expands our capacity for righteousness, peace and joy. Looking back there is not one thing I would change. Not one moment, not one experience, not one day of difficulty or suffering, for God was graciously *at work* in every situation teaching me priceless wisdom and forging righteousness, courage and character within.

God is helping me to see life in a *fallen world* for what it really is: a life-long battle against sin and its encroachment on our lives; a battle to regain what we lost in the fall—His very own holy, good and gracious image. And that makes it a *good fight.* A fight that is laced with the sweetness of victory and triumph as faith is purified, Christlike character is developed, and we become *fit vessels, useful to the Master (2 Tim. 2:21).* There's joy in that: unspeakable, unquenchable joy (1 Pet. 1:8).

Biblical Reality Therapy that works, therefore, is:

> We live in a fallen world where the consequences of sin wreak havoc all around us. Pain, suffering and death are a natural and inevitable part of this reality. But in and through Christ (obedience to His Word in the power of the Holy Spirit), we are more than conquerors over all: sin, pain, suffering…and even death! (John 11:25-26).

God never leaves us alone in dealing with the difficulties, pain and problems of life. He gives us

Himself—His Presence through His blessed Holy Spirit along with all His *precious and magnificent promises (2 Pet. 1:4)* upon which we can stand firmly and securely as we *press on*:

> *(Your) refuge will be the impregnable rock;… And He shall be the stability of your times, a wealth of salvation, wisdom, and knowledge (Is. 33:16a, 6).*

God, through Jesus, has made a way for us to <u>overcome</u> sin and its inevitable consequences in our own personal lives and to deal courageously and victoriously with the consequences of sin that come to us as a result of the fallenness of others and of our world. It is called: Trust and obey. Trust and obey the truths and promises of God in the power of the Spirit. But we must *know* the truths and promises to *obey* the truths and promises. And that is what we have been doing in this Bible Study. And that is what we, with the help of God, will continue to do long after this study is over.

Because of the redemptive, inexhaustible grace that flows from Calvary's cross, we no longer run from our difficulties and trials but rather turn to embrace them for their good God-designed purposes:

> *Consider it all joy, my brethren, when you encounter various trials, knowing that the testing of your faith produces endurance. And let endurance have its perfect result, that you may be perfect and complete, lacking in nothing (James 1:2-4).*

> *And not only this, but we also exult in our tribulations, knowing that tribulation brings about perseverance; and perseverance, proven character; and proven character, hope; and hope does not disappoint, because the love of God has been poured out within our hearts through the Holy Spirit who was given to us (Rom. 5:3-5).*

> *Now to Him who is able to keep you from stumbling, and to make you stand in the presence of His glory, blameless with great joy, to the only God our Savior, through Jesus Christ our Lord, be glory, majesty, dominion and authority… now and forever. Amen (Jude 1:24-25).*

Bible Study Supplement
Chapter 6 — Day 2 — As Sparks Fly Upward
Biblical Reality Therapy

1. Read John 16:33.

    a. What did Jesus promise for all who remain *in Him?* (vs. 33a)

    b. From what we have studied to this point, what do you think it means to be *in Jesus?*

    c. What did Jesus clearly tell us that we will have *in the world?* (vs. 16b)

    d. What kind of an attitude in the midst of trials and troubles should we have?...Why? (vs. 33b)

2. Read Job 5:7.

    a. How sure is *trouble* for man—all of us in the human race?

One of the first steps to overcoming—or avoiding being *overcome by*—the problems that inevitably befall us as a result of living in a fallen sin-cursed world is a realistic *biblical* view of life. *Man is born for trouble as sparks fly upward...in the world you <u>will</u> have tribulation, but <u>be of good cheer!</u> I have overcome the world!* (*Job. 5:7; John 16:33*). Once we accept these realities—we live in a fallen world in which we inevitably will face hardships, trials and difficulties—we can do so with confidence and *good cheer* knowing that God is with us to help us and to fight for us in our battles (Deut. 20:4; 2 Chron. 20:15-17). We can rest in God's <u>assurance of victory</u> as we look to Him and continue to walk in steadfast, trusting, obedient faith (2 Chron. 20:15-25; Deut. 20:1-4; John 14:15-26).

Ps. 107 is a psalm about God's love and faithfulness. It tells of how God delivers man from "manifold troubles". It's a psalm of hope and encouragement.

3. Read Ps. 107:1-22, 43.

    a. What is man's life like before being redeemed (vs.2) by God's mercy and grace? (vs. 4a, 5)

    b. What did God do when the afflicted cried out to Him in their trouble? (vs. 6b-7)

    c. Why did some dwell in darkness and were prisoners in misery and chains? (vs. 10-11)

    d. What did God do for them when they cried out to Him? (vs. 13b-14)

    e. Who continued to be afflicted...why? (vs. 17)

f. What did they do then...and what did God do in response? (vs. 19)

g. How did God save/heal them? (vs. 20a)

h. What should be the response of those who have experienced the deliverance of the Lord? (vs. 21a, 22b)

i. Who is wise? (vs. 43)

4. Read Ps. 34:19.
   1. How many troubles/afflictions will a righteous man have? (Circle correct answer).
      a. 1 or 2   b) a few   c) many
      b. Of these, out of <u>how many</u> does the Lord God deliver him?

This is a critical verse that will help us greatly in our Christian walk. We are not to seek or expect a trial, tribulation or pain-free life. We are to seek God and His Kingdom in which are always found an overflowing and exceedingly abundant supply of love, mercy, and grace-empowered <u>deliverance</u>!

5. Read Ps. 32:10
   a. What does life hold for the wicked?

   b. What surrounds the one who trusts in the Lord?

God is too loving and too kind to promise us a life of ease, free of pain and difficulties in a fallen world. That would be the ultimate cruelty! Rather, He tells us that *because* we are *fallen men and women* with *an innate sinful nature* and we live in a *fallen, corrupt, evil world*, there will be *enemies to face, battles to fight, pain and affliction to overcome*...as surely as the *sparks of a fire fly upward*. But in the same breath, He also offers us Himself as our Redeemer and our deliverer...*out of them all the Lord God delivers him (Ps. 34:19)*. May God help us all to *grow up*: to put away childish dreams and unrealistic lusts for *heaven on earth*. It's just not going to happen. We are not *home* yet. We are on a journey—a journey to righteousness and Christlike holiness. Jesus wants to be our Shepherd on this journey. If we closely and obediently follow Him, He promises to *lead us beside still waters*, to *make us lie down in green pasture*, to *restore our soul*, to *guide us in the paths of righteousness* so that even when *we walk through the valley of the shadow of death, we will fear no evil; for He is with us; His rod and staff comfort us… our cup of blessing overflows. Surely goodness and mercy shall follow us all the days of our lives and we will dwell in the house of the Lord forever (Ps. 23, sel.).*

Write out a Bible verse that had special meaning to you today.

Based upon what you have learned today, write a prayer to God expressing the desires of your heart in applying these truths to your life.

Chapter 6 — Day 3
You Have Need of Endurance
Fighting the Good Fight...Finishing Well

> Therefore, do not throw away your confidence, which has a great reward. For you have need of endurance, so that when you have done the will of God, you may receive what was promised (Heb. 10:35-39).
>
> I have fought the good fight, I have finished the course, I have kept the faith (2 Tim. 4:7).

Endurance: From Greek word, "Hupomeno" Meno: to abide; to remain firm and steadfast (as opposed to leaving or abandoning). Hupo: under a burden, hardship. It means to continue courageously and trustfully, regardless of the difficulties; to press on persistently through suffering and adversity. It means never giving up and never giving in (quitting). Endurance is an inner character quality. It is perseverance extended. Endurance picks up where perseverance leaves off.

You've been there and so have I. That place where life is *overwhelmingly* overwhelming! Everything hurts, the trials have gone on *too long,* and the outlook for the future appears bleak because there is absolutely no evidence that things will ever change for the better...only worse...and it all *seems* totally impossible—even *with* God!

God alone knows how many have experienced major *faith shipwreck (1 Tim. 1:9)* from which they never recovered at one of these critical junctures. Having grown weary of the battle, they jump ship to seek out a hiding place where they can get back to a more "normal" life, less fraught with conflict and daily battles. And they spend the rest of their days nursing their wounds, and resigning themselves to being satisfied that they are "going to heaven". They become content with "getting by" spiritually

while immersing themselves in the pleasures of this world in order to "enjoy" the days that remain. Far removed from God's will, they bear no fruit for the advancement of the Kingdom and contribute little to the work of the local body of believers to which they belong. It seems to *work* for awhile...until they come to the end of their days and they look back with no spiritual legacy that will go on to bless others long after they are gone and no "treasures in heaven" to joyfully anticipate—"treasures" like souls saved through their prayers and witness, along with God's special "rewards" promised for all who remain faithful to Him (Rev. 22:12; Col. 3:24). Consequently, regret, emptiness and depression haunt their final days from which there is no escape. It's a sad scenario that plays out daily in untold numbers across our nation.

What is missing in the lives of such peripheral Christians—the number of which is growing significantly as the difficulties of our days increase (2 Tim. 3:1)—is that rock solid, unshakable, inner character quality: Endurance.

Before the foundation of the world, God knew there would be difficult and overwhelming days for all who would walk this fallen planet. That is why the Bible instructs us to *continue in the things you have learned...pressing on* in *steadfast, firm, trust in God*—walking *by faith* (not *feelings* or "human" possibilities or impossibilities – 2 Tim. 2:3; Phil. 3:12, 14; Col. 1:23; Heb. 10:35). We must also recognize that true, godly endurance is not something that we can conjure up on our own. Biblical endurance—also referred to as *patience* in the Bible—is a fruit of the Spirit that is produced by the Spirit of God in those who are surrendered to Him, walking by faith and obedience as He leads them in fulfilling His good plans (the will of God) each day. And, as in all things, the *faith* that enables us to keep trusting—to *endure*—comes by *hearing and hearing by the Word of God (Rom. 10:17)*. God's Holy Spirit always leads us according to God's Word. We cannot obey what we do not *know*. We must *abide* in the Word—reading it, studying it, seeking the Holy Spirit's guidance as He enlightens the Word to our hearts and enables us to obey it. Biblical endurance, therefore, always involves a consecrated, unwavering *never give up, never turn back, fight to the finish obedience to the Word and will of God.*

Nevertheless, Father, not my will, but Thine be done (Matt. 26:39).

In times of especially difficult trials, an unflinching commitment to faithfully carry out the will of God will sustain and uphold us as we courageously face the difficulties and press on for the victory. This is what Jesus did and this is what we must do also if we are to develop that precious quality of endurance that will keep us faithful and steadfast…to the end.

I must be about my Father's business...And it came about… that He resolutely set His face to go to Jerusalem...I glorified Thee on the earth, having accomplished the work Thou hast given Me to do (Luke 2:49; John 17:4; Luke 9:51).

What a beautiful example Jesus gives us of focused simplicity in living. He did not allow Himself to get caught up in all the temptations and distractions that undoubtedly surrounded Him, just as they press in on us (Heb. 4:15). He *resolutely* set His heart on *being about the Father's business…*

accomplishing the work that <u>He</u> had given Him to do. Jesus found rest and peace and His greatest joy in that (John 15:11; 17:4). And so will we if we follow Jesus' good example.

Because it is so important, let's review what God's purpose (will) for our lives is:

1. To have a close and intimate relationship with Him—*knowing Him, loving Him and serving Him with all our heart, soul, mind and strength,* that we might *honor and glorify Him*—which should always be our deepest yearning and heart's desire in all that we do *(Matt. 22:37-39; John 17:3-4; 1 Cor. 10:31; Eph. 1:4-6, 11-12).*

2. To fulfill God's special plan for our lives, which *He preordained before the foundations of the world (Eph. 2:10; Jer. 29:11-14).*

3. To become *conformed to the image of His Son (Rom. 8:29)*—the process of transforming our fallen old nature back into it's original holy state of purity and righteousness.

4. To tell others the *good news of Christ's salvation and redemption from sin and death (Matt. 28:19-20; 2 Cor. 5:20).*

It is impossible to fulfill the latter three without first fulfilling our #1 purpose—to have a close and intimate relationship with God—because *He holds all things together (Col. 1:17).* That is why it is so important to establish a regular and consistent time in the Word daily, for it is there that we come to *know* God as He reveals Himself and His good plans to us (John 17:3; Eph. 2:10; Rom. 12:2).

He who has My commandments and keeps them, he it is who loves Me; and he who loves Me shall be loved by My Father, and I will love him, and will <u>disclose Myself</u> to him (John 14:21-23).

But what about conformity to the image of Jesus? How can that be accomplished? As in knowing the will of God it all begins with that intimate relationship with Him—accomplished through time with Him in His Word and prayer. How can we *know* what the *image of Jesus* looks like unless we look upon it often in the pages of God's Word. So it all goes back to the Bible—we must *know* the Word in order to be transformed by it.

Concerning the image of Jesus, therefore, we must ask: according to the Word of God, what is it about us that does not conform to this image? I'm sure that by now we all know the answer to this one. It is our fallen sin nature that stands between us and the image of God in which we were originally created and to which God is in the process of conforming us once again. So this—our fallen sin nature—is the ultimate enemy that must be overcome if we are to fulfill God's command to be *conformed to the image of His Son*. This, as we have mentioned many times in this study, is *the good fight* to which we have all been called—the *fight against sin, against the control of our sinful nature* in our lives that robs us of that close, intimate fellowship with God and others, keeps us from fulfilling His good purposes, and wreaks untold pain and destruction in our lives and in the lives of others.

We get a very graphic look at the pain and awful consequences of sin run amok (a result of ignoring it and not dealing with it according to God's Word) by taking a walk through Ps. 38. I find myself returning to this Psalm often when I recognize that I am dealing with a sin stronghold that refuses to be brought down. Let's listen to a little *biblical reality therapy* here:

There is no soundness in my flesh...no health in my bones <u>because of my sin</u>. For my iniquities are gone over my head; As a heavy burden they weigh too much for me. My wounds grow foul and fester. Because of my (sinful) folly, I am bent over and greatly bowed down; I go mourning all day long. For my loins are filled with burning; and there is no soundness in my flesh. I am benumbed and badly crushed; I groan because of the agitation of my heart... My heart throbs, my strength fails me; and the light of my eyes, even that has gone from me. My loved ones and my friends stand aloof from my plague. And my kinsmen stand afar off. Those who seek

my life (the devil, the world, my own sinful flesh) lay snares for me;... they devise treachery all day long... But I, like a deaf man, do not hear (sin separates us from God and closes our ears so we cannot "hear" from God)...I am ready to fall, and my sorrow is continually before me...I am full of anxiety <u>because of my sin</u>... my enemies are vigorous and strong... come quickly to help me, O Lord my Savior (Ps. 38:1-22, sel.).

Can you relate? This agonized cry of a man bent over with sin and its destructive, soul-wrenching consequences is a scene that is all too familiar to most of us. Sin hurts. It hurts to the core of our being. Sins of the past, (resulting in sin's long-range consequences), sins of the present, the ever encroaching temptations and fleshly lures of sin's future intrusions (Rom. 7:14-23). *Sin,* my greatest, most treacherous enemy surrounds me on every side. And just as we talked about yesterday, all the wishing in the world is not going to make it go away or change this reality. For the present, we live in a fallen, sin-cursed world in which the consequences of sin's pervasive presence affects us in various ways daily. But such is not a cry to discouragement or despair. I see Psalm 38 as a battle cry. A wake-up call. A summoning to rally the troops and get a lot more serious about this war in which we find ourselves. This war—against sin and the destruction and death it always causes (Rom. 3:23)—*is real.* We must stop pretending that it will somehow go away if we just ignore it long enough. It will not go away. We need to be like David and turn to God: *O Lord my Savior, come quickly to help me! (Ps. 38:22).* Then in faith and obedience, we must put on our spiritual armor every day, get out on the battlefield, face those enemies (sin habits, strongholds, and undisciplined lusts of the flesh) and *fight the good fight* for the righteous reign of Christ in our hearts and homes. And this we must do with zeal, passion and <u>endurance</u>! For our very *life* and the welfare of our family—and many others our lives touch—depend upon it (Deut. 32:46-47). We must, as never before, walk *by faith, not sight,* (or feelings or fear or being overwhelmed by "human" impossibilities) *in the power of the Holy Spirit* moment by moment, day by day, decision by decision. *Choose you this day whom you will serve*—your rebellious sinful flesh that leads to destruction and death every time, or Jesus, our Good Shepherd who leads us to life, and that *more abundantly (John 10:10).*

> *See, I have set before you today life and prosperity, and death and adversity; in that I command you today to love the Lord your God, to walk in His ways and to keep His commandments and His statutes... So* <u>*choose life*</u> *in order that you may live, you and your descendants, by loving the Lord your God, by obeying His voice, and by holding fast to Him; for this is your life (Deut. 30:15-20, sel.).*

We can win those daily battles against sin *if we choose* to *love the Lord our God, hold fast to him, obey His voice and walk in His commandments.*

Yes, it's a battle...a fight to the finish! But let our hearts take courage today because God has promised that we will overcome and we will have victory if we *choose* to *trust and obey...*and *keep on choosing...*and *enduring*!

> *Listen, all Judah...thus says the Lord to you, "Do not fear or be dismayed because of this great multitude, for the battle is not yours but God's. Tomorrow go down against them...station your-*

selves, stand and see the salvation of the Lord on your behalf... Do not fear or be dismayed; tomorrow go out to face them, for the Lord is with you"...then, the Lord set ambushes against the sons of Ammon, ...who had come against Judah; so they were routed... and (all were destroyed). *Jehoshaphat* (and his army) *were three days taking the spoil because there was so much (2 Chron. 20:15-25, sel.).*

And the God who destroyed the enemies of His people that day in the wilderness of Jeruel, is the same God who is <u>with us</u> and <u>in us</u> to fight our battles and to be *victorious over our enemies (Col. 1:27; Eph. 1:18-22; John 14:16-17, etc.).* So here we have the answer to the dilemma of being overwhelmed by human impossibility. Even when I can't <u>see</u> an answer to the difficult situation encompassing me, I can *choose* to <u>trust God</u> and continue on in faith and obedience—no matter the protests of a weak body and languishing spirit, or how impossible things *appear.* I, by the Grace of God, and the power of the Holy Spirit now resident in me, can *press on,* <u>enduring</u>...to the end!

> *Be strong and courageous, do not fear or be dismayed because of all the multitude... for the one with us is greater than the one with (them). With them is only an arm of flesh, but* <u>*with us is the Lord our God to help us and to fight our battles*</u> *(2 Chron. 32:7-8).*

Bible Study Supplement
Chapter 6 — Day 3 — You Have Need of Endurance
Fighting the Good Fight...Finishing Well

1. Read 2 Tim. 2:1, 3, 8-13.

    a. What does Paul command His spiritual son, Timothy, to do? (vs. 1)

    b. What other instruction does he give him? (vs. 3)

    c. Who are we to remember at all times? (vs. 8)

Paul was gladly willing to *suffer hardship* and to *endure* many difficulties—even imprisonment and being chained to a Roman soldier as he was at the time he wrote this letter to Timothy—because He kept His eyes on Jesus and continually remembered Jesus' great love and sacrifice for Him (Rom. 5:8). Keeping this perspective, he always considered his difficulties and sufferings as small, not even *worthy of comparison (Rom. 8:18).*

    d. Though he was in prison, what does he say is *never imprisoned/chained?* (vs. 9b)

I love this verse. It says that the Word of God is never "bound" by circumstances, trials or difficulties. It is free to work just as powerfully for the man or woman who is in prison, the housewife who finds herself in the midst of an overwhelming physical, mental or emotional situation, or the searching soul who has never met the Savior.

    e. How was he able to <u>endure</u> all things? (vs. 10)

    f. What is a trustworthy statement? (two things - vs. 11-12a)

    g. What happens if we *deny/disown* Him? (vs. 12b)

    h. If our heart is right before God and we are truly trying to serve Him, what happens even when we, in human weakness and frailty, are *faithless?* (vs. 13)

This is a beautiful promise. It reminds us of the unchanging, unwavering faithfulness of God. Even if we are unfaithful, He remains faithful to His Word and promises. We only have to repent of our sins and *return to Him* to experience once again the fullness of our Father's goodness, love, provision and protection (Luke 15:11-32). Please note, however! It does not say that if we rebel against Him and willfully disobey, we will escape the consequences of our rebellious sin. We will not. *The wages of sin is death (Rom. 6:12).* Sin always brings its "death"—separation from God, pain, suffering, loss. God wants to spare us of that. That is why He has given us His precious Word to keep us on the path of righteousness and from the snares of sin with all its painful consequences.

There is a direct link between *endurance* and *courage*. We can't *endure* unless we remain *courageous*.

2 Chron. 32:7-8 speaks of this kind of trusting, enduring courage. This passage was originally spoken by Hezekiah to God's people who found themselves in the midst of a battle against forces far greater (humanly speaking) than themselves. As God's people today who face similar situations, the message is for us as well.

   2. Read 2 Chron. 32:7-8.

      a. When we face enemies greater than our own "human" strength and resources, what are we commanded to <u>do</u> (two things) and <u>not</u> to do (two things)? (vs. 7a)

      b. Why? (vs. 7b)

      c. Describe the difference between the power our enemy has and the power we have! (vs. 8)

Now who do you think is going to win if we utilize the power God has given us through His Holy Spirit?

One of the best instructions regarding the necessity of courage when facing enemies is given to Joshua when he was about to lead the children of Israel into the promised land. We've studied this passage before, but let's take a look at it again to strengthen and re-en-**courage** our hearts.

   3. Read Josh. 1:5-9.

      a. What promise does God give Joshua as he leads the children of Israel into the promised land? (three things - vs. 5)

      b. Exactly <u>how</u> courageous is he to be? (vs. 7a)

      c. What must he do to be successful, conquer enemies, and take the land? (three things – vs. 8).

And we can be sure that those same instructions for "success" will work for us just as they did for Joshua.

   4. Read 2 Cor. 1:8-10.

      a. Why did God allow Paul to go through the difficult hardships he endured in Asia? (vs. 9b)

      b. What did God do then (and what will He continue to do for all His children when they go through similar difficulties?) (vs. 10)

5. Read 2 Tim. 1:7-12 .

Note: In verse 7 of the Niv, the word "timidity" is used when referring to what God has <u>not</u> given us. A better translation is "fear". Please use this in your answer to the first question.

   a. What has God <u>not</u> given us? (vs. 7)

   b. What has He given us? (three things - vs. 7)

   c. What was Timothy to join Paul in doing? ... and how was he to do this? (vs. 8b)

   d. Why is Paul not ashamed? (two specific reasons – vs. 12)

6. Read Heb. 10:35-39. (Use Nasb below)

35. Therefore, do not throw away your confidence, which has a great reward.

36. For you have need of endurance, so that when you have done the will of God, you may receive what was promised.

37. For yet in a very little while, He who is coming will come, and will not delay.

38. But My righteous one shall live by faith; and if he shrinks back, My soul has no pleasure in him.

39. But we are not of those who shrink back to destruction, but of those who have faith to the preserving of the soul.

   a. What are we not to throw away? Why? (vs. 35)

   b. Of what do we have need? (vs. 36a)

   c. Why do we need this character quality? (vs. 36)

   d. How are we to live? (vs. 38a)

   e. What are we <u>not</u>? (vs. 39a) What are we? (vs. 39b)

7. Read 2 Tim. 4:5, 7-8. (Use Nasb below)

5. But you, be sober in all things, endure hardship, do the work of an evangelist, fulfill your ministry.

7. I have fought the good fight, I have finished the course, I have kept the faith;

8. In the future there is laid up for me the crown of righteousness, which the Lord, the righteous judge, will award to me on that day; and not only to me, but also to all who have loved His appearing.

a. What are we instructed to do as we *continue* in our walk with the Lord? (four things - vs. 5)

b. What could Paul confidently say as he neared the end of his life? (three things - vs. 7)

c. Because of this, what did Paul know was *laid up/in store for him?* (vs. 8a)

d. For whom is this same crown also *laid up?* (vs. 8b)

May it ever be our earnest prayer that when we come to the end of our earthly days that we can say with just as much confidence and just as much joyful anticipation as Paul did:

I have fought the good fight, I have finished the course, I have kept the faith! (2 Tim. 4:7).

Write out a Bible verse that had special meaning to you today.

Based upon what you have learned today, write a prayer to God expressing the desires of your heart in applying these truths to your life.

Chapter 6 — Day 4
Sweet Hour of Prayer — Part One

> *And it came to pass, that, as he was praying in a certain place, when he finished, one of his disciples said unto him, Lord, teach us to pray (Luke 11:1).*

Today we begin a two-day study of the precious privilege God has given us to come into His presence and to commune with Him through prayer. It is in this sweet fellowship that we receive the assurance of our Father's love, forgiveness of our sins, joy in His presence, comfort and a respite from the trials and troubles of the world. It is here that we are also filled with hope, wisdom, direction from God for our lives, and the empowerment of the Holy Spirit. What a glorious privilege!

Jesus understood this. As we study His life, we see the preeminent role that prayer played for Him.

> *And in the early morning, while it was still dark, He (Jesus) arose and went out to a lonely place, and was praying there (Mark 1:35).*

It was late into the evening, on another occasion, after feeding the 5,000 (this was just the number of men—there were probably 15-20,000 present that day with women and children), gathering up the fragments of bread and fish, then ministering further to the needs of the people, that Jesus told His disciples to *get into the boat and go ahead of Him to the other side, while He departed to the mountain...to pray...* and He prayed *until the 4th watch (3:00 AM) (Matt. 14:22-23, 25).*

It was at this time (yet another occasion) that He went off to the mountain to pray, and He spent the whole night in prayer to God (Luke 6:12).

And again in Luke's gospel: *He would often slip away to the wilderness and pray (Luke 5:16).*

Jesus' ministry, indeed His whole life, revolved around prayer. Jesus began every day spending time with His heavenly Father, in communion and communication with Him, seeking His will and the wisdom and strength to carry it out. Yes, Jesus was God, but remember our study of Philippians 2 in which we learned that Jesus willingly *emptied Himself* of every *right* and every privilege of His Godhood to be a humble servant, with no greater status, position, or innate human power than any of us. He took on the *fullness of humanity (Phil. 2:7; Heb. 2:14, 17)* with all its weaknesses, frailties, and even temptations to sin. As *fully man,* Jesus knew that He must depend completely upon His Father if He was to successfully complete the purpose for which He had come (John 17:4).

Now, don't you think that if it was necessary for Jesus, the sinless, perfect Son of God, to start every morning, and to end every evening in prayer fellowship with His heavenly Father, and if it was necessary for Jesus to spend whole nights in prayer on occasion when facing important decisions (the choosing of the twelve disciples), then surely, it must be all the more necessary for us to develop this kind of dependence upon God through regular and consistent prayer fellowship with Him if we are to successfully complete the work that God has for us (Eph. 2:10).

Besides the joy of just being in God's presence, prayer is also one of the most dynamic and powerful weapons God has given us in our spiritual warfare arsenal. The Bible is replete with examples of the critical role that the prayers of God's people played in the outcome of major events: specific guidance was given through them, wars were won by them, lives were spared because of them. Jesus, Himself, had much to say about this centerpiece of our Christian walk. We won't have time in this brief overview to consider in depth all that Jesus (and the rest of the Bible) teaches us about prayer, but we will learn basic principles that will help us in our desire to become faithful men and women of God whose *fervent prayers avail much (James 5:16)*. As we look into God's Word, we will be drawn closer to the throne of grace and we will come to a deeper understanding of what a blessing, privilege, and source of power and peace spending time with our heavenly Father in prayer truly is.

Prayer, in unity with the Word of God, enables us to maintain a biblical, God-centered perspective on life, including our problems, trials and difficulties. It enables us to *set our mind on things above, not on the things below (Col. 3:2)*. It lifts us above our present, oft burdensome circumstances into the very presence of God where we enjoy intimate fellowship and communion with Him (Eph. 1:3, 2:6). It is there, in the throne room of God's presence and grace, that God dispenses to us wisdom, guidance, and every provision we need to know and do His will and to deal with all our problems and decisions with confidence and courage (Heb. 4:16; Phil. 4:19). As we yield ourselves to the control (filling) of the Holy Spirit within us, we are also given the power we need to defeat sin and Satan. That's why developing an effective prayer life will involve times of battle as well. Satan does not want

us coming to such a place of relinquishment and intimacy with God where our lives are characterized by trusting, obedient dependence upon Him (1 Thess. 5:17; Luke 18:1). But we will find that as we persevere in developing this good discipline of spending time with God in prayer, even our battles are laced with grace and the assurance of God's presence and overcoming power and victory (2 Chron. 20:15-25; Ps. 16:11). So how do we do this? How do we *enter in*—into this sacred Holy of Holies, the throne room of God's grace...into the very presence of God, Himself? And what do we do once we are "there"? How do we communicate—with God? How do we pray *effectively*?

To help us get started on developing an effective, fruitful prayer life that blesses not just us, but countless others whom we lift before God's throne of grace, we will draw from Jesus' own instructions and personal example of prayer found in Matt. 6:9-13 (Jesus' model prayer, "Our Father...") and John 17 (Jesus' high priestly prayer), as well as from other *effectual prayers that availed much* in the Bible. In so doing, we see a pattern of prayer principles that forms the acronym, ACTS – PW: Adoration, Confession, Thanksgiving, Supplication – Praise and Worship. We will talk about the first three of these today, then pick up with the last two in our study tomorrow.

Note the vertical and horizontal aspects of prayer communion with God. Our attention must first be drawn upward—to God and His majestic, transcendent holiness and glory. This awareness flows naturally into a time of confession and repentance as we recognize our own sinfulness and need for God's forgiveness and redeeming grace, which He freely bestows as we *confess our sins (1 John 1:9)*. Cleansed, renewed and restored, we move outward in our prayers—to others, interceding to our heavenly Father on their behalf. Then we pour out our hearts to God concerning our own personal needs and decisions. We conclude with a time of praise and worship as we remember all God's wonderful blessings and promises which send us out into our day with a song of joy in our hearts (Ps. 40:3; Is. 55:12).

The most important aspect of any *effective prayer* is entering into God's presence where we worship Him *in spirit and in truth (John 4:23)*. We need to be reminded of our relationship with God. He is *God, most High...holy, and lifted up (Ps. 57:2; Is. 6:1-3; Rev. 4:8-11)*. He is also our loving, caring, compassionate heavenly Father (Ps. 103:8-13). There are a number of passages in Scripture which serve as excellent sources of praise and adoration—lifting our hearts and minds heavenward, away from the troubles and tribulations of this world, into the very presence of God. For example:

Blessed art Thou, O Lord God of Israel, our Father, forever and ever. Thine, O Lord, is the greatness and the power and the glory and the victory and the majesty; indeed everything that is in the heavens and the earth, Thine is the dominion, O Lord, and Thou dost exalt Thyself as head over all. Both riches and honor come from Thee and in Thy hands are power and might, and it lies in Thy hands to make great and to strengthen everyone. Now, therefore, our God, we thank Thee and we praise Thy glorious Name (1 Chron. 29:11-13).

Praise the Lord! Praise, O servants of the Lord. Praise the name of the Lord. Blessed be the name of the Lord, from this time forth and forever. From the rising of the sun to its setting, the name of the Lord is to be praised. The Lord is high above the nations. His glory is above the heavens. Who is like the Lord, our God, who is enthroned on high; who humbles Himself to behold the things that are in heaven and in the earth? He raises the poor from the dust and lifts the needy from the ash heap... Praise the Lord! (Ps. 113:1-9, sel.).

Other excellent Scriptures of praise and adoration that you may want to incorporate into this special time of prayer fellowship with God at various times are: Is. 6:1-5; Ps. 18:1-6, 46, 49-50; Ex. 15:1-18; 1 Sam. 2:1-10; 1 Chron. 16:8-15, 23-36; 2 Kings 19:14-19, 35; 2 Chron. 20:21-22; Neh. 9:5-8; Ps. 145-150; Jer. 32:17-20; Daniel 2:19-23; Luke 1:46-55; Luke 1:67-75; Luke 2:25-32; John 12:12-13; Eph. 3:20-21; 1 Pet. 1:3-5; 1 Pet. 5:10-11; Jude 24-25.

As noted earlier, it is so important to establish this proper relationship with God—one of reverence and awe, yet intimate and personal—before proceeding to the other elements of prayer. God is the awesome and mighty ruling king and authority over all the earth (Is. 6:1; 1 Chron. 29:11-13; Ps. 113:1-4). At the same time, He is our heavenly Father, we are His children whom He loves very much and with whom He desires to commune and fellowship, guide, protect and empower. If we fail to come to Him in this spirit, our hearts will be filled with fear and doubt rather than faith and confidence. Consequently, our prayers will be ineffective and unempowered.

The next crucial element of effective *spirit and truth prayer (John 4:23)*, is *confession*—sincere, contrite, truthful, confession that leads to true repentance. We must recognize that *sin separates us from God (Is. 59:2)*. We cannot expect God to hear and answer our prayers when we are harboring unconfessed sins or bitterness against others. We should also recognize that every sin we commit is ultimately a sin against God (Ps. 51:3-4).

Behold, the Lord's hand is not so short that it cannot save; neither is His ear so dull that it cannot hear. But your iniquities have made a separation between you and your God, and your sins have hidden His face from you, so that He does not hear...If we say we have no sin, we are deceiving ourselves, and the truth us not in us... If I regard sin in my heart, the Lord will not hear...for I know my transgressions... against Thee, Thee only have I sinned (Is. 59:2; 1 John 1:8; Ps. 66:18, 51:3-4).

Search me, O God, and know my heart: try me, and know my anxious thoughts: And see if there be any wicked way in me (Ps. 139:23-24).

There are two kinds of sins: sins of commission (doing things that violate clear instructions in God's Word), and sins of omission (<u>not</u> doing something that we are instructed in God's Word to do, made clear to us by the Holy Spirit's inner convictions). As the Holy Spirit brings various sins to our remembrance (conviction), we should humbly and contritely confess them to God. But it is not enough to merely *confess* our sins. We must sincerely *repent* of them *from the heart*—experiencing true *godly sorrow*, which leads to *fruits of repentance (2 Cor. 7:10; Acts 26:20)*. We turn from our sins to God, walking in righteous obedience to Him as He leads us through His Word and prayer. This is where we often miss the joy of true repentance and forgiveness because we fail to go deeper than mere words—into the heart, into the inner motivations, into the core sin issues of our fallen nature: selfishness, greed, pride, stubbornness, rebellion, need to control, etc. If we fail to do this, our confessions become little more than lip service and the power of the sin is not broken. The result of this kind of superficial, insincere repentance is that the same sins are repeated over and over again. God wants to spare us of this terrible cyclical bondage to sin and the destructive consequences it always brings. That's why He has given us His Word to expose sin and the Holy Spirit to empower us to overcome it. But we must *listen to Him* and we must be careful to *obey Him* as He leads us out of sin's deceptive, binding snares.

Be gracious to me, O God, according to Thy lovingkindness; according to the greatness of Thy compassion blot out my transgressions and cleanse me from my sin... Purify me... and I shall be clean; wash me, and I shall be whiter than snow... if we confess our sins He is faithful and just to forgive us our sins and to cleanse us from all unrighteousness (Ps. 51:1-12 sel.; 1 John 1:9).

After we have sincerely confessed our sins, we should lift our hearts heavenward in songs of thanksgiving to God, as we remember all that He has done for us *in Jesus* because of His great, undeserved love for us: forgiveness of our sins (1 John 1:9), freedom from condemnation, (Rom. 8:1), power over sin, (Rom. 6:4-14), eternal life (John 3:16; Luke 10:20)...and so much more (Eph. 1:2-21).

It is then good to ask God to help us walk in the peace and joy of a cleansed and renewed heart.

Create in me a clean heart, O God, and renew a steadfast (righteous) spirit within me. Do not cast me away from Thy presence, and do not take Thy Holy Spirit from me. Restore to me the joy of Thy salvation, and sustain me with a willing spirit...then my tongue will joyfully sing of Thy righteousness (and) my mouth declare Your praise (Ps. 51:10-14, sel.).

Bible Study Supplement
Chapter 6 — Day 4 — Sweet Hour of Prayer – Part One

1. Read Mark 1:35.

    a. When did Jesus pray?

    b. Where did Jesus pray?

In similar passages in Luke 6:12 and 5:16 we read: *(Jesus) went off to the mountain to pray...He would often slip away to the wilderness and pray.* The point here is not that we must go outdoors to a mountain or wilderness to pray, but that it is important to find a time and place where we are alone, away from the noise and distractions of the world. Only then will we be able to focus upon God…to *be still and know…* His love, His peace, His comfort. It is also the only way that we can receive the knowledge and guidance we need to know His good will and purposes for our lives and be empowered through the Holy Spirit to walk in them. Jesus knew this. That is why He always made prayer—time alone and fellowship with His Father—a priority in His life. As sinful, weak mortals, do we not all the more *need* this?!

2. Read Is. 59:1-2.

    a. What has separated us from God—from His love, joy, peace, strength…and even from His "hearing" and answering our prayers? (vs. 2a)

3. Read Heb. 4:15-16.

    a. What kind of *high priest* do we <u>not</u> have?…What kind do we have? (vs. 15)

    b. Because of this, what can we do? (vs. 16a)

    c. What will we receive/find as we do so? (vs. 16b)

As you read the first four verses of one of the most beautiful prayers in the Bible—Jesus' High Priestly Prayer—notice the intimacy He has with His Father. Notice also His single-mindedness and clearly focused purpose.

4. Read John 17:1-4.

    a. How did Jesus address God? (vs. 1)

    b. What is "eternal life"? (vs. 3)

Notice the call to *relationship* here once again. *This is eternal life, that they may <u>know</u> Thee, the only true God and Jesus Christ whom Thou hast sent.* It is impossible to *know* someone and *love* someone without spending time with them—talking to them, listening to them, seeking to know and understand their heart...and sharing yours with them. As we read and study God's Word and as we meet with Him in prayer, we develop this relationship. Our love for God grows, our faith is increased, we develop a greater trust and dependency on Him and we become more careful and faithful in our obedience. The result: *freedom and joy unspeakable and full of glory! (John 8:31-32; 1 Pet. 1:8).*

    c. How did Jesus glorify His heavenly Father? (vs. 4)

Throughout His earthly ministry, Jesus was focused upon one thing—doing the Father's will. That's why He spent time each day alone with His heavenly Father. He wanted to maintain that close, intimate relationship so that He would always *know* and *do* His Father's will in order to please Him and bring Him honor and glory. Should we seek to do any less? Our prayer life, like Jesus', should center around *knowing God, loving God* and *fulfilling His will for our lives* that we, too, might glorify Him. And the blessing is that as we do so, our lives are made full, spilling over with joy into the lives of others (John 15:11).

There is so much more in this beautiful prayer—so much about our relationship with God and all that Jesus has done, and is doing for us as our Savior. So much about His deep, compassionate love for us and about His desire for us as brothers and sisters to walk in unity and in the joy of an intimate, loving relationship with Him and one another. Let's take just a few moments now to read through the rest of this prayer and as we do, I'm sure that our hearts will be blessed as we begin to comprehend the depth of our Savior's love for us.

5. Read John 17:6-26. (We will not ask any questions; I just want you to be encouraged by this precious prayer that Jesus prayed for our protection, unity and blessing).

6. Read 1 John 1:5-9.
    a. What happens when we walk in the light (God's truth and forgiveness)? (two things - vs. 7)

    b. If we say we have no sin, what does this mean? (two things - vs. 8)

    c What happens if we confess our sins? (two things – vs. 9).

Please keep in mind that John is referring to humble, sincere confession and repentance, not mere lip service that makes no difference in our lives. True repentance always leads to a changed heart, which leads to changes in our lives (Acts 26:20)—a progressive turning from sin to God in a life of increasing trust and obedience.

Write out a Bible verse that had special meaning to you today.

Based upon what you have learned today, write a prayer to God expressing the desires of your heart in applying these truths to your life.

Chapter 6 — Day 5
Sweet Hour of Prayer — Part Two

Pray without ceasing... devote yourself to prayer, remaining alert in it, with an attitude of thanksgiving (1 Thess. 5:17; Col. 4:2).

Today we continue our study of the precious privilege of prayer. Yesterday, we talked about the preeminent place that prayer played in the life of Jesus. Jesus lived His life around the priority of prayer. He began and ended each day in the presence of His Father in prayer fellowship with Him. And He went through the day maintaining this close, intimate, dependent and trusting relationship. He knew that His heavenly Father loved Him with a perfect and never-failing love and that He would be with Him and provide all that He needed to do His Father's good will. He found security, peace, and contentment in that assurance. It was this assurance also that gave Him the desire and power to overcome every temptation. Jesus lived His life to be pleasing to the Father (John 17:4). That is how He was able to walk in total, joyful obedience (Heb. 12:2; John 15:11). What a beautiful example Jesus gives us! As we follow His good example by maintaining an intimate, dependent and trusting relationship with our heavenly Father through prayer, we will find our own lives filled with peace, joy, security and contentment.

Drawing from the model prayers of Jesus found in Matt. 6:9-13 (the prayer Jesus gave the disciples when they asked Him to "teach us to pray") and John 17 (Jesus' "high priestly prayer"), along with other specific instructions on prayer found in the Bible, we developed a biblical pattern of prayer using

the acronym ACTS – PW (Adoration, Confession, Thanksgiving, Supplication – Praise and Worship). We learned that the first part of our prayers should be spent in reverential adoration of God—who He is and all He has done. We mentioned a number of excellent Bible passages that lift our hearts and thoughts heavenward—away from the world—and into the loving, holy presence of God.

The next element of *spirit and truth prayer (John 4:23)* is sincere confession and repentance. We talked about the importance of true *godly sorrow (2 Cor. 7:10)*—genuine remorse that produces *fruits of repentance (Acts 26:20).* This is naturally followed by a time of thanksgiving for all that God has done for us in Jesus—forgiveness of our sins, (1 John 1:9); eternal life (John 3:16); freedom from condemnation (Rom. 8:1); making us His children and all this means for us! (Eph. 1:2-21).

This is where we left off yesterday. Today, we continue our prayer fellowship with God by moving from a vertical (upward) to a horizontal focus in which we look outward—to the needs of others, lifting them before God's throne of grace. This is the supplication (or intercessory) part of our prayers.

Be on the alert... with all prayer and petition pray at all times in the Spirit... with all perseverance and petition for all the saints...and pray on my behalf, that utterance may be given to me in the opening of my mouth, to make known with boldness the mystery of the gospel (Eph. 6:18-19).

… and My servant Job will pray for you. I will accept (his prayers) *so that I may not do with you according to your folly, because you have not spoken of Me what is right … and the Lord restored* (in double measure) *the fortunes of Job when he prayed for his friends (Job. 42:8, 10).*

Moreover, as for me, far be it from me that I should sin against the Lord by ceasing to pray for you (1 Sam. 12:23).

Intercession for our brothers and sisters is clearly not an "option" in the Christian's life. It is a command from God. It is a vital and indispensable part of God's plan for the advancement of His Kingdom. What a privilege God has given us to be a part of the most important work in all the world!

After interceding for others, we are invited by God to pour out our hearts to Him on our own behalf, laying before Him our concerns and needs, our pain and sorrows, our questions and confusions, as we seek His comfort, wisdom, and guidance for our day.

… call upon Me in the day of trouble, I shall rescue you … I will answer you and tell you great and mighty things (Ps. 50:15; Jer. 33:3).

Then you will call upon Me and come and pray to Me, and I will listen to you … and you will seek me and find me when you search for me with all your heart (Jer. 29:12-13).

… casting all your anxiety upon Him, because He cares for you (1 Peter 5:7).

God wants us to come to Him with all our problems. He is our heavenly Father who loves us *with an everlasting love,* and has promised to *watch over, care for and guide us (Jer. 31:3; Matt. 6:25-30; Phil. 4:19; Ps. 25:12).* How much we miss by failing to do this.

Finally, we come to a time of praise and worship as we remember our *blessed inheritance in Christ (Eph. 1:18-21, 2:1-6)*—God's boundless blessings and promises to us, His children. As we lift our hearts in praise and thanksgiving, we are strengthened and encouraged to *press on* in all the good plans God has for us. This is my favorite time of prayer fellowship with God because I know that no matter what the day may hold, as I go out in the assurance of these promises—<u>knowing them, believing them, obeying them</u>—God will be with me and He will empower me to be victorious over every trial and difficulty and He will fill my heart with joy as I *trust and obey (Luke 1:74-75; John 15:11).*

God has done so much for us because of His great, undeserved love, mercy and grace. As we take a few moments to reflect upon this, our hearts will well up with songs of praise and thanksgiving. The following are just a few of God's endless blessings that we might include in this special time of praise and worship—*remembering* and *giving thanks to God:*

Thank You, God that I have been born again to a living hope that is imperishable and will never fade, (1 Pet. 1:3-4). Thank You that I have been crucified and buried with Christ, and it is no longer I who live, but <u>Christ lives in me</u> … so that as Christ was raised from the dead through the glory of the Father, (I), too, might walk in newness of life (Rom. 6:4). Thank You that I am dead to sin, but alive to God—to righteousness, joy and peace in the Holy Spirit (Rom.6:11, 14:17). Thank You, heavenly Father, that You know the plans You have for me … plans for welfare and not for calamity to give me a future and a hope … and that You have promised that when I call upon You and come and pray to You, that You will listen to me, and You will instruct me in the way I should go (Jer. 29:11-13 sel.; Ps. 25:12 cf. John 14:21; Rom. 12:1-2). Thank You that You have further promised: if any of you lacks wisdom, let him ask of God, who gives to all men generously and without reproach, and it will be given to him (James 1:5), and that if I make my ear attentive to wisdom and incline my heart to understanding; if I cry for discernment and lift my voice for understanding and search for her as for silver and hidden treasure… I will discover the knowledge of God… You cause wisdom to enter my heart. Your knowledge is pleasant to my soul (Prov. 2:2-123, sel); Thank You that Your sheep hear Your voice and You know them and they follow You (John 14:27).

Thank You that <u>Your grace is sufficient</u>; for Your power is perfected in (my) weakness. Most gladly, therefore, will I boast about my weaknesses that the power of Christ may dwell in me. Therefore, I am well content with weaknesses, with insults, with persecutions, with difficulties for Christ sake, for when I am weak, then I am strong (in Jesus' never failing, all-sufficient grace) (2 Cor. 12:9-10).

Thank You that You <u>are good</u> and <u>do good</u> at <u>all times and in all places</u>, and that no good thing do you withhold from those who walk uprightly (Ps. 73:1, 119:68, 84:11, cf. Rom. 8:28).

Thank You that we can be confident of Your mercy, provision and all-sufficient grace at all times knowing: You who did not spare Your own Son, but delivered Him up for us all, how will You not also with Him freely give us all things? (Rom. 8:32).

Thank you that You love me with an <u>everlasting love</u> (Jer. 31:3); and Your lovingkindness never ceases. Your compassions never fail. They are new every morning; Great is (Your) faithfulness (Lam. 3:22-23). Thank You that nothing shall ever be able to separate me from your love—not tribulation, or distress, or persecution…or peril, or sword… or demons above, or Hell below… but in all these things, we overwhelmingly conquer through (Jesus) who loved us and gave Himself up for us…I <u>can</u> do all things through Christ who strengthens me (Rom. 8:31-39, sel.; Phil 4:13).

Thank you that these things You have written that Your joy may be in us and our joy may be complete (John 15:11); Thank you that the joy of the Lord is my strength and He who believes in You, from His innermost being shall flow rivers of living water… love, joy, peace, patience, kindness, goodness, faithfulness, gentleness, self- control (Neh. 8:10; John 7:38; Gal 5:22-23).

And finally, I just want to praise and thank you God, that…there is a river whose streams make glad the (people) of God. <u>God is in the midst of her. She will not be moved</u>! (Ps. 46:4-5).

These are just a few of the more than 2,000 promises God has for us in His Word! Of course, we needn't go through the entire list above at the conclusion of every prayer time with the Lord, but we should ever be "storing up" treasures like these in our hearts as we read and study God's Word, and we should take a few minutes at the end of our prayer times to *remember* such precious promises that will strengthen and encourage us as we go out into our day… and as we walk through our day.

Just a few closing thoughts as we conclude this overview of the precious privilege of prayer:

And when you are praying, do not use meaningless repetition, as the Gentiles do, for they suppose that they will be heard for their many words (Matt. 6:7).

This is a very important caution directly from Jesus. We should not allow our prayer life to become rigid or rote. Repeating a certain phrase or "prayer" over and over is not prayer at all in God's eyes; it is vain repetition. Prayer, like all of life for the Christian is about <u>relationship</u> and the love and grace of God, not rigid rules. We will not always be able to spend an "hour" in prayer or go through our entire intercessory prayer list every day. God understands. He just wants us to "be there", fellowshipping with Him, talking to Him, listening to Him—getting to *know Him (John 17:3)*. He wants us to *freely receive His forgiveness and grace* as we *confess our sins* and *cast all our cares on Him (1 John 1:9; 1 Pet. 5:7)*. He wants us to be ever *growing* in our love for, trust in, and obedience to Him (2 Pet. 3:18; Deut. 6:4-6; Prov. 3:5-6). That is the heart of a prayer life that is pleasing to God.

Several years ago I did an in-depth Bible Study on the Lord's Prayer. It was excellent and taught me much about God's heart for prayer. I highly encourage you, if possible, to do further study on this "model" prayer after completing these lessons. And we should never forget the crucial role the Holy Spirit plays in our prayers. The Bible says that sometimes we get so overwhelmed by life with all its complexities and problems, and our own fears and doubts, that we don't even know *how to pray… but the Holy Spirit helps us in our weakness...and intercedes for us (Rom. 8:26-27, 12:2)*. I find this wonderfully comforting.

> *Pray without ceasing… devote yourself to prayer, remaining alert in it, with an attitude of thanksgiving (1 Thess. 5:17; Col. 4:2).*

Our prayers should be "continuous," steadfast and offered with an attitude of thanksgiving. Like Jesus, our lives should revolve around prayer. We should go through our day in communion with God—looking to Him, seeking His guidance, obeying Him, praising Him. Maintaining an *attitude of gratitude* in our prayer life will keep us from falling into the very destructive snares of *grumbling and complaining* and *self-pity* (Numbers 11:1, 10; Phil. 2:14-15).

These are, indeed, difficult days in which we are living. And life will surely become overwhelming if we don't take time to get alone with our heavenly Father—*away* from all the pain and problems, troubles and trials. Prayer and the Word of God are undoubtedly the most powerful *spiritual weapons* that God has given us to help us deal effectively with our problems, overcome the devil's lies and schemes and live confident, Spirit-filled, victorious lives for the glory of God—for our own blessing and joy,

and for the good of countless others our lives touch. Therefore, we can be sure that the enemy will do everything he can to rob us of these precious faith and relationship-building times with God. We must stand firm against his temptations, making time with God in His Word and prayer our number one priority. As we do this, God will reward our faith and trust. He will give wisdom, guidance and the strength we need to overcome our problems and become strong, righteous men and women of God, whose prayers—and lives—*avail much (James 5:16 cf. Matt. 6:33).*

How I look forward to these precious times with God! Every morning when I awaken, I thank God for another day in which to walk with Him, talk with Him and fulfill the good plans He has for me. I can hardly wait to get to my "quiet time corner" where I will spend time with the Lord—in His Word and prayer—because I know that there I will always find a *refuge from the storm, forgiveness for my sins, comfort for my sorrows and failures, wisdom from above to guide and direct me,* and *encouragement and strength to overcome my fears and weaknesses (Ps. 57:1, 61:3-4, 62:5-7; Prov. 2:2-12; 2 Cor. 12:9-10).* This time, along with our family devotions at bedtime are my favorite times of the day. I don't know what I'd do without these precious restorative and refreshing times of fellowship with God and one another.

Finally, remember that few battles are actually won on the battlefield. The outcome of nearly all serious warfare is determined on our knees as we seek the wisdom and power of God through fervent prayer. Without such, there will be no *godly wisdom*, no *divine power*, and *no lasting victory*.

> *Keep watching and praying, that you may not enter into temptation; be on guard… praying in order that you may have strength to escape all these things about to take place (Matt. 26:40; Luke 21:36).*

Bible Study Supplement
Chapter 6 — Day 5 — Sweet Hour of Prayer – Part Two

1. Read 1 John 5:14-15.
   a. How can we be sure that God will *hear* and *answer* our prayers? (vs. 14b)

2. Read James 4:1-3.
   a. Why do we <u>not</u> receive what we ask for? (vs. 3)

There is a little verse tucked away at the end of the book of Job that would be of incalculable blessing to all of us if we practiced it regularly—particularly when we are going through especially difficult trials or affliction.

3. Read Job 42:10, 12-13.

Here we are told that God brought about restoration, healing and a double portion of blessing to Job.

   a. When did God do this? (vs. 10)

I wonder how much more effective our prayers—and greater and more consistent our victories—would be if we followed the good example of Job (and principle of prayer) that God gives us here.

4. Read 1 Sam. 12:23.
   a. What did Samuel realize he would be doing if he failed to pray for God's people? (vs. 23a)

How long has it been since we stopped to ponder what the Bible says about our responsibility before God to pray for our brothers and sisters and that to fail to do so is…<u>*sin*</u>.

God is pleased when we come to Him in loving compassion on behalf of others. He blesses this kind of obedience, adding to our own lives as well as to the lives of those for whom we pray. This is so encouraging, because even when we are too sick, too weak, or too overwhelmed with our own problems and difficulties and just don't have the time or the physical resources to get out and witness or share the love of Jesus in practical ways with others outside the home, we can still pray for them. And we can pray for those who do not yet know Jesus—that God's Holy Spirit would break through the deception, pride, hardness of heart or fear, help them realize their need for Him, and open their hearts to receive Him as their personal Lord and Savior. We should also remember others going through especially hard times—that God would be merciful and help and strengthen them. God hears every sincere prayer, prayed in faith and trust, and He always answers in the very best way for all involved. How many blessings have we withheld from our family and friends (and ourselves, in turn) because we failed to *pray for them*?

5. Read Luke 1:45-55. (Note: This prayer is often referred to as "Mary's Song" or "Mary's Magnificat (song of praise). It was lifted to God on the occasion of her visit with her cousin, Elizabeth, when Elizabeth was six months pregnant with John the Baptist and Mary had just been told she would bear the Savior of the world. It truly is a beautiful *song of praise*.

    a. Who is blessed? (vs. 45)

    b . What did Mary's soul and spirit do? (vs. 46-47)

    c. Why was Mary's heart so full of joy? (vs. 48a, 49)

    d. To whom is His mercy extended? (vs. 50)

We have just as great a reason to be full of joy as Mary, for indeed, God in Christ, has done *great things for us!* (*John 3:16; Rom 5:8; Eph. 1:2-22, 2:1-6, 3:16-20 etc., etc., etc.*)!

6. Read Phil. 4:6-7.

    a. About "how much" in life should we be "anxious"? (vs. 6)

    b. What should we do instead? (vs. 6)

    c. What should be our "attitude" as we come to God in prayer? (vs. 6 - Complete the following sentence): We should make our requests to God with _____ in our hearts.

    d. If we obey God in this good command—refuse to get anxious in times of trials and difficulties, but instead, turn to God in prayer with a believing, thankful heart—what will be the result? (vs. 7)

7. Read 1 Thess. 5:16-18.

    a. What are we instructed to do *always?* (vs. 16)

    b. What else are we to do *without ceasing/continually?* (vs. 17)

    c. What should be our attitude at all times…in *every situation/circumstance?* (vs. 18)

Do you see the link here between constant, fervent prayer and joy and thanksgiving. People who *pray without ceasing* will also develop a thankful, joyful heart. This may not happen immediately. *Fervent, effective* prayer, like every other spiritual discipline takes time and devotion (exercise and practice) to develop. Let's ask God to help us persevere in this pursuit, for in so doing, we will become *faithful, righteous* men and women of God whose *fervent prayers avail much* for the glory of God and the advancement of His great kingdom (James 5:16).

Write out a Bible verse that had special meaning to you today:

Based upon what you have learned today, write a prayer to God expressing the desires of your heart in applying these truths to your life.

Chapter 7

Bible Memory Verse: *Looking for the blessed hope and the appearing of the glory of our great God and Savior Christ Jesus (Titus 2:13).*

Bonus Memory Verse: *Therefore, my beloved brethren, be steadfast, immovable, always abounding in the work of the Lord (1 Cor. 15:58).*

Day 1

Biblical Health and Healing

An Overview – Part One

Day 2

Biblical Health and Healing

An Overview – Part Two

Day 3

The Sons of Issachar and the Signs of the Times

Day 4

Heaven – Better By Far – Part One

Strangers and Aliens

Day 5

Heaven – Better By Far – Part Two

Storing up Treasures

Keeping An Eternal Perspective …One Day at A Time

Epilogue

A Preview of Things to Come

Overview of Book Three: *That Your Joy May be Full*

Chapter 7 — Day 1
Biblical Health and Healing
An Overview — Part One

> *Before I was afflicted I went astray, but now I keep Thy Word… It is good for me that I was afflicted, that I may learn Thy statutes. (Ps. 119:67, 71).*

I had planned on devoting the entire sixth week to studying the important topic of biblical health and healing but there were just too many other subjects that needed attention this time, so we will pick this topic up again in book three of this series, dealing with it more comprehensively there.

However, since we all face the reality of pain and suffering in a fallen world, and since we live in an age of incredible deception with a plethora of unbiblical teaching concerning it—which, sadly, has resulted in much additional, unnecessary suffering and heartache—we need to take at least a couple of days here to get an overview of what the Bible says about health and healing.

One of the most dangerous teachings that permeates our Christian community today is the "health, wealth, and prosperity gospel." We talked about this briefly in a previous lesson, but we need to mention it again here because so many of our precious brothers and sisters have been devastatingly hurt and their faith shaken because they have trusted the bold claims of the preachers and teachers of this *false gospel*. Contrary to what many radio and television evangelist—and sadly preachers in far too many pulpits—preach, it is not *God's will*, according to the *whole counsel of God's Word (Acts 20:27)*, that all God's people be "in perfect physical health, immune from disease and pain free". It is God's will that we enter into a personal relationship with Him through repentance and faith in what Jesus accomplished for

us on the cross and through His resurrection, and that we grow in this relationship through the process of sanctification—being set apart for His holy purposes and becoming conformed to the image of His Son (2 Thess. 2:13; Rom. 8:29; 1 Pet 1:15-16). It is, therefore, God's will that we *know Him* and *love Him* and *walk with Him* day by day in a trusting, obedient, growing relationship (John 17:3; Matt. 22:37; John 10:29, 14:21, 23). In so doing, we bring honor and glory to God—our ultimate goal in all that we do—just as Jesus always did (Is. 43:6-7; 1 Cor. 10:31; John 17:4). Sometimes God uses affliction to accomplish these, His highest purposes for us.

> *And we know that God causes all things to work together for good to those who love God, to those who are called according to His purpose (Rom. 8:28).*

Everything God does and everything God allows is for a purpose—a *good* and a *blessed* purpose—for *those who love Him*. If only we really believed this and had the faith to walk in this assurance, our lives would be radically transformed and we would experience a lot less anxiety, stress and bitterness and a lot more peace, joy and contentment.

The area that is the most difficult for most of us to embrace by faith, believing God for His goodness in it, is the area of human pain and suffering. We are quick to judge all suffering as bad and undesirable. That is really sad because we miss so much of God's "good" by failing to trust Him and to be blessed as He works His good purposes in and through our pain.

If we are to develop the kind of faith that sees beyond what we *feel* and what our *sinful flesh demands*, we will need to develop an accurate biblical definition of health and healing. So we must, as always, return to the Word of God to search out God's purposes in human suffering. In so doing we will clear up a lot of confusion, our faith will become stronger and purer, and *the peace and joy of Jesus will rule in our hearts (Col. 3:15; John 15:11).*

A BIBLICAL VIEW OF SUFFERING

Before I was afflicted I went astray, but now I keep Thy word...It is good for me that I was afflicted, that I may learn Thy statutes (Ps.119:67, 71).

For the truly born again Christian, difficulties and affliction always draw us closer to God and deeper into His Word for wisdom, strength and comfort. And in so doing, we are made more aware of the necessity of God's Word in our lives. It elevates the value of God's Word to its rightful place— God's very own revelation of Himself, essential for *knowing Him,* for comprehending His great love for us and for guiding us in all His good plans for our lives. God's Word truly is a *light unto our feet and a lamp unto our path (Ps. 119:105),* including the path through suffering. As we are drawn into a closer relationship with God through His Word, we find not only the encouragement we need to endure momentary pain and affliction, but also the wisdom and power (through the Holy Spirit within us) to overcome sin and to *press on* to Christlike holiness (Phil. 3:12-14; Rom. 8:29).

But He knows the way I take; when He has tried me, I shall come forth as gold (Job. 23:10).

Take away the dross from the silver, and there comes out a vessel for the (Master) (Prov. 25:4).

Suffering refines, purifies and perfects. It brings to the surface the ungodly, unrighteous dross so that

it can be removed, making us *vessels for honor, sanctified, useful to the Master (2 Tim. 2:21).*

Consider it all joy, my brethren, when you encounter various trials, knowing that the testing of your faith produces endurance. And let endurance have its perfect result, that you may be perfect and complete, lacking in nothing (James 1:2-4).

Trials, including physical, mental and emotional pain, purify our hearts, strengthen our faith, produce endurance, and make us *complete* so that we can stand strong in all of life's adversities.

And as He passed by, He saw a man blind from birth. And His disciples asked Him, saying, "Rabbi, who sinned, this man or his parents, that he should be born blind?" Jesus answered, "It was neither that this man sinned, nor his parents; but it was in order that the works of God might be displayed in him (John 9:1-3).

Suffering provides the greatest platform from which we can *display the works of God.* When we sing the praises of God's sustaining mercy and grace as we walk through our pain with courage and unwavering, trusting faith, others *see and believe and put their trust in the Lord (Ps. 40:3).* Anyone can praise God when they are "healthy, wealthy and pain free". It takes true godly character to praise God in the midst of pain and suffering. It is such a life that both proves and reflects the magnificent magnitude of God's mercy, grace, and glory.

For we do not want you to be unaware, brethren, of our affliction which came to us in Asia, that we were burdened excessively, beyond our strength, so that we despaired even of life…in order that we should not trust in ourselves, but in God who raises the dead; who delivered us from so great a peril… and will deliver us, He on whom we set our hope. And He will yet deliver us (2 Cor. 1:8-10).

But we have this treasure in earthen vessels, that the surpassing greatness of the power may be of God and not from ourselves (2 Cor. 4:7).

Suffering starkly reminds us of our human frailty and inability to handle life with all its difficulties and perplexities—alone. If we allow suffering to work its good purposes in us, it will break our stubborn independent spirit and thrust us into the arms of God who is our *very present help in time of trouble, our faithful Savior* and *great deliverer (Ps. 46:1, 18:1-6, sel., 34:19).*

> *…that I may <u>know</u> Him, and the <u>power of His resurrection</u> and the <u>fellowship of His sufferings</u> (Phil. 3:10).*

Affliction/pain draws us into an intimate fellowship with Jesus—the fellowship of His sufferings—that enables us to experience a depth of love and oneness with our Savior that we could never know any other way. It also introduces to us the *power of His resurrection* as we put our faith and trust completely in Him and experience His triumphant empowerment working in us to lift, sustain, and bring victory.

> *…and He Himself bore our sins in His body on the cross, that we might die to sin and live to righteousness; for by His wounds you were healed (1 Peter 2:24).*

This is a beautiful promise. Sadly, however, this verse has been taken out of context, twisted and misused more than any other to promote the unbiblical teaching of the "health, wealth and prosperity" gospel. Preachers and teachers of this false doctrine are quick to point out that the wounds inflicted upon Jesus were the payment for all human affliction, therefore, true "saving" faith in Jesus and in His atoning sacrifice on the cross results in "healing" of every kind of sickness and infirmity. But it is clear, according to *the whole counsel of God's Word* (evidenced in the texts already discussed above, along with dozens more, and from this verse itself), that the "healing" referred to here is a spiritual healing from sin and death and the power they once held over us…*that we might die to sin and live to righteousness.* To be sure, we will all be perfectly healed—physically, mentally, emotionally and spiritually—

one day when our sanctification is complete and we enter into the blessed state of perfected glorification with Christ. But that will not happen until we are taken out of these sin-corrupted bodies and receive our new glorified bodies in heaven. In the meantime, God gives us His amazing, always sufficient grace to enable us to be *more than conquerors* over every type of difficulty, pain and affliction.

> *…there was given me a thorn in the flesh, a messenger of Satan to buffet me…Concerning this I entreated the Lord three times that it might depart from me. And He has said to me, "My grace is sufficient for you, for power is perfected in weakness."… Therefore, I am well content with weaknesses, with insults, with distresses, with persecutions, with difficulties, for Christ's sake; for when I am weak, then I am strong (in Jesus' strength-giving grace) (2 Cor. 12:7, 9-10).*

Paul prayed earnestly that God would take away his affliction. God's answer came in the above response. God did not physically *heal* Paul of his affliction, troublesome as it was. But He did give Paul something far better: His abundant, all-sufficient grace to carry him through every situation victoriously. Paul believed God for the overcoming power of His grace and wisely chose to live in the triumphant joy of that assurance rather than focusing upon His affliction and the inadequacy of his own human weaknesses (2 Cor. 12:9-10; Phil. 4:4-13).

It is clear again here that *immediate* physical healing was not "in the atonement". The apostle Paul was one of the most committed, godly men of faith and perseverance that ever walked the face of this earth. Yet God did not *heal* him of his affliction—even though he prayed earnestly for it. And there have been countless other saints through the ages who have also served God and believed Him wholeheartedly for His power to heal them, for whom physical healing did not come. Yet these same trusting men and women of God lived vibrant, joyful, contented lives and were mightily used of God to bring scores of souls into the kingdom. I cannot help but think of a modern day "Paul" who also prayed with complete faith for healing, but did not receive it. So she wisely and courageously followed the biblical example of Paul and put her faith in God and in His always abundant, always sufficient grace rather than in having a fully functioning, pain free body. Her name is Joni Eareckson Tada, and for over 40 years since her diving accident in which she became a quadriplegic, Joni has encouraged hundreds of thousands of people all around the world—from her wheelchair—with her beautiful example of total trust and faith in God and in His promises for overcoming grace. God alone knows how many have come to faith in Christ as they observe Joni faithfully and consistently living in the power and joy of Christ's victory over sin and its consequences—including physical pain and difficulties. I thank God for Joni and I pray that He will richly bless her in all the good work she continues to do for His glory and the advancement of His kingdom. And I pray that He will help me to follow her good example, walking daily in the same trusting, triumphant faith and victory.

> *We have been born again to a living hope… I would have despaired if I had not believed that I would see the goodness of the Lord in the land of the living (1 Pet. 1:3; Ps. 27:13-14).*

Suffering awakens within us a *living hope* that assures us that we <u>will</u> see the goodness of the Lord…

in the land of the living. When our trust is in God, we know that suffering will never defeat us, it will only help us to know and love our Savior in an ever greater more intimate way. Suffering—my suffering, your suffering—is always personal and specific. It is not random or universally administered. God knows each one of us and He knows what is the very best for our long-term sanctification, fulfillment, peace and joy. There's comfort and rest in this assurance *(1 Pet. 5:10; James 1:2-4).*

> *But whatever things were gain to me, I count as loss… rubbish… in order to gain Christ and be found in* (His) *righteousness… for I consider that the sufferings of this present time are not worthy to be compared with the glory that is to be revealed to us (Phil. 3:7-8, sel.; Rom. 8:18).*

Suffering loosens our grip on the things of this world and begins to formulate within us a hopeful, eager, anticipation of a far *greater glory* yet to be revealed.

> *Eye hath not seen, nor ear heard all that God has prepared for those who love Him… Therefore we do not lose heart, but though our outer man is decaying, yet our inner man is being renewed day by day. For momentary, light affliction is producing for us an eternal weight of glory far beyond all comparison! (1 Cor. 2:9; 2 Cor. 4:16-18).*

Bible Study Supplement
Chapter 7 — Day 1 — Biblical Health and Healing – An Overview – Part One

Because this is such an important lesson, we will use our "Bible Study Supplement" time today to review the biblical reasons for suffering so that we will be able to stand strong in times of personal pain and suffering, and also to encourage others when they walk through their own trials and seasons of affliction.

Please turn back to the meditation for today, and beginning with the section: A BIBLICAL VIEW OF SUFFERING, review the Bible verses (in italics) that relate to God's reasons for allowing suffering in our lives. Please note any verses that have special meaning to you. When you are finished, write out at least two of these verses below.

Bible verses that had special meaning to me today:

Based upon what these verses teach, write a prayer to God asking Him to help you believe and, through His enabling grace and the power of the Holy Spirit in you, to live in the assurance and joy of these precious promises today and in the days to come.

Chapter 7 — Day 2
Biblical Health and Healing
An Overview — Part Two

> ...that I may know Him, and the power of His resurrection and the fellowship of His sufferings (Phil. 3:10).
>
> For I consider that the sufferings of this present time are not worthy to be compared with the glory that is to be revealed to us (Rom. 8:18).

When I was ministering to a woman who had been suffering for eight years with the same affliction as I—*medically* "incurable", causing chronic pain which was at times, severe, nearly unbearable—she asked me: "How can a 'God of love' leave us in such a snake pit of relentless physical and mental torment?" Of course the woman's assessment was biblically inaccurate. God hadn't *left us (Heb. 13:5; Matt. 28:20),* nor would she have found her situation a 'snake pit' had she viewed it through the eyes of faith, and the truths of God's Word. God's promises for mercy, grace, and overcoming strength, are just as real and just as powerful—and all the more so—in times of suffering as they are at any other time. Her thinking, like all of ours so often, had been clouded by her experience, her fleshly, sin-tainted *emotions,* (feelings) and deceptive worldly evaluations. She was living *by sight* (feelings and circumstances) not *by faith,* trusting and obeying God.

Most assuredly, it is not *easy* to walk *by faith* and to maintain a joyful, thankful spirit when pain is your daily companion—be it physical, mental, emotional, or a combination of all three—for months, years, decades of years. It is not *easy* to trust God and to praise Him when you are, as Paul was, *burdened excessively, beyond our strength, so that we despaired even of life (2 Cor. 1:9).* It is not *easy* to get out of bed on those days when you are

experiencing the kind of pain and *excessive burden* that causes everything in you to "hurt". It is not *easy* when the relentless pain and distress has gone on so long that you *feel* like pulling the covers over your head and staying there until Jesus comes back. No, it is not *easy.* But it is possible. I know. Because, by God's grace, I have done that for more than 25 years—not perfectly, of course, and certainly not because of any special strength or merit of my own. It was God, and God alone who, in His infinite mercy and grace, sustained, lifted, encouraged and so often *carried* me each step of the way on my own journey to that precious promised land of true biblical faith and obedience where we dwell daily in God's presence, enjoying the sweet, blessed fruits of *righteousness, peace and joy in the Holy Spirit (Rom. 14:17, cf. Is. 46:3; 58:11, 60:5; Ps. 34:5).* And I can tell you honestly, I would not change one day, one minute of it for anything, not one! God has accomplished so much more than anything I could have even *hoped or dreamed (Eph. 3:20)* through every situation of suffering and challenge. The scarlet thread of His presence, compassion, mercy and grace woven into each experience has resulted in a unique resilience and radiance in His unfolding tapestry. He has also taught me that when the heart is right and the thinking is truly biblical, even our pain and difficulties are permeated with peace and laced with joy as we recognize the opportunity they give us to *know Christ* and the *power of His resurrection and the fellowship of His sufferings* while at the same time, learning the good disciplines of relinquishment, submission and true godly contentment...*in whatever circumstances I am (Phil. 4:11).* There's freedom in that—broad, secure, joy-producing freedom! (Ps. 18:19; James 1:2-4; John 8:31-32, 36).

Another, and even greater, motivation that gets me out of bed every day is recognizing that it wasn't *easy* for Jesus to go to the cross either, enduring unimaginable pain and suffering—on <u>my</u> behalf, and on the behalf of every other man, woman and child that would ever be born. And He didn't <u>have</u> to. He was God. He could have done whatever He pleased. But He did it because of His unfathomable love for you and me and in obedience to His heavenly Father whose very character and nature of divine, transcendent holiness and justice demanded payment for sinful man's rebellion and disobedience. It was the only way that the clearly stated righteous, "just" payment for sin—death—could be satisfied. It was also the only way that God's love would be forever displayed so that not one searching soul would ever again be able to doubt it. *For God <u>demonstrated</u> His love for us, in that while we were yet sinners, Christ died for us (Rom. 5:8).* And because Jesus conquered sin and death, we will never have to face our pain and our difficulties alone or without the assurance of a sure and lasting victory one day, because <u>all</u> suffering on this earth is *temporary!* (Rev. 21:3-4; 2 Cor. 4:16-18).

We must be very careful to view our hardships and problems through the perspective of God's Word and His eternal truths—<u>not</u> through human reasoning and evaluations or our *emotions—feelings*—including feelings of pain and suffering (1 Cor. 1:18-30; 2 Cor. 4:16-18). If we fail to do this, our thinking quickly becomes distorted and we begin to develop bitterness and anger towards God, just as my friend did, and just as most of us have been guilty of doing far too often.

How can we avoid this trap? How can we discover the enduring joys of intimate fellowship with

Jesus *in* our suffering (Phil. 3:10)...along with those good, blessed disciplines of relinquishment, submission and true godly contentment...*whatever circumstances we are in (Phil. 4:11)?*

> *Come unto Me all you who are weary and heavy laden, and I will give you rest...learn from me for I am gentle in heart and you will find rest for your souls...In the morning, O Lord, Thou wilt hear my voice; in the morning I will order my prayer to Thee and eagerly watch...cast all your burdens on Him because He cares for you (Matt. 11:28-30; Ps. 5:3; 1 Pet. 5:7).*

The pain and problems of this world are much too big, too complex, and too overwhelming for any of us to handle on our own. That is why we need to set aside time every day to *come to Jesus (Matt. 11:28),* sit at *His feet (Luke 10:39), talk to Him (Ps. 5:3; Phil. 4:6), listen to Him (Ps. 27:13,14), cry out to Him, (Ps. 34:6) be comforted by Him (2 Cor. 1:3-4), learn from Him (Matt. 11:29),* and *grow in our love for, intimacy with, and dependency upon Him (Ps. 18:1; Matt. 22:37-39; Phil. 3:10).*

It is my heart's desire, and I know it is yours as well, to walk daily in this kind of loving, trusting communion with God and faithful obedience to His Word because we know that God's Word is true and that as we are faithful to believe and obey it, we become *more than conquerors* over all our problems, including the problem of pain (Rom. 8:37). In so doing, we bring honor and glory to God. I have walked with God long enough now to realize that some of life's greatest, most treasured joys are found, not in the absence of pain, but in the presence of our Savior—comforting us, strengthening us—as we go *through* our pain and problems. As we look to Jesus, and trust Him to accomplish God's good purposes in and through our trials and difficulties, our *hearts are purified,* our *faith is strengthened,* and we are *made complete, lacking in nothing (James 1:2-4).*

What then is true biblical health and healing? According to the verses we studied yesterday and today—and many others we won't have time to examine individually here that comprise the *whole* counsel of God's Word (Acts 20:27)—we can now give an accurate definition:

<u>*Biblical health and healing*</u> *is: Being born again by the Spirit of the living God into God's kingdom, receiving forgiveness of sins, eternal life and the unfailing love, grace and power of God through the indwelling Holy Spirit to overcome every difficulty and affliction with courage and confidence, as we fulfill God's good purposes for us… day by faithful day.* In so doing we bring honor and glory to God, contentment and joy to our own lives, and blessing to others.

May God help us all to live in the light of the all-sufficient *healing* we have already received so that we firmly and resolutely resist the temptations that afflictions often bring that would turn us aside from God's good path, choosing instead to remain faithful to fulfilling all God's good plans for us each and every day God gives us… in *sickness* (pain, difficulties, hardships), *and in health.*

Take away the dross from the silver, and there comes out a vessel… for honor, sanctified, useful to the Master (Prov. 25:4; 2 Tim. 2:21).

Before I was afflicted I went astray, but now I keep Thy Word… It is good for me that I was afflicted, that I may learn Thy statutes. Oh, how I love Thy law! It is my meditation all the day. Thy commandments make me wiser than my enemies; they are sweet to my taste. Yes, sweeter than honey to my mouth… they are the joy of my heart! The law of Thy mouth is better than thousands of gold and silver pieces (or health, wealth and prosperity!) (Ps. 119:67, 71, 97-98, 103, 111, 72,).

Bible Study Supplement
Chapter 7 — Day 2 — Biblical Health and Healing – An Overview – Part Two

James 1:2-4 is a classic text for teaching us how to respond to our trials. It is full of hope and promise for the future. Though we have looked at it in previous lessons, we need to take one more focused, concentrated look at it so that the truth it proclaims may be indelibly impressed upon our hearts and the next time we *encounter various kinds of trials,* we will be able to respond as God intends—a response that will bring joy and blessing.

1. Read James 1:2-4.

    a. How are we to respond to trials of many/various kinds (pain, suffering, hardships)? (vs. 2)

    b. Why? (Why should we respond this way—what are our trials doing <u>for</u> us?) (vs. 3)

    c. What will happen if we allow the trials that come to us to accomplish God's good purposes? (vs. 4b)

2. Read Rom. 5:1-5.

    a. Besides rejoicing in "the hope of the glory of God", in what else do we exalt/rejoice? (3a)

    b. What does suffering/tribulation produce? (vs. 3b)

    c. What does this, in turn produce? (vs. 4a)

    d. And again, what does this latter quality produce? (vs. 4b)

    e. What does this final good quality <u>not</u> do…and why? (vs. 5)

3. Read Ps. 119:67-72.

    a. What happened to the psalmist *before he was afflicted?* (vs. 67a)

    b. What happened as a result of his affliction? (vs. 67b)

    c. What did the psalmist discover about God through his suffering? (two things - vs. 68a)

    d. What does the psalmist do now? (vs. 69b)

e. What is the psalmist's conclusion regarding his afflictions?...Why? (vs. 71)

f. Describe the Word of God (law of God's mouth) to the psalmist after his affliction. (vs. 72)

4. Read Rom. 8:28.

a. Fill in the blanks:

_____ things work together for _____ to those who love God.

b. How many things? _____ (Write answer in capital letters this time).

c. Does this include troubles and trials, pain and suffering? Yes No (Circle correct answer)

d. Do you <u>really</u> believe this? Yes No

e. Does your life and the way you handle trials, pain and difficulties demonstrate and confirm your "belief"? Yes No

I hope that you have been encouraged today to truly begin to see your trials as God intends: not as unwanted intruders that rob and destroy and lead to bitterness and anger with God, but rather as friends to be welcomed for all the good He wants to do in them and through them.

Write out a Bible verse that had special meaning to you today.

Based upon what you have learned today, write a prayer to God expressing the desires of your heart in applying these truths to your life.

Chapter 7 — Day 3
The Sons of Issachar and the Signs of the Times

> *And the sons of Issachar (were) men who understood the times, with knowledge of what Israel should do (1 Chron. 12:32).*
>
> *Tell us, what will be the sign of your coming and of the end of the age? And Jesus answered and said to them, "See to it that no one misleads you" (Matt. 24:3-4).*

And you will be hearing of wars and rumors of wars; <u>see that you are not frightened</u>, for those things must take place, but that is not yet the end. For nation will rise against nation, and kingdom against kingdom, and in various places there will be great earthquakes… and plagues and famines; and there will be terrors and great signs from heaven… But all these things are merely the beginning of birth pangs (Matt. 24:6-9; Luke 21:11, sel.).

And Jesus answered and said to them, "See to it that no one misleads you. For many will come in My name, saying, 'I am the Christ,' and will mislead many… And many false prophets will arise, and will mislead many… For the mystery of lawlessness is already at work…in accord with the activity of Satan, with all power and signs and false wonders, and with all the deception of wickedness for those who perish, because they… took pleasure in wickedness… and did not receive the love of the truth so as to be saved (Matt.24:4-5, 11; 2 Thess. 2:7-12, sel.).

The Bible clearly warns that the end times will be times of incredible demonic deception. In fact the deception will be so great that there will be an apostasy, (falling away from, abandonment of God) the likes of which

has not occurred since Noah's era just prior to the world-wide flood.

Now we request you, brethren, with regard to the coming of our Lord Jesus Christ and our gathering together with Him, that <u>you not be quickly shaken from your composure or be disturbed</u>… let no one deceive you, for it will not come unless the apostasy comes first, and the man of lawlessness (the Antichrist) is revealed, the son of destruction, who opposes and exalts himself above every so-called god or object of worship, so that he takes his seat in the temple of God, displaying himself as being God (2 Thess. 2:1, 3-4).

Paul is clear here that there are two events that must transpire before Jesus' return: the great apostasy and the revealing of the Antichrist. The latter has not yet happened, but we are seeing the former unfold as man-centered humanism rises in popularity, dethroning God and becoming the "god" of the age. Self replaces God and rules in hearts, homes, governments and even apostasized churches.

But realize this, that in the last days difficult times will come. For men will be lovers of self, lovers of money, boastful, arrogant, revilers, disobedient to parents, ungrateful, unholy, unloving, irreconcilable, malicious gossips, without self-control, brutal, haters of good, treacherous, reckless, conceited, lovers of pleasure rather than lovers of God (2 Tim. 3:1-4).

It reads like the evening newspaper, doesn't it? It is exactly as God said it would be in *the last days.*

And because lawlessness is increased, most people's love will grow cold (Matt. 24:12).

With the ascendancy of *self* will come an incredible *lawlessness* and a *growing cold of love*—for God, and for one another. And with the coldness and rejection of God will also come a time of unprecedented violence and physical, mental and emotional disturbances and difficulties—the inevitable consequences of rejecting and abandoning God. God speaks directly to those who choose this path of rebellious disobedience in the 28th chapter of Deuteronomy:

The Lord will send upon you curses (and) confusion in all you undertake to do, until you are destroyed on account of the evil of your deeds, because you have forsaken Me. The Lord will make the pestilence cling to you until He has consumed you from the land…The Lord will smite you with consumption and with fever… with inflammation and with fiery heat and with boils and with tumors and with the scab and with the itch, from which you cannot be healed…The Lord will smite you with madness and with blindness and with bewilderment of heart; and you shall grope at noon, as the blind man gropes in darkness, and you shall not prosper in your ways; but you shall only be oppressed and robbed continually, with none to save you. In the morning you shall say, 'Would that it were evening!' And at evening you shall say, 'Would that it were morning!' because of the dread of your heart… And you shall be driven mad by the sight of what you see (Deut. 28:20-29, 67 sel.).

And there will be signs in the sun and moon and stars, and upon the earth dismay among nations, in perplexity at the roaring of the sea and the waves… men's hearts failing them for fear and the expectation of the things which are coming upon the world; for the powers of the heavens will be shaken (Luke 21:25-26, Nasb, Kjv).

Then say to the people of the land, 'Thus says the Lord God concerning the inhabitants of Jerusalem in the land of Israel, "They will eat their bread with anxiety and drink their water with horror, because their land will be stripped of its fullness <u>on account of the violence</u> of all who live in it… so you will know that I am the Lord (Ezek. 12:19-20).

The rejection of God is already bringing its natural consequences: separation from God and His protective hand, judgment of wickedness. The condition of our nation and of our world confirms this. We are experiencing unprecedented affliction, plagues and turmoil of body, mind and spirit, just as God said would happen. Plagues: there are over <u>5,000 rare diseases</u> affecting more than 25 million Americans for which there is no medical cure.[9] Heart disease is a leading killer among men, and is increasing among women as well. Serious mental and emotional affliction is at an all-time high with suicide now the 2nd leading killer among <u>teenagers</u> in our country! People are groping for answers, for escape. *In the morning you shall say, "Would that it were evening!" And at evening, "Would that it were morning!" because of the dread of your heart (Deut. 28:67).* But they won't find answers, nor an escape from the troubles apart from repentance and a right relationship with God.

Therefore when you see the abomination of desolation standing in the holy place (the Antichrist sets himself up as "God" and initiates pagan worship in the temple), which was spoken of through Daniel the prophet…then there will be a great tribulation, such as has not occurred since the beginning of the world until now, nor ever shall. And unless those days had been cut short, no life would have been saved; but for the sake of the elect those days shall be cut short (Matt. 24:15-22).

The abomination of desolation will usher in the *great tribulation*…the accompanying destruction of which *has not occurred since the beginning of the world until now, nor ever shall. And unless those days had been cut short, no life would have been saved (Matt. 24:21-22).* The tribulation will be a time of severe, unrestrained judgment as God pours out His wrath upon sin and those who have repeatedly and rebelliously rejected His Son and His loving invitation to enter into a relationship with Him. It is the beginning of the final purging of the world of sin.

> *(But) God has not destined us for wrath, but for obtaining salvation through our Lord Jesus Christ… For the Lord Himself will descend from heaven with a shout, with the voice of the archangel, and with the trumpet of God; and the dead in Christ shall rise first. Then we who are alive shall be caught up together with them in the clouds to meet the Lord in the air, and thus we shall always be with the Lord… Therefore comfort one another with these words (1 Thes. 4:16-18, 5:9).*

Before that terrible and awful "day of the Lord" (Is. 13:6, 9) when God's wrath is poured out upon the sin and wickedness of the world, God will bring to Himself, His children—all those who have sincerely repented and made a true confession of faith in Jesus, making Him their personal Lord and Savior.

> *But when these things begin to take place, straighten up and lift up your heads, because your redemption is drawing near. And He told them a parable: "Behold the fig tree and all the trees; as soon as they put forth leaves, you know for yourselves that summer is near. Even so you, too, when you see these things happening, recognize that the kingdom of God is near" (Luke 21:28-31).*

These are days of perplexity, anxiety and despair for those outside of Christ, unprotected by God's mercy and saving grace. But it is, at the same time, a period of great hope, anticipation and opportunity for the believer as he sees first hand *these things taking place* and recognizes that indeed, his *redemption draweth nigh!* Yes, we ought every day to *straighten up and lift up our heads* in eager anticipation. At the same time, we need also to be on the alert, strong and steadfast in our faith, courageously facing, and in God's grace, overcoming sin's intrusions, difficulties and trials. The opportunities we have for witness in these times will be great, for the world is desperately in need of, and troubled hearts are searching for…a Savior (Rom. 10:13-15).

> *Be on guard, that your hearts may not be weighted down with dissipation* (sinful lusts and pleasures of the world), *drunkenness and the worries of life, and that day come on you suddenly like a trap; But keep on the alert at all times, praying in order that you may have strength to escape all these things that are about to take place (Luke 21:34-36, sel.).*

It's a call to vigilance and a rekindling of our *blessed hope (Titus 2:13).*

> *…for the grace of God has appeared, bringing salvation to all men, instructing us to deny ungodliness and worldly desires and to live sensibly, righteously and godly in the present age, looking for the blessed hope and the appearing of the glory of our great God and Savior, Christ Jesus (Titus 2:11-13).*

Bible Study Supplement
Chapter 7 — Day 3 — The Sons of Isachaar and the Signs of the Times

1. Read 1 Chron. 12:32.

   a. What did the sons of Issachar understand? (two things) ... Do you?

2. Read Daniel 12:10.

   a. What will happen to "many" in the end times? (three things - vs. 10a)

   b. What will the wicked do?...will they understand what is going on? (vs. 10 - middle of verse)

   c. What will characterize those who have insight/are wise? (vs. 10b)

3. Read 2 Tim. 3:1-4.

   a. The "last days" will be times of... (vs. 1 - Circle correct answer).

   1) Carefree, fun and easy living   2) Difficult/terrible times

   b. How many characteristics described in verses 2-4 do you see happening in our world today?

4. Read Luke 21:12-13, 18-19.

   a. God says here that some of His faithful will be arrested, persecuted and "brought before kings and governors." What opportunity will this give? (vs. 13)

   b. What does God promise in the midst of times of hatred and persecution? (vs. 18-19)

Here is a beautiful promise for God's remnant. A promise of protection and deliverance even in the midst of persecution and difficulties. I do not know exactly how God is going to do this, but God says that *not a hair on the head of His children will perish* and I believe God!

Every time I read these verses I cannot help but think of Shadrach, Meshach and Abednego. They were cast into the fire, yet immediately there was with them, *a fourth Man who walked about... in the midst of the fire without harm. Then the king's high officials gathered around and saw that the fire had no effect on the bodies of these men nor was the hair of their head singed, nor were their trousers damaged, nor had the smell of fire even come upon them* (Daniel 3:27).

5. Read Matt. 24:32-33.

   a. What can you know when the fig tree begins to put forth its leaves? (vs. 32b)

b. What does this parable tell us about the return of Jesus...how near is it/Jesus? (vs. 33b)

6. Read Matt. 25:1-13.

   a. What did the five prudent (wise) virgins do? (vs. 4)

   b. What happened at midnight? (vs. 6)

   c. What did the foolish virgins say to the wise? (vs. 8)...did the wise do what they asked? (vs. 9)

   d. What happened when the foolish went away to purchase more oil? (three things - vs. 10)

   e. What happened when the foolish came to the house and asked to enter? (vs.12)

   f. What is Jesus' warning regarding preparedness? (vs. 13)

7. Read Matt. 24:37-39.

   a. What will it be like at the time of the second coming of Jesus? (vs. 37).

I find these verses very comforting. According to what Jesus tells us here, there is not going to be a world-wide cataclysmic event that falls upon the earth bringing mass destruction and chaos <u>before</u> Jesus returns for His children. Rather things are going to go along *as in the days of Noah*. People will be *eating and drinking, marrying and giving in marriage*. God will mercifully hold back His hand of wrath and, even though times will be *difficult (2 Tim. 3:1)*, life will go along pretty much as "usual"...until He takes His children out.

Daniel 12:3 is among my favorite verses in all the Bible. It, along with the first verse in the same chapter, offers special hope, assurance, and encouragement for these challenging end-time days.

8. Read Daniel 12:1, 3.

   a. What will happen to those whose names are found in the book of life? (vs. 1b)

   b. Describe those *who are wise/have insight* and *lead many to righteousness*. (two characteristics - vs. 3)

Write out a Bible verse that had special meaning to you today.

Based upon what you have learned today, write a prayer to God expressing the desires of your heart in applying these truths to your life.

Chapter 7 — Day 4
Heaven — Better by Far! — Part One

> *Looking for the blessed hope and the appearing of the glory of our great God and Savior, Christ Jesus (Titus 2:13).*
>
> *He has set eternity in their heart (Eccles. 3:11).*

Strangers and Aliens

As we come to the close of this second book in our journey to true freedom and joy in Christ, we will be getting just a very brief "sneak preview" of one of the most precious and glorious topics in the entire Bible: Heaven! After all, it is, as the beloved Apostle Paul said:

> *But if there is no resurrection of the dead, not even Christ has been raised; and if Christ has not been raised, then our preaching is vain, your faith also is vain… and you are still in your sins. Then those also who have fallen asleep in Christ have perished. If we have hoped in Christ in this life only, we are of all men most to be pitied.(1 Cor. 15:13-19).*

If I thought for one minute that life on this fallen planet with all its pain and suffering, injustices and evil of every nature perpetrated upon the innocent by wicked, depraved men and women, was "it", I would be depressed—and stay that way! It would be very hard to get out of bed every morning and impossible to find true joy in life with such a meaningless, hopeless end. But this is not "the end". This is only the beginning, the training ground where God has chosen for us to live while He teaches us many things—about Himself and ourselves, the terribleness of sin and its consequences, and what real love, happiness and joy is all about. It is the place where He is ever at work, fulfilling His good purposes in His children, making us like His Son and preparing us for the real life yet to come when we will be *with Him* in that glorious *eye-hath-not-seen* paradise called Heaven (1 Cor. 2:9-10).

Oh, how I long for that day when my own training and the work that God has for me on this present sin-polluted planet is complete and I will join my blessed Savior—and my dad and grandmas and grandpas, uncles and cousins, and all my family and friends who trusted Jesus as Savior who are already *there*, in His presence, waiting for me. I think often of that grand reunion and how glorious that will be! There is so much about Heaven with all its majesty and glory that we will not be able to cover here in this brief overview. For example: where exactly is Heaven? What will it be like? Who will be there? What will we do in Heaven—for an eternity? What will we eat, drink, wear? Will we recognize each other? Will we actually "see" God?...and much more. That we will have to save for another time (book three), but we need to at least introduce this capstone of our Christian faith—this enduring *blessed hope*—to keep our hearts encouraged as we *press on* in our heavenward journey.

Whenever I think of Heaven, my mind often returns to an earlier time in my life which I remember so vividly. I was a recent college grad on a grand travel adventure to *see the world*. It was the fulfillment of a life-long dream. How I had looked forward to the excitement of experiencing first hand the old world culture of Europe—the architecture, history, art, food and customs—along with that ethereal romance that came from mixing that rich heritage with the new European way of life that I'd seen depicted so often in the movies. It was exciting...at first. I was met at Árlanda International Airport in Stockholm, Sweden by my cousin who took me to "Moster" (Aunt) Maj-Britt and "Morbror" (Uncle) Yngve's home where I was sheltered and protected and showered with that ever so warm, generous Scandanavian hospitality—for which I will always be grateful! They treated me like one of the family, going out of their way to make my time there special and memorable in every way. It was wonderful! But then I left that protective environment and began to travel on my own. That wasn't so fun. I found myself in difficult situations so often—in remote areas where I didn't know anyone and could not find even one person who spoke my language. I was homeless, jobless, separated from family and friends...alone... and very lonely. With tears streaming down my cheeks, I longed for home—for my mom and dad, my brothers and sister, the comfortable familiarity of our farmhouse, my room, "meat and potatoes" for supper, and mom's wonderful bread pudding with vanilla sauce. Thoughts of that great day when I would be home again was all that kept me going many times.

After I became a Christian, I learned that as God's children we are *called out* (set apart) people—*in the world,* but not *of the world.* We now belong to another kingdom with a new ruler. We are, in reality, *strangers and aliens* on this planet (Phil. 3:20). Our real home is in Heaven. And as I continued in my Christian walk and the trials and tribulations came, often with great intensity and longevity, I found myself experiencing those same longings—for comfort, for departed family members now so far away, for *home.* And the longer I lived *in the world,* the more aware I became of its hostility and "foreignness" to the things of God. This was not my home, my language or my country. I was just *passing through.* Oh, how I yearned to be...home!

God's Word became all the more precious and with further study, I began to realize I was in pretty good company of homesick ones. Abraham longed for *the city whose architect and builder is God...*as did Moses and David and Job and Daniel and Jeremiah and Amos and Peter and John and Paul...and Jesus. So I guess it's OK to get a little homesick sometimes. In fact I think it is very healthy. Because if we get really comfortable and settled in here, we will lose our vision and we will forget that we really don't *belong here.* We are but *passing through.* That is one reason for the trials we experience—they help us to remember that. They also keep us close to God, ever reminding us of the utter depravity of the human (fallen) heart, the terrible consequences of sin, the brevity of this mortal life and the eternality of the life to come.

> *For our citizenship is in Heaven, from which also we <u>eagerly wait</u> for a Savior, the Lord Jesus Christ; who will transform the body of our humble state into conformity with the body of His glory (Phil. 3:20-21).*

How we all long for that! And God longs for it, too. Even more marvelous is the fact that He doesn't want us to wait until Heaven to experience a foreshadow of "Heaven's glories" here on earth—*Christ in you, the hope of glory (Col. 1:27).* He desires to *dwell among us*—to fellowship and have a close, intimate relationship with us. Do you remember how we began this study? We began by talking about this very basic fact: God desires to have a personal, loving, intimate, growing relationship with us. That's really what this thing called *life* is all about.

To illustrate, let's pull out a Biblical scrapbook, and take another look at a few scenes we've visited that confirm God's wonderful plan for us to experience such a fellowship with all its wonder and joy!

> Scene #1 – *The Garden of Eden: Then God said, "Let Us make man in Our Image, according to Our likeness...Then the Lord God formed man of dust from the ground, and breathed into his nostrils the breath of life; and man became a living being (Gen. 1:26, 2:7).*

God, Himself, personally *formed* us in *His Image* with a *soul, mind, spirit* that could *know Him* and fellowship with Him in the fullness and beauty of His love, joy, majesty and glory. We were His royal offspring—joint heirs with Him in His glorious kingdom.

Scene #2 – *And they heard the Lord God walking in the garden in the cool of the day (Gen. 3:8).*

I love this scene. God, walking in the Garden in the cool of the day, coming to His children to fellowship with them. That's how it's going to be in Heaven. God *dwelling among us*, fellowshipping with us, blessing us with His presence. What joy to think of such oneness and intimacy—*with God!*

Then we have some not so pleasant scenes about man's rebellion against God and the awful consequences of that. But even before the proud, ungrateful, disobedient man and woman were put out of the garden because of their rebellious rejection of God's love, God promised a Savior who would pay the terrible penalty for their sin—*death*—and would restore them to fellowship with Him. Then, later, we see God, in His infinite mercy and grace going *with* His children, His presence leading them out of the bondage and captivity that sin had brought upon them to that *promised land* where He would be their God once again and dwell among them.

Scene #3 – *And the Lord was going before them in a pillar of cloud by day to lead them on the way, and in a pillar of fire by night to give them light, that they might travel by day and by night. He did not take away the pillar of cloud by day, nor the pillar of fire by night, from before the people (Ex. 13:21-22).*

What a beautiful picture! God's presence with His people—night and day. It sounds a lot like Jesus doesn't it? *I will never leave you or forsake you (Heb. 13:5).*

Scene #4 – *No man will be able to stand before you all the days of your life. Just as I have been with Moses, I will be with you; I will not fail you or forsake you. Be strong and courageous, for you shall give this people possession of the land which I swore to their fathers to give them. Only*

be strong and very courageous; be careful to do according to all the law which Moses My servant commanded you; do not turn from it to the right or to the left, so that you may have success wherever you go (Josh. 1:5-7).

God kept His promise and He led His children—*by great signs and wonders (Deut. 6:22)*—to the promised land. But it wasn't long before the proud, selfish rebels turned once again away from God. And back into captivity they went. And so they remained for 400 years.

Scene #4 – *But when the fullness of the time came, God sent forth His Son...demonstrating His own love toward us, in that while we were yet sinners, Christ died for us...and as many as received Him, to them gave He the right to become children of God! (Gal. 4:4; Rom. 5:8; John 1:12). God sent Jesus to die for our sins so that our sins could be forgiven and we could be born again of the Spirit of God never, ever again to be separated from Him! Then Jesus told us more about that beautiful place He was going away to prepare for us.*

Scene #5 – *Let not your heart be troubled; believe in God, believe also in Me. In My Father's house are many dwelling places; if it were not so, I would have told you; I go to prepare a place for you. And if I go and prepare a place for you, I will come again, and receive you to Myself; that where I am, there you may be also (John 14:1-3).*

And that's what Jesus is doing at this very minute—preparing a home in that glorious place called Heaven, for you…and me! But in the meantime…there is yet a huge problem here on this fallen planet. There is another *presence* that is not so welcomed. It is the relentless, never gives up, never goes away opposition of three powerful enemies of God and of our relationship with Him: 1) *the devil and his demons,* 2) *the corrupted, sin-polluted "world"* (ruled by the devil) *with all its enticements,* and 3) *our own fallen rebellious, selfish, sinful nature (flesh).* All three of these very real enemies of God and enemies of our own soul are ever at work, wreaking havoc so often upon our sincerest desires to walk in loving, obedient fellowship with God. God knew this. And God loves us too much to leave us alone in the battle against these strong and powerful enemies. That's why He sent His blessed Holy Spirit.

> Scene #7 – *And I will ask the Father, and He will give you another Helper, that He may be with you forever; that is the Spirit of truth, whom the world cannot receive, because it does not know Him, but you know Him because He abides with you, and will be in you. I will not leave you as orphans; I will come to you. In that day you shall know that I am in My Father, and you in Me, and I in you. If anyone loves Me, he will keep My Word; and My Father will love him, and We will come to him, and make Our abode with him (John 14:16-23, sel.).*

God has given us His blessed Holy Spirit to be with us—to dwell *in us*! He will be our helper, our comforter, our teacher, our dispenser of truth, wisdom and strength. He will be our *very present help in time of trouble (Ps. 46:1).*

> Scene #8 – *For we are the temple of the living God; just as God said, "I will dwell in them and walk among them; And I will be their God, and they shall be My people. Therefore, come out from their midst and be separate," says the Lord. "And do not touch what is unclean; And I will welcome you. And I will be a father to you, and you shall be sons and daughters to Me (2 Cor. 6:16-18).*

God wants to be our *Father* and *dwell among us* right here on earth—in *relationship* with us—loving us, protecting us, providing for us, until we are *with Him* in the transcendent glories of Heaven.

Do you see the scarlet thread of unbroken covenant love woven into all these scenes? *God with us—in relationship*—loving us, fellowshipping with us and preparing us...for **Heaven!**

> *Who for the JOY set before Him endured the cross, despising the shame, and has sat down at the right hand of the throne of God. For consider*

> *Him who has endured such hostility by sinners against Himself, so that you may not grow weary and lose heart (Heb. 12:1-3).*

And what was that wonderful joy that kept Jesus' heart encouraged all the way to and through the cross? It was the joy of Heaven—the perfected completion of His glorious kingdom. It was the joy of you and me and all His redeemed children in union and eternal fellowship with Him. It was the joy of His precious, holy Bride, adorned in the beauty of His righteousness being there *at home* with Him in the heavenly mansion He prepared for her...forever!

It is the same joy that keeps our hearts encouraged...all the way to and through any trials and difficulties that may come our way as we walk this grand *Highway of Holiness* to the portals of Heaven!

Before we close this Biblical scrapbook for today, come a little closer and stretch upward on your tiptoes to gaze upon just one more glorious scene:

> *And I saw a new Heaven and a new earth; for the first Heaven and the first earth passed away... And I saw the holy city, new Jerusalem, coming down out of Heaven from God, made ready as a bride adorned for her husband...And I heard a loud voice from the throne, saying, "Behold, the tabernacle of God is among men, and He shall dwell among them, and they shall be His people, and God Himself shall be among them, and He shall wipe away every tear from their eyes; and there shall no longer be any death; there shall no longer be any mourning, or crying, or pain;... And He who sits on the throne said...I am the Alpha and the Omega, the beginning and the end. I will give to the one who thirsts from the spring of the water of life without cost. He who overcomes shall inherit these things, and I will be his God and he will be My son (Rev. 21:1-7).*

> *I, Jesus, have sent My angel to testify to you these things... And the Spirit and the bride say, "Come." And let the one who hears, "Come." He who testifies to these things says, "Yes, I am coming quickly. Amen. Come, Lord Jesus" (Rev. 22:16-21).*

Bible Study Supplement
Chapter 7 — Day 4 — Heaven — Better by Far! — Part One
Strangers and Aliens

1. Read Gen. 1:1.

    a. What did God create *in the beginning* – besides the earth?

I think we get too "earth-bound" far too often and forget that.

2. Read Dan. 2:28.

    a. What did Daniel affirm to King Nebuchadnezzar? (vs. 28a)

3. Read 2 Kings 2:11.

    a. Where did the Lord take Elijah? (vs. 11b)

4. Read Ps. 73:23-28.

    a. Where was God in the psalmist's life? (vs. 23)

    b. What did the Lord do for the psalmist here on earth and where was He taking him? (vs. 24)

    c. Who was in Heaven for the psalmist and what/who did the psalmist desire on earth? (vs. 25)

    d. What was *good* for the psalmist … and what did he "make" God? (vs. 28)

5. Read Heb. 11:8-10, 13-16.

    a. For what was Abraham looking? (vs. 10)

    b. Verse 13 says that Abraham and his descendants viewed the promise of being *home with God* in Heaven as sure! They welcomed this beautiful promise from a distance peering *with faith* into the very portals of Heaven itself. What did they confess/admit? (vs. 13b)

    c. What is God not ashamed to be called by all who seek after a *better, heavenly country?*... What has He prepared for them? (vs. 16b)

6. Read Rom. 8:18.

    a. To what are our present sufferings *not worthy to be compared?*

7. Read 2 Cor. 4:16-18.

a. Why do we not lose heart? (vs. 16b)

b. What is momentary light affliction producing for us? (vs. 17)

Every time I read these verses I am once again amazed at Paul's courage and joy in serving God. It is nearly unfathomable to me that Paul would consider _his suffering_ as _light and momentary_ when we look at the list:

> *Are they servants of Christ? I more so; in far more labors, in far more imprisonments, beaten times without number, often in danger of death. Five times I received from the Jews thirty-nine lashes. Three times I was beaten with rods, once I was stoned, three times I was shipwrecked, a night and a day I have spent in the deep. I have been on frequent journeys, in dangers from rivers, dangers from robbers, dangers from my countrymen, dangers from the Gentiles, dangers in the city, dangers in the wilderness, dangers on the sea, dangers among false brethren; I have been in labor and hardship, through many sleepless nights, in hunger and thirst, often without food, in cold and exposure. There is (additionally), the daily pressure of concern for all the churches (2 Cor. 11:23-28).*

For Paul the hardships came one upon another—throughout his lifetime! Yet Paul never lost his joy or thankful, rejoicing spirit in serving God because he was always looking forward, upward, _pressing on...to the eternal glories of Heaven_ yet to come that _far outweighed_ His present _temporal_ difficulties. We do well to look at Paul's beautiful example when we feel weighed down by our trials and troubles for I am sure that if we did this, most of us would find that ours really are _light and momentary_ in comparison.

c. How can we maintain a confident, hopeful and joyful perspective as Paul (and Jesus) did? (vs. 18a)

d. What are the things that are _seen?_ _____ _unseen?_ _____ (vs. 18b)

Note: The _unseen_ refers to the spiritual part of our lives that human eyes cannot "see", but is of primary concern to God: things such as our relationship with Him, our faithfulness in trusting and obeying Him, watching over our heart that we _might not sin against Him (Ps. 119:11)_, longing for Heaven and being with Him forever! When our hearts are rightly focused upon these things, the "seen" will take its place according to God's good plans, and _the peace of Christ will rule in our hearts (Col. 3:16)_ as we press ever onward and upward to Heaven's eye-hath-not-seen majesty, glory and joy! (1 Cor. 2:9).

Write out a Bible verse that had special meaning to you today.

Based upon what you have learned today, write a prayer to God expressing the desires of your heart in applying these truths to your life.

Chapter 7 — Day 5
Heaven — Better by Far! — Part Two

> I have fought the good fight, I have finished the course, I have kept the faith; in the future there is laid up for me the crown of righteousness, which the Lord, the righteous Judge, will award to me on that day; and not only to me, but also to all who have loved His appearing (2 Tim. 4:6-8).
>
> Behold, I am coming quickly, and My reward is with Me, to render to every man according to what he has done (Rev. 22:12).

Storing up Treasures…Keeping An Eternal Perspective …One Day at A Time

Some of my sweetest memories as I think back over the years are the times I have sat at the feet of precious venerable widow and widower friends as they shared their wisdom, spiritual insights, and meaningful memories gleaned over many years of walking closely with the Lord. As I began working on this lesson, I could not help but think of my dear friend and encourager for over 20 years, Ms. Ethel Westmoreland. I can still see the scene vividly now as I reflect back on these cherished times: sitting with Ms. Ethel on the cozy closed-in back porch of her 100-year old "add on" country farmhouse, rocking gently in well-worn, hand-hewn rockers as we shared together. I learned a lot from Ms. Ethel. One of my favorite stories was about the time Ms. Ethel's papa sent her to the bean patch to hoe the weeds. Ms. Ethel didn't feel like hoeing the weeds that day. She felt like going off with her sister to have a little fun in the woods. She said to herself. "Papa's not here. He won't know if I hoe the bean patch or not. I'll just have a little fun today. I can hoe the bean patch tomorrow."

So off she went to the woods with her sister. When Ms. Ethel came back home later her mama asked her if she'd obeyed her papa and hoed the bean patch. Ms. Ethel had been to Sunday School enough to know that she shouldn't lie, so she just got real quiet and pretended she didn't hear her mama, then announced quickly that she was going back outside to play. But Mama could tell something wasn't quite right. When she pressed her young daughter further, Ms. Ethel confessed that she hadn't hoed the beans, but that she planned to do it the very first thing in the morning. It wouldn't hurt anything to be just one day later in chopping those silly old weeds. But Mama said that it did matter: "You think you got by with something because Papa didn't see you go off and he didn't know that you hadn't hoed the garden like he asked you. But Jesus saw what you did. He was right there with you all the time. He saw you disobey your Papa. Do you think that this pleased Jesus? Just remember Ethel that Jesus is with you wherever you go. He sees everything you do and He hears every word you speak. Don't ever forget that."

And Ms. Ethel never did…and neither should we.

Whatever you do, do your work heartily, as for the Lord rather than for men; knowing that from the Lord you will receive the reward…It is the Lord Christ whom you serve (Col. 3:23-24).

When we go through our days with a continual awareness that "Jesus is with us" and He sees everything we do, we will work a lot more heartily, and be a lot more joyful in our labors. We will sense His smile when we have persevered and completed what He asked us to do knowing that this pleases Him and brings joy to His heart (3 John 4; Ps. 103:1-5; Prov. 23:15-16; Zeph. 3:17).

One of the greatest motivations for me is to think about that wonderful moment when I will actually *see* Jesus and stand in His presence. My heart's desire, above all else is to hear my Savior say, *"Well done, good and faithful servant, enter into the JOY of your Master"* (Matt. 25:23). I try to think about this often as I go through my day. Then, when I am preparing for bed, I ponder this scene again as I reflect upon the day's activities. If Jesus had come today, what would He have said? Peace and joy fill my heart when I have been faithful and I have loved Him and obeyed Him and served Him *heartily.* A smile breaks across my face as I lay my head upon my pillow and hear Jesus speak those sweet words: *Well done, good and faithful servant.*

Laying up Treasures in Heaven

Do not lay up for yourselves treasures upon earth, where moth and rust destroy, and where thieves break in and steal. But lay up for yourselves treasures in Heaven, where neither moth nor rust destroy, and where thieves do not break in or steal; for where your treasure is, there will your heart be also (Matt. 6:19-21).

The Bible is filled with promises of rewards for God's faithful children who *lay up treasures in Heaven.* Every good deed I do in humble service and obedience to Jesus is a *treasure* that will be gloriously *rewarded* (Matt. 26:31-45; Rev. 22:12). The greatest treasure that we can store up in Heaven are the souls of other people that we have faithfully and fervently prayed for, personally led to Christ, or been a part of God's work of salvation through supporting others who led them to Jesus. This is the treasure God loves best to reward! (1 Tim. 2:4; Matt. 28:19-20; Jude 1:21-23). So let's try to keep this in mind as we go about our work, asking Jesus to help us make the best use of our time as we walk in obedience to Him, so that we can store up lots of precious *treasures in Heaven.*

Keeping an Eternal Perspective

Therefore, we do not lose heart, but though our outer man is decaying, yet our inner man is being renewed day by day. For momentary, light affliction is producing for us an eternal weight of glory far beyond all comparison, while we look not at the things which are seen, but at the things which are not seen; for the things which are seen are temporal, but the things which are not seen are eternal (2 Cor. 4:16-18).

One of the best kept secrets to living a consistently joyful, victorious life is keeping an eternal perspective by focusing upon the *spiritual* things that *are not seen*—the truths and promises of God's Word, the presence of God, the power of the Holy Spirit, and the incomprehensible, inexpressible JOYS (1 Cor. 2:9) <u>yet to come</u>: Heaven, the wedding supper of the lamb and being with Jesus and all God's children forever, totally and completely free of pain and problems, temptations, trials and tribulations, separation and sorrow…free of sin! In Heaven we will experience life in a whole new glorious dimension that we cannot even imagine at the moment! (1 Cor. 2:9). If we keep our hearts and minds focused on such *inexpressible, full of glory, soon-to-be* <u>realities</u>, we will be able to face all those things that come our way that are *seen*—the momentary, passing pains and problems, difficulties and trials—with courage and the assurance of God's presence and power to *bring us through (Ex. 14:21-22).* When our hearts and minds are firmly fixed upon the eternal and *being about the Father's business* till we get there, *the things of earth* really do *grow strangely dim, in the light of His glory and grace!* [10]

If then you have been raised up with Christ, keep seeking the things above, where Christ is, seated at the right hand of God. Set your mind on the things above, not on the things that are on earth. For you have died and your life is hidden with Christ in God (Col. 3:1-3).

Here is another encouraging reminder that will keep our eyes ever *looking up* and filled with joyful anticipation. As we make it our ambition daily to *seek the things above*—knowing God, loving God, pleasing God, obeying God, praising God, bringing glory to God, being filled with and walking in the power and joy of God's Holy Spirit—we are lifted above the trials and tribulations of this temporal passing world into the very presence of God, where there is *unending love* and *fullness of joy* (Jer. 31:3; Ps. 16:11).

> *Therefore… let us run with endurance the race that is set before us, <u>fixing our eyes on Jesus</u>, the author and perfecter of faith, <u>who for the joy set before Him</u> endured the cross, despising the shame, and has sat down at the right hand of the throne of God. For consider Him who has endured such hostility by sinners against Himself, so that you may not grow weary and lose heart (Heb. 12:1-3).*

> *I have fought the good fight, I have finished the course, I have kept the faith; in the future there is laid up for me the crown of righteousness, which the Lord, the righteous Judge, will award to me on that day; and not only to me, but also to all who have loved His appearing (2 Tim. 4:7-8).*

When I *fix my eyes on Jesus*, ever living with anticipation of that *crown of righteousness* and the *eternal glories that await me*, my heart is filled with a *living hope* and *joy unspeakable and full of glory (1 Pet. 1:3, 8)*. All has purpose; all has value when it is lived according to God's good plans with an *eternal perspective*.

One Day at a Time

For this reason I say to you, do not be anxious for your life, as to what you shall eat, or what you shall drink; nor for your body, as to what you shall put on. Is not life more than food, and the body more than clothing? Look at the birds of the air… they do not sow, neither do they reap, nor gather into barns, and yet your heavenly Father feeds them. Are you not worth much more than they? And which of you by being anxious can add a single hour to his life's span? And why are you anxious about clothing? Observe how the lilies of the field grow; they do not toil nor do they spin, yet I say to you that even Solomon in all his glory did not clothe himself like one of these. But if God so arrays the grass of the field, which is alive today and tomorrow is thrown into the furnace, will He not much more do so for you, O men of little faith? Do

not be anxious then, saying, 'What shall we eat?' or 'What shall we drink?.. for your heavenly Father knows that you need all these things. But seek first His kingdom and His righteousness; and all these things shall be added to you…Therefore do not be anxious for tomorrow; for tomorrow will care for itself (Matt. 6:25-34).

I love these wise, beautiful words from Jesus. He is reminding us that our heavenly Father cares about us and He will take care of us as we look to Him with trusting, obedient faith… *one day at a time*. He clearly instructs us <u>not</u> to *worry* about tomorrow. Our heavenly Father is already there, just as He is with us today. He will see us through today, just as He will see us through tomorrow as we *keep our eyes on Jesus* and *follow Him* as He leads us…one moment, one step at a time.

God has promised that *His grace will be sufficient* for us as we do this. He does not promise grace for tomorrow, but grace for today and for every need that comes to us as we walk through it. As we look to Him, refusing to become anxious and worried, but rather choosing to trust him completely for the grace we need—for this moment, this step—He guides and provides and even opens up *impassable seas* for us when necessary, that we might *walk through on dry land* (Ex. 14:21-22).

There is yet one more thought that comes to mind every time I think about Heaven and *going home!* It has to do with Christmases…and funerals. Can you recall those sweet nostalgic feelings you always got at Christmas time when the neighborhood is aglow with pretty lights and manger scenes, or you see a kid's program at church, listen to a beautiful Christmas cantata or go caroling with friends? Then, at last, the special day arrives. Family and friends gather together. Some have traveled from far away. You haven't seen them for such a long time and it's so good to just be together again. The fellowship is sweet as you sit down around the table, join hands as "Papa" prays his special Christmas prayer of thanksgiving for sending Jesus, for making us His children and for providing so graciously and so abundantly for everyone through the year. Then everyone digs into the sumptuous Christmas feast. The cares and worries of the world fade into total oblivion as you become absorbed in the joy of fellowship, good food and fun with your family. Don't you fight back nostalgic tears as your heart yearns for a more permanent experience of this precious camaraderie? God's in that. "Heaven comes down" in these moments. It's God's way of giving us little "tastes" of Heaven and the sweet unity with Him and one another—along with all the other endless joys—we will experience together there!

I often get that same nostalgic feeling at funerals when a dear friend or loved one who served the Lord faithfully through the years...*goes home.* I miss them...but there is something sweet in the anticipation of that glorious *reunion* soon to be, that takes the sting out of the tears (1 Cor. 15:55).

He has set eternity in their hearts (Eccles. 3:11).

The nostalgia we feel in these special times of fellowship, and even when we've had to say a temporary good-bye to a dear loved one, is from God. It is His way of communicating to our hearts: "I'm here; I'm waiting. And your grandma and grandpa, your papa and uncle and all those who are already *home* are waiting for you, too. We can hardly wait to welcome you and give you lots of heavenly hugs! So just hang on, because one day we will be together and nothing will ever again be able to separate us—nothing...ever!"

I want to close this brief overview of Heaven and the wonderful, endless joys and glories that await us there, by sharing a story that has been a special encouragement to me through the years. This true story took place a number of years ago when overseas travel was done primarily by ship. It's about a devoted missionary couple who were both well up in years. They served the Lord faithfully and sacrificially on the mission field in a remote jungle location for more than 40 years. There were health issues and they were no longer capable of dealing with the strenuous physical requirements in the primitive culture. They were finally coming home after a long, faithful ministry with many souls won to Christ. As their ship was nearing the dock, they noticed that many people

were gathered there. It brought great joy to their hearts to think that so many had come to welcome them home. They could hardly wait to get a closer look at these loving, faithful friends! As they began to disembark, they were a bit surprised that there were no familiar faces, outstretched arms, "welcome home" shouts or joyful applause. The people seemed to be looking right past them. Didn't they recognize them? Suddenly, there erupted a roar of clapping, shouting and waving of flags as a figure emerged from the shadows into the view of the people. It was Teddy Roosevelt. He was returning from a hunting safari in Africa, and had been sequestered away in one of the ship's luxury cabins so he could have privacy and rest. As the enthusiastic cheers continued, the wife noticed a painful look on her kind, hard-working husband's face. She nudged closer, placing her head on his chest and wrapping comforting arms around him. She listened as with a hurting, broken voice he said: "All I wanted was for someone to 'be here' to meet us when we returned. Surely someone would have cared enough…after all…we served the Lord faithfully in those remote jungle villages for all those years. We never had the comforts of a modern home with running water, electricity, or even a telephone. And we were so far from our families…oh, how we missed them at times—especially at Christmas! Day and night we labored, sharing the love of Jesus and telling the people about him so they could come to know Him and be with us in Heaven one day, too. We went through many difficult times and trials, but we didn't quit. We just kept trusting the Lord and serving Him…I mean…I'm not complaining. God was good and He took care of us through all those years. I've got no regrets about one minute of it because the Lord called us and we just obeyed…and He was with us and blessed us in so many ways. I'm thankful for that…but still…couldn't a few people have taken the time to come and welcome us back? It would have meant so much…" His wise, loving wife gently brushed away the tears as she cupped his furrowed, disappointed face in her hands and said: "Don't be sad, my strong, faithful husband. Just remember... we're not home, yet!"[11]

Bible Study Supplement

Chapter 7 — Day 5 — Heaven – Better By Far – Part Two

Storing up Treasures…Keeping An Eternal Perspective …One Day at A Time

The Bible clearly teaches that there are rewards in Heaven for faithfulness and for good deeds done on earth in Jesus Name, out of love and devotion to Him.

1. Read Col. 3:23-24.

    a. How should we do our work? (two characteristics – vs. 23)

    b. What ought to motivate our hearts to do this with joyful anticipation? (vs. 24)

2. Read Matt. 6:19-20.

    a. What kind of treasures should we be storing up? (vs. 20)

It is very exciting to think about the fact that every time we do something out of obedience to God and His kingdom-building purposes that may involve momentary sacrifice and no immediate tangible "reward" here on earth, we are *storing up treasures in Heaven!*

3. Read 2 Chron. 15:1-2, 7.

    a. What did the prophet Azariah tell King Asa concerning the Lord? (three things – vs. 2)

    b. What was King Asa encouraged to do? (two things – vs. 7a) Why? (7b)

4. Read Gal. 6:9.

    a. What are we commanded <u>not</u> to do?

    b. Why?

5. Read 1 Cor. 15:58.

    a. How are we to be as we serve the Lord? (three characteristics - vs. 58a) Why? (vs. 58b)

6. Read Rev. 22:12. (Jesus is speaking)

    a. Who is coming quickly?

    b. What is with Him?

One of the great motivations of every Christian is the knowledge that we serve a God who abounds in lovingkindness and loves to reward and bless His children whose hearts are right before Him—

humble, repentant, obedient (Matt. 19:29; Rev. 22:12; Matt. 6:19-20; Deut. 28:1-13; Heb. 10:6).

7. Read Rev. 22:17-21.

   a. What do the Spirit and the Bride say? (vs. 17a)

   b. What clear warning concerning "adding to God's Word" does Jesus give us? (vs. 18)

   c. There is a second warning involving even greater tragic consequences if disobeyed in verse 19. What is it?

May God help us all to recognize the seriousness of these warnings that we not ignore them to our peril. And may He also help us to be joyfully about our Father's business, knowing that indeed we shall reap a harvest of blessings here, and treasures in Heaven, if we are faithful and *faint not (Matt. 19:29, 6:20; Rev. 22:12; Gal. 6:9).*

And now, as we bring this study to a close, I want to <u>congratulate you</u> and also <u>thank you</u> for your diligent labors in completing the assignments. I pray that the Lord will *bless you, and keep you… make His face shine upon you, and be gracious to you; The Lord lift up His countenance on you, and give you peace (Num. 6:24-26)* as you *press on* in all the good plans He yet has for you. And I pray also that the Lord will help you to trust and obey every new truth and promise discovered while you *continue in God's Word* becoming an ever stronger, more beautiful *oak of righteousness, the planting of the Lord that He may be glorified! (Is. 61:3).*

Just one final thought to leave with you as you continue your journey on this triumphant *Highway of Holiness* to Heaven's glories: never forget…*we aren't home yet! Press on*, faithful saint… *press on!*

Write out a Bible verse that had special meaning to you today.

Based upon what you have learned today, write a prayer to God expressing the desires of your heart in applying these truths to your life.

NOTE: There is an update to my personal testimony in the appendix if you are interested.

There is also a preview of book three, *That Your Joy May be Full,* in the Epilogue (next page). In this final book of the series, we will be studying more truths from God's Word that will encourage our hearts, filling them with *Rivers of Joy.*

Epilogue

A Preview of Things to Come – Overview of Book Three
That Your Joy May Be Full

I am so thankful to God for all that He has taught us thus far in this Bible Study series. I eagerly look forward to continuing upon this good *path of righteousness… that grows brighter and brighter until the full day! (Prov. 4:18)*.

I am, therefore, excited about the topics we will be studying in book three, the final book in the series. As we dig even deeper into God's precious Word, we will uncover yet more *hidden treasures (Prov. 2:4)* that will encourage our hearts, strengthen our faith, and increase our joy… *that our joy may be full (John 15:11)*.

Here are some of the topics we will be studying:

- Bringing Down Strongholds – God's Solution to addictive/compulsive behavior.
- Be on the Alert! – The power of an alert mind in successful spiritual warfare.
- How Can I Know the Will of God?
- Learning to Discern: The Key to Obedience (Crucial to hearing from God).
- When You 'Can't' Obey – Hope for those who truly *want* to obey, but just can't seem to move past the fears and unbelief that keep them bound in hurtful, sinful behavior.
- The Freedom of Forgiveness.
- From Fear to Faith… Worry to Worship – A study of Habakkuk that will keep your heart secure!
- Beyond Condemnation – Living in the freedom and joy of God's boundless grace.
- He, Himself is our Peace – Beyond fretting to a peace that passes human understanding.
- A Biblical Health and Nutrition Primer.
- Time Management – Making the most of God's precious gift of time.
- Heart of Hospitality – Recapturing the lost art and blessing of Christian hospitality.
- Growing Old Gracefully – Truly enjoying and finding a sweet richness in the second half.
- Heaven – Better by Far! – More wonderful thoughts on Heaven, our *real* home.
- From My Heart – Some very personal and honest thoughts on the difficult and oft *humanly* overwhelming challenges of bipolar and chronic pain and how, by God's Grace, we truly can become *more than conquerers (Rom. 8:37)* over these—and all other afflictions—living meaningful, fruitful, and yes, even <u>joyful</u> lives in spite of the challenges (Eph. 3:20; Jude 24).

End Notes

1. MacArthur, John, First Love (Victor Books, Wheaton, IL, 1995, pg. 22).

2. Brown, Walt, PH.D, In the Beginning, Center for Scientific Creation, Phoenix, AZ 85016, pg. 15-16, 64-65.

3. Creation Moments: P.O. Box 839, Foley, MN 56329; ph. 1-800-569-5959; www.creationmoments.com.

4. Heitzig, Skip, "The Rise and Fall of Man" tape series, Connection Communications, San Juan Capistrano, CA 92693.

5. Although countless books have been written on this subject—the false teachings of the Roman Catholic Church—the one that I found most helpful was: The Gospel According to Rome, McCarthy, James G., Harvest House Publishers, Eugene, Oregon 97402. Mr. McCarthy also wrote the booklet entitled "What You Need to Know About Roman Catholicism", Quick Reference Guide, from which the select Doctrines in today's meditation are taken. I found this booklet of immense help. This booklet is available through The Berean Call, Box 7019, Bend, OR 97708; Ph. 1-800-937-6638; www.thebereancall.org. The Berean Call is an excellent source of information on this topic.

6. Bobgen, Martin and Diedra, Ministry Statement, PsychoHeresy Awareness Letter, May-June 2007, pg. 8.

7. Lemmel, Helen H., "Turn Your Eyes Upon Jesus", The Baptist Hymnal, Convention Press, Nashville, TN, #320. (Original copyright, Singspiration Music, 1922).

8. I have, since that time, read the Bible through many times using a number of different reading programs. But the program that I have benefitted from the most, and the one to which I return for this purpose, is: Bible Pathways. I have found the Bible Pathway program especially effective because of it's very helpful devotionals each day that further explain the text, giving clear insight into "hard to understand" passages. My faith has also been strengthened by the way Dr. Hash (the author of the devotionals) demonstrates the continuity between the Old and New Testaments by showing "Christ" in every book of the Old Testament—profound and ever so encouraging proof of God's love for His people!). For more info, contact: Bible Pathways, P.O. Box 20123, Murfreesboro, TN 37129, web: www.biblepathway.org; e-mail mail@biblepathway.org.

9. Info obtained from National Organization for Rare Disorders (NORD) Web Site – www.rarediseases.org.

10. Lemmel, "Turn Your Eyes Upon Jesus".

11. The story of missionary Henry Morrison and his wife, "Wisdom from the Word" radio broadcast - Series on Job, Stephen Davey, Pastor/teacher.

12. Bobgan, Martin, Psychological Seduction, DVD from The Berean Call Conference 2006.

Appendix

Gospel Presentation

Catholic Doctrine vs. the Word of God

Biblical Proofs of Salvation

Psychology: A Biblical Analysis

Update on Personal Testimony

Resources

Gospel Presentation

He has set eternity in their hearts (Eccles. 3:11)

In the book of Ecclesiastes, God tells us that when He created man (Adam and Eve and every man and woman since them) He *set eternity in their hearts (Eccles. 3:11)*. This means that every person that is born has within him a heart/soul that *knows* (whether he admits it or not) that there is an eternity and a place he will go after he dies. In presenting the gospel, therefore, one of the best questions to ask is: If you died today, do you know where you would go? This is a great "door opener" because people who are not saved do not *know*—they may "think" or "hope" they know (which you will hear them express), but they do not *know*. And you can share with them God's *good news*—that they can *know (1 John 5:13)*. Here are the main points of the *good news* you can share.

God is holy. Heaven is where God lives. Heaven is a holy place and only holy people can live there. Sinful people are not holy people. Have you ever committed a sin? Have you ever lied about anything? Gotten angry and said a harsh, unkind word to someone? Used God's Name in vain? Grumbled or complained? (The answer is an obvious "yes"). Then you have sinned and you cannot go to God's Heaven. But there's good news. Let me share that with you. *In the beginning, God created the heavens and the earth* (Gen. 1:1). Then He created man (Adam and Eve) *in His image*—holy—to have *fellowship with Him* (Gen. 1:26-27; Col. 1:16); There was only one rule in order to maintain this wonderful, intimate fellowship with God. God clearly instructed Adam and Eve not to *eat of the fruit of the tree of the knowledge of good and evil…for in the day you eat of it, you will surely die"* (Gen. 2:16-17). But Adam and Eve rebelled against God by partaking of the forbidden fruit. That act of rebellion was called "sin". So sin entered Adam and Eve's (man's) "holy" heart and corrupted it.

Man now had a sinful, rather than a holy heart/nature. And every child born after Adam and Eve has inherited this corrupt, unholy nature (Rom. 5:12). Sin separated man from God because God is holy and "sin" and "holy" cannot dwell and fellowship together (Is. 59:2). The penalty for sin is death, just as God said (Gen. 2:17; Rom. 3:23). Man's only hope was for a Savior to pay the penalty for his sins—death. God loved man (Adam and Eve…and you and me) so much that He sent His very own Son, *Jesus*, to pay this sin debt (John 3:16). Jesus, who was sinless and holy, willingly died for our sins (Rom. 5:8). But He didn't stay in the grave. He arose from the dead, defeating not only sin, but also death. When we repent of our sins and put our faith in Jesus and what He accomplished on the cross and in His resurrection—paying our sin debt through His death then rising victoriously over sin and death—God no longer sees us as "sinners" but as "saints", redeemed and sanctified (made holy) by the blood of Jesus (2 Cor. 5:21). God declares us righteous and welcomes us into His eternal family (John 1:12). This is what it means to be "born again". We are spiritually born into the family of God. And that is the only way that any of us can go to Heaven. Jesus said: *I am the way, the truth and the life, no man comes to the Father (to Heaven) except through Me…there is no other name given among men whereby we must be saved (John 14:6; Acts 4:12)*. God offers this free gift to all who sincerely repent of their sins and receive Jesus as their personal Lord and Savior (John 1:12). He not only gives them a home in Heaven when they die, but He also gives them an *abundant life* filled with blessing, purpose and joy here on earth (John 10:10, 15:11).

Would you like to receive this wonderful gift?…

If the person says "yes", tell him simply how he can do this: 1) Recognize that he is a sinner and cannot save himself. 2) Believe that Jesus died on the cross to pay the penalty for his sins, then rose from the dead to give him eternal life. 3) Repent of his sins. 4) Ask Jesus to come into his heart to be his Lord and Savior and help him to live a new life, pleasing to God. If he says that he believes all these things, you can then lead him in a prayer expressing his repentant heart and faith in Jesus. For example: "Lord Jesus, I know I am a sinner. I believe that You died on the cross to pay the penalty for my sins and rose again from the dead to give me eternal life. I repent of my sins and ask You to come into my heart to be my Lord and Savior. Help me to trust and obey You in this new life that You have given me. Amen."

Roman Catholic Doctrine that Opposes the Word of God

Here are a just a few of the major conflicts of the Catholic faith with the Word of God. This is but a small sampling. There are dozens more.

Bracketed numbers refer to official doctrinal statements of the Catholic Church Catechism, the governing document of the church. "Doctrine" = Foundational Authoritative Teaching of the Church.

Note: If you are a member of the Catholic church, your membership affirms your acceptance of these doctrines—whether or not you may personally "believe them". This is very serious.

Catholic Doctrine – Initial justification is by means of baptism, most commonly, infant baptism [1262-1274].

Word of God – Justification is by personal faith in Christ alone (John 3:16; Acts 16:31; Rom. 10:9).

> Catholic Doctrine – Christ's work of redemption was not complete. Justification must be furthered by sacraments and good works [1212, 1292, 2010].

> Word of God – Christ's work of redemption was complete; justification is the imputation (putting on by God) of the perfect righteousness of Jesus. In Christ the believer has been completely redeemed from the penalty of sin—death, separation from God (Rom. 3:28; 2 Cor. 5:21; 1 Pet. 3:18).

Catholic Doctrine – Grace is merited by good works [2010, 2027].

Word of God – Grace is a free gift (Rom. 3:28, 6:23, 11:6)

> Catholic Doctrine - Acts of penance make satisfaction for the punishment of sin [1434, 1459-1460]

> Word of God – Jesus paid the full penalty for sin. His payment is complete (1 John 2:1-2; 2 Cor. 5:21).

Catholic Doctrine – Mary is a co-redemptrist (co-redeemer) with Christ and has the same power to "redeem" us as Christ [628, 964, 968, 970].

Word of God – Christ alone is the Redeemer, for He alone suffered and died for sin (1 Pet. 1:18-19).

> Catholic Doctrine – Mary—and a host of other "saints"—are co-mediators to whom we can entrust all our cares and petitions [968-970, 2677]

> Word of God – Jesus Christ is the one and only mediator between God and man to whom we are to entrust all our cares and petitions (1 Tim. 2:5).

Catholic Doctrine – Indulgences dispensed by the Church for acts of piety release sinners from punishment [1471-1473].

Word of God – Jesus releases believers from their sins by His blood (Rev. 1:5). It is impossible for us to pay our sin debt (Is. 53:6, 64:6; Eccles. 7:20; Ps. 143:2

> Catholic Doctrine – Purgatory is necessary to atone for sin and cleanse the soul. The soul can be "bought" out of purgatory [1030-1031].

<u>Word of God</u> – Purgatory does not exist. (Not one Bible reference to it). Jesus made purification for sins on the cross (Heb. 1:3). It is impossible for a soul to be "redeemed" after death (Heb. 9:27).

<u>Catholic Doctrine</u> – Poor souls suffering in purgatory can be helped by those alive on earth offering up prayers, good works, and the sacrifice of the Mass [1032, 1371, 1479].

<u>Word of God</u> – No one can be "helped" after they die. Those who have died in Christ are safe and secure in the presence of Jesus (2 Cor. 5:8). Those who have not (did not have a personal relationship with God, through Chirst, when they died) are eternally separated from Him in Hell (Luke 16:19-26).

> <u>Catholic Doctrine</u> – No one can know if he will attain to eternal life [1036, 2005].

> <u>Word of God</u> – The Bible clearly teaches that we <u>can</u> <u>know</u> we have eternal life (1 John 5:13).

<u>Catholic Doctrine</u> – Eternal life is a merited reward based upon good works, participation in the sacraments etc. [1821,2010].

<u>Word of God</u> – Eternal life is a *free gift of God (Rom. 6:23)*. There is nothing we can do to earn it.

> <u>Catholic Doctrine</u> – The Roman Catholic Church is the final authority in all matters of belief and practice (above the Word of God) and is necessary for salvation [846].

> <u>Word of God</u> – The Bible is the final authority regarding all matters of belief and practice, and Jesus is the only way to God and to eternal life (salvation): *All Scripture is inspired by God… Holy men of God spoke as they were moved by the Holy Spirit… there is salvation in no one else; for there is no other name under Heaven that has been given among men, by which we must be saved… I (Jesus) am the Way, the Truth and the Life; no man cometh unto the Father except through Me (Acts 4:12; John 14:6, Kjv, Nasb).*

Sadly, as we can see here through their very own doctrinal statements, the Catholic faith glorifies the church (the Roman Catholic church), church tradition, Mary, and a thousand and one other "icons"(human "saints", idols) over God. It makes a mockery of the finished work of Christ on the cross and the authority of Scripture.

If you are a member of a Roman Catholic church—or any other church steeped in church tradition—I urge you, with the deepest of love and concern, to take this matter very seriously for truly your eternal destiny is at stake. Make this an urgent matter of prayer and study. Look up the Bible verses and study them for yourself, asking God to help you *know* the truth. Then, with God's help, "do" whatever you must to come out from under such teaching and practice—for your sake, and for the sake of your precious children, whose eternal destiny is likewise at stake. You will be responsible for how you led them when you stand before God (Deut. 6:6, 11:19; Heb. 9:27).

You may also wish to contact The Berean Call, a Christ-centered organization with a passion for ministering to Catholics and others caught in deceptive church tradition practices. One of the co-leaders of this organization was himself a devout Catholic for many years. For contact information see "End notes #5". (End notes are located at the back of the book just before the appendix.)

(Please return to the Bible Study Supplement for the conclusion of today's study).

THE SALVATION TEST

BIBLICAL PROOFS OF THE NEW BIRTH

<u>Before you begin the test</u>, pause for a moment and ask the Holy Spirit to help you keep an open and honest heart so that your answers accurately reflect your standing regarding each proof—whether you possess it or not.

As you go through the test, place a "yes" beside each proof that you do possess and a "no" beside those that you do not. A "yes" answer means that you already possess this proof, verified by "fruit" in your life. (Obedience – You sincerely seek to "do" what you say you "believe"). In some cases the "proof" may be weak and in need of improvement, but you sense conviction in your heart to do something about it and you have a <u>sincere desire</u> to work on this area so that you can fully possess and reflect this "proof". A "no" answer indicates that there is no assurance in your heart or evidence in your life that you possess this proof. Nor is there even a desire (conviction) to do so. If you are confused about whether or not you actually possess a proof, place a question mark beside it.

1. I will give you a new heart and put a new spirit within you… if any man be in Christ, He is a <u>new creature</u>, old things passed away, new things have come… Christ's love compels us… that (we) should no longer live for (ourselves) but for Him who died for us (Ezek. 36:26; 2 Cor. 5:17, 14-15 Niv).

The born again believer whose confession of faith in Christ is genuine will have a new heart and a new spirit that produces new desires to know, love, and obey God—not out of duty, but out of love and a thankful heart for God's great love for him and for the *new life* and secure future he now has as His child (John 3:16; 1 John 4:19; Rom. 8:32; 2 Cor. 5:9).

2. You also after you believed were sealed in Him with the Holy Spirit who is given as a pledge of our inheritance… you are not in the flesh but in the Spirit, if indeed the Spirit of God dwells in you. But if anyone does not have the Spirit of Christ, he does not belong to Him (Eph. 1:13-14; Rom. 8:9).

The moment a genuine confession is made, the Holy Spirit comes to indwell the born again believer. His very real presence serves as a *seal* of salvation. This is that deep unshakable assurance in the heart that says: I know that <u>I know</u> that <u>I know</u> that I am a child of God. I have a personal, forgiven, relationship with Him now and will enjoy *life eternal* with Him in the glories of Heaven one day.

3. And by this we know that we have come to know Him, if we keep His commandments (1 John 2:3, cf. John 14:21, 23).

The truly repentant sinner will have a love for and desire to obey the Word of God. He recognizes that it is impossible to obey the Word of God if he does not know the Word of God. Therefore, he has a hunger and thirst for God's Word, spending time consistently in it that he might please His heavenly Father and bring honor and glory to Him by upholding and obeying what His Word teaches.

4. We know that we have passed out of death into life because we love the brethren. He who does not love abides in death. Everyone who hates his brother is a murderer; and you know that no murderer has eternal life abiding in him (1 John 3:14-15).

God's love (John 3:16) and hate cannot dwell together in the same heart. Hate must go. The *born again* believer will repent of any residual hatred or bitterness towards his brothers and sisters and offer to them the same forgiveness that has so graciously been extended to him by God.

5. Who is the liar but the one who denies that Jesus is the Christ (1 John 2:22).

The born again believer will not deny or refute the deity or the Lordship of Jesus. He believes all God says about him in His Word and lives his life accordingly. He loves to talk about His Savior, and does so freely with others, bringing honor and glory to Him.

6. Not everyone who says to me, 'Lord, Lord,' will enter the Kingdom of Heaven; but he who does the will of My Father... even so, every good tree bears good fruit...So then, you will know them by their fruits (Matt. 7:17–23).

Those who are *born again* are ever seeking—through prayer and studying God's Word—to know and do the will of God, gratefully, joyfully bearing fruit for His kingdom (John 15:8).

7. My sheep hear My voice, and I know them, and they follow Me (John 10:27).

God's true sheep *hear (listen to)* His voice—through His Word and prayer—so that they can gladly and carefully *follow (obey)* Him.

8. My son, do not regard lightly the discipline of the Lord, nor faint when you are reproved by Him; for those whom the Lord loves He disciplines... God deals with you as sons; for what son is there whom his father does not discipline? But if you are without discipline, then you are illegitimate children and not sons (Heb. 12:5, 8).

True sons of God will welcome the discipline of their loving, heavenly Father, knowing that it is *for their good*, that they may *share in His Holiness... becoming partakers of the divine nature and bearing the peaceful fruit of righteousness* (Heb. 12:10-13; 2 Pet. 1:4). The person who can sin without any sense of conviction or discipline from God has reason to be greatly concerned about his sonship.

The gift of salvation is, by far, the greatest, most precious possession in all the world! Wonderful and magnificent as it is, however, it is but the beginning of all that God has for His children. There is beyond this glorious gift, a vast, blessed *inheritance in Christ* (Eph. 1:1-21, 2:1-6; 1 Pet. 1:1-9; 2 Pet. 1:3-10, 2:9-10; 1 Cor. 2:9-13 etc.). God has so much more for all who receive Jesus as their personal Lord and Savior which we'll look at in upcoming chapters. No wonder Jesus said to His disciples when they returned from their first evangelistic outreach mission, *"Do not rejoice that the spirits are subject to you, but rejoice that your names are recorded in Heaven!"* (Luke 10:19-20).

That is why I am praying that if there is anyone who fails this salvation test, or for whom there is any doubt about his relationship with God and his eternal destiny, that he will not wait one more day to settle this issue once and for all.

... and the Spirit (says) "Come" and let the one who hears, "come." Let the one who is thirsty, "come" and take of the Water of Life... for God so loved the world that He gave His only begotten Son that whosoever believeth in Him should not perish but have everlasting life... But as many as received Him, to them He gave the right to become children of God (Rev. 22:17, 20; John 3:16, 1:12, NASB, KJV).

Repent... believe... and you shall be saved! (Acts 2:38, 16:31).

Please return to the Bible Study Supplement to complete today's assignment.

This following article was originally published in the *PsychoHeresy Avareness Newsletter,* Sept/Oct. 1999. It was reviewed and revised July, 2007.

Psychology: A Biblical Analysis
by Mel and Gloria Blowers

Then the sons of Israel did evil in the sight of the Lord… they forsook the LORD… and followed other gods from among the gods of the peoples around them, and bowed themselves down to them; thus… (they fell) into the hands of plunderers, who plundered them… so that they could no longer stand before their enemies (Judges 2:11-14, sel.).

The precious Body of Christ today is being weakened and plundered so that it can *no longer stand before its enemies* because it has *forsaken the Lord* to *follow the god* of humanistic psychology, whose unbiblical goal is to make people "feel good about themselves," rather than to *love the Lord your God with all your heart, soul, mind and strength,* to *glorify Him in all things,* and to be *conformed to the image of His Son (Deut. 6:5; Matt. 22:37; 1 Cor. 10:31; Rom. 8:29).*

Psychology is a very deceptive and dangerous "science" (though it is not a science at all—part of the deception) conceived in the mind of unredeemed man in his state of rebellion against God as the answer to his mental, emotional and moral problems. It has been the revered "god" of the people for such problems since the late 1800's, when Freud systematized his atheistic assessments about the psyche (soul) of man. "Feel good" psychological concepts have replaced the clear teachings of Scripture. Even Christians stream to its practitioners for affirmation, comfort, and guidance, rather than to God and His Word.

Because psychology, like the god of Baal, helps people temporarily "feel better about themselves", it is deceptively appealing, and thus, highly regarded and worshiped by many. Great energies and time are invested in seeking out and practicing its modern new "insights". But the Bible says, *Like the Holy One who called you, be holy yourselves in all your behavior…*

do not touch what is unclean… come out from them and be separate (1 Pet. 1:16; 2 Cor. 6:14-18, sel.).

Rather than *coming out from* the *unholy, unclean* practice of psychology, we have embraced it, incorporated it, and twisted and distorted Scripture to "prove" unbiblical man-centered psychological theories!

I will destroy the wisdom of the wise, and the cleverness of the clever, I will set aside…has not God made foolish the wisdom of this world? (1 Cor. 1:19-20).

There are currently over 500 conflicting and contradicting "psycho"-therapies being taught and practiced today. That in itself shows the foolishness of the wisdom of the world.

Common to all psychological teaching is a biblically defective view of the nature of man: that man is basically good and able to solve his problems, when properly "enlightened". Nothing could be farther from the truth.

For all of us (are) unclean; Every one… has become corrupt… The heart is deceitful above all else, and desperately wicked: who can understand it? (Is. 64:6; Ps. 53:3; Jer. 17:9, KJV, NASB).

The gods that psychology has created— "self"-obsession, materialism, pain-free living, and a thousand other "feel good" fantasies are as ungodly and pagan as the Ashtoreth of the Sidonians (1 Kings 11:33). God says we should destroy these heathen idols and cling to Him alone, seeking holiness and righteousness, not preoccupation with "self". He does this because He loves us and He knows that idols and the false hope they offer will never help or heal any of us. It will only weaken and eventually destroy us.

For they will turn your sons away from following Me to serve other gods… But thus you shall do to them: you shall tear down their altars, and smash their sacred pillars, and burn their graven images with fire. For you are a holy people to the LORD your God (Deut. 7:4-6, sel.).

Whenever we attempt to "mix" the unholy with the Holy—such as "Christian Psychology"—we profane the precious Holy Name of God (Ezek. 36:22), and we make a mockery of His sovereignty, authority and sufficiency. We imply that God is not capable of dealing with a certain class of problems—"psychological". History clearly illustrates that anytime the people of God attempted to mix the Holy with the profane it was only a matter of time before they "forsook" the Holy and were "consumed" by the profane (2 Chron. 28:22-23). Surely, we would be wise to heed the call to purity and obedience.

Now these things happened as examples for us, that we should not crave evil things, as they also craved (1 Cor. 10:6).

It is not that we doubt for one moment the sincerity or intelligence of many Christian "experts," who boldly promote "psychological techniques" today. Many undoubtedly are saved, sincere and extremely intelligent. But even saved, sincere, and intelligent people can be deceived. All of us are, at times, deceived by the schemes of Satan (2 Cor 2:11), as he appeals to certain presuppositions based on personal experiences, unsanctified "personality bents" (sinful weaknesses), and circumstances. That is why the Bible exhorts us to *not forsake the assembling of ourselves together (Heb. 10:25)*; to *teach, exhort, and admonish one another (Col. 3:16; 2 Tim. 3:16-17)*, and to have a humble *teachable spirit (James 3:13-18).* That is the purpose of the body of Christ. God calls preachers and teachers to speak forth the clear teachings of Scripture, warning of waywardness (Ezek. 33:7-9). In obedience to God, faithful, godly men and women today who recognize the dangers of psychology are "crying out from the wilderness" concerning its many subtle and harmful deceptions. But who is heeding the cry?

The first six books of the Bible are dedicated to establishing the Lordship and sovereignty of God:

Hear, O Israel: The LORD is … God; the LORD is one … You shall fear only the LORD your God, and you shall worship him. You shall not go after … the gods of the people which are round about you … For you are a holy people unto the LORD your God (Deut. 6:4, 13-15; 7:6).

The new testament builds upon this foundation of God's sovereignty and sufficiency:

… His divine power has granted to us everything pertaining to life and godliness, through the true knowledge of Him … do not add to the (words) of this book nor take away from (them) (2 Pet. 1:3; Rev. 22:18-19).

Whether we recognize it or not, psychology adds "enlightened" man-centered theories to Scripture. Satan is a master counterfeiter. Our fallen minds and deceitful, lustful hearts are bent towards rebellion and satisfying our own unholy cravings, thus making us extremely vulnerable to deception. In the area of psychology, scriptural terms are carefully chosen to create "biblical models" that affirm various psychological theories and techniques so that few are able to recognize the deception. We must keep in mind at all times that "Psychology" as we understand it today was born out of the theories of rebellious men who hated God and refused to acknowledge His involvement in man's life and problem solving. And God's Word clearly teaches that we are not to join or identify ourselves with such (2 Cor. 6:14-17; Deut. 7:2-4). Yet, respected "Christian Psychologists" have convinced troubled, hurting people that it is not only possible to *integrate* psychology and the Bible, it is desirable and superior!

To *prove* the "goodness" of this marriage, psychologists are quick to reference anecdotal examples (experiences) of people who have been "helped" by their techniques. All outside indication would support their arguments. But is it not more deception? Since the devil is the perpetrator of sin, sickness and disease—especially mental and emotional disturbances—he can quite strategically lift his heavy hand of oppression for a time to make it "appear" as if the psychological technique is actually bringing healing when in reality the "healing" is superficial and not true healing at all. It is but a temporary reprieve, a lull in the battle. Lacking a disciplined, seasoned discernment, the already weakened, unstable person is eventually led down another path of deception and failure. A vicious cycle develops: therapy, a reprieve, a new crisis, more therapy, a reprieve, a new crisis, more therapy...

We are fully aware that in some instances people are genuinely helped during a period of time they are under the treatment of a "Christian Psychologist." But again, it is clear that the healing did not come from the "therapist" or the "psychological technique." The healing came from a compassionate touch of the grace of God—usually as these people received salvation or renewed their commitment to Christ and to the study and application of His Word (obedience).

At the heart of our concern in all this is that the wrong "gods" are receiving the glory—the therapist, "Christian Psychology," psychological techniques, or the newly resurrected god of "self-esteem." The Bible clearly warns:

> "I am the Lord, that is my name: and my glory will I not give to another" (Is. 42:8).

The vast majority of "psychological" problems are, in reality, spiritual problems that have never been properly dealt with according to God's Word. When we try to wed God's ways of dealing with the problem of sin (the cross, forgiveness, personal responsibility, obedience) with man's ways (blaming others, "getting in touch with our past", self-pity/victimization, and catering to and building up "self"), we are playing the harlot, and the new "gods" we have embraced will become a *snare and a trap* (Josh. 23:8-13).

Sin and its devastating consequences—shame, guilt, feelings of worthlessness—cannot be dealt with by any other means than the redemptive blood of Jesus and the sanctifying work of the Holy Spirit of God. Putting a psychological band-aid on these spiritual problems only covers an *incurable wound* (Jer. 30:12). It is true: *With men this* (difficult problem) *is impossible; but with God all things are possible... Behold, the Lord's hand is not so short that it cannot save* (Matt. 19:26; Is. 59:1).

It is tragic that many have been led to believe that victory over various "psychological" problems can be obtained only through "professional" *psychological* counseling. This is not only untrue, (as proven by extensive research[12]), it is a devastating witness to the already perceived impotence of the Church.

By implying that some *soul* problems are "too serious" to be dealt with through the proper application of Scripture, we not only deny the sovereignty and power of God, we begin to develop within people a dependence on psychology, a therapist, or a "coping technique", instead of dependence on God. That is why the body of Christ is so weak. We are literally sucking the life blood out of one another in a sincere attempt to be "compassionate" apart from obedience to the Word of God in the power of the Holy Spirit.

Did God leave His people "in the dark" for over 1800 years after Christ returned to the Father until Freud appeared on the scene in the late 1800's to shed his enlightenment upon the various problems of the human psyche - "soul"? Contrarily, history confirms that some of the most productive, fruitful saints lived during this very period, and people in general were much more "stable" before this new era of enlightenment than today. In truth, countless individuals through the ages have experienced complete, perfect, and lasting victory over the most severe *soul* problems as the truths of God's Word were received, believed and applied (obeyed) through the power of the Holy Spirit, the loving mercy and grace of God, and the support and encouragement of the Body of Christ.

It is time we tore down the Ashtoreth of Psychology and returned in pure and holy allegiance to God who lovingly invites us:

> *Return, faithless (ones)... I will not look upon you in anger. For I am gracious... only acknowledge your iniquity, that you have transgressed against the Lord your God and have scattered your favors to strangers; you have not obeyed My voice... return... I will restore you to health and I will heal your wounds... I will build you and you shall be rebuilt (Jer. 3:12-14, 30:17, 31:4, sel.).*

Update on Personal Testimony

So much has transpired since I wrote my testimony. There just won't be time here to tell *the rest of the story* concerning the more than twenty-year battle (so far) with the strange affliction, the oft confusing pain and difficulties that accompanied it, and the matchless mercy and grace of God that overcame (and continues to overcome) it. God taught me *so* much that I am longing to share. But that we will have to save for book three. For now, I just want to mention a couple highlights and give praise to God for His unfailing love, grace and faithfulness.

Of all that God has done in the past twenty five years since my rebirth into His glorious Kingdom, the most treasured has been the way He has transformed our marriage and my relationship with my husband. Daily, I stand in awe! A Christian home and marriage surely is God's way of giving us a little taste of Heaven right here on earth. How I thank God every day for my godly husband and for our Christian home. I realize more and more how blessed I am! Mel's gentle but strong, Christlike leadership keeps our home secure and filled with blessing and joy beyond anything I could have hoped or dreamed (Eph. 3:20). And as God continues His good work, perfecting me in my role as Mel's helpmeet, the joy only increases.

Another special joy has been sharing God's love and the wonderful good news of His redemption and new life in Jesus with others, then seeing again and again the power of the Word of God transforming lives, rebuilding marriages, filling hearts and homes with love and peace.

I've learned to stay *grafted into the vine (John 15:5)* through daily Bible study and prayer, and to live very close to the cross, confessing immediately sins and shortcomings, then thanking God for His forgiveness and restoration. I've learned the ever-increasing joy of discovering more and more of all that we are and all that we possess in Jesus (Eph. 1:1–23; Col. 1:27; Col. 2:9–15).

God's Word has become even more precious to me. As I grow in *the wisdom and grace of our Lord Jesus (2 Peter 3:18)*, I never cease to be amazed at the power and practicality of God's Word. As I apply its life-giving principles to every area of my life (Matt. 4:4; John 6:63), I find victory and peace that truly does *pass all human understanding (Phil. 4:7)*. I think so often of the beautiful promise in *Prov. 4:18: For the path of the righteous is like the light of dawn that grows brighter and brighter until the full day.* How unfailingly true I have found it to be. As I walk in the wonderful *light of God's Word each day (1 John 1:7; John 8:12), my path is made clear, my footsteps established and secured (Ps. 43:3; Prov. 4:26; Ps. 18:36)*. I walk confidently knowing that *God holds my hand and will keep me from stumbling (Ps.18:36, 37:23-24; Prov. 3:23)*. I thank God for these and for hundreds of other precious promises that keep *a song in my heart, encouragement in my spirit, and joy in the journey (Psalm 40:3; John 15:11; Phil. 1:6)*.

The longer I walk with God, the deeper the roots of my once fledgling faith extend, and, by God's ever-abounding grace and faithfulness, the stronger and fuller grows the fruit-bearing tree (Lam. 3:22-23; Jer. 17:8; John 15:5–8). All of those common, early doubts regarding basic foundational, unalterable truths have long since been settled. I know that God is real: *the heavens declare the glory of God (Ps. 19:1)*, and every Word of the Bible is true: *All Scripture is inspired by God… Holy men of God spake as they were moved by the Holy Spirit (2 Tim. 3:16; 2 Pet. 1:20,21)*. God gave us all a soul that is eternal (Eccles. 3:11). Heaven is a very real place (Matt.13:31–52) and so is hell (Matt. 13:50; Rev. 20:9,10, 14:11). One day, we will all go to one place or the other, for eternity. God leaves the choice to us (John 3:16; Josh. 24:15).

How can I ever thank Him enough that He never gave up on me through all those years of prideful, obstinate rebellion, and paralyzing fears. And how can I thank Him enough for His *unspeakable gift: salvation through the redemptive blood of Jesus shed on the cross to take away my sins and the sins of the world (John 3:16; Rom. 5:8; 1 Pet. 3:18)* or for all He has done for me since that glorious day I accepted Jesus into my heart (John 1:12; 2 Cor. 3:18). Truly, *God is good; His compassions never fail. They are new every morning. Great is His faithfulness (Ps. 73:1;Lam. 3:22-23; Ps. 84:11).* I pray that you will join me in the wonderful pursuit of knowing, loving, and obeying God in all His good plans and purposes for our lives with courage, joy and sweet contentment (Matt. 22:37–39; Jer. 29:11–14; John 17:4; Luke 1:74,75; Rom. 14:17). For, as we do this, we will discover the most glorious promise of all: that nothing in all the world will ever, ever again be able to *separate us from the love of God, which is in Christ Jesus our Lord (Rom. 8: 31–39).*

To God be the glory;
great things He has done!

Resources

We live in an age of abundance. God has blessed us with a myriad of Study Bibles, books, teaching tapes, videos, and a host of other helpful discipleship materials from which to gain further understanding and fortify our growing faith and freedom in Christ. But we must heed the warning of Jer. 15:19 in which God's people are exhorted to be very careful to *extract the precious from the worthless.* There is a lot of precious, solid, Bible study material easily available, but, sadly there is far more that attempts to mix the Holy with the profane (worldly), something that is an abomination to God, concerning which He clearly warns and bids us not to partake because of the harm and destruction it will cause us (2 Cor. 6:14–18; 1 Cor. 1:18–29).

The following is a list of ministries where Bible Study and other discipleship resources may be obtained. If you are interested, just give them a call and ask for a catalogue.

Caveat: Though I am personally familiar with all these ministries and have found them, for the most part, to be trustworthy in their commitment to the authority and sufficiency of God's Word, I have discovered material available from some of them to be in error to *the whole counsel of God's Word,* so I urge you always to be like the Bereans: *For these were more noble-minded…for they received the word with great eagerness, examining the Scriptures daily, to see whether these things (that they were being taught) were so (Acts 17:11).* Everything we read should always be held up to the plumb line of God's Word. If it contradicts the clear teaching and principles of Scripture, it is false doctrine and must be rejected.

Answers in Genesis (Ken Ham)
P.O. Box 510, Hebron, KY 41048
Phone 1-800-350-3232 or (859) 727-2222
www.answersradio.com

Ken Ham's "Answers in Genesis" ministry is an excellent resource for obtaining information regarding creation including a solid defense of the young earth theory, literal 24-hour creation days. He also very clearly establishes other crucial foundational doctrines of our faith.

The Berean Call (Dave Hunt, T. A. McMahon)
P.O. Box 7019, Bend, OR 97708-7019
Ph. 1-800-937-6638
www.thebereancall.org

Great resources for developing spiritual discernment. Try a sample newsletter. You'll be blessed and your faith will be strengthened.

Bible Pathway Ministries (John Hash)
P.O. Box 20123, Murfreesboro, TN 37129
Phone: 1-800-598-7884 or (615) 896-4243
www.biblepathway.org

Bible Pathway is a very special "Read Through the Bible in One Year" program. Please go to end of resource list for additional information about this excellent program—highly recommended!

Bold Christian Living (Jonathan Lindvall)
P.O. Box 820, Springville, CA 93265
Phone for orders: 1-800-4LINDVALL (1-800-454-6382) Other information 1–559-539-0500
www.BoldChristianLiving.com
Lindvall@BoldChristianLiving.com

Jonathan has a heart for ministry and a love for the Word of God. Though he specializes in parenting and biblical youth ministry, his tapes and videos cover subjects pertaining to all areas of spiritual growth. When I am having an especially hard day, I grab one of Jonathan's tapes for *strengthening the weak arms (Heb. 12:12)* and getting that shield of faith back into proper position. Jonathan's clear, biblical teachings are always like a breath of heaven—a real spirit booster and faith builder.

Creation Moments
P.O. Box 839, Foley, MN 56329
Phone 1-800-569-5959
www.creationmoments.com

This is an excellent resource for information on Creation Science. An extensive catalogue of books, tapes, and videos offers infallible proof supporting the biblical account of the creation of the universe and substantially refutes the unstable, unprovable theories and fallacies of evolution. This is also where you can obtain Paul Bartz's devotional books, *Let God Create Your Day*, about all the unique plants and animals God has created that defy evolutionary theories mentioned in Chapter 1, Day 3.

Creation Moments also offers an excellent two-part video series produced by Moody Institute of Science called: "Journeys to the Edge of Creation" Part 1: Our Solar System; Part 2: The Milky Way and Beyond. The is an excellent presentation of the vastness of our universe! I have watched these videos several times and stand all the more in awe of God's awesome creation every time.

NANC – National Association of Nouthetic Counselors
3600 West 96th Street, Indianapolis, IN 46268
317 337-9100
www.NANC.org

NANC (National Association of Nouthetic Counselors) is the primary educational and certifying agency for Biblical Counseling Training. Its requirements are strict and arduous. All who complete the classroom training and practicums (supervised counseling) will be well equipped to *handle accurately the Word of God (2 Tim. 2:15)*. NANC has a number of conferences, training schools and seminars through the year. These are recorded and made available electronically so that excellent teaching material can be found on every type of mental, emotional, psychological and spiritual problem. See the NANC web site for more information.

PsychoHeresy Awareness Ministries – Martin and Deidre Bobgan
4137 Primavera Road, Santa Barbara, CA 93110
Ph. 805-683-0864; Orders: 1-800-216-4796
www.psychoheresy-aware.org

The infiltration of humanistic psychology into the church is a very real and dangerous problem because it is so popular and widely accepted and the deception is so very powerful and destructive in nature. This unholy integration of man-centered, anti-God secular psychological theories and therapies with the Bible has proliferated into every aspect of church life through books, tapes, videos, seminars, youth ministry, preaching, etc. The body of Christ was in desperate need of a *watchman on the wall (Ezek. 3:17)* to cry out the warnings of this serious corruption of truth and doctrine. Martin and Deidre Bobgan heard that call and responded with careful, thorough attention to the subject from a biblical viewpoint. They share their warnings and call to biblical discernment through their many books and bi-monthly newsletter. If you have never read any of their material, it would be good to get a sample copy of their newsletter. The Bobgans do an excellent job of exposing the subtle deceptions of psychological indoctrination through thorough biblical examination.

Revive our Hearts Ministries (Nancy Leigh DeMoss)
P.O. Box 83500, Lincoln, NE 68501
Phone 1-800-569-5959
www.ReviveOurHearts.com
info@ReviveOurHearts.com

This is an excellent resource for women. Nancy is a knowledgeable, gifted Bible teacher and committed to the authority of Scripture. I have ordered dozens of tapes and am always blessed and encouraged in my walk with the Lord through them. (Pray for protection for Nancy that she remains strong and faithful to the authority and sufficiency of Scripture, as the encroachment of man-centered psychological compromise infiltrates the church).

Truths That Transform (Dr. D. James Kennedy)
P.O. Box 33, Fort Lauderdale, FL 33302
1-800-229-WORD

Dr. Kennedy wrote the excellent book, *Why I Believe . . . in the Bible, God, Creation, Heaven, Hell, etc.* It is a very helpful tool in putting together one's personal testimony and ready defense of the Bible, God, Creation, etc. It is also an excellent resource in ministering to skeptics.

"Unshackled" Radio Program
Pacific Garden Mission
646 So. State St. , Chicago, IL 60605
Phone 312-922–1462
unshackled@pgm.org
www.unshackled.org

The "Unshackled" radio program airs testimonies of lives that have been transformed by the gospel. The stories are incredible true accounts of God's love reaching out to lost sinners. For many years, I listened to nearly every broadcast and still listen as often as possible. Hearing these testimonies always encourages me and reminds me of the greatness of God's mercy and amazing grace towards His wayward children. If you haven't heard this program or haven't heard it for some time, do listen and be encouraged. You can write or call for a catalogue of all the programs by main subject, i.e., addictions, depression, anger, drugs, alcohol, unhealthy striving for achievement/approval of others, etc. The programs are also available on-line, anytime.

Zion's Hope Ministries (Marv Rosenthall)
P.O. Box 121048, Clermont, FL 34712
1-888-781-9466 or (352) 241-9085

Zion's Hope is a wonderful ministry for helping us understand end-time prophecy and other core doctrines of our faith. An excellent resource for all believers is a book entitled *The Pre-Wrath Rapture* (book and workbook) by Marv Rosenthal, which makes understanding the Books of Daniel, Amos, Joel, Isaiah, Revelation (and other prophesies) much easier through clear, simplified explanations, while remaining solidly biblical. You will definitely want to get the supplemental workbook to go with the main text book. This corresponding Bible study helps so much in explaining more clearly and solidifying the truths of Scripture on this important topic.

A Special Word About Bible Pathway

I must take a moment here to point out one resource in particular that has been of incalculable value to both my husband and me—and countless others—in our walk with the Lord. It is the Bible Pathway, "Read Through the Bible In One Year" program. I have read through the Bible a number of times since becoming a Christian. But of all the outlines/study programs I have followed, the Bible Pathway Study Series has been by far the most edifying and faith-building. God has blessed Dr. Hash (founder and writer of the Bible Pathway meditations) with an incredible Holy Spirit inspired clear and accurate understanding of the Word of God from Genesis to Revelation. In nearly every lesson, he ties the Old Testament to the New Testament showing their interrelatedness and continuity of the promises and purposes of God. He also helps the reader to understand those passages that are often difficult to discern accurately.

Every Christian should read through the Bible at least once every three to five years in order to maintain a good understanding of *the whole counsel of God's Word (Acts 20:28).* (Even better is to read it through every year as my husband does!) I prefer to start the Bible Pathway's program at the beginning of a new year. It just seems to start the year off in a special anticipation and hope-building way. Also, by planning ahead you can make sure that you have the material and are ready to begin on January 1. If, however, it is not convenient for you to start then, Bible Pathways has a comprehensive study book that you can use to begin the program at any time in the year. Whichever plan will work best for you, I strongly encourage you to set a goal to do this as soon as possible. Your love for God will grow as you come to understand more clearly His nature, goodness and faithfulness, and in so doing, your faith will be strengthened, and your joy multiplied.

Blessings!